PENGU

THE 108 UPANISHADS

Roshen Dalal was born in Mussoorie and has lived in various places in India, including Hyderabad, Mumbai and Delhi, before settling in Dehradun, where she now resides. She has an MA and a PhD in ancient Indian history from Jawaharlal Nehru University, New Delhi. She has taught both at school and university, and been involved in research in the fields of history, religion, philosophy and education. She is the author of the bestselling two-volume *The Puffin History of India; The Puffin History of the World*, also in two volumes; *India at 70: Snapshots since Independence; The Religions of India: A Concise Guide to Nine Major Faiths; Hinduism: An Alphabetical Guide; The Vedas: An Introduction to Hinduism's Sacred Texts* and *The Compact Timeline History of the World*. Her latest book is a novel, *The Guru Who Came Down from the Mountain*.

ROSHEN DALAL

The

1⦿8
UPANISHADS

an introduction

PENGUIN BOOKS

An imprint of Penguin Random House

PENGUIN BOOKS

USA | Canada | UK | Ireland | Australia
New Zealand | India | South Africa | China

Penguin Books is part of the Penguin Random House group of companies
whose addresses can be found at global.penguinrandomhouse.com

Published by Penguin Random House India Pvt. Ltd
7th Floor, Infinity Tower C, DLF Cyber City,
Gurgaon 122 002, Haryana, India

Penguin
Random House
India

First published in Penguin Books by Penguin Random House India 2018

10 9 8 7 6 5 4 3 2 1

ISBN 9780143428596

Typeset in Adobe Caslon Pro by Manipal Digital Systems, Manipal
Printed at Thomson Press India Ltd, New Delhi

www.penguin.co.in

For Shahnaz

Mandukya Upanishads *Ki*

Contents

Preface

THE UPANISHADS ARE Sanskrit texts that form part of Vedic literature. The rishis who composed the Upanishads were not composing historical texts, but were attempting to convey great spiritual truths. The main concept in these texts is that Brahman, the incomprehensible supreme source of all creation, is ultimately the same as the atman, the soul in each living being, which, thus, is also a universal soul. When this truth can be comprehended, there can be no division in society, no 'I' or 'you', in fact, no 'other'. Over the centuries, these and other concepts in the texts have been interpreted in different ways, and *The 108 Upanishads* presents the key ideas in the Upanishads along with summaries of the texts. It is hoped that this book will provide a starting point for a deeper study and understanding of these texts.

This book is a sequel to my book on the Vedas, *The Vedas: An Introduction to Hinduism's Sacred Texts*, and should be read in conjunction with it, as the Upanishads form the last part of Vedic literature. *The Vedas* deals with all aspects of the four Vedic Samhitas, that is, the *Rig Veda*, *Yajur Veda*, *Sama Veda* and *Atharva Veda*. It also looks at related literature, including the Brahmanas and Aranyakas, along with later texts such as the Pratishakyas, which provide information on the Vedas. It examines the possible date of the *Rig Veda* and takes an in-depth look at theories of the origin of the Rig Vedic people. There are detailed chapters on the Indo-Europeans, their languages and possible homeland, as well as an investigation of the Indo-Iranians, the Iranian and Avestan connection with the Rig Veda, and the relationship of Avestan and Vedic texts. Numerous texts are included in the Avesta, a term for the corpus of early Zoroastrian texts in the languages termed Old and Younger Avestan. Most scholars have still not looked at these texts in depth and continue to randomly use the texts without analysing their comparative dates. *The Vedas*, however, looks at these texts in detail. It then goes on to situate every place, river, mountain, tribe and clan mentioned in Vedic texts, along with an analysis and interpretation of every plant, herb and animal referred to, providing the socio-economic context for the Vedic texts. There is a separate chapter on the plants and mantras used to cure diseases, found mainly in the *Atharva Veda*. Other chapters deal with the deities and rishis of the Vedic Samhitas, and also with aspects of ritual. Conventional and spiritual interpretations are also described. Apart from this, the book provides an overview of the archaeological cultures across the entire subcontinent from pre-Harappan times up to around 1000 BCE. Some aspects of this book on the Vedas are summarized in *The 108 Upanishads*.

Part I of this book contains a general introduction to the Upanishads. As noted above, more on Vedic texts and their background will be found in *The Vedas*. More details on philosophies described in the Upanishads, on the additional topics in the Upanishads, on the various deities and people mentioned and on the dating of various texts will be found in another book of mine, *Hinduism: An Alphabetical Guide*, while for further information on Buddhism and Jainism, readers can check *Religions of India: A Concise Guide to Nine Major Faiths*.

Part II is an account of the 108 Upanishads mentioned in the *Muktika Upanishad*, which are considered the main Upanishads. Among the thousands of works on the Upanishads, very few look at all 108 of the *Muktika Upanishad*, as in this book. For each Upanishad described here, the original Sanskrit text, along with translations and commentaries, have been consulted. There are numerous variations in translations, and the best are those done by Indian translators and particularly those well-versed in the spiritual traditions of the Upanishads. Without an understanding of these, the translations are academic and often incorrect. At times, even Indian translators merely repeat parts of old translations; thus, in every case, reading the Sanskrit text is essential. Wherever a particular translator has been quoted, the name is mentioned; in other cases the summaries are created from the text and various translations and quotes are direct translations from the Sanskrit. After summaries of all 108 Upanishads, a detailed account of the *Brahma Sutra* is given. The *Brahma Sutra* is the earliest available text that systematizes the main themes of the Upanishads. Finally, a conclusion looks at the influence of the Upanishads across the world and their relevance today.

Academic works use diacritical marks which indicate the exact Sanskrit letters used, but as this book is for the general reader, phonetic spellings have been used. Standard phonetic spellings for the titles of the Upanishads have been used throughout the book, except where they form part of the title of a book or article.

There are innumerable sources for the Upanishads, including the Sanskrit texts, translations, old and new, commentaries, interpretations and analyses, as well as works that situate the Upanishads in a historical context. Even Sanskrit texts have variations. An extensive Bibliography in two parts provides details of the sources used. In many places in this book, Sanskrit terms have been used, as there is no adequate translation for these. On the whole, these terms are explained in the narrative, but a glossary provides explanations for some. We often hear the phrase 'the wisdom of the Vedas'. The seeds of this wisdom are contained in the Vedic Samhitas, but it is in the Upanishads that this wisdom is fully explained.

Part I

One

An Introduction

THE UPANISHADS ARE a series of Sanskrit texts which contain
a profound philosophy. They form part of the literature of the
Vedas, the most sacred texts of Hinduism. The term 'upanishad'
is often interpreted as 'sitting near the feet of a master', the word
being broken up into 'upa' (near) and 'nishad' (sitting down).
However, different interpretations arise when 'ni' and 'shad' are
separated. 'Ni' means 'totality', and one of the meanings of 'shad'
is destruction', and 'upanishad' therefore, is 'that which destroys
ignorance'. Shankara (Adi Shankaracharya), the eighth- to ninth-
century philosopher and the greatest exponent of the Upanishads,
suggests this meaning. However, the original meaning of the
word, provided in early texts, is 'secret doctrine'. Yet another
meaning of Upanishad is 'a connection' or 'equivalence'; thus, the
texts discover and reveal the connections between different topics.

Vedic Literature

How do the Upanishads fit in with the rest of Vedic literature?
'Veda' comes from the Sanskrit root 'vid', to know, and the word

implies 'divine knowledge'. The main texts of Vedic literature are the four Vedic Samhitas, that is, the *Rig Veda*, *Yajur Veda*, *Sama Veda* and *Atharva Veda*, along with the Brahmanas, Aranyakas and Upanishads. All these texts are said to be 'shruti' or 'heard', and are believed to be directly revealed from a divine source. These four categories of texts are broadly divided into two parts, the first consisting of the Samhitas, and the second of the rest.

These texts are interrelated, yet different. Even the four Samhitas differ. The *Rig Veda* is the earliest text, usually dated between 1500 and 1000 BCE, though it could be earlier. We will look at some more aspects of dating below, as the date of the *Rig Veda* has a bearing on that of the Upanishads.

The *Rig Veda*

The *Rig Veda* has 1028 hymns arranged in ten *mandala*s or sections. The hymns are composed mainly by rishis (sages) and rishi families, though some are by rishikas (female rishis), kings and sometimes deities. Of course, they are not considered the actual authors but those who 'heard' and transmitted the hymns.

This text mainly consists of prayers to various deities, including Indra, the god of war, Agni, the god of fire, Soma, the deity representing divine nectar, Surya, the sun god, and many others. Some hymns, which are considered slightly later than the others, mainly in the tenth mandala, have a concept of one supreme being, but most of them are addressed to individual deities, often personifications of nature, or of an attribute or ideal. These hymns also contain references to socio-economic data, to names of chiefs and clans, to wars and battles, as well as to plants and animals. The Rig Vedic people sometimes refer to themselves as Arya, meaning 'noble'. In English they are often called 'Aryans' and on the basis of language are thought to be connected with Indo-Iranians and Indo-European groups of people. The text also refers to other groups of people, such as the Dasas and Dasyus, which have been variously interpreted.

The Later Vedas

The three other Samhitas—the *Sama*, *Yajur* and *Atharva*—are usually grouped together in a time period known as 'Later Vedic'. The probable time when these were composed would be dependent on the date of the *Rig Veda*, which remains inconclusive, but in general they could be dated before 1000 BCE. The *Sama Veda* provides the musical method of chanting the verses. The text has two parts—the Archika and the Uttararchika—which in the Kauthuma version amount to 1810 verses or 1549 without repetitions. Most of these are taken from the *Rig Veda*—though they have some variations—and have been modified for chanting. *Gana*s or song books, which are somewhat later than the text, are also attached to the *Sama Veda*.

The *Yajur Veda* contains the mantras and prayers to be chanted and used in yajnas or sacrificial rituals. Numerous sacrificial rituals are described, including the new and full moon sacrifices, the ashvamedha or horse sacrifice and the various Soma sacrifices.

The *Atharva Veda*, or the fourth Veda, is also known as the *Brahma Veda*, though this is a late name. *Atharvan-Angirasa* is an an early name of the *Atharva Veda* which occurs once in the text and several times in the Brahmanas. The term 'Atharvana' (Veda) occurs in the *Chhandogya Upanishad*, and is earlier than the term Atharva Veda, which came to be used later. Bhrigvangirasah is another name of this Veda—from Bhrigu and Angirasa, who were two ancient rishis.

Its hymns include a number of different topics and can be prayers to deities, or incantations and spells. There are some beautiful prayers to Rig Vedic deities, as well as to others. Overall, the text deals with health, prosperity and the daily concerns of people, and not with grand sacrifices. A major part of the text consists of songs and spells. Several of these deal with the healing of diseases and include detailed descriptions of the body; it is therefore considered the first text containing aspects of medicine. Diseases are sometimes personified and hymns are addressed to them, while in other cases there are spells to banish demons considered responsible for ill-health. There are prayers to curative herbs or to healing waters and fires, chants for health and long life and for harmony within the family. There are spells to win someone's love or for protection from demons and people with evil intentions. There are hymns specially for the protection and blessing of kings, as well as battle chants and songs of war.

There are also philosophical hymns which almost reach the high philosophy of the Upanishads. Of the twenty *kanda*s or books, the nineteenth and twentieth seem to be later.

'Atharvan' originally meant 'fire-priest', corresponding with Athravan of the Zoroastrian collection of texts known as the Avesta; therefore, this may have an Indo-Iranian origin, though in its present form it is later than the *Rig Veda*. The *Atharva Veda*, in the best-known Shaunaka recension, consists of 731 hymns, with about 6000 verses divided into twenty books or sections. Some of the Rig Vedic hymns are repeated in the *Atharva*, and, according to estimates, around one-seventh of the verses are the same as in the *Rig*. Around one-sixth of the text is in prose.

The Priests

Passages from all these four texts were together used in elaborate rituals conducted by brahmana priests. The main priests were the *hotr* for the *Rig Veda*, the *udgatr* for the *Sama Veda*, the *adhvaryu* for the *Yajur* and the brahman for the *Atharva Veda*.

The number of priests was expanded to sixteen and they were classified into four groups: (1) hotr, *maitravaruna, achavaka, gravastut*; (2) udgatr, *prastotr, pratihartr, subrahmanya*; (3) adhvaryu, *pratisthatr, neshtr, unnetr*; (4) brahman, *brahmnachchhamsin, agnidhra, potr*. Thus, elaborate yajnas (sacrificial rituals) had a total of sixteen *ritvik*s (priests) or sometimes seventeen. These priests were assisted by other workers for the various tasks that formed part of the rituals. The purohita, spiritual adviser to the king, was usually a different priest, though he may have carried out the functions of the hotr in Rig Vedic times. Each priest was an expert in the particular text to which he was assigned. He knew the details and background of the hymns or verses used in the rituals, as well as how exactly they were to be used. These details were also codified in additional texts.

The Shakhas

Different versions or recensions of the texts emerged as they were studied in various regions under individual teachers, thus forming *shakha*s, schools or branches. Though the Samhita texts were memorized and relatively unchanged over the centuries, there were still regional variants. Shaunaka, Ashvalayana, Pippalada and Kaushika were among the Vedic teachers. There were once a number of different shakhas, but now texts belonging to only a few of these are known. Each shakha specialized in the study of one Vedic Samhita and seems to have had a slightly different version of the text. Even more variations can be seen in the directions for rituals in the prose Brahmanas as these were modified according to the area where they were performed.

Apart from the Samhita itself, shakhas studied various associated texts, which could include a Brahmana, Aranyaka or Upanishad along with other texts. This, however, was not essential.

Patanjali's *Mahabhashya* of about the fourth century BCE refers to twenty-one shakhas of the *Rig Veda*, 101 of the *Yajur Veda*, nine of the *Atharva Veda* and 1000 paths of the *Sama Veda*.

The Mahabharata and some of the Puranas also describe and list a number of shakhas. Over 1000 shakhas are listed in various texts, but of all these probably only ten are current today. Two shakhas sometimes used some of the same texts.

At one time, the Vedas in their various shakhas were studied across much of India. As communities of brahmanas moved from one place to another when invited by kings or patrons to attach themselves to a temple or settle in a particular area, the shakhas and *charanas* moved to different geographical areas. The Upanishads indicate that members of different castes could engage in such study. Later, however, their study was confined to members of the brahmana caste, and they were not accessible to the general population. It was only in the nineteenth century that attempts started being made to make them known and available to others.

Though, as seen above, the *Mahabhashya* refers to twenty-one shakhas, but according to the *Charana Vyuha*—a text attributed to the rishi Shaunaka—there were five Rig Vedic schools or shakhas: the *Shakala, Bashkala, Ashvalayana, Shankhayana* and *Mandukeya*. The only complete recension of this text known today is of the *Shakala* school. The *Shankhayana* and *Bashkala* shakhas are said to still be known in some parts of the country, but this is uncertain.

There are no variants in the extant versions of the *Rig Veda*.

There are a number of different schools or shakhas for the *Yajur Veda*, though they are nowhere near the original number of 101 referred to in the *Mahabhashya*. The two main versions of the *Yajur* are known as the *Shukla* or *White Yajur Veda* and the *Krishna* or *Black Yajur Veda*. The first is also known as the *Vajasaneyi Samhita*. Of this, texts of two shakhas are known, the *Kanva* and the *Madhyandina*, which are quite similar. Of the *Black Yajur Veda*, five shakhas are known, the *Taittiriya* (Apastamba), *Kapishthala* (Hiranyakesi), *Katha, Kathaka* and *Maitrayani* (Kalapa), with four closely related recensions known as the *Kathaka Samhita*, the *Kapishthala-Katha Samhita*, the *Maitrayani Samhita* and the *Taittiriya Samhita*.

The *Vajasaneyi Madhyandina* was originally prevalent in Mithila (north Bihar), while the *Kanva* was in Koshala (east Uttar Pradesh).

The *Sama Veda* had a number of different recensions. As seen above, Patanjali's *Mahabhashya* says the *Sama Veda* had 'a thousand paths'. The Puranas also mention 1000 paths. This may refer to the many different options and modes of singing in the ganas, which could have led to a number of different shakhas. Thirteen shakhas are listed in texts, but only three are known today. These are the *Kauthuma*, *Jaiminiya* or *Talavakra* and *Ranayaniya*. The exact number of verses varies in the different recensions. The *Ranayaniya* recension was commented on by the medieval scholar Sayana and has been translated by several people from the nineteenth century onwards. It has minor variations from the *Kauthuma* recension.

Nine shakhas of the *Atharva* are listed in Shaunaka's *Charana Vyuha*. These are *Paippalada*; *Stauda*; *Mauda*; *Shaunaka*; *Jajala*; *Jalada*; *Kuntapa*; *Brahmavada* and *Devadarsha*. The *Atharva Veda* is known today in two recensions belonging to two shakhas: the *Shaunaka* and the *Paippalada*. The *Shaunaka* recension is known from various parts of India and consists of 731 hymns with about 6000 verses divided into twenty books or sections. Its oral traditions had been maintained in Gujarat and were recently revived in parts of south India. The *Paippalada* recension has been found both in Kashmir and Odisha.

The Brahmanas

The Brahmanas form the next category of Vedic texts. Many Brahmanas are lost but each of those available is attached to one of the four Vedic Samhitas.

Attached to the *Rig Veda*: *Aitareya Brahmana*, common to the *Shakala* and *Ashvalayana* shakhas; *Kaushitaki Brahmana* and *Shankhayana Brahmana*, almost identical with *Kaushitaki*.

Attached to the *Sama Veda*: *Tandya* or *Panchavimsha Brahmana*; *Shadvimsha Brahmana*, which includes *Adbhuta*; *Samavidhana Brahmana*; *Arsheya Brahmana*; *Devatadhyaya Brahmana*; *Chhandogya* or *Mantra Brahmana*; *Samhitopanishad Brahmana*; *Vamsha Brahmana*; *Jaiminiya* or *Talavakra Brahmana*; *Jaiminiya Arsheya Brahmana*.

Attached to the *Black Yajur Veda* or *Taittiriya Samhita*: the *Taittiriya Brahmana*.

Attached to the *White Yajur Veda* or *Vajasaneyi Samhita*: *Shatapatha Brahmana*. The *Shatapatha* has two different recensions: the *Kanva* and the *Madhyandina*.

Attached to the *Atharva Veda*: the *Gopatha Brahmana*.

The sacrifices described in the *Yajur Veda* are further explained in the Brahmanas, along with some legends and stories.

The subject matter of the Brahmanas can be divided into two main topics of *vidhi* (rules) and *arthavada* (explanations). Thus, the rules for conducting a sacrifice are supplemented by a commentary on everything connected with the sacrifice, including stories and legends used to explain a point. The sacrificial ritual was believed to be a means to fulfil one's wishes and gain or augment one's power. The deities too are invoked in the sacrifice, and each item used in the rituals has a deeper symbolic meaning. Rules for the sacrifice were laid out in minute detail and any deviation led to its failure. This led to the increased exaltation of the brahmana (caste) priests who conducted the sacrifices. Stories and legends in these texts include those of Manu and the flood, Harishchandra and Shunahshepa, and Pururava and Urvashi. There are early creation myths in which Prajapati, or sometimes Manu, is the creator. Some philosophical concepts are also mentioned here.

The Brahmanas are considered later than the Vedic Samhitas but contain some archaic elements. Their exact date would depend on that of the Samhitas and is therefore uncertain. Various scholars provide different relative dates for the Brahmanas. The prose portions of the *Yajur* (*Taittiriya Samhita*) which really constitute a Brahmana are considered the earliest. The *Panchavimsha Brahmana* and *Taittiriya Brahmana* are probably next in date, followed by the *Jaiminiya, Kaushitaki* and *Aitareya Brahmana*s, in that order. Sometimes the *Aitareya* is considered older than the *Kaushitaki*, and the *Jaiminiya* older than the *Panchavimsha*. The *Shatapatha* is later than these and the *Gopatha* and other short Brahmanas of the *Sama* the latest. These views are based on linguistic analysis. These Brahmana texts are generally dated to between approximately 1000 BCE to 600 BCE but they could be earlier.

The Aranyakas

The Aranyakas or forest texts ('aranya' means forest) usually form the second part of the Brahmanas. Their contents indicate that they constitute a bridge between the Brahmanas and the Upanishads. The Aranyakas include descriptions of special sacrifices, along with comments on their mystical symbolism. There are philosophical sections as well as techniques of focusing on various symbols in order to attain the Absolute.

The *Aitareya Aranyaka* forms part of the *Aitareya Brahmana*, attached to the *Rig Veda*, and has five books or sections that describe sacrifices and philosophical concepts. It contains the *Aitareya Upanishad*.

The *Kaushitaki Aranyaka*, attached to the *Kaushitaki Brahmana* of the *Rig Veda*, has contents similar to the *Aitareya Aranyaka*. It includes the *Kaushitaki Upanishad*.

The *Taittiriya Aranyaka* is a continuation of the *Taittiriya Brahmana* which is attached to the *Krishna Yajur Veda*, and has ten chapters or *prapathaka*s. Chapters seven to nine form the *Taittiriya Upanishad*. The tenth chapter, known as the *Maha-Narayana Upanishad*, is a late addition.

The *Brihad-Aranyaka*, or *Brihadaranyaka Upanishad*, is attached to the *Shatapatha Brahmana* of the *Shukla Yajur Veda*, but is considered an Upanishad.

The *Chhandogya Upanishad* of the *Sama Veda* has a first section similar to an Aranyaka, while the *Jaiminiya Upanishad Brahmana* is really an Aranyaka, containing the *Kena Upanishad*.

The Upanishads

The Upanishads form the last part of Vedic literature, and again each Upanishad is attached to one of the Vedic Samhitas. While the early Upanishads can form part of a Brahmana or Aranyaka, the later ones were composed independently. Though the Upanishads have some continuity with the Samhitas, Brahmanas and Aranyakas, they are distinguished by their focus on philosophy— particularly on the concept of Brahman—and reflect a new stage in thought. All commentators and scholars recognize that of the four groups of texts, the Upanishads form a different category. The first three formed the karma marga—the path of action—while the Upanishads formed the jnana marga—the path of knowledge. The Vedic Samhitas were not rejected in the Upanishads, but a continuity was sought to be maintained between them and later ideas. As S. Radhakrishnan points out, passages from the Vedic Samhitas are often quoted in the Upanishads, but new meanings are given to them.[1] Sri Aurobindo and others have pointed out numerous passages from the Samhitas that are explained in the Upanishads.[2] Most of the early Upanishads are named after these shakhas. The Upanishads of a later date were attached to the *Atharva Veda* and many of them were not named after schools but after their subject matter.

We will examine the number and classification of the Upanishads after a look at views on the origin of the Vedic people and the reasons why the dates of these texts remain uncertain.

The Four Ashramas

The four categories of Vedic texts are often linked with the theory of *varnashrama* dharma; that is, of the traditional four stages of life. The first stage was that of the *brahmacharya* or student, the second of the *grihastha* or householder, the third of the *vanaprastha*, when the householder's life had been renounced and the person had retired to the forests, and the fourth of the sannyasi, when everything had been renounced. It is said that the Brahmanas were meant for the householder, the Aranyakas for the vanaprastha, and the Upanishads for the sannyasi. Not all agree with this, though. For instance, certain complex sacrifices such as the Mahavrata and Pravargya described in the Aranyakas were meant to be practised outside the town area, and that could account for the name 'aranyaka' or forest text. However, others feel that though they may not initially have been intended for the vanaprastha, they were used by them when the theory of the four ashramas or four stages of life was well-established. Another theory is that the four-ashrama system came into being to accommodate the new ideas and concepts that were gradually being formulated.

Texts As Shruti

Another aspect of all these four categories of texts is that they are sacrosanct. As they are considered *shruti* (heard), revealed by god, they cannot be questioned but only explained. However, there are two differing views on how the Upanishads are to be used. Should followers of Upanishadic philosophy reject the performance of Vedic rites and rituals? This is the view of many commentators including Shankara and is clearly stated in his commentary on the *Brahma Sutra* (see Chapter 11) where he also lays down guidelines and prerequisites for beginning an enquiry into Brahman. Others such as Ramanuja, however, believe that Vedic rituals should be practised as a preliminary stage, with philosophical enquiry forming the second stage.

The Origin of the Vedic People

One of the key questions regarding the Vedas has been about their origin. Did the Vedic people originate outside the territory of India, or were they part of cultures that already existed in the region where the text was composed? This question has been extensively analysed with a focus on the *Rig Veda* as this is the earliest text.

Vedic Sanskrit is classified as an Indo-Aryan language belonging to the larger group of Indo-European languages. The theory owes its origin to William Jones in the eighteenth century. Jones, who came to India in 1783 and became a judge of the Calcutta High Court, knew several languages, including English, Persian, Latin, Greek, Gothic (an old form of German) and Welsh. In India, he began to study Sanskrit in order to understand local and customary laws. In 1786 he put forward his views, laying the base for hundreds of years of further study. He said:

> The Sanskrit language, whatever be its antiquity, is of a wonderful structure: more perfect than the Greek, more copious than the Latin, and more exquisitely refined than either; yet bearing to both of them a stronger affinity, both in the roots of verbs and in the forms of grammar, than could possibly have been produced by accident; so strong indeed that no philologer could examine them all three, without believing them to have sprung from some common source, which perhaps no longer exists.'

He also added that Persian, Celtic and Gothic probably belonged to the same family.

Jones provided the hints which later led to the theory of a group or family of Indo-European languages. This term was first used by an English scholar, Thomas Young, in 1813, and after that became the standard term for all these related languages. These languages are spread across Asia and Europe and are today spoken by about three billion people, more than any other language family. In addition, they include some extinct languages.

These Indo-European languages are believed to have been derived from a common language called Proto Indo-European (PIE). This is a hypothetical language reconstructed on the basis of key and root words in various Indo-European languages. The spread of Indo-European languages has usually been related to the migration of people across Europe and Asia. These people were not genetically similar but are presumed to have once spoken the same language, PIE, and to have had certain cultural similarities. As the language spread to different regions through the migration of this linguistic group, it changed and several languages arose. Where was its original home? And did such a migration take place at all? Several linguists and archaeologists have worked on this, including Morris Swadesh and Colin Renfrew.

There is no agreement on the answers to these questions. The concept of a homeland for PIE presumes: (a) that PIE did exist; (b) that its time frame can be correctly estimated; (c) that language probably spread through migration or conquest, or through certain activities such as farming.

Many archaeologists and linguists believe that such a homeland did exist. The most likely date for the existence of a PIE homeland is taken as 5000–3000 BCE. Many different regions are suggested, but the region of Anatolia or of the Andronovo culture located in Ukraine and southern Russia are thought to be among the most likely. However, there is no consensus on the date of PIE or on how and when it spread. Some even doubt whether it ever existed.

Indo-Iranian is one of the languages believed to be derived from Indo-European, from which both Iranian (with Gathic as the earliest) and Indo-Aryan languages (of which Rig Vedic Sanskrit is the earliest) are thought to have developed. The theory is that after the PIE language had emerged and possibly after the first PIE speakers began to move out of their original homeland, the Indo-Iranian group lived together for some time before separating. There are again many theories about their possible homeland and the date when they separated. Gathic or Old Avestan, in which the Gathas, the earliest Zoroastrian text, is composed, is extremely similar to the language of the *Rig Veda*. The similarity is so marked that there can be no doubt that the two languages were once closely connected. In fact, minor changes enable one to 'translate' or transpose much of the Gatha text into Sanskrit. Younger Avestan, later than Old Avestan, also has similarities with the language of the Vedas.

Did the two groups once speak the same language and did they migrate to these regions from a common homeland? As we saw earlier, this is a major theory regarding their origin, but the same uncertainties that arise when searching for the Indo-European homeland can apply to the Indo-Iranian homeland as well.

A steppe homeland is a popular theory both for the Indo-European and Indo-Iranian languages. According to this theory, while Indo-European languages began to spread across Europe, Indo-Iranian developed in the Indo-European homeland of Ukraine and southern Russia. Alternatively, it reached here from Anatolia and then began to cross Central Asia to Iran and India. There are other theories regarding an original Indo-Iranian homeland, too; for instance, Western Asia and Central Asia, or alternatively within India. From ancient days, Western, Central and South Asia have been linked by sea and land routes.

Boundaries in those days were more fluid and did not reflect the political concerns of today. Instead of migration, J.F. Jarrige and others suggest that the entire region of Afghanistan, Iranian Seistan, west Baluchistan and central Asia were involved in bidirectional exchanges around 2500 BCE, hence, there were elements of similarity along with the existence of local cultures.[4] Based on the analysis of available human bones, Brian Hemphill and others suggest this may be correct and such interactions continued to 1000 BCE and later. There were, therefore, no great migrations but trade and cultural exchanges, including marriage. This theory follows the current trend all over the world that seeks an indigenous origin for language and culture. This is the case not only in India, but in several other countries as well, for instance, Greece and Scotland.

Attempts have been made to identify an archaeological culture that would correspond with the time of the *Rig Veda* but there is no consensus on this.

Dates

It is not known when the *Rig Veda* was first written down, and the hymns were transmitted orally for generations. The earliest available written text dates to around the eleventh century.

Many different suggestions have been put forward for the date of its composition, with estimates varying from 11,000 BCE to 1000 BCE. It was the German scholar Max Muller who in 1859 rather arbitrarily dated the *Rig Veda* between 1200 and 1000 BCE, based on the date of Buddhism, as he believed Buddhism's development was linked with anti-brahmanical feelings and, therefore, Vedic literature, including the Samhitas, Brahmanas, Aranyakas and the main early Upanishads, must have existed before this. He dated the Vedangas, the auxiliary texts, to between 600 and 200 BCE, that is, roughly contemporary with the early years of Buddhism. Presupposing the Brahmanas to be earlier than this, he placed their date between 800 and 600 BCE. As the Vedic Samhitas had to be earlier than this, he chose 1000–800 BCE for the three later Samhitas: the *Sama*, *Yajur* and *Atharva* Vedas. The *Rig Veda* had to be earlier, therefore, he allowed another 200 years, bringing its composition to between 1200 and 1000 BCE. Max Muller only suggested these dates, stating that at the latest, the *Rig Veda* must have been composed by 1000 BCE, and did not believe these dates were inviolable. In 1889, in his Gifford lectures, he said: 'Whether the Vedic hymns were composed in 1000, or 1500, or 2000 or 3000 BC, no power on earth will ever determine.'[5] Yet, somehow, the dates of which he himself was not convinced gained acceptance by others. As M. Winternitz pointed out, 'Max Muller's hypothetical and really purely arbitrary determination of the Vedic epochs in the course of years received more and more the dignity and character of a scientifically proved fact, without any new arguments or actual proofs being added.'[6]

Winternitz disagreed with Max Muller and said there was nothing against the assumption that Vedic literature was at least as old as the third millennium BCE. German indologist Albrecht Friedrich Weber also felt the *Rig Veda* must be earlier than Max Muller's postulated date. Two early scholars, H. Jacobi in Bonn and B.G. Tilak in India, independently placed the Vedic texts between 6000 and 3000 BCE, using astronomical data. Modern and contemporary writers provide a wide variety of dates. Many Western scholars stick to the conventional dates of 1500 to 1000 BCE for the *Rig Veda*, with the succeeding texts being dated somewhat later. Several others push the date far back. Among them, Subhash Kak put forward his views in his book *The Astronomical Code of the Rig Veda* and dated the *Rig Veda* to 4500–2500 BCE. There are also dates based on information in the epics and the Puranas. Using these texts, a date for the battle of the ten kings, a crucial event in the *Rig Veda*, is between 2000 and 1000 BCE.

Archaeology has also been used to date the texts, but equating the culture described in the Vedas with an archaeological culture is difficult and often arbitrary.

My own analysis of the socio-economic aspects of the text reduces the earliest possible date of the *Rig Veda* to around 4000 BCE. This is based on various factors, including references to metal used, that is, copper, and the types of animals mentioned in the text.[7]

Number of Upanishads

There are almost 300 Upanishads available today, but not all have the same value. In this book, we will look at the 108 Upanishads listed in the seventeenth-century *Muktika Upanishad*, while touching on some of those in other groups. How was this *Muktika* list of 108 put together? Why were these chosen out of other available Upanishads? As will be seen, those listed here include the major Upanishads and provide a selection of different types of Upanishads. There were other collections available as well, but those seemed to be a more random selection.

The *Muktika* List

Two differently arranged lists of the 108 classical Upanishads are provided in the *Muktika Upanishad*. One list has the names of the Upanishads attached to each Vedic Samhita. The numbers are as follows: *Rig Veda*: 10; *Shukla Yajur Veda*: 19; *Krishna Yajur Veda*: 32; *Sama Veda*: 16; *Atharva Veda*: 31.

According to the *Muktika*, the ten Upanishads attached to the *Rig Veda* are: 1. *Aitareya*; 2. *Kaushitaki Brahmana*; 3. *Nada-bindu*; 4. *Atmabodha*; 5. *Nirvana*; 6. *Mudgala*; 7. *Akshamalika*; 8. *Tripura*; 9. *Saubhagyalakshmi*; 10. *Bahvricha*.

Those attached to the *Shukla Yajur Veda* are: 1. *Ishavasya;* 2. *Brihadaranyaka;* 3. *Jabala;* 4. *Hamsa;* 5. *Paramahamsa;* 6. *Subala;* 7. *Mantrika;* 8. *Niralamba;* 9. *Trishikhi-brahmana;* 10. *Mandala-brahmana;* 11. *Advaya-taraka;* 12. *Paingala;* 13. *Bhikshu;* 14. *Turiyatita;* 15. *Adhyatma;* 16. *Tarasara;* 17. *Yajnavalkya;* 18. *Satyayani;* 19. *Muktika.*

Attached to the *Krishna Yajur Veda* are: 1. *Kathavalli;* 2. *Taittiriyaka;* 3. *Brahma;* 4. *Kaivalya;* 5. *Shvetashvatara;* 6. *Garbha;* 7. *Narayana;* 8. *Amrita-bindu;* 9. *Amrita-nada;* 10. *Kalagnirudra;* 11. *Kshurika;* 12. *Sarvasara;* 13. *Shukarahasya;* 14. *Tejo-bindu;* 15. *Dhyana-bindu;* 16. *Brahmavidya;* 17. *Yogatattva;* 18. *Dakshinamurti;* 19. *Skanda;* 20. *Shariraka;* 21. *Yogashikha;* 22. *Ekakshara;* 23. *Akshi;* 24. *Avadhuta;* 25. *Katharudra;* 26. *Rudrahridaya;* 27. *Yoga-kundalini;* 28. *Panchabrahma;* 29. *Pranagnihotra;* 30. *Varaha;* 31. *Kalisantarana;* 32. *Sarasvatirahasya.*

Attached to the *Sama Veda* are: 1. *Kena;* 2. *Chhandogya;* 3. *Aruni;* 4. *Maitrayani;* 5. *Maitreya;* 6. *Vajrasuchika;* 7. *Yoga-chudamani;* 8. *Vasudeva;* 9. *Mahat;* 10. *Sannyasa;* 11. *Avyakta;* 12. *Kundika;* 13. *Savitri;* 14. *Rudraksha-jabala;* 15. *Darshana;* 16. *Jabali.*

Attached to the *Atharva Veda* are: 1. *Prashna;* 2. *Mundaka;* 3. *Mandukya;* 4. *Atharvashiras;* 5. *Atharvashikha;* 6. *Brihad-jabala;* 7. *Nrisimhatapini* (*Purvottara*); 8. *Narada-Parivrajaka;* 9. *Sita;* 10. *Sarabha;* 11. *Tripadvibhuti-Maha-Narayana;* 12. *Ramarahasya;* 13. *Ramatapini* (*Purvottara*); 14. *Shandilya;* 15. *Paramahamsa-Parivrajaka;* 16. *Annapurna;* 17. *Surya;* 18. *Atma;* 19. *Pashupata-Brahma;* 20. *Parabrahma;* 21. *Tripuratapini;* 22. *Devi;* 23. *Bhavana;* 24. *Bhasma-jabala;* 25. *Ganapati;* 26. *Mahavakya;* 27. *Gopalatapini;* 28. *Krishna;* 29. *Hayagriva;* 30. *Dattatreya;* 31. *Garuda.*

The *Muktika* also provides a list of the 108 in a particular order, which are then classified into groups.

Muktika-integrated List

1. *Isha*; 2. *Kena*; 3. *Katha*; 4. *Prashna*; 5. *Munda*; 6. *Mandukya*; 7. *Taittiriya*; 8. *Aitareya*; 9. *Chhandogya*; 10. *Brihadaranyaka*; 11. *Brahma*; 12. *Kaivalya*; 13. *Jabala*; 14. *Shvetashvatara*; 15. *Hamsa*; 16. *Aruni*; 17. *Garbha*; 18. *Narayana*; 19. *Paramahamsa*; 20. *Amrita-bindu*; 21. *Amrita-nada*; 22. *Atharvashira*; 23. *Atharvashikha*; 24. *Maitrayini*; 25. *Kaushitaki Brahmana*; 26. *Brihad-jabala*; 27. *Nrisimhatapini*; 28. *Kalagnirudra*; 29. *Maitreya*; 30. *Subala*; 31. *Kshurika*; 32. *Mantrika*; 33. *Sarvasara*; 34. *Niralamba*; 35. *Shukarahasya*; 36. *Vajrasuchika*; 37. *Tejo-bindu*; 38. *Nada-bindu*; 39. *Dhyana-bindu*; 40. *Brahmavidya*; 41. *Yogatattva*; 42. *Atmabodha*; 43. *Narada-Parivrajaka*; 44. *Trishikhi*; 45. *Sita*; 46. *Yoga-chudamani*; 47. *Nirvana*; 48. *Mandala-brahmana*; 49. *Dakshinamurti*; 50. *Sharabha*; 51. *Skanda*; 52. *Tripadvibhuti-Maha-Narayana*; 53. *Advaya-taraka*; 54. *Ramarahasya*; 55. *Ramatapani*; 56. *Vasudeva*; 57. *Mudgala*; 58. *Shandilya*; 59. *Paingala*; 60. *Bhikshu*; 61. *Mahat*; 62. *Shariraka*; 63. *Yoga-shikha*; 64. *Turiyatita*; 65. *Sannyasa*; 66. *Paramahamsa-Parivrajaka*; 67. *Akshamalika*; 68. *Avyakta*; 69. *Ekakshara*; 70. *Annapurna*; 71. *Surya*; 72. *Akshi*; 73. *Adhyatma*; 74. *Kundika*; 75. *Savitri*; 76. *Atma*; 77. *Pashupata*; 78. *Parabrahma*; 79. *Avadhutaka*; 80. *Tripuratapini*; 81. *Devi*; 82. *Tripura*; 83. *Katharudra*; 84. *Bhavana*; 85. *Rudrahridaya*; 86. *Yoga-kundali*; 87. *Bhasma*; 88. *Rudraksha*; 89. *Ganapati*; 90. *Darshana*; 91. *Tarasara*; 92. *Mahavakya*; 93. *Panchabrahma*; 94. *Pranagnihotra*; 95. *Gopalatapini*; 96. *Krishna*; 97. *Yajnavalkya*; 98. *Varaha*; 99. *Shatyayani*; 100. *Hayagriva*; 101. *Dattatreya*; 102. *Garuda*; 103. *Kalisantarana*; 104. *Jabali*;

105. *Saubhagyalakshmi*; 106. *Sarasvatirahasya*; 107. *Bahvricha*;
108. *Muktika*.

This list includes Upanishads of different types and therefore is most often used for a discussion of these texts. There were other collections made which were not as comprehensive.

Dara Shikoh's Collection

In 1656, Dara Shikoh, the son of the Mughal emperor Shah Jahan, later killed by his brother Aurangzeb in the struggle for the throne, was in Kashmir when he heard about the Upanishads. He invited the pandits of Benares to help him in translating them into Persian. Fifty Upanishads were then translated. Anquetil Duperron, the first translator of some of the Avesta texts, translated Dara Shikoh's Persian text into Latin, and this was published in 1801–02. Though rather erratically translated, Arthur Schopenhauer (1788–1860), the German thinker and philosopher, came upon this text and was deeply influenced by it. He said, 'It has been the solace of my life, and it will be the solace of my death.'[8]

The fifty were given Persian names and were together known as the Oupnekhat in Latin. Reconverted from the Persian and Latin into Sanskrit, they are: 1. *Chhandogya*; 2. *Brihadaranyaka*; 3. *Maitrayaniya*; 4. *Mundaka*; 5. *Isha*; 6. *Sarva*; 7. *Narayana*; 8. *Tadeva=Vajasaneyi Samhita* 32.1–2; 9. *Atharvashiras*; 10. *Hamsananda*; 11. *Sarvasara*; 12. *Kaushitaki*; 13. *Shvetashvatara*; 14. *Prashna*; 15. *Dhyana-bindu*; 16. *Maha*; 17. *Atmaprabodha*; 18. *Shatarudriyam* (abridged as *Nila-Rudra Upanishad*); 20. *Yogashikha*; 21. *Yogatattva*; 22. *Shiva Sankalpa=Vajasaneyi Samhita* 34.1–6; 23. *Atharvashikha*; 24. *Atma*; 25. *Brahmavidya*; 26. *Amrita-bindu* (more correctly *Brahmabindu*); 27. *Tejo-bindu*; 28. *Garbha*; 29. *Jabala*; 30. *Maha-Narayana*; 31. *Mandukya*; 32. *Paingala*; 33. *Kshurika*; 34. *Paramahamsa*; 35. *Arunika*; 36. *Kena*; 37. *Kathaka*;

38. *Anandavalli=Taittiriya* 2; 39. *Bhrigavalli+Taittiriya* 3; 40. *Purushasuktam* + *Rig Veda* 10.50 and *Uttaranarayaniyam*, *Vajasaneyi Samhita* 31.17–22; 41. *Chulika*; 42. *Mrityu-langala*; 43. *Amrita-nada*, also known as *Amrita-bindu*; 44. *Bashkala*; 45. *Chagaleya*; 46. *Taraka=Tarasara* and *Ramottaratapaniya*; 47. *Arsheya*; 48. *Pranava*; 49. *Shaunaka*; 50. *Nrisimha*.

This includes both major and minor Upanishads as well as some not included in the *Muktika* list. In addition, sections of the *Vajasaneyi Samhita* are included as Upanishads. It is presumed by German Indologist Paul Deussen[9] that this was an existing collection that Dara Shikoh found and got translated.

Colebrooke's Collection

Henry Thomas Colebrooke (1765–1837), a scholar of classical languages, studied Sanskrit after joining the East India Company in 1782. In 1801, Colebrooke had provided a collection of fifty-two Upanishads, expanded from an earlier list of thirty-four, and from his statements and from those of the German indologist Albrecht Weber (1825–1901), who also listed them, it would seem that this was an existing collection and not compiled by Colebrooke. This list included the following: 1. *Mundaka*; 2. *Prashna*; 3. *Brahmavidya*; 4. *Kshurika*; 5. *Chulika*; 6. *Atharvashiras*; 7. *Atharvashikha*; 8. *Garbha*; 9. *Maha*; 10. *Brahma*; 11. *Pranagnihotra*; 12–15. *Mandukya*, with Gaudapada's *Karika*; 16. *Nilarudra*; 17. *Nadabindu*; 18. *Brahmabindu*; 19. *Amrita-bindu*; 20. *Dhyanabindu*; 21. *Tejo-bindu*; 22. *Yogashikha*; 23. *Yogatattva*; 24. *Sannyasa*; 25. *Aruniya*; 26. *Kanthashruti*; 27. *Pinda*; 28. *Atma*; 29–34. *Nrisimhatapaniya*; 35–36. *Kathaka*; 37. *Kena*; 38. *Narayana*; 39–40. *Brihannarayana*; 41. *Sarvopanishatsara*; 42. *Hamsa*; 43. *Paramahamsa*; 44. *Anandavalli*; 45. *Bhriguvalli*; 46. *Garuda*; 47. *Kalagnirudra*; 48–49. *Ramatapaniya*; 50. *Kaivalya*; 51. *Jabala*; 52. *Ashrama*. 44–45 form the *Taittiriya Upanishad*.

Narayana's Selection

Another list of Upanishads was provided by the commentator
Narayana. Narayana, son of Ramakra, probably belonged to the late
fourteenth century. Narayana is later than Shankara and also than
Shankarananda of the first half of the fourteenth century (flourished
circa 1350), the guru of Madhava, the Advaita Vedantist. He wrote
commentaries on several Upanishads and provided a list of fifty-two.
Many of these are the same as Colebrooke's list, and identical with
his from 1 to 28.[10] After this we have 29–30. *Nrisimha*; 31. probably
Kathaka; 32. probably *Kena*; 33. *Narayana*; 34. *Maha-Narayana* =
Brihannarayana; 35–36. *Ramatapaniya*; 37. *Sarvopanishatsara*; 38.
Hamsa; 39–42 are unclear, but probably 39. *Paramahamsa*; 40. *Jabala*;
41. *Kaivalya*; 42. *Taittiriya*; 43. possibly *Ashrama*; 44. *Garuda*; 45.
Kalagnirudra; 46–7. *Gopalatapaniya*; 48. *Krishna*; 49. *Vasudeva*; 50.
Gopichandana; 51–2. *Varadapurva* and *Uttara-tapini*.

    However, one cannot find any reason for this collection. As
Deussen says, these collections 'exhibit such a lack of principle
that they make an impression of having been mixed up confusedly
by mere accident'.[11]

Classification of the 108 Upanishads

Deussen and others have classified the Upanishads in similar ways,
though with minor variations. Ramachandreshvara Sarasvati,
more popularly known as Upanishad Brahmayogin, lived in the
late eighteenth to early nineteenth centuries. He commented on
and classified the 108 Upanishads of the *Muktika Upanishad*.

Major Upanishads

A group of ten to thirteen are referred to as the 'major Upanishads'.
Of these ten, or according to some sources, eleven, were

commented on or referred to by the great philosopher Shankara (Adi Shankaracharya). Shankara's dates are uncertain, though most scholars feel he was born in 788 CE and died in 820 CE. *Isha, Kena, Katha, Prashna, Mundaka, Mandukya, Taittiriya, Aitareya, Chhandogya, Brihadaranyaka* are the ten major Upanishads commented upon by Shankara. These correspond with the first ten of the integrated list provided in the *Muktika Upanishad*. The eleventh Upanishad, the *Shvetashvatara*, has a commentary attributed to Shankara, though some doubt if it was his. In addition, in his commentary on the *Brahma Sutra*, he refers to the *Kaushitaki, Jabala, Maha-Narayana* and *Paingala* Upanishads. He is also said to have commented on the *Atharvashikha, Atharvashiras* and *Nrisimhatapaniya* Upanishads. Ramanuja in his *Brahma Sutra* commentary refers to most of these Upanishads as well as to the *Maitrayaniya* or *Maitri*, the *Subala* and the *Chulika*. He has some references to the *Garbha, Jabala* and *Maha* Upanishads. Madhva too used many of these Upanishads in his *Brahma Sutra* commentary. A number of other Upanishads also contain the highest philosophical ideas while some deal with various rituals, deities or aspects of Yoga. The *Maitrayani* and *Kaushitaki* are also often classified as major Upanishads.

The remaining Upanishads have been classified as the Samanya Vedanta, Deity Upanishads, Sannyasa Upanishads and Yoga Upanishads. There is some variation in the texts grouped under these heads.

Samanya Vedanta Upanishads

The Samanya Vedanta Upanishads are those that elaborate on aspects of Vedanta. Between twenty-one and twenty-seven are grouped under this category. The twenty-one are *Akshaya, Adhyatma, Annapurna, Atma, Atmabodha, Ekakshara, Garbha,*

Maha, *Mantrika*, *Muktika*, *Mudgala*, *Niralamba*, *Paingala*, *Shariraka*, *Shukarahasya*, *Sarvasara*, *Savitraya*, *Subala*, *Surya*, *Skanda Vajrasuchika*. Some include three ancient Upanishads, that is, the *Shvetashvatara*, *Maitrayani* and *Kaushitaki*, thus reaching twenty-four.

Deity Upanishads

The Deity Upanishads are classified into Shaiva, Vaishnava and Shakta.

There are fifteen Shaiva Upanishads: *Akshamalika*, *Atharvashikha*, *Atharvashira*, *Kalagnirudra*, *Kaivalya*, *Ganapatya*, *Jabalya*, *Dakshinamurti*, *Panchabrahma*, *Brihad-jabala*, *Bhasma-jabala*, *Rudrahridaya*, *Rudraksha-jabala*, *Sharabha* and *Shvetashvatara*. Though in some lists there are twelve.

There are eight Shakta Upanishads: *Tripura*, *Tripuratapini*, *Devi*, *Bahvricha*, *Bhavana*, *Sarasvatirahasya*, *Sita* and *Saubhagyalakshmi*. (The Annapurna listed above as Samanya Vedanta is sometimes classified with these.)

There are fourteen Vaishnava Upanishads: *Avyakta*, *Kalisantarana*, *Krishna*, *Garuda*, *Gopaltapaniya-Purva* and *Uttara*, *Tarasara*, *Maha-Narayana*, *Dattatreya*, *Narayana*, *Nrisimhatapini-Purva* and *Uttara*, *Ramatapini-Purva* and *Uttara*, *Ramarahasya*, *Vasudeva*, *Hayagriva*.

Sannyasa Upanishads

Seventeen Upanishads are classified as the Sannyasa Upanishads.

These are *Aruni*, *Avadhuta*, *Bhikshu*, *Brahma*, *Jabala*, *Katharudra*, *Kundika*, *Maitreya*, *Narada-Parivrajaka*, *Nirvana*, *Parabrahma*, *Paramahamsa*, *Paramahamsa-Parivrajaka*, *Sannyasa*, *Shatyayaniya*, *Turiyatita Avadhuta* and *Yajnavalkya*.

Yoga Upanishads

The Yoga Upanishads seek to reach Brahman through methods prescribed by yoga. The following are classified as Yoga Upanishads: *Advaya-taraka Upanishad, Amrita-bindu Upanishad, Amrita-nada, Brahmavidya, Darshana/Jabala Darshana, Dhyana-bindu, Hamsa, Kshurika, Mahavakya, Mandala-brahmana, Nada-bindu, Pashupata-brahma, Shandilya, Tejo-bindu, Trishikha-brahmana* or *Trishikhi-brahmana, Varaha, Yoga-chudamani, Yoga-kundalini, Yoga-shikha, Yogatattva.*

Topics in the Upanishads

With all this diversity, the Upanishads have numerous topics, including Brahman, the source of all creation, the atman or soul, the jiva, or individual soul, the nature of consciousness, the different worlds, reincarnation, the body, the chakras and inner power centres, as well as meditations on deities and a lot more (see Chapter 3 for more on these). However, the concept of Brahman can be said to be the most important aspect of these texts, and the main theme that of ultimate realization and transcendence. Long ago, this common and main aspect was recognized and compressed into a single text, the *Brahma Sutra*, composed before the first century CE (see Chapter 11 for more on the *Brahma Sutra* and its date.)

Though the Upanishads use some of the terminology of the Vedic Samhitas, they provide new meanings and interpretations to them. They comment on and reinterpret passages from the Vedas in the context of spiritual thought. They are a continuation of the Vedas, Brahmanas and Aranyakas, but convey a deeper symbolic meaning. They are not merely intellectual texts, but accounts of those who have a vision of the divine. Explaining this vision is not easy, and different methods are used. There are some direct explanations and many that are indirect, that hint at deeper truths.

Commentaries and explanations of the Upanishads have been written from ancient days. There were also attempts to distil the main teachings of the Upanishads.

Sri Aurobindo called the Upanishads 'the supreme work of the Indian mind'.[12] Upanishadic ideas form the basis for several later streams of thought in India, and have a similarity with certain ideas in the works of Plato, Pythagoras, the Gnostics, Neo-Platonics, German metaphysics and Sufis, and other profound philosophies.

After the texts became known in the West, they were also used by nineteenth- and twentieth-century writers and philosophers.

Date of the Upanishads

To arrive at conclusions regarding the dating of the texts, we can begin with the *Muktika*, which lists the 108 Upanishads. This has been dated to around 1650, thus all the 108 were composed by this time. At the other end of the spectrum, dating is done by examining the archaicness of the language, by looking at early commentaries and texts related to the Upanishads, by the relationship of the texts to Buddhism, and by their relative dating based on the date of the *Rig Veda*. Some of the texts can clearly be dated before the Buddha while others indicate a knowledge of its principles. In addition, the texts mention certain places and territories which also provide indications of the date.

The earliest Upanishads that we know today are the *Aitareya*, *Kaushitaki*, *Taittiriya*, *Brihadaranyaka*, *Chhandogya* and *Kena*, while slightly later are the *Katha*, *Shvetashvatara*, *Maha-Narayana*, *Isha*, *Mundaka*, *Prashna*, *Maitrayaniya* and *Mandukya*. These fourteen can be dated to before the third century BCE. Various scholars vary slightly in the relative dating of these texts, though all agree that the prose Upanishads are the earliest. Patrick Olivelle, based on a consensus of various views, provides the following sequence: 1. The earliest are the *Brihadaranyaka* and *Chhandogya*, probably seventh to sixth centuries BCE, though they may include passages that belong to much earlier times; 2. These are followed by the *Aitareya*, *Taittiriya* and *Kaushitaki*, sixth to fifth centuries BCE. All these are prose Upanishads; 3. Next is the verse *Kena*; 4. This is followed by the *Katha*, *Isha*, *Shvetashvatara* and *Mundaka*; 5. After this are the *Prashna* and *Mandukya*, two prose Upanishads. The *Brihad*, *Chhandogya* and *Kaushitaki* seem to have separate strands which were then put together. Some stories and ideas are repeated in several Upanishads, hence must be drawn from some earlier sources.

As for other scholars, David Knipe places the earliest Upanishads in the eighth century BCE. Sigme Cohen, in his recent exhaustive study, provides a relative chronological dating of the early Upanishads, placing them in the following order without fixing any dates: 1. The *Madhyandina* recension of the *Brihadaranyaka Upanishad*; 2. *Chhandogya*; 3. *Aitareya*; 4. *Kaushitaki*; 5. The *Kanva* recension of the *Brihadaranyaka*; 6. *Taittiriya*; 7. *Isha*; 8. *Prashna*; 9. *Mundaka*; 10. *Katha*; 11. *Shvetashvatara*; 12. *Kena*; 13. *Maitri*; 14. *Mandukya*; 15. *Maha-Narayana*; 16. *Kaivalya*; 17. *Bashkalamantra*; 18. The later Vaishnava, Shaiva, Shakta, Sannyasa and Yoga Upanishads. He places this latter category after the eleventh century.[13]

The Upanishads are also linked with the date of the Buddha, as some are placed earlier than Buddhism and some later. The dates of the Buddha vary according to chronologies provided in different sources. Dates generally accepted in India are 566 BCE for his birth and 486 BCE for his death. Other dates are 624–564 BCE and 448–368 BCE.

If, as according to some theories, the date of the Buddha is placed in the fourth century BCE instead of 486 BCE, all these texts may be later. Ruben dates some of the individual teachers as follows. Shandilya, 670–640 BCE; Uddalaka Aruni and Yajnavalkya, 640–610 BCE; and Shvetaketu, 610–580 BCE.

On the whole, scholars agree on which are the earliest Upanishads and on the broad dating of each Upanishad. More precise dates will be provided under the individual Upanishads.

Location

An analysis of the rivers and places mentioned in the *Rig Veda* indicate that the core area of the clans and people mentioned was in present north-west India and in Pakistan, in the region of the Sapta Sindhava, or seven rivers—the Indus and its tributaries, along with the Sarasvati and Drishadvati, all located to the west of the river Yamuna. In the later Vedic period, the core area moves to the east of the river Yamuna, within the Ganga plains. Gradually, the clans and tribes were acquiring fixed territories and forming states known as *janapada*s, which were later consolidated into *mahajanapada*s, clearly described in Buddhist texts. These texts list sixteen mahajanapadas which existed by the sixth century BCE: Gandhara, Kamboja, Matsya, Surasena, Kuru, Panchala, Koshala, Kashi, Vatsa, Malla, Vajji, Anga, Magadha, Chedi, Avanti and Asmaka. Most of them were monarchies, while Malla and Vajji were confederacies. We find many of these, along with other states, particularly Kekaya, Madra, Ushinara and Videha, mentioned in the Upanishads. The kingdom of Magadha expanded and developed into the empire of the Nandas and later of the Mauryas.

In general, it is presumed that the region of composition of the early Upanishads was broadly northern India up to the Vindhyas in the south. The *Brihadaranyaka Upanishad* is thought to have been composed mainly in the state of Videha. The *Aitareya Upanishad* may also be in Videha, while the *Chhandogya*, *Kaushitaki*, *Taittiriya* and *Jaiminiya* may have a core area somewhere in Kuru–Panchala. The *Jaiminiya Upanishad* may alternatively belong to northern Madhya Pradesh or east Rajasthan.

The most prominent janapadas mentioned in the early Upanishads are that of the Kurus and Panchalas. The Kuru–Panchalas are referred to together in the *Kathaka Samhita* and both together and separately in several Brahmanas and Upanishads. Together they seem to have occupied the area from the west of the Yamuna across much of the upper Ganga plains up to Allahabad. A passage in the *Kanva* recension of the *Kathaka Samhita* shows that they had one king. The Kurus were within the western doab and to the west of the Yamuna in the Kurukshetra region. Kauravya in the *Atharva Veda* enjoyed prosperity under Parikshit, who ruled at Asandivat, identified with Asandh. Both the Kurus and Panchalas were probably groups in which several different clans were amalgamated. The Kurus included the Bharatas and Purus. The *Chhandogya* refers to the assembly of the Panchalas, where the king Pravahana, son of Jivala, ruled.

Further east were the Kashis, who can be identified with the later Kashis in the Varanasi region. Ajatashatru, a king of Kashi, is prominent in the Upanishads. The Koshalas, mentioned in the Brahmanas, can be located north of the Kashis. The Kashis and Videhas, the latter probably in north Bihar, were connected. Janaka, king of Videha, is frequently mentioned as a great scholar. The *Kaushitaki Upanishad* mentions the Vashas along with the Matsyas. In earlier texts, the Vashas were located near the Ushinaras and seem to have united with them. The Shalvas and Matsyas were probably in the present region of Rajasthan. However, M.R. Singh places the Vedic Shalvas, Matsyas, Ushinaras and Vashas in the northern part of the Kurukshetra region. In the *Atharva Veda*, the Shalvas are said to live on the banks of the Yamuna. Gandhara is mentioned in the *Chhandogya Upanishad*, in which Uddalaka Aruni refers to it in a question to King Janaka, and is located in present-day Pakistan. From other texts, particularly the Buddhist *Setaketu Jataka*, Uddalaka and his son Shvetaketu went to Takshashila, one of the capitals of Gandhara, to study.

Kekaya, whose king Ashvapati is referred to in the Upanishads, was adjacent to Gandhara. Ashvapati, Janaka and Uddalaka Aruni were contemporaries. The Madras were also in the north-west.

The mahajanapadas represent a time of urbanization—the use of baked bricks in urban areas and the beginnings of coinage. Several Upanishads reflect the time of urbanization with references to courts, kings, capital cities and states. At the same time, agriculture and pastoralism continued. The *Brihadaranyaka* mentions agriculture and various crops that were grown, and a number of early Upanishads refer to pastoralism and the importance of cows. Horses, prominent in earlier texts, are also mentioned, but both in the Vedic Samhitas and later, cows and horses also have a metaphorical meaning, representing knowledge and light. According to the *Brihadaranyaka Upanishad* (6.3.22), there were ten kinds of cultivated (*gramyani*) grains; *vrihi-yava* (rice and barley); *tila-mashah* (sesamum and beans); *anu-priyangavah* (millets, *Panicum miliaceum* and *italicum*); *godhuma* (wheat); *masurah* (lentils); *khala*-kulah (khalvah and *Dolichos uniflorus*). *Kulmasha* is referred to in the *Chhandogya Upanishad*. The Nirukta explains it as sour gruel, but the commentator feels it is bad or sour beans (masha). The *Brihadaranyaka Upanishad* also records the storing of grain in villages.

Did urbanization influence Upanishadic thought? According to Olivelle,[14] the new ideas of asceticism and celibacy reflect a society in transition. On the whole, though, the new ideas in the Upanishads present a continuity in thought and a gradual development towards a higher philosophy.

Later verse Upanishads were after urbanization and even after the Mauryas.

Caste in the Upanishads

The brahmana, kshatriya or rajanya, vaishya and shudra were the four main castes at the time of the Upanishads. Among the two higher castes—the brahmana and the kshatriya or rajanya—the brahmana gradually gained importance, though at times there was some ambivalence about their relative positions. In the *Atharva Veda*, brahmanas refer to themselves as *deva*s or gods. The king's purohita, who was hereditary, was the most important brahmana in the kingdom, while other brahmanas were village priests. All of them received special privileges, though reverence for them was also a reverence for the values they embodied, of learning, teaching and simplicity. Not all brahmanas retained these values. Though brahmanas had religious authority, in the Upanishads they were sometimes instructed by kings.

Kshatriyas consisted of the king's relatives, warriors, some nobles and minor chieftains under his control. Vaishyas were artisans, traders and agriculturalists. The practice of crafts was to some extent hereditary, thus creating castes.

In some passages, shudras are considered inferior. The first three castes were known as *dvija*, or twice-born, as they were entitled to perform the *upanayana*, which was a kind of rebirth. The three upper castes could also install *agni* at the *agneyadheya*, or first installation of the fire. But according to the *Kathaka Samhita*, the shudra is not allowed to milk the cow for the *agnihotra* milk. In the *purushamedha*, different castes were offered to different deities.

*Chandala*s or outcastes are also referred to, particularly in the later Upanishads. Olivelle remarks[15] that Vedic literature was produced by and largely intended for brahmanas. However, the concept of caste was not developed in the *Rig Veda*, where there is only one verse, the Purusha-sukta, on the different castes. The three later Vedas, along with the Brahmanas, mention caste, which was gradually getting crystallized. As sacrifices became more complex, the brahmana's role in the sacrifice was essential, leading to their prominence in the caste system, with the shudra gradually being looked down upon. Thus, the *Aitareya Brahmana* (35.3) says the shudra should obey the orders of others. However, the caste

system was not rigid and the same text (8.36.4) states that through
the Rajasuya sacrifice different castes attained different qualities.
The brahmana received *tejas* (ascetic fervour), the kshatriya *virya* or
bravery, the vaishya *prajati* or the power to have children, and the
shudra *pratishtha*, meaning firmness or stability. Here, though the
four castes are differentiated, each received something worthwhile.

The *Brihadaranyaka Upanishad* (1.4) suggests that each caste
had a valuable role and says that each emerged out of Brahman,
the Absolute. It states: 'At first the kshatriya and other castes
were Brahman, who was alone. Being alone, he did not prosper.
He created a noble form, the kshatriya, consisting of those who
are kshatriyas among the gods: Indra, Varuna, Soma, Rudra,
Parjanya, Yama, Mrityu, Ishana. Therefore, there is none superior
to the kshatriya. Hence, in the Rajasuya sacrifice, the brahmana
adores the kshatriya from a lower seat.' However, the verse goes
on to say that it is the brahmana who is the source of the kshatriya.
Thus, though the king attains pre-eminence, he is ultimately
under the brahmana. The next verse says that he (Brahman) still
did not prosper, therefore he created the vaishyas, that is those
gods who are in groups, the Vasus, Rudras, Adityas, Vishvadevas
and Maruts. As he still did not prosper, he created the shudra
varna, Pushan. 'This earth indeed is Pushan for it nourishes all
that exists.' He then created a noble form (*shreya rupam*) which
is dharma (righteousness). He also equates dharma with satya or
truth. Thus, the four varnas were created through the divine varnas.
The Shrauta Sutras indicate different methods of performing
sacrifices according to the caste of the sacrificer (*yajamana*). In
the Soma sacrifices, different results were sought for each caste.
The *Shatapatha Brahmana* allots a place to the shudra in the Soma
sacrifice.

Certainly, the ritual texts were primarily for brahmanas, as the
priesthood developed, but the Upanishads were more diverse. The
story of Satyakama Jabala, who did not know who his father was,

but could still study with a teacher (see the *Chhandogya Upanishad* in Part II) is often told to reinforce this. In fact, with their emphasis on 'one without a second', the Upanishads could not promote or support caste divisions. Yet, as caste became entrenched in society, shudras began to be excluded even from the study of the Upanishads. Later Upanishads suggest that one needs to be a dvija (a twice-born, one of the three upper castes) even to renounce the world and become a sannyasi. Even the *Brahma Sutra* has a passage on shudras not being allowed to study the Vedas.

In this context, a story is told of Shankara's encounter with an untouchable (Dalit). According to the story, when walking on the road, he asked a lower-caste person (a chandala) coming towards him to move out of the way. Instead of moving away, the chandala questioned him. 'Should I move my atman, which is eternal, or my impermanent body? Is my untouchability in my body or my soul?' Shankara then realized that he had in fact been going against his own philosophy, that there was only One. He saw the chandala as the god Shiva and composed five verses, *Manisha Panchakam*, where he says he is ready to accept as his guru anyone with the knowledge of Brahman, whether a chandala or a brahmana. The story may not be true, but it indicates the fallacy of restricting access to the Upanishads on the basis of caste. However, such restrictions continued. The medieval Mahanubhava sect used a secret coded literature to avoid brahmanical caste restrictions. This would not have been required if caste was not entrenched. Bahinabai, a woman devotee of the Maratha saint Tukaram, revealed that she was not allowed to utter 'Om' or listen to the Vedas. Bhakti was a method of bypassing caste restrictions, which was one of the reasons for its popularity in medieval times. But even while the Upanishads may not have been available to all, concepts similar to those in the Upanishads reappeared in regional literature of all types and thus must have been well-known. Among such literature is the *Amritanubhava*, composed in Marathi by the thirteenth-century saint Jnaneshvara, and the literature of the Mahima Dharma, a religious sect that emerged in nineteenth-century Odisha.

Women

When we look at the position of women in the Upanishads, Maitreyi and Gargi are mentioned most often. Maitreyi, one of the two wives of the rishi Yajnavalkya, wished to know about Brahman, while his other wife Katyayani is described as being interested only in women's affairs. Gargi questioned Yajnavalkya twice, appearing as an independent woman, posing philosophical questions. (See the *Brihadaranyaka Upanishad* for more on these.) Yet these two instances cannot be taken to mean that women had a status equal to men. Steven E. Lindquist points out that the Upanishads were composed by men, not a single Upanishad is composed by a woman. Were these few references in the Upanishads to real women or were their conversations inserted into the text for some purpose? The *Brihadaranyaka* also has other passages on women which indicate that a married woman was usually subservient to her husband. The same Upanishad also says (1.4.3) that the creator, Prajapati or Viraj, was alone and not happy. Therefore, he divided his body into two, and the husband and wife (*pati–patni*) came into being. In a later section, the Upanishad (6.4) provides some instructions for the union of man and woman. At the time of procreation there should be sublimation through meditation. The implication here is that a man should approach his wife in a calm and reverential way. Those men who unite with their wives without this meditation destroy all their merit. A man should try to win a woman over by giving her desired objects, but if she refuses he can hit her and curse her. If she does yield to him, he recites a mantra and then both become reputed parents.

Instructions follow for what to do if the man's wife has a lover. Mantras are chanted and certain rituals undertaken so that the man the brahmana curses 'departs from the world, impotent and devoid of merit'. Men should therefore be very careful in their dealings with the wife of a Vedic scholar who knows these rites and not even joke with her. When the wife has her periodical impurity, she should drink from a bell metal vessel for three days, and no shudra man or woman should touch her. After this she should bathe and wear fresh clothes and the husband should ask her to thresh rice (this is obviously related to fertility). Next, there are instructions for what to eat to produce ideal sons, and in one case even an ideal daughter. The *Brihadaranyaka Upanishad* (6.4.17) reads: 'He who wishes, "May a daughter be born to me who will be a scholar [pandita] and attain longevity" should have rice and sesamum cooked together, and with his wife eat it mixed with ghi. Then they would be able to produce such a daughter.'[16]

Though the Upanishads are considerably later, there was probably some continuity in the position of women from Rig Vedic times. In the *Rig Veda*, several references indicate that girls reached maturity before they were married. They did not have a free choice in marriage, though one hymn mentions marriage through elopement, and courtship and love are also referred to. On the whole, women definitely had an inferior position, though the status would have differed among different classes and in different clans and areas. Marriage was of various types, including polygamy and monogamy. One indication of the inferior position of women is the nature of the goddesses in the *Rig Veda*. Though goddesses are known, they are relatively few. Aditi and Usha are the most important goddesses, but they do not have the same prominence as the gods. At the most fifteen hymns were composed by women in the *Rig Veda*, out of 1028, and Michael Witzel,[17] in his article on female rishis and philosophers in the Veda, doubts even these. He adds that in the patriarchal society of the Vedic tribes, poets were male bards. Women may have composed poems, but these were not thought to be valuable enough for preservation. He

emphasizes that the so-called equality of women in Vedic times
is elusive. There are no women priests who conducted sacrifices.
Several prayers in the *Rig Veda* are for children in general and
specifically for sons.

In later Vedic times, women still seem to have married
after puberty. Polygamy existed and two, four or more wives are
mentioned. As seen above, the rishi Yajnavalkya had two wives,
whereas a king was said to have four wives, of whom the mahishi
was the chief queen and the vavata the favourite. Passages in
the *Atharva Veda* suggest that a widow could remarry and that
polyandry too existed. The *Vajasaneyi Samhita* refers to illicit
relationships and to the son of an unmarried girl (*kumariputra*).
The father had some control over the daughter and there are
instances where he gave her as an offering to a brahmana. Dowries
were sometimes given. The marriage ceremony was probably
much the same as in the Rig Vedic period as the marriage hymn
is repeated in the *Atharva* without much change. There is a
reference in the *Atharva* (18.3.1) to the ancient practice of sati.
Initially, the sacrificer (yajamana) was accompanied by his wife,
but she could not initiate a sacrifice on her own. Slightly later,
the priest often replaced the wife in the sacrificial ritual, perhaps
indicating a decline in her status. The *Shatapatha Brahmana* says
that a wife is half her husband and without her he is incomplete,
but in another passage suggests her inferior position when it states
that she should eat after her husband. The *Aitareya Brahmana*
says that a good woman does not talk back. In another passage
it says that a daughter is a source of misery and a son is a saviour
for the family. Widow remarriage is permitted in some texts and
prohibited in others.

In the later Upanishads, the evils of associating with women
on the path towards attaining Brahman is pointed out. Women
are one of the categories that are not allowed to study the Vedas
or Upanishads.

Commentators

There have been numerous commentaries on the Upanishads and today the texts can hardly be read without the work of the commentators. In the *Brahma Sutra*, early commentators such as Audolomi are mentioned.

Gaudapada, who lived in the seventh or eighth century, provides the earliest available commentary on the Upanishads, simultaneously laying the foundations of the philosophy of Advaita. Though Advaitic ideas were known earlier, Gaudapada explained its principles in a systematic way. He was the teacher of Govinda, who was the guru of Shankara, who firmly established Advaita in India. Gaudapada put forward his ideas in the *Karika*, which has four sections. The first consists of a commentary on the *Mandukya Upanishad*, while the next three explain Advaitic concepts. He incorporated Buddhist principles in his system of thought, particularly those of the Madhyamika and Vijnanavada. S. Dasgupta feels he was initially a Buddhist[18] while according to S. Radhakrishnan he accepted Buddhist principles when they were not in conflict with his own and adjusted Buddhist doctrines 'to the Advaita design'. Gaudapada's ideas were further elaborated by Shankara.

Shankara (CE 788–820) commented on the *Brahma Sutra*, a text which distils the essence of the Upanishads, as well as on several other Upanishads, as seen above. Several other works are assigned to him: *Shariraka-mimamsa-bhashya; Aparokshanubhava*; commentary on Gaudapada's *Mandukya-karika*, known as *Gaudapadya-bhashya* or *Agama-shastra-vivarana*; commentary on the Bhagavad Gita; *Eka-shloka*; the *Upadesha Sahasri*, the *Viveka Chudamani; Atma Bodha* (Knowledge of the Soul); *Atmanatma-viveka; Atmopadesha-vidhi; Chidananda-stava-raja*, also known as *Dashashloki; Drig-drishya-prakarana; Laghu-vakya-vritti; Vakya-vritti*. According to others, only his commentaries on the *Brahma Sutra*, Upanishads, *Yoga Sutra* and Bhagavad Gita, along with the 'Upadesha Sahasri' and 'Bhajagovinda' hymns, are authentically his. In addition, other works assigned to him are the *Dakshinamurti Stotra, Harimide Stotra, Advaitanubhuti, Tattvopadesha, Praudhanubhuti* and *Saundarya Lahiri* (including *Ananda Lahiri*), as well as several others.

In his works, Shankara not only explained his own theories but provided a critique of existing philosophies. Shankara's theories in turn had several critics, giving rise to different schools of philosophy such as Vishishtadvaita, Dvaita, Dvaitadvaita and others. Later Advaita philosophers attempted to address the questions raised by different philosophical systems and to substantiate and expand on the views of Shankara. Another general criticism of his philosophy is that Shankara's metaphysical concept of oneness was not given a practical application during his lifetime and did not promote egalitarianism. This is true of later times, too, though Shankara is often quoted and revered.

From the standpoint of Dvaita, Madhva commented on the *Aitareya, Brihadaranyaka, Chhandogya, Taittiriya, Isha, Kathaka, Mundaka, Mandukya, Kena,* and also on the *Brahma Sutra* and Bhagavad Gita, among other texts. There were numerous other commentators of all branches of Vedanta as well as of other philosophies (see Chapter 2).

Among the noted commentators was Mandana Mishra, a disciple of Kumarila Bhatta and an exponent of Purva Mimamsa philosophy, who lived in the eighth to ninth centuries. He wrote *Vidhiviveka* and *Mimamsanukramani* on the Mimamsa philosophy. His other works include *Bhavana-viveka, Sphotasiddhi* and *Vibhrama-viveka.* However, his work *Brahma Siddhi* has Vedantic ideas. According to tradition, he was defeated by Sri Shankara in a philosophical argument and became his follower, modifying his earlier views. He was then known as Sri Sureshvara Acharya and was installed by Shankara as head of the Sringeri Matha. As

Sureshvara, he wrote commentaries on Shankara's works, including *Manasola Varttika* on the *Dakshinamurti Stotra*. His *Naishkarmya Siddhi* summarizes the teachings of Shankara. In addition, he wrote the *Balakrida*, a commentary on the *Yajnavalkya Smriti*, and elucidated Shankara's commentaries on the *Taittiriya* and *Brihadaranyaka* Upanishads. Vishvarupa is considered another name of Sureshvara.

Sayana was a commentator on the *Rig Veda* and other Vedic texts. He lived in the fourteenth century and was a minister of several kings of Vijayanagara, particularly Bukka I (1344–77) and Harihara II (1377–1404). Sayana wrote commentaries on the *Rig Veda*, *Taittiriya Samhita*, *Sama Veda*, *Atharva Veda*, a number of Brahmanas and the *Aitareya Aranyaka*. In addition, he compiled the *Subhashita-sudhanidhi*, a collection of moral sayings, *Prayschitta-sudhanidhi* on dharma, *Purushartha-sudhanidhi* on the goal of human life, *Yajnatantra-sudhanidhi* on Vedic rituals and a number of other texts, including some on grammar. Sayana's commentary on the *Rig Veda* is extensive and deals with each hymn, mentioning the rishi who is said to have composed it, the deity, the metre and its use in sacrifice. Other texts and stories are used in explaining the verses. Sayana was probably assisted by other scholars, but was himself extremely learned. He is sometimes given the title 'Sarvajna', 'one who has all knowledge'. He was the brother of Madhava, and, according to some accounts, the son of Mayana, a brahmana of the Bharadvaja gotra.

Vidyaranya was a philosopher of the fourteenth century. His identity is not very clear. His original name is not known, but is thought to have been Madhava; he is said to have taken the name Vidyaranya after he became a sannyasi in 1377. Vidyaranya is generally identified with Madhavacharya, the author of *Sarvadarshana Samgraha* and *Shankara-digvijaya*. According to some accounts, Madhavacharya or Vidyaranya was the same as Madhava, the brother of Sayana, commentator on the Vedas.

However, records of the Sringeri Matha have a different account. According to this, Vidyaranya was born in about 1296 in Ekasila Nagara, present-day Warangal in Andhra Pradesh, and was the elder brother of Sri Bharati Krishna Tirtha, whom he succeeded as the twelfth acharya of the Sringeri Matha from 1380 to 1386. He was involved in the foundation of the Vijayanagara kingdom in 1336. The Sringeri accounts state that the two brothers Madhava and Sayana came to him for his blessings. Vidyaranya gave them his unfinished Veda bhashyas along with some other works and they completed them. Madhava and Sayana became the ministers of the Vijayanagara kings Harihara and Bukka, who were also blessed by Vidyaranya.

Vidyaranya composed a number of texts, the most popular being *Panchadashi* on Advaita Vedanta. He also wrote *Dhatu-vritti*, on Sanskrit grammar, *Jaiminiya Nyayamala*, on Mimamsa, and *Parasara-smritivyakhya*, a commentary on the *Parasara-smriti*. Other texts assigned to him are *Smriti Sangraha, Vyavahara Madhava, Sri Vidyartha Dipika, Vivaranaprameya Sangraha, Drik Drishya Viveka, Aparokshanubhuti Tika,* as well as commentaries on the Upanishads. *Jivan-mukti-viveka* is also assigned to Vidyaranya. This deals with attaining liberation while alive (*jivan-mukti*) and includes quotations from earlier texts. However, S. Dasgupta feels this could be a later text, written by a different Vidyaranya.[19]

According to some sources, not all the texts were solely written by him, and Bharati Tirtha also contributed to the *Panchadashi*. One theory is that Bharati Tirtha was the same person as Vidyaranya, though the Sringeri Matha clearly distinguishes between them. In spreading the truths of Advaita, Vidyaranya had a reputation that came close to that of Shankara. Vidyaranya travelled to several sacred sites and tirthas. He died in 1386 at Sringeri.

Upanishads continued to be composed in medieval times and were seen as a distinct category of literature. They were collected, listed, read and translated, but were not easily accessible for the

common person. The knowledge of the Vedic Samhitas and the
Upanishads were largely confined to brahmanas who did not
explain them to the people but used the Samhitas in rituals. In
the nineteenth century, this began to change with an increasing
number of translations being made available. Rammohan Roy
(22 May 1772–27 September 1833), a scholar in Bengal who had
studied Persian, Arabic and Sanskrit, as well as Hebrew and Greek,
was determined to make the Vedic texts known as they seemed
the answer to the social injustice, superstition and idol worship
prevailing in the country. He also saw that these texts promoted
equality and could be used to improve the position of women and
the lower castes. He translated the *Mandukya*, *Kena*, *Katha* and *Isha*
Upanishads into English and also made translations into Bengali
and Hindi. His works on Vedanta include an explanation of it,
establishing that there is one universal supreme being. Rammohan
Roy also wrote on Islam and Christianity.

He founded the Brahmo Samaj, which was inspired by
Upanishadic thought. The Brahmo Samaj is an organization for
social and religious reform, inaugurated in Kolkata (Calcutta) on
20 August 1828. It was open to people of all castes and religions.
Initially, the Samaj held a weekly meeting at which parts of the
Vedic Samhitas were recited and the Upanishads explained.
Following this, bhajans were sung. Despite his best efforts, the
Telugu brahmanas who recited the Vedic passages refused to let
non-brahmanas attend; however, the Upanishadic explanations
were open to all. After Rammohan Roy, the Samaj went through
many phases, but on the whole continued to base its philosophy
on Upanishadic thought.

Other reform movements of the nineteenth century used these
texts. For instance, the Atmiya Sabha which preached the worship
of one god was established in 1814.

Swami Dayananda Saraswati, founder of the Arya Samaj,
based his work on the Vedic Samhitas but believed that the

Upanishads also had value, particularly those commented upon by Shankara. He did not see the Upanishads as divine revelations but as the knowledge of rishis which could clarify portions of the Samhitas. In his main book, *Satyartha Prakasha*, he quoted verses from the Upanishads. Others in the Arya Samaj did write on the Upanishads later, among them being Mahatma Narayan Swami, Satyavratta Siddhantalankara, Swami Darshanacharya and Swami Satya Prakash.

Shri Upanishad Brahmayogin, who followed the philosophy of Advaita, is the only one to have commented on all 108 Upanishads. The son of Shivakameshvara, his original name was Shivarama and he was born in Brahmapuram village near the river Palar, probably in the mid-eighteenth century. He became a sannyasi and was given *diksha* (initiation) by Vasudevendra Sarasvati of Kanchipuram. As part of the Sarasvati order of sannyasis, he received the name Ramachandrenda Sarasvati. He founded his own math at Kanchipuram and came to be known as Upanishad Brahmayogin because of his commentary on all 108 Upanishads listed in the *Muktika Upanishad*. On the ten major Upanishads, he largely follows Shankaracharya's commentary with some divergences and additional explanations.

Sri Aurobindo also commented on and reinterpreted some of the Upanishads. In modern times, in the twentieth and twenty-first centuries, commentators have been numerous. Swami Veda Bharati, Swami Madhavananda, Swami Nikhilananda and Swami Chinmayananda are just a few of this vast number.

Related Texts

From very early times, the Vedas, that is the Vedic Samhitas, were considered difficult to understand. Additional texts were composed which commented on, clarified or explained aspects of the Vedic Samhitas.

Padapathas and Anukramanis

Among these were the Padapathas and Anukramanis. The Samhita texts had words in their conjoined forms whereas the Padapatha or word texts present the words in various ways, without *sandhi* (sandhi rules join words together in a particular way, changing the ending or beginning). Anukramani is a Sanskrit term for a list, catalogue or index. Some Anukramanis classify and provide details that are not available in the Samhitas. They include lists of hymns, rishis who composed the hymns and lists of metres.

Vedangas

The Vedangas, another group of associated texts, deal with six subjects that are considered essential for an understanding of the Vedas. These are: *shiksha*, phonetics or the science of pronunciation; *vyakarana*, grammar; *chhandas* or metre; *nirukta*, etymology or glossary; *jyotisha*, astronomy and astrology, essential to fix the right time for ceremonies and sacrifices and *kalpa*, or rules for sacrifices. There are several texts on these topics. Shiksha, vyakarana and nirukta are connected and the subject matter overlaps to some extent. Shiksha as a term for phonetics is first used in the *Taittiriya Upanishad*, which gives its various components including varna (individual sounds) and *svara* (accent).

The Pratishakhyas are among the earliest texts on shiksha. Pratishakhya literally means 'belonging to each shakha' and there were pratishakhya texts for the various Vedic shakhas or schools. The Pratishakhyas describe how the verses in the Vedas are to be pronounced and also deal with sandhi rules (methods of joining words), accents, vowels and some aspects of grammar useful for pronunciation. They were composed later than the Vedas and are related to the Padapatha texts described earlier. There are several other texts on shiksha, most of which were later than the Pratishakhyas.

At least sixty-five such texts on shiksha are known.

Nirukta, in the sense of etymology or glossary, is another of the Vedangas. Nirukta texts are important for understanding the archaic language of the *Rig Veda*. There must have been several Niruktas but the one that is still extant is that of Yaska, who probably lived before Panini.

Vyakarana or grammar is another important topic necessary to study and understand the Vedas. The Brahmanas, Aranyakas and Upanishads contain some aspects of grammar. The Padapatha texts and some of the Pratishakhyas described above also contain elements of grammar and so does the Nirukta. Yaska in fact mentions that in his time there were already two schools of grammarians, the eastern and northern. However, the earliest available complete Sanskrit grammar was written by Panini and is known as the *Ashtadhyayi*. Not much is known of his life but Panini is thought to have lived sometime between the seventh and fourth centuries BCE.

Panini was, however, not the first to write a grammar, and is believed to have had sixty-four predecessors. There were also several later texts on grammar.

*Chhanda*s is a Sanskrit term with several meanings and is usually translated as 'prosody' but in general it refers to metres occurring in sacred texts.

A knowledge of chhandas as metre is considered essential for an understanding of the Veda.

Elements of *jyotisha* and of a calendric system appear from the Rig Veda onwards. The times, dates and duration of many of the sacrifices described in the *Yajur Veda* and later texts were based on a knowledge of the solar and lunar calendars.

The *Yajur Veda* texts as well as the *Atharva Veda* name the *nakshatra*s (constellations), though the names differ. The *Yajur*

Taittiriya Samhita says there are twenty-seven nakshatras, while the *Atharva* and *Yajur Maitrayani Samhita* give twenty-eight. The nakshatras listed in succession formed a sort of lunar zodiac. Based on a passage in the Brahmanas, the early scholars Tilak and Jacobi felt the Krittikas (Pleiades) was the starting point of the nakshatra system. The Vedic texts also seem to refer to an older calendar, when the vernal equinox was Mrigashiras (Orion). In the *Chhandogya Upanishad*, the study and knowledge of nakshatras is considered worthwhile. The Grihya Sutras have references to astronomical phenomena.

The *Vedanga Jyotisha*, compiled by Lagadha, is the earliest known text on the subject.

A special category of texts were concerned with ritual. These are broadly termed the Kalpa Sutras. They have three categories: the Shrauta Sutras, which provide instructions for the agnihotra and other sacrifices; the Grihya Sutras, which describe domestic sacrifices; and the Dharma Sutras, which explain laws and customs. Each of these are attached to one of the four Vedic Samhitas, but are considered smriti (remembered) and not shruti or divinely revealed, that is, they have less sanctity than the Vedic Samhitas and other texts closely associated with them. The Kalpa Sutras belong to different Vedic Samhitas and schools, and though each text is separate, some series of texts form a connected sequence. For instance, the Apastamba and Baudhayana schools of the *Krishna Yajur Veda* have closely related Shrauta, Grihya and Dharma Sutras. For certain schools, only a single type of sutra is now available, that is, a Shrauta Sutra or a Grihya Sutra, while some have only two.

The Dharma Sutras form the earliest sources of Hindu law and were originally composed between the sixth and seventh centuries BCE, with additions being made later. The customs and ethics described in these are written in short aphorisms or 'sutras' and were later expanded and written in verse, forming the Dharma

Shastras. The Dharma Sutras are attributed to different authors, among them being the sages or rishis Apastambha, Baudhayana, Gautama and Vasishtha. There are many Dharma Shastras probably composed from the second century onwards, which expand on the Dharma Sutras. Some of these are idealistic, whereas others were used as legal texts; each is assigned to a mythical or real author. The *Manava Dharma Shastra* (of Manu), also known as the *Manu Smriti*, is the earliest, while those of Yajnavalkya, Vishnu and Narada are probably of the third to fifth centuries CE. There are several others.

Upavedas

Another category or branch of knowledge is known as Upaveda. Aspects of these are contained in the Vedic Samhitas and associated texts, but they were further developed as separate branches of knowledge. The four classes of the Upavedas are: Ayurveda, the science of medicine; Gandharvaveda, of music and dancing; Dhanurveda, of archery or military science; Sthapatyaveda, of architecture.

References to the Vedas in Other Sources

References to the Vedas are found in many other sources, including the epics, Bhagavad Gita, Puranas, later regional literature and in the six early systems of Hindu philosophy.

The two north Indian epics, the Mahabharata and the Ramayana, mention the Vedic Samhitas. In addition, some of the Vedic myths are retold or recast in the Mahabharata. On the whole, the Mahabharata has a closer connection with the Vedas than the Ramayana. Names mentioned in the Vedic Samhitas are also found in the Mahabharata. Several deities known in the Vedas are referred to, and some of the same myths occur, though in a different form. The Mahabharata contains references to sacrifices and to sacrificial material such as *darbha* grass. Some scholars also suggest that events such as the Mahabharata war represent a kind of ritual, purificatory sacrifice. The Puranas have numerous references to the Vedas as well as to Vedic deities. There are elaborations of old stories and new legends on Vedic deities and personalities.

The six orthodox systems of philosophy—Nyaya, Vaisheshika, Samkhya, Yoga, Mimamsa and Vedanta—were developing around the same time that the early Upanishads were composed, or a little later. We will look at these systems, all of which accept the authority of the Vedas, in the next chapter.

About This Book

This book will provide information on the 108 Upanishads, with an analysis of the main topics, along with a summary of each text.

The Upanishads are all composed in Sanskrit. Every word in Sanskrit has multiple meanings and translators and commentators have interpreted the words and terms differently. For each Upanishad, the Sanskrit text has been consulted, along with different translations and commentaries.

One can read and study the Upanishads for many reasons. It could be to complete one's understanding of Vedic literature from a historical or intellectual standpoint, or to understand Brahman and gain liberation. Which Upanishad should one begin with, or should one proceed directly to the *Brahma Sutra* and their innumerable commentaries?

The *Muktika Upanishad*, though not an early one, is a good starting place to understand the essence of the Upanishads. The *Muktika* not only provides a list of the 108 classic Upanishads and the Vedas that each is assigned to, but also a perception into the true meaning of what a deity is.

It begins with a description of Rama and Sita seated in a gem-studded pavilion in Ayodhya, worshipped by all, and proceeds with Rama explaining to Hanuman how to attain mukti, liberation. Perfect liberation is 'videha-mukti', that is, liberation also from the body and the concept of the body.

Obviously, Rama is liberated, and must also have videha mukti. How then is he still seated in Ayodhya? Towards the end of the *Muktika*, Rama indicates that this form has something beyond it when he says: 'Contemplate me as without sound, touch, form, taste and smell, eternal, indestructible, without name and family' (2.2.72).

Two

The Philosophical Context

AS WE SAW in the previous chapter, the Upanishads form the last part of the Vedic Samhitas and present some continuity in thought from the Samhitas, Brahmanas and Aranyakas. In addition, these texts are considered 'shruti', or divinely revealed, and therefore cannot be altered in any way; they can only be explained. As the Upanishads have numerous topics and different strands of thought, great scholars of the past have tried to understand their essence and explain them using their own divine intuition and knowledge along with their understanding of other texts. Today, they cannot be understood without the commentaries of these thinkers, whose works almost form an integral part of the texts.

The Upanishads, though, were just one strand in the development of philosophy in India. Philosophical thought began even before the Upanishads, right from the time of the *Rig Veda*. Even in the *Rig Veda*, questions are raised on the origin of the universe and the beginnings of life. The Brahmanas, which are attached to the Vedic Samhitas, deal mainly with the magical power of ritual, but along with this there was some speculative thinking. This philosophical thinking proceeded further in the Aranyakas, reaching a height in the Upanishads.

The school of philosophy based on the Upanishads is known as Vedanta. The term Vedanta also refers to the Upanishads themselves, which form the last part of the Vedas (Vedanta: Veda and anta: end or last). Vedanta is mentioned in the Mahabharata as a category of literary works and probably here refers to the Upanishads.

Apart from these, there were many other early schools of thought. They were broadly divided into astika and nastika, the former being those that accepted the authority of the Vedas and the latter those that did not. Vedanta itself is one of the six main astika schools of classical Indian philosophy which began to develop around the sixth century BCE, if not earlier. The others are Mimamsa, Nyaya, Vaisheshika, Samkhya and Yoga. Purva Mimamsa, or early Mimamsa, focused on the Vedic Samhitas and on ritual. Mimamsa and Vedanta were initially different, but later were thought to form a unified system, and Uttara Mimamsa, or later Mimamsa, became identical with Vedanta. Samkhya uses some of the terms in the Upanishads but creates a system of philosophy that is substantially different. Samkhya is said to have been founded by the sage Kapila. Elements of the Samkhya philosophy are found in the Upanishads and the Mahabharata and are also explained in the Bhagavad Gita.

Nyaya and Vaisheshika use logic and experience to understand the nature of reality. Though initially divergent, these two schools of thought later almost merged. Nyaya literally means that by which the mind reaches a conclusion and is based on logic and analysis. Nyaya's methods of analysis have been used to understand the Vedas, and hence it has been called an *upanga* (auxiliary limb) of the Vedas.

Vaisheshika deals with physics, metaphysics, logic and methods of knowledge, and its central feature is considered its theory on the atomic structure of the universe. As with Nyaya, its methods of analysis can be used to understand the Vedas.

Both Vedanta and the others had early origins but continued to develop in succeeding centuries. In fact, many of them were defined by their later commentators. Vedanta developed numerous branches as its principles were analysed and refuted. These commentators were much later than the Upanishads; however, their work is so closely linked with the texts that the texts cannot be fully understood without them.

The most important nastika schools were Buddhism and Jainism, along with the philosophies of Ajita Keshakambalin, the Ajivikas, and the Charvakas or materialists. In a Buddhist text (the Brahmajala Sutta of the *Digha Nikaya*), sixty-two heretical schools of thought are mentioned, though not all of these are known. Some scholars include only materialistic schools which do not believe in an afterlife, and thus exclude Buddhism and Jainism from nastika schools.

In this chapter, we provide an overview of the main philosophical systems of early India, as well as some later philosophical developments. All the six early orthodox systems uphold the sanctity of the Vedas. Though Nyaya, Vaisheshika, Samkhya and Yoga did not directly comment on them, they incorporated some aspects of the Vedic Samhitas.

Vedanta

As seen above, the term Vedanta comes from 'Veda' plus 'anta', indicating that the Upanishads form both the last part of the Vedas and its ultimate or highest part. The basis for the analysis of Vedantic principles was laid by Badarayana (500 BCE to first century CE) who summarized the main teachings of the Upanishads in the *Brahma Sutra*, also known as the *Vedanta Sutra*. The *Brahma Sutra*, the Upanishads and the Bhagavad Gita are the texts most often quoted by Vedantic scholars, though others are also used. They are known as the *prasthana-traya*, or the three starting points for any discussion of Vedanta. The early Vedantic teachers are those mentioned in the Upanishads themselves, and in the *Brahma Sutra*. The *Brahma Sutra* refers to several teachers of ancient days who spanned different philosophies, including Ashmarathya, Atreya, Audulomi, Badari, Jaimini, Kashakritana and Karshnajini. Among these, Kashakritana was probably a Vedantist. Other early Vedantists referred to in various sources include Dravidacharya, Tanka, Upavarsha, Bodhayana, Brahmadatta and Sundara Pandya.[1]

Vedantic commentators interpreted the Upanishads and other basic texts in different ways, thus developing various schools of philosophy within the broad framework of Vedanta. These schools that developed over the years include Advaita, Vishishtadvaita, Dvaita, Dvaitadvaita, Shuddhadvaita and Shivadvaita. Each school arrives at different understandings on the nature and relationship of Brahman, Ishvara or god, the atman or soul—which can be a universal soul—the jiva or individual soul, and the world. Each also focuses on understanding the *mahavakya*s, the great sacred sentences (see Chapter 3), and in addition goes into several other subtle and intricate concepts.

Advaita

In Vedanta, Advaita, meaning monism, is the most widespread and influential school of thought. Traditionally, Advaita is said to have been first revealed by the god Narayana or by the god Sadashiva—both of them seen as representing the supreme deity—to the god Brahma. Brahma imparted it to the rishi Vasishtha, who taught it to his son Shakti, from whom it passed on to Parashara, Vyasa and Shuka. The god Brahma, as well as the rishis Vasishtha, Shakti and others, are mentioned in the

Upanishads. Teachers such as Kashakritana, and some of the others referred to in the *Brahma Sutra*, seem to have followed the philosophy of Advaita, though nothing much is known about them. However, as seen in the introduction, the earliest available texts are those of Gaudapada, a philosopher who lived in the seventh or eighth century, followed by those of Shankara of the ninth century.

Gaudapada put forward his main ideas in the *Karika*, a commentary on the *Mandukya Upanishad*. This has four parts, of which only the first is actually a commentary and the rest expands on Advaitic principles. Shankara provides a further commentary on Gaudapada's text. He also explains Advaita in several other commentaries and texts.

In his introduction to his commentary on the *Brahma Sutra*, Shankara questions what is generally perceived as reality. He says that experiences, senses and memory may deceive us. However, all consciousness and knowledge presupposes that there is an atman, a self through which everything is known. The nature of the atman can be nothing other than pure consciousness (*chaitanyam*) and eternal knowledge but it is not the same as what we perceive as consciousness. And if there is the atman, Brahman must exist, as the substratum of all atmans.

Brahman, the One Reality, has always existed and will always exist. Beyond time and space, it never changes, grows or diminishes. It is complete and perfect and is not similar to anything else. The true Self, the atman or individual soul within, is identical with this, and both have the characteristics of true being, consciousness and bliss (sat-chit-ananda). Brahman and the world, which has space, time, causality and a multiplicity of forms, cannot both be real, hence the world is unreal, an illusion. This unreality is known as maya, and is a product of *ajnana* or *avidya*, that is, of ignorance. The world is always changing, and whatever changes and is non-eternal cannot be real. Similarly, the ego or the individual personality, which is subject to birth, growth and death, cannot be real. Realizing the Self as Brahman brings bliss, joy and freedom. Jnana or wisdom is the direct route for such realization.

Within this framework, Shankara developed certain other ideas. He put forward the concept of Ishvara or a personal god, though he said that logic and rationality cannot prove its existence. However, shruti (scripture) states that it exists. If one accepts shruti, which is a source of knowledge (jnana) then Ishvara too must exist and can be reconciled with reason. Ishvara is the creator and destroyer of the world. Ishvara creates because that is its nature (svabhava). It is Saguna Brahman (Brahman limited by qualities), related to the world, to maya (which is not only a term representing unreality, but refers to an illusory creative power), and to the individual consciousness or jiva. The jiva incorporates the *antahkarana* or personal inner Self, including the mind, ego and thought, and thus is not the same as the atman. It is subject to rebirth and to its individual karma. Yet, in essence all is the same as all is Brahman.

The concepts of Shankara, such as the relationship of Brahman and Ishvara, the atman and the jiva, maya and the world, as well as of jnana and ajnana, were further clarified by commentators on Shankara's work, who explained them in different ways.

Commentators on Advaita soon after the time of Shankara include Sureshvara (according to tradition, this was the later name of Mandana Mishra), Vachaspati Mishra, Padmapada and Anandagiri. Among other writers on Advaita were Sarvajnatma Muni (circa 900), Shriharsha (twelfth century), Chitsukha (flourished circa 1220), Amalananda (thirteenth century), Vidyaranya (fourteenth century), Appayya Dikshitar (sixteenth century), Anandabodha Yati, Anandajnana, Vimuktatman, Ramadvaya, Nrisimhashrama Muni, Prakashananda and Madhusudana Sarasvati (circa 1565–1665). Upanishad Brahmayogin, the commentator on the 108

Upanishads on Advaitic lines, belonged to the mid-eighteenth- to-nineteenth centuries. Also in the nineteenth century, Vivekananda as well as various reform groups used the principles of Advaita in their attempts to revive and reform Hinduism. Vivekananda emphasized 'Tat tvam asi' (You are That, meaning 'You are god') as the essence of Advaita Vedanta. He said that with the recognition that within each being was the same universal Self, the Vedantic ideal was realized. In the twentieth century, several scholars and gurus have explained Shankara's ideas, among them Swami Chinmayananda and his disciples and various teachers of the Ramakrishna Mission.

Advaita is considered the most influential philosophical system in Indian society even today.

Vishishtadvaita

Vishishtadvaita can be defined as 'qualified monism'. The main proponent of this philosophy was Ramanuja of the eleventh century. Ramanuja's *Shribhashya* and other texts form the first full delineation of the philosophy but its principles can be traced to earlier philosophers and mystics, including Nathamuni, Pundarikaksha, Rama Mishra and Yamunacharya. Vishishtadvaita is also known as Ubhayavedanta as it includes both (*ubhaya*) Vedantic concepts and bhakti.

According to Ramanuja, Brahman is the only true reality, but matter and the soul are not unreal as they are pervaded by Brahman. The soul is created by god from his own essence. Through karma, various forms such as gods, people, animals and plants came into existence but their souls are essentially the same. Each soul is divine and eternal but always remains distinct from Brahman and conscious of itself. If it were to lose this, it would not exist. Worship and devotion to god lead to the soul being released from matter, realizing its divine nature and attaining eternal communion with god. However, such souls are not identical with Brahman, which is all-pervasive and which alone has creative power. According to Ramanuja, moksha or liberation is a state where all limitations disappear, but the individual soul continues to exist. The individual soul remains atomic in nature and Brahman contains a unity of perfected souls.

The material world is also a part of god and is not an illusion. God has love and compassion for his creation and incarnated in different forms to show them the path to salvation. According to Ramanuja, Rama was the highest of these incarnations.

The philosopher Radhakrishnan said that both Shankara and Ramanuja were great exponents of Vedanta; they examined the same texts and based their ideas on the same assumptions, yet reached different conclusions. He said, 'Ramanuja trusts firmly to the religious instinct, and sets forth a deeply religious view which reveals god to man through creation.'[2]

In its social and religious manifestation, Vishishtadvaita is known as Shrivaishnavism (see below). After Ramanuja, the two best-known proponents of Vishishtadvaita were Pillai Lokacharya and Vedanta Desika, who founded the Tengalai and Vadagalai branches of Shrivaishnavism. Other philosophers who contributed to Vishishtadvaita theories include Meghanadri, Ramanujacharya or Vadihamsa, Sudarshana Suri, Parakala Yati, Ranga Ramanuja, Shrishaila Shrinivasa, Ramanujadasa, Shrinivasa Dasa, Ahobila Ranganatha Yati and Manavala Mamuni, among others.

Dvaita

Dvaita has been explained as dualism. Its main proponent was Madhva, who lived in the thirteenth century. His works laid the foundations for Dvaita, particularly his commentaries on the *Brahma Sutra*, certain Upanishads, the Bhagavad Gita, the Bhagavata Purana and on the first forty hymns of the *Rig Veda*.

His work *Anuvyakhyana* explains his interpretation of the *Brahma Sutra*. *Bharatatatparyanirnaya* is a work on the Mahabharata, while his Prakaranas explain some philosophical themes. His main principles were summarized in ten short texts known as the Dashaprakaranas. All these works are collectively known as the Sarva Mula Grantha.

Madhva challenged Shankara's concept of One Reality. Brahman is supreme, an independent (*svatantra*) and self-created entity who can be identified with the god Vishnu. The existence of all living beings (chit or jiva) and non-living entities (*achit*) is dependent on Brahman. But though unable to exist without it, the individual soul and the world are distinct from it.

According to Madhva, the statement in one of the mahavakyas that Brahman is One without a second ('Ekam evadvitiyam brahma') only means that it is unequalled and supreme. Brahman is perfect in every way. He is the ultimate creator and destroyer, transcendent and immanent, and is the inner ruler (*antaryamin*) of all souls. He manifests himself in forms (*vyuhas*) or incarnations (avataras). Lakshmi is the personification of his creative energy and is *nityamukta*, eternally liberated.

As Madhva accepted the supremacy of Brahman, it is not true dualism in the sense of two equal principles. Regarding jivas or individual souls, he stated that they are infinite in number. The jiva cannot exist without Brahman, yet it is an active agent with its own responsibilities. Madhva distinguished between three types of jivas. These were those who were eternally (nitya) free, like the goddess Lakshmi; those devas, rishis, people and pitris who have freed themselves from samsara or the bonds of the world; and those who are still bound. The last category included those who could achieve release (*mukti-yugya*) and those who could not. Sattvic souls would be able to attain release and go to heaven, the rajasic would constantly revolve in samsara, while the tamasic were destined for hell. Thus, he differed from Ramanuja in stating that individual souls were not of the same essence and not all were eligible for salvation.

He analysed five categories of differences (*panchabheda*) in the world. These are: between god and matter; god and sentient beings; matter and sentient beings; various sentient beings themselves; and between material objects.

Though he believed that Vishnu was the supreme deity, his philosophy accommodated other deities. Vishnu is the supreme creator, but Brahma creates the world on his command. Vayu is the intermediary between the souls and god and is known as the son of Vishnu (*hareh-sutah*) or the dearest image (*pratima preyasi*). Some of Madhva's followers composed hymns to Shiva and there was no major conflict with Shaivites. According to some accounts, he may have belonged to a Smarta group, now known as Bhagavatasampradaya. Madhva often used Pancharatra texts, which he felt were as authentic as the Vedas. In the *Tantrasara Sangraha*, he describes Pancharatra-style temple worship (For the Pancharatras, see Vaishnavism, discussed later).

Madhva advocated Bhakti and the worship of god in the form of the avataras or incarnations of Vishnu, Shiva or the Panchayatanas or five deities. He did not recognize the worship of Radha, the consort of Krishna, who is an incarnation of Vishnu. According to his philosophy, knowledge and a moral life led to the love of god and salvation was attained by the grace of god. However, even those who had attained liberation remained separate individuals, connected with but not identical to god. Some have suggested the influence of Christianity on his ideas, such as his concept of the individual soul and the concept of Vayu as an intermediary. Others deny the possibility of such influence.

Madhva established eight mathas or monastic centres of worship and the heads of these were among those who continued to contribute to this philosophy. Among other notable exponents of Dvaita were Madhva's immediate disciples, Padmanabha Tirtha (pontiff 1318–24), Narahari Tirtha (1324–33), Madhava Tirtha (1330–50) and Akshobhya Tirtha (1350–65), Hrishikesha Tirtha (1250–1330), the founder and first pontiff of the Palimar Matha, Jaya Tirtha (fourteenth century), one of the most notable developers of Dvaita thought, Vyasaraya or Vyasa Tirtha, Vadiraja Tirtha and Raghavendra Tirtha, among many others. Dvaita thought continued to develop in the nineteenth and twentieth centuries. Among later scholars were Adavi Jaya Tirthacharya alias Vishnu Tirtha (1756–1806), Vedagarbha Padmanabhacharya (eighteenth century), Hulugi Shriyahpatyacharya, Kashi Timmannacharya, Annepacharya, Kochi Rangappacharya and many more.

Dvaitadvaita

Dvaitadvaita states that both duality and non-duality are real. Its main proponent was Nimbarka, who probably belonged to the twelfth century. Like Dvaita, this philosophy believes that the soul and the world are distinct from, yet dependent on, Brahman. The relationship between Brahman, the soul and the world is natural and uncaused, hence this type of philosophy has been called *svabhavika* (natural) *bhedabhedavada*, that is, 'unity in difference'. Nimbarka's two main works are a commentary on the *Brahma Sutra* called *Vedanta Parijata Saurabha* and a work of ten verses, *Dashashloki*. At least seven other works are attributed to him, but all may not be his. In the *Vedanta Parijata Saurabha*, he differentiates between chit, corresponding to the jiva or soul, achit, corresponding to jagat or the world, and Brahman. The soul and the world possessed attributes different from Brahman, yet could not exist independently, being a transformation of Brahman and dependent on Brahman. The universe was not an illusion as it was the manifestation of the nature of god. Nimbarka questioned the concepts of both Shankara and Ramanuja, and believed that neither maya nor ajnana (ignorance) or any of its aspects could create the world. Ajnana was a quality of the individual being, associated with the person's own karma. The pure nature of the jiva or soul is clouded by its karma. Nimbarka was thus different from Bhaskara, an earlier exponent of Bhedabhedavada, as he emphasized not only unity but the differences of the individual from god or Brahman while in the state of bondage. Only with a true realization of Brahman could karma and ajnana be removed. Even so, the individuals retained consciousness of themselves. When emancipated, they lived in the essential being of god as His distinct energies and could be used by god for any divine purpose, but never again returned to Earth.

Nimbarka believed the person seeking Brahman should first study the literature on Vedic duties and understand that the enjoyments and beneficial results provided by these were only temporary, and that only the realization of Brahman could lead to eternal bliss. Following this, a person should go to one who had realized Brahman and accept him as his teacher with due reverence. Then the seeker should try and organize his thoughts and constantly meditate on the truths revealed by the teacher. Through submission to god as well as devotion or Bhakti and an ethical life, one could realize god. Nimbarka stressed devotion to a personal god, Krishna, along with Radha. Brahman is identical with Krishna.

Another name of this philosophy, Sanakadi Sampradaya, is traced to its mythical origins. According to this, Hamsa, an incarnation of Vishnu and a unity of Radha and Krishna, was the first teacher; he taught it to Sanaka, Sananda, Sanatana and Sanat Kumara, Brahma's mindborn sons—that is, sons born through the power of his mind—who taught it to Narada, from whom Nimbarka learnt it. Nimbarka was followed by a long line of teachers. His own chief disciple was said to be Shrinivasa. Among other notable exponents of this school was Keshava Kashmiri Bhatta who revived and spread Nimbarka's teachings and wrote a number of texts; among the others were Purushottama Prasada, Madhava Mukunda and Harivyasadeva.

Dvaitadvaita, Dvaita and Vishishtadvaita

There are very subtle differences between these three philosophies, all of which believed that Brahman was supreme and that souls and the world emanated from Brahman but were not identical with it. These three also identified Brahman with the god Vishnu or one of his forms. The differences are seen only through an analysis of the philosophical details. For instance, Madhva believed that individual souls were of different types whereas for Ramanuja all souls had the same substance.

Shivadvaita

Shivadvaita sees the god Shiva as identical with Brahman. Its main exponent was Shrikanthacharya, who lived in the twelfth century. Shrikantha wrote a *bhashya* or commentary on the *Brahma Sutra* in which he identified Brahman with Shiva. He said that the unchangeable Brahman has the nature of being, consciousness and bliss. However, within Brahman is the energy not only of consciousness but of the material nature of the universe. This Shakti or energy, which can be termed maya or prakriti, is the cause of creation, though Brahman remains transcendent. Thus, the material world is not identical with, nor entirely different from, Brahman.

Shrikantha described the nature of Shiva as the supreme being. He is known as Sarva as all things are absorbed in him and as Ishana and Pashupati because he is the lord of all.

The deeds of people are responsible for pleasure and sorrow in the world but the law of karma depends on the will of Shiva. When karma is exhausted and minds become pure, self-knowledge arises, leading to the bliss of liberation. The philosophy was similar to that of Bhedabhedavada.

Shivadvaita agrees with other Vedanta schools on certain basic premises, for instance, that Brahman, the Absolute, transcending time and space, is the ultimate cause of all creation and that its true nature is concealed because of ignorance.

Appayya Dikshitar is among those who commented on this system.

Bhedabhedavada

As seen above, Dvaitadvaita is a form of Bhedabhedavada, a philosophy that holds that both unity and multiplicity are real. However, a slightly different version of Bhedabhedavada was put forward by Bhaskara, who lived around CE 900, on the basis of even earlier philosophers. Bhaskara wrote a commentary on the *Brahma Sutra* called *Bhaskarabhashya.* According to him, Brahman, the underlying reality of the world, is One in its causal state, but has multiplicity in its evolved state. These two aspects coexist and are equally real. The world is not an illusion, but real, yet is essentially the same as Brahman. The jiva or individual soul is also of the same essence, but limited by matter. Karma or right action is the means to knowledge (jnana), which leads to moksha (liberation).

Thus, in Bhaskara's view, a person should live an active life and withdraw from the world only after fulfilling his dharma.

Yadavaprakasha, a philosopher of the eleventh century, also put forward this theory. Achintya Bhedabheda, or incomprehensible unity in difference, was part of the philosophy of Chaitanya Mahaprabhu.

Shuddhadvaita

Shuddhadvaita is another Vedantic school founded by the Vaishnava philosopher Vallabhacharya, who lived in the fifteenth century. Vallabhacharya was familiar with the Vedas and Puranas. He accepted the authority of the Upanishads, the Bhagavad Gita, *Brahma Sutra* and the Bhagavata Purana as well as the works of Vishnusvamin, a philosopher of the thirteenth century. His philosophy of Shuddhadvaita, revealed through his writings, is considered pure (*shuddha*) non-dualism. Vallabha sees god as the whole and the individual as the part, but both have the same essence and hence are essentially the same. Yet, the highest goal for the individual is not union with god, or liberation, but the service of Krishna. He, in fact, expounded his philosophy after receiving a vision of Krishna.

Vallabha travelled to different parts of the country and became known as Acharya, or teacher. He started a sect known as Pushtimarga, which flourished in western and central India. This sect is still important today. He also established the worship of Krishna as Shrinathji, with the main temple being located today at Nathdwara in Rajasthan.

Mimamsa

Mimamsa is one of the astika schools of philosophy. Jaimini, from between the fourth and the second century BCE, is said to have founded this school, and his work *Mimamsa Sutra* explains its philosophy. This early form of Mimamsa, known as Purva Mimamsa or Karma Mimamsa (analysis of action), focused on the Vedas as the ultimate source of divine knowledge and the correct performance of rituals and sacrifices. As there were many different texts describing rituals, some guidelines or rules (nyayas) were required, and Jaimini's Sutra provided these. The interpretation of the Vedas was only possible through the understanding of each *shabda* or word and thus the Sutra focused on both sound and meaning.

The text has twelve chapters. The first discusses the sources of knowledge and the truth of the Vedas. Other chapters describe various sacrifices and what can be gained from them, the theory of *apurva*, and some other philosophical concepts. Apurva is a concept related to action, the hidden force that brings, at some point in time, the result of the action performed. Jaimini also wrote *Samkarshanakanda*, or *Devatakanda*, on methods of worship. He is referred to several times in the *Brahma Sutra*, where his views are refuted.

Other commentators elaborated on Jaimini's Sutras. Shabara, who has been variously dated from the first century BCE to the sixth century CE, was the chief commentator on the Sutras, with all later Mimamsa writings being based on his work. He said that not merely right knowledge but dharma and right conduct were essential. Kumarila Bhatta of the eighth or ninth century, Mandana Mishra, his disciple, and Prabhakara were among other commentators on Mimamsa. Mandana Mishra wrote some works on Mimamsa, but according to tradition was later converted to Advaita by Shankara after being defeated by the latter in a philosophical argument. Kumarila and Prabhakara have different views on some aspects of Mimamsa, leading to two different schools of thought. Parthasarathi Mishra of about the ninth century (though Radhakrishnan places him around 1300), Sucharita Mishra, Ramakrishna Mishra and Somanatha were among other scholars who followed Kumarila's line of thinking. Another school is associated with the name of Murari, though its details are not known. Vachaspati Mishra (c. 850) composed *Nyayakanika*, expanding on Mandana's *Vidhiviveka*. In addition, Vachaspati Mishra has commented on Prabhakara and divided his followers into two schools: Jaratprabhakara and Navyaprabhakara. Other notable works on Mimamsa were the *Jaiminiya Nyaya Mala Vistara* of Madhava, *Subodhini*, *Mimamsabala Prakasha* of Shankara Bhatta, *Mimamsa Paribhasha* of Krishnayajvan, *Bhattachintamani* of Gaga Bhatta and several others. Among later works, those of Apadeva or Anantadeva and Khandadeva of the seventeenth century are significant.

Purva Mimamsa examines the nature of dharma and tries to show that every part of the Vedic texts can be related to dharma. It accepts a plurality of selves, and the early writers do not concern themselves with moksha or ultimate liberation; they accept a number of deities, the worship of whom leads to heaven. Later commentators began to deal with higher philosophical concepts and this philosophy became almost identical with Vedanta, known as Uttara Mimamsa or later Mimamsa. Badarayana's *Brahma Sutra* is also known as Uttara Mimamsa. According to some commentators, Jaimini's Purva Mimamsa and Badarayana's Uttara Mimamsa formed one whole, the former emphasizing dharma, ethics and ritual, and the latter philosophical aspects.

Purva Mimamsa, with its emphasis on dharma, is an important source of Hindu law.

In myths, Jaimini was a great rishi and teacher, a disciple of Vyasa. He is said to have received the knowledge of the *Sama Veda* from Vyasa. According to tradition, Jaimini was one of the people to whom the rishi Vyasa narrated the Mahabharata, after which he wrote the Jaimini Mahabharata, of which only the *Ashvamedhika* is available today.

Samkhya

Samkhya, one of the six early astika schools of philosophy, is said to have been founded by the sage Kapila. Elements of Samkhya philosophy are found in the Upanishads and the Mahabharata, and are also explained in the Bhagavad Gita. The legendary Kapila is said to have existed sometime between the seventh century BCE and sixth century BCE, but the texts assigned to him, the *Samkhyapravachana Sutra* and the *Tattvasamasa*, seem to be much later. In fact, the former is assigned by some scholars to the fourteenth century CE. The earliest available text is the *Samkhya Karika* of the second to third century CE, written by Ishvarakrishna.

Among other major works explaining Samkhya philosophy are Vachaspati's *Samkhyatattvakaumudi* of the ninth century CE, Narayana's *Samkhyachandrika*, Aniruddha's *Samkhyasutravritti* of the fifteenth century, Mahadeva's *Samkhyasutravrittisara* of the sixteenth century and Vijnanabhikshu's *Samkhyapravachanabhashya* of the sixteenth century CE.

Samkhya sees the world as a result of two principles, Purusha and prakriti.

Prakriti is the active principle, the potentiality of all nature, through which the material and non-material world comes into being. It is not the same as matter and has three components (gunas) through which it arises: *sattva, rajas* and *tamas*. Sattva is potential consciousness and indicates perfection, goodness and happiness. Rajas is the source of all activity, producing both enjoyment as well as restlessness and pain. Tamas resists activity, leading to indifference and slothfulness. The three are never separate, but one or the other predominates. Sattva is the essence of that which is to be realized, tamas the obstacles preventing its realization and rajas the force that overcomes the obstacles. Prakriti evolves for Purusha. The process of evolution has been extensively described. After the pralaya or dissolution of the world, prakriti remains in a state of rest. This is a result of the mutual opposition of the three gunas, which produces a state of equilibrium. The equilibrium is disturbed by the action of the gunas and creation begins through a gradual evolution.

Mahat: In the first stage, prakriti becomes *buddhi* (higher mind or intelligence), in which sattva predominates. This is actually a re-emergence of the minds of all the purushas that continue to exist in a dormant state after the pralaya. This stage is called *mahat* (the great one), holding within it the Buddhitattva (all the Buddhis). It is also known as linga (sign) as it is the sign of what is to come.

Ahamkara: From mahat, *ahamkara*, or the ego, develops, which is of three kinds, the first being the sattvika or *vaikarika* ahamkara. From this, through the action of rajas, the various senses develop, including those of sight, hearing, touch, smell, taste and movement as well as *manas* (mind). From the *tamasika* ahamkara, also known as *bhutadi*, again with the help of rajas, the *tanmatras*, which are the preceding cause of gross elements, come into being. These contain the potential elements from which the five classes of atoms (*paramanus*) develop.

Twenty-five Principles

Though there can be variations, most texts of Samkhya believe that this evolution results in twenty-five *tattvas* (aspects or principles). These include prakriti and Purusha, along with twenty-three manifestations from prakriti.

Using different methods, Samkhya, however, can have between three and twenty-five principles.

Purusha can be translated as soul and is similar to the concept of Brahman. In each living being there is a Purusha, yet essentially all purushas are the same. According to Radhakrishnan, it is 'not the mind, life or body, but the informing and sustaining soul, silent, peaceful, eternal'. It illuminates all the activities that take place but does not participate in them. It is pure inactive intelligence. Yet, the concept of Purusha in Samkhya philosophy indicates that it is different from Brahman as it is not the direct agent of creation. Creation arises from prakriti by itself, though the reason for it coming into being is Purusha. Purusha 'excites prakriti to activity and development', for prakriti exists only to serve Purusha. The empirical Self is the union of the free spirit, Purusha, and of prakriti. Purusha is the knower and the known is prakriti. The purpose of Samkhya is to free the knower from the known.

Samkhya believes the world is full of sorrow and all experience is sorrowful. It therefore creates a field of experiences for Purusha.

Purusha is eternally free, but to realize its nature, the empirical Self requires virtue, including unselfish activity, and *vairagya* or detachment, as well as higher knowledge. The buddhi reflects the Purusha but when the buddhi realizes its difference, the Purusha is finally freed and can never again be bound. Thus, with the right knowledge and discrimination (*viveka*), freedom from bondage is achieved.

The Samkhya system states that Vedic sacrifices do not lead anywhere and the path of liberation is only through knowledge and understanding. There is no Ishvara or god, but only a natural process of causation. Though the first cause is Purusha, it is only a mechanical cause.

Involution

Samkhya is concerned with both evolution (*avirbhava*) and involution (*tirobhava*). The world evolves from prakriti, but through correct knowledge, Purusha is freed from prakriti.

Later Theism

While Ishvarakrishna's *Karika* does not bring god into the picture, Vijnanabhikshu attempts to reconcile Samkhya with theistic Vedanta. He puts forward the theory of a universal Purusha, which would be similar to Brahman. He felt that Kapila did not dwell on god so that people would reflect and develop discriminative knowledge. Elsewhere, he says that Samkhya may have been created to mislead evil men and prevent them from reaching the truth.

The basics of Samkhya philosophy were accepted by the system of Yoga, with the addition of the concept of Ishvara or god. The Samkhya theory of evolution is also described in the Upanishads and in the later Puranas, though with some modifications.

Vaisheshika

The traditional founder of Vaisheshika, another astika school, was the rishi Kanada, also known as Uluka Kanada, who probably lived between 250 BCE and 100 CE. Some feel he lived even earlier, before the time of the Buddha. His real name is said to have been Kashyapa, and he composed the *Vaisheshika Sutra*, which forms the basis for this philosophy. According to one story, the god Shiva appeared to Kanada in the form of an owl (*uluka*) and revealed the philosophy to him, which, therefore is also known as Aulukya Darshana.

The *Vaisheshika Sutra* has ten books or sections. While Book I looks at the categories of substance, quality, activity, generality and particularity, Book II analyses different substances. Book III deals with souls, the mind and the nature of inference, Book IV mainly explains the atomic structure of the universe and Book V analyses karma along with the nature and type of action. Book VI takes a look at ethical issues and Book VII analyses quality, the Self and inherence. Books VIII–X look at problems of perception, inherence and causality.

Several writers later elaborated and commented on the Sutras, among the most prominent being Prashastapada of the fourth century CE. Later writers include Vyomashekhara, Shridhara, Udayana and Shivaditya. Shrivatsa, Langakshi Bhaskara, Shankara Mishra, Annam Bhatta, Jagdisha and Jayanarayana were other commentators. The term *vaisheshika* comes from *vishesha* or 'particularity'. It has similarities with the Nyaya system of philosophy, and by the medieval period the two schools almost merged.

Vaisheshika deals with physics, metaphysics, logic and methods of knowledge, and its central feature is considered to be its theory on the atomic structure of the universe. Four valid types of knowledge are perception, inference, remembrance and intuition (*arshajnana*).

These are subdivided into various categories. Vaisheshika uses intensive methods of analysis to understand the components of the world. Central to these methods is its theory of *padartha*s, or categories, literally, the meaning of a word, an object which can be thought of and named. Objects can be analysed according to substance (*dravya*), quality (guna), activity (karma), generality (*samanya*), particularity (vishesha) and inherence (*samavaya*), to which later a seventh aspect of non-existence (*abhava*) was added. Substances can also be eternal and include souls, which according to this philosophy are several; they are bound by their own deeds and can attain liberation. The supreme soul is distinct from these individual souls.

Other dravyas or substances include earth, air, water, light, space and time. Earth, air, water and light are concrete and made up of atoms (paramanus) which combine to form objects but are never destroyed, even when the world ends. Atoms have both a primary and a secondary nature and thus have different qualities. True knowledge, that is, recognizing the atomic structure of the world, is essential for liberation.

Kanada's Sutras do not directly refer to god, though Prashastapada sees Ishvara as the cause of the universe, but souls and atoms are coexistent. Later writers accepted a divine principle because of existing contradictions in the philosophy. Summing up this philosophical system, S. Radhakrishnan says, 'The many-sided context of human life is ignored by the Vaisheshika, and its physical philosophy and moral and religious values are not worked into a unified interpretation. An atomistic pluralism is not the final answer to the intellectual demand for a rational interpretation of the universe.'[3] In his commentary on the *Brahma Sutra*, Shankara criticized the Vaisheshika concept of atoms (paramanus), particularly the theory that when atoms combine they create a product which can be different from the original components.

Nyaya

Nyaya literally means that by which the mind reaches a conclusion, and is based on logic and analysis. It is one of the astika schools of philosophy and accepts the authority of the Vedas.

According to tradition, it was founded by Akshapada Gautama, though some hold that Akshapada and Gautama were two different people who both contributed to its philosophy. The basic text is Gautama's *Nyaya Sutra*. This Sanskrit text contains five books, each with two sections. The first book states the sixteen subjects that will be analysed in the other books. These are: means of right knowledge (*pramana*s); object of right knowledge (*prameya*); doubt (*samshaya*); purpose (*prayojana*); illustrative instances (*drishtanta*); accepted conclusions (*siddhanta*); premises (*avayava*); argumentation (*tarka*); ascertainment (*nirnaya*); debates (*vada*); disputations (*jalpa*); destructive criticism (*vitanada*); fallacy (*hetvabhasa*); quibble (*chala*); refutations (*jati*) and points of opponents' defeat (*nigrahasthana*). By exploring these, the highest good can be attained. Some aspects of these sixteen topics are explained in this book. The second looks at the nature of doubt, the means of proof and their validity. The third book describes the Self, body, senses, their objects, cognition and mind. The Self or atman is that which integrates sense perception. It provides arguments to prove the existence of a permanent soul. Salvation (*apavarga*) is attained when the manas (mind) separates from the soul (atman) after all karma has been destroyed. The fourth analyses the sorrow involved in daily life and the means of liberation. It looks at the root cause of dosha (defects) and states it is *moha* (usually greed, but here it refers to ignorance) that leads to other doshas such as *raga* (attachment) and *dvesha* (antipathy). All births lead to sorrow, but in salvation all sorrow is removed. This book also discusses other topics, such as the nature of atoms (*anu*). The fifth book discusses jati (refutations) and nigrahasthanas (points of opponents' defeat). The text uses logic to arrive at religious and philosophical understandings. At least part of the text belongs to the third century BCE, though some parts are later, from about the first century CE.

The *Nyaya Bhashya* of Vatsyayana, probably of the fourth century CE, is an important commentary on the *Nyaya Sutra*. Other notable commentaries and sub-commentaries include Uddyotakara's *Nyayavarttika* of the seventh century, Vachaspati Mishra's *Nyayavarttikatatparyatika* of the ninth century and Udayana's *Tatparyatikaparishuddhi* of the tenth century. In addition, there is the *Nyayamanjari* of Jayanta (880 CE). Gangesha's *Tattvachintamani* (dated between the eleventh and thirteenth centuries) is the standard text of the modern school, known as Nava Nyaya. Nava Nyaya developed further at Navadvipa, a centre of learning in Bengal, in the sixteenth century and thereafter. Later, Nyaya became similar to Vaisheshika. Both Nyaya and Vaisheshika analysed the world through logic and experience. Nyaya accepted the six padarthas or categories of Vaisheshika: dravya, guna, karma, samanya, vishesha and samavaya. In some texts, these were brought under prameya or objects of knowledge, or under *artha*, one of the twelve types of prameya. Both also put forward the theory that the natural world is composed of atoms (anu or paramanu), which are eternal, unalterable, and have an independent existence. Regarding the soul, Nyaya states that there are eternal souls which are attached to a body from time to time, but each soul is individual and independent. Neither knowledge nor intellect form the soul.

Ishvara or god is mentioned, though not prominent in the *Nyaya Sutra*, but later Nyaya was clearly theistic, with Shiva as the chief deity and cause or origin of the universe. The rigorous analytical methods of Nyaya contributed to other philosophical systems as well, and its categories are still used in philosophical debate and discussion.

Some Nyaya schools exist in Bengal today.

Yoga Philosophy

An important astika school, the earliest available text for the
philosophical system of Yoga is Patanjali's *Yoga Sutra*. Yoga
literally means union, implying the union of the individual Self
with the divine. This is attained when the individual Self, the
atman or jiva, also known as the Purusha, realizes its true being
by stilling the mind and body. In its philosophical base, Yoga is
similar to Samkhya. Yoga accepts the Samkhya theories of Purusha
and prakriti, but adds to these the concept of Ishvara or god. It
differs from Samkhya in its method of reaching the goal. In Yoga,
a systematic effort is required to detach Purusha from prakriti,
and Patanjali describes this unified system. Patanjali's Yoga was
later called Raja Yoga to distinguish it from other forms of Yoga.
This form is also known as Ashtanga Yoga or the Yoga with eight
limbs, or eight parts, sometimes translated as eight steps.

Patanjali begins his text by stating that he will now describe the
practice of Yoga. In the second verse he says that Yoga is 'Chitta-
vritti-nirodha' (cessation of thought). He states that vrittis, or
things that affect the mind, can be classified into five: pramana,
or valid states of knowledge through perception, inference or
study of the scriptures; *viparyaya*, false knowledge, including
illusion and other states; *vikalpa*, abstraction, construction or
imagination; *nidra*, sleep; and smriti, memory. These states
of mind can be either good or bad and can be used to lead one
towards liberation or to further sorrow. Patanjali further explains
a graded and methodical way of attaining liberation. Both *abhyasa*
(practice) and *vairagya* (dispassion) are required to follow this
path that consists of eight steps or stages. These are: (1) Yama,
or five ethical restraints of ahimsa (non-violence), satya (truth),
asteya (non-stealing), *brahmacharya* (always being aware of god,

often translated literally as celibacy), *aparigraha* (non-greed); (2) *Niyama*, or five positive observances, which are *shaucha* (purity), *santosha* (contentment), *tapasya* (ascetic practices), *svadhyaya* (self-study), Ishvara *pranidhana* (surrender to god). In addition to these niyamas, there are other practices prescribed. *Pratipakshabhavana* involves replacing a negative thought with its opposite; *maitri* is friendliness towards all; *karuna* is compassion; *mudita* is to feel happy for the good of all beings; *upeksha* is to cultivate indifference to the vices of others; (3) Asana, or postures to stabilize and improve the body; (4) *Pranayama*, or breathing practices; (5) *Pratyahara*, or withdrawal of the senses from the outer world; (6) *Dharana*, or concentration; (7) *Dhyana*, or meditation; (8) *Samadhi* or union. These are explained in the *Yoga Sutra* and in numerous commentaries and form the basis for all later systems of Yoga.

Aspects of Yoga were known at the time of the Buddha and Mahavira. Several later Upanishads deal with Yoga and will be looked at in the section on the Yoga Upanishads. The Mahabharata describes Samkhya and Yoga as two aspects of one whole, the former being the theory and the latter the practical aspects. The Bhagavad Gita also relates Samkhya and Yoga. The Gita uses the term Yoga in many different ways but basically in the sense of 'joining' or 'union'. Yoga or union can be attained when all desires have ceased and the mind has been controlled, becoming single-pointed in its focus on god.

Vyasa's *Bhashya* or commentary on the *Yoga Sutra*, from about the fourth century CE, explains the basic principles of the system. A commentary on Vyasa's *Bhashya* was written by Vachaspati in the ninth century. Other early works on Yoga include Bhoja's *Rajamartanda* and Vijnanabhikshu's *Yogavartika*. Additional texts on Yoga do not exactly follow Patanjali and some list ten yamas and niyamas. Later texts explain various forms of Yoga in detail, such as Hatha Yoga, Mantra Yoga, Bhakti Yoga, Jnana Yoga, Kundali Yoga, Likhita Yoga, Laya Yoga, Siddha Yoga, Integral Yoga, Tantra

Yoga, as well as several modern hybrid forms, such as Power Yoga. Texts on yoga include the *Gheranda Samhita*, the *Goraksha Samhita* of Gorakhanatha and the *Hatha Yoga Pradipika*, among others. All traditional forms of Yoga are not mutually exclusive, each employing some of the techniques used by other forms, though the emphasis is different. The prerequisites of each form are basic ethics, morality (dharma) and discipline or regular practice (sadhana).

Yoga is also described in Vaishnava, Shaiva and tantric texts, in the Puranas, and in the works of several other writers.

Other Philosophies

Between the sixth and fourth centuries BCE, other types of philosophies coexisted. Buddhism and Jainism developed and they are also commented upon by Upanishadic philosophers. The Ajivikas, Keshakambalins and Lokayats or Charvakas were other streams of thought. The Shaivite Pashupata sect developed slightly later. In later centuries, there were further developments in Shaivism, Vaishnavism, Shaktism and Tantrism, which also have relevance for the later Upanishads.

Buddhism

Buddhism originated in India and Nepal, later spreading to other parts of the world. It was founded by Gautama Siddhartha, later known as the Buddha. As seen earlier, there is some controversy about the date of his birth. Western and Indian scholars take the date of his birth as circa 566 BCE and for his death 486 BCE. Buddhists in Sri Lanka and Southeast Asia generally follow the traditionally accepted dates of 624 BCE for his birth and 564 BCE for his death. Several Japanese scholars take the date of his birth as 448 BCE and of his death as 368 BCE. These various dates are based on chronologies given in different sources.

Though the Buddha was born in what is now Nepal, he lived and preached mainly in present-day Bihar and eastern Uttar Pradesh. He developed his new philosophy against the background of prevailing ideas and philosophical systems. While the Upanishads presented concepts of oneness and liberation, there were at the same time Vedic sacrifices and a caste system that was growing increasingly rigid. By the time of the Buddha's death around 486 BCE, his teachings already had a large following and the sangha or monastic system was well-established. Further developments are marked by the four Buddhist Councils which were held over the next few hundred years. The patronage of Ashoka, the Mauryan emperor, helped in spreading Buddhism. Out of the vast number of texts and ideas, the basics of Buddhism are found in the Pali Canon, consisting of the early teachings of the historic Buddha. The Pali Canon includes a number of texts in three groups: the Vinaya Pitaka, Sutta Pitaka and Abhidhamma Pitaka. There are some variations in these texts in different Buddhist schools. These basic teachings consist of the Four Noble Truths on suffering and its cause, and the Eightfold Path, which is the way to liberation. Other early concepts include the impermanence of everything (*anichcha*, *anitya*). Not realizing this truth, people were caught in ignorance and sorrow. There was no permanent individual Self; this was another delusion. Thus, the Buddha put forward the concept of *anatta* (*anatman*) or non-ego, and of the five aggregates (*skandha*s) which create human existence. Related to this is the law of dependent origination or *patichcha samutpada* (*pratitya* samutpada), in which one state of being arises out of the previous state. Understanding these basic concepts and following the Eightfold Path, nirvana or enlightenment could be reached. The sangha or community provided the means to reach the goal. The Buddha himself was born in a kshatriya family, and after his birth his future was predicted by 108 brahmanas. He studied with yogis and ascetics before gaining enlightenment. The main Buddhist shila, the precepts or code of ethics, are similar to the yama and niyama of Yoga.

The Buddha accepted certain prevailing beliefs such as those of karma, rebirth and samsara. However, he was against sacrifices, ceremonies, rituals and the rigidities of the caste system.

Early Buddhism, incorporating these basic ideas, is known as Hinayana Buddhism, though within this there were several different schools and variations. In fact, by the first century BCE, there were already about thirty different sects and schools. A later development from the first century CE was Mahayana Buddhism, which retained the basic principles and ideas but developed certain aspects further. Two key developments were the ideal of the Bodhisattva and the incorporation of a number of Buddhist deities, along with more complex philosophical concepts. Mahayana Buddhism too had different schools of thought. Vajrayana Buddhism then arose, which included tantric practices. Each of these historical stages is seen as a valid expression of Buddhist ideas.

Logical analysis and intellectual enquiry were parallel developments in Buddhist and other early systems of philosophy. Philosophical texts often comment on and refute Buddhist concepts. Some believe the theory of the four ashramas or stages of life could have been a response to the Buddhist sangha or monastic order.

In the context of the Upanishads, the dates of the Buddha and the Hinayana and Mahayana schools of thought are important. As seen above, some of the Upanishads were dated on the basis of their familiarity or non-familiarity with Buddhist ideas. As for developments in later Mahayana Buddhism, Gaudapada, the teacher of Shankara's teacher, accepted certain principles of the Madhyamika and Vijnanavada schools of Mahayana Buddhism. Both Shankara and his teacher Govinda are thought to have been influenced by Buddhism, and Shankara has often been called a 'crypto-Buddhist'. In fact, even Ramanuja used this term (*pracchana bauddha* in Sanskrit).[4] Incorporating Buddhist principles in his thought provided a perfect answer to the growth of Buddhism.

In the Mahayana form of Buddhism, the concept of *shunya* or the void is thought to be closely related to Upanishadic concepts and later to Shankara's Advaita. In a regional context there are several indications of the interaction between Hinduism and Buddhism and of the subtle influence of Buddhism. For instance, in some temples of Himachal Pradesh and the northeast of India, the same image is worshipped as a Buddhist deity by Buddhists and as a Hindu deity by Hindus. In Odisha, the concept of shunya was integrated into the writings of the Panchasakhas of the fifteenth to sixteenth centuries, and into the later Mahima Dharma.

The Vijnanavada or Yogachara school of Mahayana Buddhism expresses the importance of cultivating the Self, particularly through meditation. According to this school, there is nothing but mind or that perceived by the mind. Meditating and analysing the mind reveals the source of consciousness. The school basically consists of theories of consciousness (*vijnana*) and therefore is called Vijnanavada. Its main exponents were Maitreyanatha, Asanga (310–390) and Vasubandhu (320–400).

Yogacharabhumi, the basic text of the school, is assigned to Maitreyanatha, or sometimes to Asanga. The school explains the ideas of consciousness derived from the practice of meditation. In deep mediation, ecstasy is experienced, indicating that the world is nothing but mind (*chittamatrata*) or else something that is perceived by the mind (*vijnaptimatrata*). When meditating, one becomes aware of different levels of the mind, and deep within is the *alaya vijnana*, the storehouse of consciousness, containing the seeds of past actions and therefore of karma. Vasubandhu focuses in his writings on the nature of the mind while Asanga deals more with the storehouse of consciousness.

There were subtle differences in the various branches of the Yogachara school, particularly at Nalanda and Vallabhi. The Vallabhi school led by Sthiramati (500–560) held that the storehouse of consciousness is pure and has no forms, while the Nalanda school, systemized by Dharmapala (530–561) and based on the work of Dignaga, stated that consciousness does contain forms.

The Madhyamika, another school of Mahayana Buddhism, literally means 'the middle way'. Founded by Nagarjuna in about 150 CE, its basic text is the *Madhyamika Karika*, written by him. The school rejects both affirmations and negations of all metaphysical systems and sees *shunyata* (the void) as the middle way between being and non-being. Shunyata is the only reality, samsara and nirvana being the same and unreal. Cosmic change is unreal and the consciousness that perceives it has no reality either. Yet, the world has a qualified practical reality and shunyata is the essence that pervades the world, which according to some texts is identified with the Adi Buddha and the source of bliss. Nagarjuna's disciple Aryadeva also made notable contributions to this school. By about 500–550 CE, two branches of Madhyamika developed, the Prasangika and Svatantrika. Later, Madhyamika absorbed other philosophies, including that of Yogachara.

Another Buddhist concept similar to aspects of Advaita is that of the Pudgala. According to some schools of Hinayana Buddhism, in each individual was a permanent entity called Pudgala, which transmigrated from life to life and could attain liberation. The Vatsiputriya and their subdivisions followed this concept, which was strongly opposed by other schools that did not believe in any permanent entity.

Jainism

Jainism, the religion of the Jains, also developed around the same time. In early literature, Jains were known as Nirgranthas. In historical times, Vardhamana Mahavira, who was probably born in 599 BCE, explained this religion, but he was not the first to reveal its principles, which are said to have always existed.

Though Jainism has the two main sects of the Shvetambaras and Digambaras as well as several sub-sects, the basic philosophical concepts are common to all.

According to Jain theory, there is no creator god; the universe exists by itself. The aim of every living being is to attain moksha or liberation. This is possible by understanding the nature of the world and by following an ethical and ascetic path.

Jain ethics are different for the ascetic and the layperson. Even a layperson, however, has to observe eight basic lifestyle disciplines, such as not eating after sunset, avoiding certain foods and following twelve vows or *vrata*s. Eleven *pratima*s or stages in the life of a Jain householder are also laid down.

Like the Eightfold Path of Buddhism, Jainism has the three ideals of right belief (*samyak darshana*), right knowledge (*samyak jnana*) and right conduct (*samyak charitra*), known as the three jewels or Ratnatraya. Right conduct includes truth, brahmacharya, ahimsa and non-attachment to material possessions—similar to the five basic yamas or restraints of Yoga. These form part of the vratas or vows. The most important ethical aspect of Jainism is ahimsa or not harming any living being, including plants and insects. Ahimsa in Jainism has several aspects, including vegetarianism and also a restriction on types of vegetarian food. Agriculture is forbidden as ploughing leads to the death of small creatures and insects.

Jain ascetics observe some of the same vows at a higher level, as well as additional ones.

Jainism explains the nature of the world in detail.

There are two main categories in the universe: jiva (life or soul) and ajiva (non-living substance). Various aspects of the universe are also classified into astikayas or basic realities, dravyas or substances, tattvas or principles and padarthas or categories. Karma, which in Jainism is a material substance, prevents the jiva from attaining its natural blissful state. Following an ethical life, penance and austerities are necessary to eliminate karma and this may take several lifetimes.

Jainism has a complex classification of jnana or knowledge, and of the means of understanding reality. Scholars compare its logical approach to that of the Samkhya philosophy.

Charvaka

Charvaka is a materialistic school of thought in ancient India, also known as Lokayata. It was said to have been founded by a philosopher named Charvaka, but 'Charvaka' was also a generic name for materialistic philosophy. Charvaka philosophy is known mainly through Hindu, Jain and Buddhist texts that are extremely critical of this system. The focus of the philosophy is on sense perception and matter. Matter is the only reality and perception through the senses the only method of gaining knowledge. The four elements of earth, water, fire and air combine in different ways, leading to all forms of life, which end in death. There is no soul or atman, no gods, demons or superior beings, but only the natural world and the forces of nature. Moral rules are created by people and the aim or goal in life is pleasure. Sorrow is part of the world, and has to be accepted for the sake of the joy that is also found.

Materialist philosophers were against the Vedas, sacrifices and rituals, and probably emerged because of the dominance of brahmanas and the focus on rituals. Scholars such as S. Dasgupta feel these ideas existed before the rise of Buddhism and Jainism.[5]

The Charvakas are described in Jayanta's *Nyayamanjari* and in other later works including the *Tattvopaplavasimha*, written in the eighth century CE by Jayarashi, who criticizes all existing religious systems and attempts to show that they were false. Madhava of the fourteenth century also describes the Charvakas.

Ajivika

The Ajivikas belong to an ancient non-orthodox sect which existed from before the time of the Buddha. It was probably founded by Nanda Vachchha, who was succeeded by Kisa Samkichcha, but became widespread under Makkhali Gosala, also known as Gosala Maskariputra, who lived in the sixth century BCE at the time of the Buddha and Mahavira. Gosala was at first a follower of Mahavira but later founded his own sect. There are no Ajivika texts existing, but records of their practices are found in Buddhist and Jain sources. The Ajivikas are also mentioned in inscriptions.

The Jain *Bhagavati Sutra* states that the Ajivika scriptures consisted of ten Puvvas (Purvas), while the early Jain texts comprised fourteen Puvvas. The language too was similar to the Ardha Magadhi of the Jain texts. Tamil sources mention a text called the *Navakadir* (Nine Rays), probably a translation into Tamil from the original.

Gosala believed that living beings had no force or power of their own, and were completely controlled by niyati or fate. There were six classes (*sangati*) of beings, and their experiences depended on the class to which they belonged and their inherent nature. There were also five classes of atoms, which are eternal: air, water, fire, earth and life. Of these, only life is endowed with knowledge. A living being passes through 84,00,000 *maha* or great kalpas (aeons), followed by twenty-eight lives, including seven as a deity, after which the being finally attained bliss. Nothing could be done to speed up the process. No one could attain perfection by their own efforts or help others. Existence was like a ball of yarn, slowly unwinding, the end of the yarn being similar to the end of the series of lives.

Despite this fatalistic attitude, Ajivika monks wandered about nude and practised strict moral observances. They abstained from eating plants with roots as well as certain types of fruit.

The *Bhagavati Sutra* also states that they worshipped various deities, while according to a Tamil text they worshipped the Ashoka tree. Gosala was also revered as a deity in south India.

The Ajivikas lived in several parts of India. Initially in the north, they moved to the region at the foot of the Vindhyan mountains and to south India. Two caves of the Barabar hills near Gaya have inscriptions recording they were dedicated by Ashoka, the Mauryan emperor, and his successor Dasharatha to Ajivika monks.

Ajita Keshakambalin

Ajita was the founder of a non-orthodox sect, who lived at the time of the Buddha in the sixth century BCE. 'Keshakambalin' means 'hair-blanket', which is evidently what he and his followers wore, and accounts of the sect occur in Buddhist and Jain texts.

Ajita believed a person consisted of four elements. At the time of death, the earth element returned to earth, the water to water, the fire or heat to fire and the air to air. The various faculties (*indrayani*), including the five senses and the mind, returned to space (*akasha*). He said that there was no life after death and no result of one's deeds, whether good or evil. Thus, there was no point in sacrifices, offerings or reverence of one's parents. No person had attained knowledge of the next world.

Some of Ajita's followers were monks, though their type and level of asceticism is not described.

Shaivism

Shiva is one of the two most important gods of Hinduism, the other being Vishnu. Three gods, Brahma, Vishnu and Shiva, represent creation, preservation and destruction, but Brahma, the creator, is less important than the other two. Shiva is not only part of the trinity, but also a supreme deity, the ultimate source and goal.

The god Shiva and Shaivism find a place in the Upanishads, particularly in the Shaiva Upanishads. Shaivism centres around the worship of the god Shiva in his various forms, of the linga, his emblem and of other deities associated with him, particularly Parvati, Ganesha and Karttikeya. His *vahana* or vehicle is Nandi, a white bull, and his favourite weapon is a *trishula* or trident.

In general, Shiva, in his lesser aspect as one of the trinity, exists outside established society. As a wandering ascetic, he has to be lured by Parvati into a domestic setting with a family. Even so, they never live in a settled home, but in caves, mountains and forests. In the Himalayas are several places where Shiva is said to have lived and visits even now, though his main abode is on Mount Kailasha.

Shiva can be worshipped along with Parvati, or alone. A special form with Parvati is Ardhanarishvara, where the two are conjoined. Shiva is also depicted in family scenes along with his wife and sons.

There are innumerable Shaivite texts, as well as Shaivite sects and cults, and Shiva is also described in the Mahabharata, Puranas and Tulasidasa's Ramayana. The literature on Shaiva and Shaivism is vast, but here we look at some aspects of the deity and three sects that have a relevance on his portrayal in the Upanishads. Shivadvaita, as seen above, is a philosophical school of Shaivism.

Rudra, an early form of Shiva, is mentioned in the *Rig Veda*. In the *Yajur Veda*, Rudra's other names are given as Kapardin, Sharva, Bhava, Shambhu, Shankara and Shiva, thus leading to his later identification with Shiva, whereas Shiva is first referred to in the *Shvetashvatara Upanishad*.

The Pashupata, Shaiva Siddhanta and some other sects view Shiva as equal to or even greater than Brahman. This view occurs in texts of these sects, in the Shaiva Puranas, and in the Shaiva Upanishads. As the supreme reality, Shiva is both the formless Absolute and the personal god and saviour, representing love. The whole world operates through his *anugraha* or grace, which has five aspects: of creating, maintaining and destroying the world, concealing the truth, and, finally, giving liberation. Certain Shaiva texts explain that the supreme Shiva is the creator of the trinity. There is a similar concept of a supreme Vishnu in Vaishnava texts.

Pashupata

The Pashupata was a Shaiva sect, which according to tradition was founded in the second century CE by Lakulisha (also known as Nakulisha), who is said to have been an incarnation of the god Shiva. In this, the supreme deity, a form of Shiva, is known as Pashupati. He is the lord of all souls and the cause of all existence.

As a form of Shiva, he is also the protector of animals, particularly of domestic herds, and the patron of reproduction in all forms of life. In south India he is represented in this form as a four-armed man holding an axe and a small deer.

The sect probably existed earlier as it is mentioned in the Mahabharata and referred to in the *Brahma Sutra*. The *Pashupata Sutra* is the earliest text of this school, said to have been written by Shiva himself in his incarnation as Lakulisha. The earliest bhashya or commentary on this is by Kaundinya, who probably belonged to the sixth century. *Ganakarika* is another text describing the principles of this sect.

Kaundinya states that Pashupati created the whole world, beginning from Brahman, for the good of all. He says that five aspects are discussed in the system, *karya* (effect), *karana* (cause), yoga (union or contact), *vidhi* (behaviour) and *dukhanta* (ending of sorrow). All sorrow can be removed by the grace of Shiva, who is Pashupati, the lord and protector of all. According to

Kaundinya, liberation cannot be attained by jnana (knowledge), vairagya (detachment), dharma (right action) or *aishvarya-tyaga* (surrendering miraculous powers), but only by the grace of Shiva. This path to freedom from sorrow can be explained by a teacher to one who is fit for it. (In this text it says he should be a brahmana with keen senses.) The individual Self must understand the karana or cause and come into contact (yoga) with god through the right behaviour. Certain yamas and niyamas, codes of behaviour, are laid down to be followed on the path.

Three aspects of creation were *pashu*, the individual soul, *pati*, god or the lord, and *pasha*, the world. (Pasha also means bonds or bondage.) Pashu includes all living beings, as well as knowledge and the *pramana*s or means of knowledge. Whatever is known or visible (*pashyana*) is called pasha. These three were separate and distinct. The path to enlightenment is described in these texts and has five stages: the first two being external and the next three involving meditative and other internal practices. Despite all one's efforts, enlightenment could finally be achieved only by the grace of god.

The sect existed up to the end of the fifteenth century.

Pratyabhijna

Pratyabhijna is a philosophical concept, implying a recognition of the world as a manifestation of Shiva. Somananda (circa 875 and 925) founded the Pratyabhijna system, further elaborated by Utpaladeva (circa 900 and 950) and Abhinavagupta (circa 975 and 1025).

Somananda's most notable work is *Shivadrishti*, which consists of seven chapters and approximately 700 verses. He explains that Shiva is the ultimate reality and the highest consciousness. He is both immanent and transcendent and he pervades the world yet is at the same time beyond it. His immanent aspect, which manifests as the world, is known as Shakti, and is not different from or independent of Shiva. Chit or consciousness, *ichchha*, will or desire, *kriya* or action and jnana or knowledge are all aspects of Shakti. In Paramashiva, the supreme Shiva, Shakti has two aspects: *prakasha* or self-luminosity, and *vimarsha* or self-consciousness. This two-fold Shakti is the same as Shiva, shining with his own light and conscious of the whole. When prakasha is emphasized, Shakti is jnana or knowledge, and when vimarsha is emphasized, she is kriya or action. Sadashivatattva corresponds to the first and Ishvaratattva to the second. Maya Shakti (the power of illusion or obfuscation) hides the truth of the real nature of Shiva and the world. The individual has the same nature as Shiva but cannot recognize this. Through instruction and guidance, pratyabhijna, recognition of the true state, is achieved.

Shaktavijnana is another short work of Somananda's.

Utpaladeva further developed the philosophy. His works include the *Ishvara Pratyabhijna Karika* as well as a number of verses in praise of Shiva. Utpaladeva was the son of Udayakara, the disciple of Somananda, and the teacher of Padmakara and of Lakshmanagupta, who was the teacher of Abhinavagupta. Abhinavagupta's *Pratyabhijna Darshana* is the most important text for this school.

Shaiva Siddhanta

Shaiva Siddhanta developed between the seventh and fourteenth centuries.[6]

Literally, it means 'the doctrine of the followers of Shiva'. It bases its philosophy on the Vedas, Upanishads and the Shaiva Agamas, which are all Sanskrit texts, as well as the Tamil texts of the Nayanar saints, the twelve Tirumurai and the Meykanta Shastras, apart from other Shaivite works. It sees the supreme reality as Shiva, who is both the formless Absolute and the personal god and saviour representing love. As in other Shaiva systems,

Shiva's anugraha or grace has five aspects, of creating, maintaining
and destroying the world, concealing the truth, and finally, giving
liberation. Shiva operates through his Shakti, which, though a part
of him, forms the link between pure consciousness and matter.
Through Shakti, knowledge, action and desire come into being,
creating the world and the individual souls. Shiva is pati, the lord,
and all the souls are pashu (literally, cattle). They are in bondage
(pasha) to the world of material existence. Shiva, the source of all,
is not affected by the material world, which is unconscious (achit).
Pashu is a term for all souls, but each individual soul or jiva is
different. It is pure consciousness that is clouded by impurities. It
has the same essence as Shiva but is not identical. Pasha, which
constitutes bondage, includes karma and maya (illusion). *Mala* or
impurity is part of pasha and is embedded in maya. It is of various
kinds. *Sahaja* mala is that associated with the soul from the very
beginning and remains until liberation. *Agantuka* mala refers to
the senses and sense objects. *Sumsargika* mala is that produced by
the interrelationship of the first two. It is actually Shiva's Shakti
(Maheshvari Shakti) that is the cause of bondage, but at the same
time it is acting for the good of all. It helps people to develop and
grow in their own way, and though one may seem to suffer, the
Shakti is always directed for one's own good.

The world has thirty-six tattvas or principles that arise from
Maya. The world is real but is constantly evolving through the
grace of Shiva. This evolution is designed to benefit all.

Acting in the world, the souls, which are eternal and have
knowledge and the ability to act, become bound by false ideas
and wrong actions. Destroying these bonds by right action and
devotion to Shiva, the soul is freed from impurities and united with
Shiva, though it retains its separate identity. Divine knowledge
is obtained through Shiva, either directly through intuition or
through a guru. Four stages on this path are said to be charya, kriya
or action, yoga or union and jnana or knowledge, though these can

exist simultaneously as well. Daily rituals are an essential part of
this school. Certain principles of this school, that is, of the three
forms of pati, pashu and pasha, are the same in the Pashupata form
of Shaivism, though the interpretation of these is not identical.
There are differences of thought even within Shaiva Siddhanta.
While most hold that Shiva is the instrumental cause of the world,
some veer towards the Advaita concept that Brahman (identified
with Shiva) is the instrumental and the material cause. There
are also some differences on whether the individual soul remains
separate after liberation or attains identity and unity with Shiva.

Vaishnavism

Vaishnavism centres around the god Vishnu, the preserver in the
trinity of Brahma, Vishnu and Shiva. Vishnu is first mentioned in
the *Rig Veda*, where he joins the god Indra in his battles. In this
and other Vedic texts, he is mentioned as a god who takes three
steps, traversing heaven and earth, which later becomes the story
of his incarnation as Vamana. His incarnations, however, are not
directly mentioned in the Vedas. In the Mahabharata, Matsya,
later one of his incarnations, is identified with Prajapati. In the
Shatapatha Brahmana (14.1.1), he is identified with sacrifice
(yajna).

The name Vishnu is said to come from the word 'vish', to
pervade, as Vishnu pervades the world. He is the quality or guna
of sattva, which leads to light and truth. He dwells in everything
and overcomes all. He is the inner cause and the symbol of life.

According to Puranic myths, after the great deluge, when
creation ends and before the next cycle of creation begins, there
is deep silence, and Vishnu sleeps on a banyan (*vata*) leaf on the
surface of the water in his form as Bala Mukunda. Slowly, he
awakes, a lotus stalk grows from his navel and on this appears
Brahma, who gains the power to create from Vishnu. Other myths

state that between cycles of creation Vishnu sleeps on the serpent Ananta. The developed form of Vishnu incorporates earlier deities, including Narayana, later one of his names, and Krishna, one of his main incarnations.

Vishnu lives in a heaven known as Vaikuntha and is married to Lakshmi, also known as Shri Devi. His other consorts include Bhu Devi and Nila Devi. Through his mind, Vishnu once created a son named Viraja, but more important is his son Shasta, actually born through Shiva when Vishnu took the form of a woman, Mohini. Shasta is popular in south India as Ayyappa. Vishnu's vahana or vehicle is the bird Garuda.

Vishnu is thought to have been the most important deity during the period of the composition of the epics and Puranas. As the concept of Vishnu developed, he began to be worshipped in five aspects: *para*, the highest supreme form; *vyuha*, emanation; *vibhava*, incarnation; archcha, images or representations of god; and *antaryamin*, the inner controller, known in the heart.

Para, meaning the highest, refers to the supreme form or aspect of the deity. He directs his wishes (ichchha) towards his consort, Shri Lakshmi, who represents matter (*bhuti*) and action (kriya). From these three powers (shaktis), six qualities (gunas) come into being: jnana (knowledge), *aishvarya* (lordship), Shakti (ability), *bala* (strength), virya (virility) and tejas (splendour). These powers are embodied in the vyuhas. The concept of the vyuhas seems to have been known by the second century BCE and it forms an important part of the Pancharatra sect. Initially, there were four vyuhas: Vasudeva (Krishna), Samkarshana (Balarama), Pradyumna and Aniruddha, but later the number was raised to twenty-four. Vishnu is born in the world in different forms and these are known as his incarnations or avataras. The vyuhas are not the same as the vibhavas, though the vyuhas can become incarnations. The ten main incarnations of Vishnu listed in the *Matsya Purana*, *Agni Purana*, *Varaha Purana* and other texts are: Matsya, Kurma, Varaha, Narasimha, Vamana, Parashurama, Rama, Krishna, Buddha and Kalki. Some of these are only partial incarnations, that is, they do not embody the complete essence of Vishnu but only a part of it. This list became the standardized version in all later texts. However, in earlier texts, there are several different lists and versions of the incarnations. The Mahabharata refers to the incarnations and in one list provides the names of ten. These are: Hamsa, Kurma, Matsya, Varaha, Narasimha, Vamana, Rama (Bhargava), Rama (Dasharathi), Satvata (Krishna or Balarama) and Kalkin. The *Matsya Purana* contains both the standard list and a different version, where it states that Vishnu had seven human incarnations because he killed the rishi Brighu's wife. These were: Dattatreya, Mandhata, Jamadagnya (Parashurama), Rama, son of Dasharatha, Veda Vyasa, Buddha and Kalki. His three other incarnations were Narayana, Narasimha and Vamana (47.46). Some texts provide lists of twenty-two and even thirty-nine incarnations, while others state that there are thousands of incarnations. The twenty-two incarnations given in the *Bhagavata Purana* are: (1) Sanat Kumara, the eternal youth; (2) Varaha; (3) the rishi Narada; (4) the two saints, Nara and Narayana; (5) the rishi Kapila; (6) Dattatreya; (7) Yajna, personification of sacrifice; (8) Rishabha, a king; (9) Prithu, the first ruler; (10) Matsya; (11) Kurma; (12) Dhanvantari, the divine physician; (13) Mohini, the divine enchantress; (14) Narasimha; (15) Vamana; (16) Parashurama; (17) the great rishi Vyasa; (18) Rama; (19) Balarama; (20) Krishna; (21) Buddha; (22) Kalki. The *Garuda Purana* has a similar list. However, in this his third incarnation was of a Devarishi, the eighth was Urukrama, the son of Nabhi and Meru, the eighteenth was the rishi Narada and the nineteenth was Rama. Another shorter list in the *Garuda* includes Hayagriva, Makaradhvaja and Naga as incarnations. The *Satvata Samhita* and *Ahirbudhnya Samhita*, both Pancharatra texts, have a list of thirty-nine incarnations.

His main consort, Lakshmi, takes different forms in his various incarnations.

Vishnu is usually worshipped in the form of an image. If an image is not available, a *shalagrama* is the preferred object of worship. Images of the god represent him in his incarnations, emanations or as the supreme form. The exact way he is to be depicted in each form is laid out in texts. Vaishnavism includes not only devotion and worship but also a complex philosophy.

An early Vaishnava sect was the Bhagavata, focusing on the worship of Vasudeva Krishna. A later development was the Pancharatra, with its theory of emanations, or vyuhas. Between the seventh and tenth centuries were the Alvar saints who worshipped Vishnu with bhakti, or love and devotion. The Alvars were followed by the Vaishnava Acharyas, including Nathamuni and Yamunacharya. Ramanuja, in the eleventh century, took over from them and established the most influential Vaishnava school of philosophy known as Vishishtadvaita, and Madhva in the thirteenth century established the school of Dvaita (see above). Two branches of southern Vaishnavism around this time were the Tengalai and Vadagalai, while the Haridasa sect focused on bhakti. Meanwhile, in Bengal, Jayadeva wrote the famous *Gita Govinda* in the twelfth century on the love between Radha and Krishna, which contributed to the growth of Radha–Krishna cults.

Another major sect was established by Vallabhacharya (1489–1531). In central India, including Maharashtra and Karnataka, the cult of Vitthala, a form of Vishnu, was important, worshipped by Jnaneshvara, Namadeva, Tukaram and others, while in north India, Ramananda, Ravidas, Mirabai and Sur Das were among the noted Vaishnava saints. Others included Nimbarka, Nabhadas (circa 1525), Biharilal (1603–63), Ramdas (1608–81) and Jagjivan Das (1632–1720). Chandidas, Chaitanya Mahaprabhu and Shankara Deva were Vaishnava saints in eastern India. In modern times, the International Society for Krishna Consciousness (ISKCON) carries on the tradition of Krishna worship. Nimbarka, Vidyapati, Umapati, Chandidas and Chaitanya Mahaprabhu are among those who focus on Radha–Krishna worship influenced by Shaktism.

The Vedas, Upanishads, *Brahma Sutra*, *Harivamsha* and the Puranas are all utilized in the development of Vaishnava philosophy, while the Bhagavad Gita, *Pancharatra Agamas* and bhakti compositions of all saints and writers and the complex works of philosophers form part of Vaishnava literature.

Thus, Vaishnava sects include the Pancharatras, Sahajiyas, Varkaris or worshippers of Vitthala, Shrivaishnavas and followers of the various Vaishnava saints and philosophers, including Chaitaniya Mahaprabhu, Vallabhacharya, Ramanuja, Madhva and Ramananda.

Shrivaishnavism

Shrivaishnavism is a Vaishnavite sect in which the goddess Shri or Lakshmi is considered an inseparable part of the god Vishnu. The sect is based on the poems and teachings of the Alvars, compiled by Nathamuni of the tenth century, in the text *Nalayira Divya Prabandham*. Nathamuni's grandson, Yamunacharya, translated some of these into Sanskrit in his text *Stotraratna*. His disciples were among the teachers of Ramanuja, who modified the teachings and made Shrivaishnavism a part of the Vedantic tradition. Thus, Shrivaishnavism has been called the socio-religious manifestation of Ramanuja's Vishishtadvaita. After his death, the sect split into two, known as the Vadagalai (northern) and Tengalai or Tenkalai (southern). The northern school, led by Vedanta Desika, preferred the use of Sanskrit and believed that to achieve liberation or moksha human effort was also necessary. The southern school led by Lokacharya Pillai used Tamil texts and considered that god's grace was sufficient to attain moksha. The Vadagalai is often described as the school of the baby monkey, as the animal makes an effort to cling to its mother, whereas the Tengalai approach is compared to a kitten, which is carried by the mother without any effort on its part. There were several other doctrinal differences. The Vadagalai believe that Lakshmi is infinite and equal to Vishnu, the Tengalai that she is a liberated soul. Minor differences include the shape of the Vaishnava emblem and the order of dishes to be served during a meal.

Shaktism

Tantrism and Shaktism also find a place in the later Upanishads. Shaktism had its base in the Samkhya concept of Purusha and prakriti.

Shaktism is based on the concept of Shakti or divine feminine energy. The Shaktas, or those who primarily worship Shakti, see the feminine principle represented by Devi or Mahadevi as inherent in every aspect of the universe. The Shakta sect not only worships the outer form of the deity, who can transform herself into all forms, but the inner aspect. Thus, the Kundalini is identified with Shakti and the advanced Shakta attempts to raise it from the Muladhara to the Sahasrara Chakra. The Samkhya theory of Purusha and prakriti is also part of Shakta philosophy, where Shiva represents Purusha and Shakti, prakriti. The sect has ascetic, philosophic and tantric practices and was initially prominent in Bengal and Assam, though the worship of Shakti is widespread all over India.

The worship of the female principle has been traced back to the Indus Valley civilization and even earlier, where 'mother goddess' figurines and ring stones, thought by some to represent the Yoni, have been found. But without textual corroboration it is not possible to say whether these items were worshipped or in what way. In the Devi-sukta hymn of the *Rig Veda* (10.125) the concept of feminine energy inherent in creation is explained. The goddess or Devi is supreme and all-pervading. In this hymn, the goddess says: 'I am the Kingdom, the giver of wealth, the knower of all. I am the first of all rituals . . . I dwell in all things.' Two Durgastotras in the Mahabharata and the Aryastava in *Harivamsha* further expand the concept, while the Devi Mahatmya section of the *Markandeya Purana* is the most important text describing different forms of Shakti. In Samkhya philosophy, prakriti is the equivalent of Shakti. Other Puranas too contain passages on Shakti. Shaktis are named as consorts of some of the gods and depicted in images as the Matrikas, representing aspects of one supreme feminine deity. Two texts, *Saundarya Lahiri* and *Lalitasahasranama*, assigned to the philosopher Shankara, are expositions on the powers and aspects of Shakti. Shakti is most commonly associated with Shiva, but also forms a part of other sects and religions. In Vaishnavism, eight Shaktis are named as channels for the energies of the gods. These are Shri, Bhu, Sarasvati, Priti, Pushti, Tushti, Kirti and Shanti. The feminine principle is an integral part of Vajrayana Buddhism and is seen in Jainism in the Vidyadevis and Shasana Devis. Reverence and worship of Shakti forms a part of all tantric cults.

Tantrism

Tantrism is a form of religion or spiritualism which originated in ancient days but gained popularity around the eighth century CE. The word comes from the Sanskrit root *tan*, to spread, or *tanu*, body, or *tadantara*, inner.

As a method of religious practice, its exact origin is not known, but certain concepts and practices are traced back to the *Atharva Veda*.

Tantrism aims to gain control over all the forces of nature and to obtain the power to accomplish any task. At its highest level it seeks union with the divine, while at its lowest its powers can be used to harm others.

There are numerous tantric texts describing various practices, as well as a number of tantric sects, many of which still exist. Extant Hindu tantric literature includes a vast number of texts dating from the seventh to the seventeenth and eighteenth centuries, much of which is still untranslated. There are, in addition, later works, as well as a number of modern explorations of tantra. The Tantras contain both high philosophy and practical methodology. The texts are composed both in Sanskrit and in regional languages. An ideal Tantra should have four themes: (1) jnana or knowledge, both that obtained through philosophical enquiry and secret and mystical knowledge; (2) methods of Yoga, or union with the Supreme; these methods include concentration, meditation and the acquisition of siddhis or powers; (3) kriya or action, creating and consecrating images, temples and other objects of worship, and methods of worship of various deities; (4) *charya* or conduct, concerning rituals, festivals and daily duties. Most Tantras include aspects of these topics as well as theories regarding the creation and destruction of the world and various stories and legends. Tantras may also deal with the worship of specific deities, or with the use of the Pancha-makaras under specific conditions. A number of Tantras consist of a dialogue between Shiva and Shakti. The tantric method includes sadhana or practice, shuddhi or purification, uddhara or elevation, and chaitanya, the reaffirmation of identity in consciousness. Several Tantras focus on the chakras, raising the Kundalini and the practice of *nyasa* (see Chapter 3).

Other Philosophical Developments

A vast body of philosophical literature exists in India. The early schools of philosophy used the same or similar terminology, though in different ways. There was more interaction between Buddhist and Hindu ideas, though some Jains such as Haribhadra and Gunaratna were also involved in these discussions. Philosophical texts in Sanskrit use a number of technical terms which are rather complex. These, in addition, are used in terse statements known as sutras, each of which is difficult to interpret. Depending on the school of philosophy, these terms and sutras have different meanings. To understand any philosophical text, therefore, study with a teacher, a guru well-versed in that school of philosophy, was essential. Apart from the vast quantity of purely philosophical literature, philosophy is embedded in most religious texts including various Samhitas, Agamas and Puranas.

Each school of thought continued to develop in medieval times. There were also new ideas and concepts, such as the development of ideas on bhakti formulated by bhakti saints, and its philosophical development in Gaudiya Vaishnavism, the esoteric concepts of the Panchasakhas and many more. The Siddhas and Natha Yogis contributed to a different stream of philosophical development and, as seen above, philosophical concepts developed in both Shaivism and Vaishnavism. Some of the ideas of the philosophical schools originated in very early days but were now clearly formulated. Many of these combined philosophy with theism and devotion, seeing one particular deity as supreme. Each system of thought developed separately through an unbroken line of scholars and teachers, but simultaneously commented on and referred to other systems. They used the same terminology, though the terms could have different meanings in each system. They discussed Brahman, atman, Ishvara, jiva, maya, the composition of the world, the pramanas or means of knowledge, logic, fallacy, the doctrines of karma, transmigration, god's grace, bhakti and means of moksha or liberation.

In early days, the method of discussion between different groups and philosophies followed a set pattern. A statement would be made and then the opposing view (*purvapaksha*) would be presented. Following this, the opposing view would be refuted (*uttarapaksha*).

Islam, Sufi ideas, the growth of Sikhism and Christianity all contributed in some way to philosophical development. Social and religious movements in the nineteenth century such as the Brahmo Samaj, Arya Samaj, Mahima Dharma, Radhasoami and others brought in new trends.

Philosophical speculations have continued into modern times. Some noted philosophers such as J. Krishnamurti, U.G. Krishnamurti, Osho and Sri Aurobindo may have their origins in Hindu or Buddhist philosophy but developed their own terminology that went beyond any specific religion.

Some Important Texts

We end this chapter with a summary of four important philosophical texts, three of which are related to Advaita, while the fourth is encyclopaedic in nature. These provide a small sample of innumerable philosophical and religious texts composed over the centuries. While the first three texts were composed in Sanskrit, the fourth was written in Kannada, representing the development of philosophical literature in regional languages.

Upadesha Sahasri

This philosophical text was composed in Sanskrit by the ninth-century philosopher Shankara. *Upadesha Sahasri* literally means 'A Thousand Teachings' and in this text Adi Shankaracharya reiterates certain important truths of Advaita. The first chapter explains the method of enlightening a disciple. True knowledge should be explained again and again to a disciple until the truth is grasped. The teacher should understand the nature of the disciple and remove the causes of non-comprehension such as past and present sins, laxity, absence of firm knowledge of discrimination between the real and unreal, desire for popular esteem, vanity based on caste or lineage, etc. In addition, the teacher should ensure that the student is following the *yama*s (ethical restraints) and other rules of conduct. Then, the essential teachings of the shruti texts should be conveyed. A number of verses from the Upanishads as well as a few from other texts are quoted in this. The second chapter explains the cause and nature of ignorance and conveys the knowledge of the changeless and non-dual Self. True knowledge brings the transmigratory state to an end.

This text in effect provides a summary of the key statements that reveal the truths of Advaita Vedanta.

Viveka Chudamani

This philosophical text is also assigned to the ninth-century philosopher Shankara. The *Viveka Chudamani* consists of 581 verses in Sanskrit. It describes the basic principles of Advaita and provides guidance to the sincere seeker on how to attain moksha.

In the first verse, Shankara says: 'I bow down to Govinda, who is the goal of all Vedanta, who is beyond words and thought, who is supreme bliss, and who is my guru.' Here, Govinda has a dual meaning of referring to both god and Shankara's own guru, Govindapada. Shankara goes on to say that a human birth is difficult to attain and when one has attained it one should use it to reach the true end of life. Liberation cannot be attained through rituals, worship of deities or by acquiring wealth. To go beyond life and death, one must focus on realizing and identifying with the atman. Work can purify the mind but does not lead to liberation. Bhakti is important on the path but this bhakti is not devotion to god but to inquiry into the truth of the Self. A guru who is himself immersed in Brahman can guide the aspirant on the path. In this text, Shankara explains how moksha or liberation can be attained only through jnana or knowledge. True knowledge is obtained through discrimination (viveka), an understanding of the difference between the real and the unreal, between what is eternal and what is transient.

Yoga Vasishtha

This text is said to have been composed by the ancient rishi Valmiki, famous as the composer of the Ramayana, though it was probably composed in the seventh or eighth century CE and records the philosophical teachings given to Rama by the rishi Vasishtha. The text has 23,734 verses, though there are different recensions in which the number of verses vary. It has six *prakarana*s or sections: Vairagya; Mumukshuvyavahara; Utpatti; Sthiti; Upashama and Nirvana.

The greatest contribution of this text is in its discussion on the nature of the mind and how to control it. The mind has great potential and by gaining control over it its inherent powers can be developed. The *Yoga Vasishtha* guides the individual to think for himself rather than depend on the authority of the shastras, a guru or divine grace. To one who has gained control over the mind, everything in life can be achieved, including health, wealth, power and position. When a great effort is made in any course of action, without violating righteous principles, victory is assured. Thus, past karma can be overcome by present actions and the life of an individual is not predetermined. Both liberation and bondage are only states of mind.

Among other topics, the text discusses seven stages of spiritual progress. In the first stage, there is enquiry and association with spiritual persons. In the second stage, the aspirant develops the ability to discriminate (*vicharana*). The third stage involves detachment. In the fourth stage, the unreal nature of the world is realized while the fifth is the state of pure knowledge and bliss. The sixth is deep bliss, a kind of samadhi similar to dreamless sleep. In the seventh, which cannot be experienced when alive, all states are transcended. Thus, the sixth corresponds to the state of consciousness known as *Turiya*, and the seventh to *Turiyatita*.

The book discusses desire as the root of all problems and states that to progress all passions and desires must be controlled and removed. To help in this, breath control (*prananirodhana*) can be practised. Both jnana and karma (knowledge and action) can be combined on the path.

The text as a whole has its own unique philosophy, though there are some similarities with the philosophy of Advaita as well as with Buddhism and Shaivism. The *Yoga Vasishtha* agrees with Advaita that Brahman is the only reality. It denies the existence of the external world even more categorically than Shankara's Advaita. Such a denial existed earlier in Buddhist philosophy and was later followed by the Advaitin Prakashananda. The state of mukti or liberation is described as identical with Brahman and is the same as shunya (the void) or vijnana (consciousness). Brahman in this text is described as a formless entity without any characteristics, a state beyond experience. Its doctrine of spanda or immanent activity is similar to that of Shaiva philosophy.

Viveka Chintamani

This encyclopaedic work on various aspects of religion and philosophy was composed in Kannada in the fifteenth century by Nijaguna Shivayogi.

The text has ten chapters and the first chapter begins by explaining the names and qualities of the lord. It then describes various types of texts and philosophies including the Vedas, Vedangas, Upanishads, Puranas, six systems of philosophy, Vaishnavism, Buddhism, Jainism and materialism. The second chapter is on Shaiva Siddhanta and explains the essence of the Shaiva agamas and the methods of worshipping Shiva. The third describes Brahmanda, the cosmic egg, and fourteen *loka*s or worlds, while the fourth and fifth focus on *bhuloka* (earth), and particularly on Jambudvipa, the continent in which India is said to be located. The sixth describes Devaloka or the world of the gods and other heavenly realms, while the seventh analyses the principles of existence on the earth, including descriptions of buddhi, ahamkara, the senses and the various Rudras. The eighth chapter discusses knowledge and the characteristics of Ishvara, Shiva, Maheshvara, Sadashiva, Shakti and Shambhulinga. The ninth explains how wrong thinking leads to atheism and how the best action is that performed without thought of a reward. The tenth chapter is on the traditional system of time. This text thus provides a handy summary of the main streams of religious thought. It has been translated into Sanskrit, Tamil, Telugu, Marathi and other languages.

Three

The Main Topics

THE 108 UPANISHADS include several different topics. Some of the ideas represented and terms used have been explained in the previous chapter. A few of the main topics are also discussed here.

Shanti Mantras

Each of the Upanishads is preceded by a Shanti Mantra or invocation of peace. Though there are some variations, on the whole those belonging to the *Rig Veda* have the mantra that begins: 'Vanme-Manasi pratishthata. Mano me vachi pratishthatam . . .' The mantra is translated as 'Om, may my speech rest on my mind. May my mind rest on my speech. O self-manifested Brahman, reveal yourself to me. May both these [mind and speech] lead me to the Veda. May that Vedic knowledge not forsake me. By that Vedic study I unite day and night. I shall speak of ritam [the real or, what is right]. I shall speak the truth [satyam]. May that protect me. May that protect him who taught me. Protect me. Protect him who taught me. Om, Peace, peace, peace.'

The Upanishads attached to the *Shukla Yajur Veda* begin with the mantra 'Purnamada purnamidam', translated as 'Om. That is whole. This is whole. The whole comes from the whole. Taking the whole from the whole, only the whole remains.'

Those of the *Krishna Yajur Veda* begin with 'Om. Sahanavavatu . . .' This is translated as 'Om. May He protect us both [student and teacher]. May He sustain us both. May we work together to acquire strength [wisdom]. May our study lead to illumination. May there be no differences between us. Om, Peace, peace, peace.'

The *Sama Veda* has the mantra beginning 'Apyayantu . . .', translated as 'Om. May my limbs grow strong, and also my speech, prana, eyes, ears, and all my senses. All is the Brahman of the Upanishads. May I never deny Brahman. May Brahman never deny me. May there be non-denial. May non-denial be mine. May the dharmas proclaimed in the Upanishads be in me, who am devoted to the atman. May they be in me. Om. Peace, peace, peace.'

The *Atharva Veda* Shanti Mantra begins with 'Bhadram Karnebhih . . .', the whole translated as 'May we hear with our ears what is auspicious, O devas. May we who are engaged in sacrifices see what is auspicious with our eyes. While praising the gods, with strong limbs and bodies, may we live a life that is beneficial to the devas. May Indra of ancient fame be auspicious to us. May Pushan the all-knowing be propitious to us. May Tarkshya Arishtanemi be propitious to us. May Brihaspati be propitious to us. Om. Peace, peace, peace.'

The Mahavakyas

If one wants to understand the vast and varied Upanishads, one should begin with the mahavakyas, or 'great sentences', identified as such by early philosophers. These are the most important or key statements in these texts.

The mahavakyas include: 'Brahma-asmi' (I am Brahman) and 'Tat tvam asi' (You are That); 'Ayamatma Brahma' (The soul is Brahman); 'Prajnanam Brahma' (Pure consciousness is Brahman) and 'Ekam evadvitiyam brahma' (Brahman is One without a second). These key sentences state the nature of Brahman, which is further explained below.

The Eternal and Non-eternal Soul: Brahman, Atman and Jiva

Brahman is the most important concept discussed in the Upanishads. Every Upanishad, including the early and late Upanishads, Upanishads focusing on a deity or on the paths of sannyasa or yoga, affirm that the ultimate goal of all existence is Brahman. But what exactly is Brahman? Brahman can be defined as the substratum of the world. The Upanishads agree that everything originates from Brahman, which is uncreated and has always existed. It is eternal, infinite and has no form or shape. It is beyond time and space. Its nature is 'sat-chit-ananda', that is, 'truth or true being, consciousness and bliss'. Even though Brahman is responsible for the creation of the world and is identical with or part of the soul in every living being, Brahman retains its original, unchangeable, eternal nature. Brahman is beyond thought and words which is why no description can ever reveal it. Only through knowledge of it would one know its reality.

The origin of the term Brahman can be traced to the *Rig Veda*, though the concept was not clearly developed there. In the *Rig Veda*, Brahman is linked to the idea of power. Power existed in the mantra or sacred word and was generated by rituals. It could also be a wider, underlying power, but it was nothing like the later concept. The philosopher S. Dasgupta also traces the concept of Brahman to the idea of power, the power obtained through sacrifice.[1] In some late Rig Vedic hymns, there are elements of monotheism. Vishvakarma, Hiranyagarbha, Brahmanaspati, Prajapati and Purusha, referred to in the *Rig Veda*, have aspects of a supreme creator, but this creator is outside the person, not within. These deities are also referred to in the Upanishads. For instance, Vishvakarma is mentioned in the *Shvetashvatara Upanishad* (4.17) and so is Hiranyagrabha (3.4 and 4.12), where he is called the first created being, not the creator. Deussen refers to Sarvahammani Hiranyagrabha, which appears in the *Nrisimha Upanishad*, but as this is a late Upanishad, it could not have contributed to the Brahman concept. Brahmanaspati is not mentioned in the Upanishads but there are several references to Prajapati, mainly in the later Upanishads. Purusha, described as having 1000 heads, 1000 eyes, etc. (*Rig Veda* 10.129) may come closest to the concept of Brahman. The term Purusha as later used in Samkhya or Yoga philosophy has no connection with this early idea of Purusha. However, Purusha in the Upanishads is often identified with or used as a synonym for Brahman.

The concept of Brahman is difficult to grasp and the Upanishads go to great lengths to explain it in different ways. Brahman has two aspects: saguna and nirguna. The word 'guna' means a quality, therefore Saguna Brahman is that which can be described, that which has certain attributes and qualities. Nirguna is not limited by a description, though attempts to describe it refer to its eternal, unchanging and blissful nature, as given above. Nirguna, or that which is beyond form or specific qualities, can also take on attributes and become saguna, with qualities. Nirguna Brahman is also referred to as Para Brahman.

Below, we look at some select passages of how some of the main Upanishads describe Brahman.

The *Aitareya Upanishad* identifies Brahman and the atman. The atman is that through which everything is known, by whom one sees, hears and tastes. It goes on to say it is the heart, mind, wisdom, sorrow, memory, purpose and various other attributes, and all these are just names of consciousness (prajnanam), which can be identified with Brahman.

The *Kaushitaki Upanishad* describes the two paths of *pitriyana* and *devayana* (the path of the ancestors and the path of the gods) and how crossing through the devayana one first reaches the world of the god Brahma, and finally Brahman. It identifies Brahman with prana (breath) and *uktha* (recitation). The *Kena Upanishad* sees Brahman as the power behind our actions. Brahman is different from both the known and the unknown. It cannot be revealed by speech, understood by the mind, seen, heard or smelt, yet it is that by which all these actions take place. It can be known only to the one who has no trace of individuality left, who has no sense of duality. When Brahman pervades consciousness, only That is seen and nothing else. When the atman is realized (that is, its identity as Brahman), it attains immortality.

The *Taittiriya Upanishad* states that the one who knows Brahman attains the supreme. Brahman is reality, knowledge and infinity, hidden in the cave of the heart and in the highest akasha. Brahman is described as the self-created (2.7.1) and as satya (the true) (2.6.1). Next, the bliss of Brahman is explained. It is hundreds of times more than anything that can be experienced. The one who knows it loses all fear (2.9.1).

The *Kena Upanishad* says that it is Brahman through which everything is known, yet Brahman is neither the known nor the unknown. It can only be understood by those who have no other thoughts or aims, that is, by one who is immersed in it.

The *Katha Upanishad* says, 'Brahman, the immortal, contains all worlds in it, and no one goes beyond it.' Brahman has never been created and can never be destroyed.

The *Brihadaranyaka* (2.3) says that Brahman has two forms, gross and subtle, mortal and immortal, limited and unlimited, seen and unseen. In succeeding verses in this text the rishi Yajnavalkya explains Brahman in many ways. He says that just as different types of smoke come from a fire, in the same way everything including the Vedas comes from limitless reality (*mahat bhutasya*), which can be equated with Brahman. And everything merges with it just as all sorts of water merge in the sea, as all sounds merge in the ear, all thoughts in the mind and as salt in water pervades all of it. He also explained that when everything is Brahman, there can be no duality.

There are innumerable references to Brahman in these texts but at times other aspects of life such as light or Prana (breath) or a deity are referred to as supreme and identified with Brahman. The *Brahma Sutra*, a text composed by Badarayana, puts together various references to show the supremacy of Brahman.

As one reads through the Upanishads, one will begin to get a clearer idea of Brahman, which, in fact, cannot be described as it has no attributes. Through various dialogues and explanations by commentators, methods of reaching Brahman are suggested.

How does Brahman relate to god, the world and the individual soul? This is analysed in various philosophies, particularly in those together known as Vedanta. (A brief idea of these has been provided in Chapter 2). In Advaita, Brahman is the only true reality and is essentially the same as the atman or soul in every living being, while in other philosophies there are different interpretations, corresponding to different interpretations of the atman. Brahman can limit itself and take the form of Ishvara or any personal deity or can become Hiranyagarbha, the golden womb, the soul of the universe.

Closely related to the concept of Brahman is that of the atman and jiva. Both these terms indicate the individual soul but they are used differently. In the *Rig Veda*, the term atman means breath or vital essence, but by the time of the Upanishads the atman is a term for the Self or soul, which is imperishable, beyond time and eternal. The atman is not the same as the body, mind or consciousness, but is something beyond which permeates all of these. The Upanishads explore the concept of the atman from all possible angles and most later schools of philosophy base themselves on these texts. The atman is often seen as identical with Brahman, and moksha or liberation is achieved when its true identity is perceived or realized.

The jiva, also called the *jivatma*, is another term for the individual soul. According to the great philosopher Shankara, jiva is in essence identical with the atman and Brahman. However, in practice it is different and undergoes the experiences of successive lives, but ultimately there is unity. However, various philosophies have different views on the atman and its relationship with Brahman and jiva. According to Ramanuja, the individual soul is a form of the Supreme, yet is unique, endowed with intelligence and self-consciousness. It remains unchanged through a series of lives, retaining its identity, and is different from the body, the breath or the intelligence. According to Madhva, the number of jivas are infinite, and they are different from Brahman. Though dependent on Brahman, the jiva is an active agent with its own responsibilities. The three types of jivas were those fit for liberation (mukti yogya), including the gods, rishis and other advanced people; ordinary jivas, subject to transmigration; and other beings such as asuras and bhutas. Nimbarka believed that the jiva is both different from and united with Brahman. According to some theories, the atman and jiva are the same and do not unite with Brahman even in liberation, but remain in blissful communication with the divine.

In Samkhya philosophy, there is a plurality of souls. In both Samkhya and Yoga the term Purusha indicates both the individual soul and the universal. However, in the Upanishads, Purusha is also used as a term for Brahman. In Jainism, everything in the universe is classified into two categories, jiva and ajiva, which broadly mean life and non-life. Jiva is also used to refer to the individual soul, of which there are any number, and the liberated jiva, freed from matter, is known as the atman. Early Buddhist philosophy states that there is no permanent entity and if only an eternal entity can be known as the atman, everything is *anatta*, or *anatman*, that is, with no atman or soul.

Purusha and Prakriti

Literally, Purusha means man. But in different contexts, Purusha refers to the soul, to god, or in the Upanishads to Brahman. The term is most often used in Samkhya philosophy, where Purusha represents the eternal male principle, the passive or fixed aspect of creation. It is the eternal Truth that sets creation in motion. It is beyond form and shape, the subtle essence of creation. In the *Rig Veda* (10.90), Purusha represents primeval man, from whom creation emerged. This famous hymn states that Purusha pervades the earth and has a thousand heads, a thousand eyes and a thousand feet. Purusha is the past, present and future, and all creatures are a part of him. Viraj was born from him and he again from her. Purusha was the sacrificial offering and spring was the clarified butter, summer the fuel, and autumn the oblation. The four castes arose from him, as well as the sun and moon, Indra and Agni, the elements and space. Thus, here, Purusha is similar to the concept of Brahman. The *Brihadaranyaka Upanishad* (1.4) states that Purusha was the first, but, feeling lonely, he made his body swell and divided it into two parts, male and female. These united, and from them human beings and other creatures were born. Purusha as the creative principle is further described in later texts, while prakriti is the female principle.

The nature of Purusha and prakriti are extensively analysed in Samkhya philosophy. According to this philosophy, Purusha and prakriti are separate and distinct, and creation arises from prakriti by itself. Yet, the aim of creation is to serve Purusha, the soul, and to enable it to attain freedom. Purusha is also known as Puman. In later Samkhya philosophy, as well as in Yoga and in most of the Puranas, Purusha is identified with Ishvara or another form of god. In the *Vishnu Purana*, Purusha is the same as Brahma, the creator; he is part of Vishnu and is the first principle of creation. According to the *Devi Bhagavata Purana*, Purusha and prakriti emerged together from Brahman.

Mahat

Mahat generally means 'great' or 'large'. In a philosophical context, it refers to the intellect or buddhi. Mahat can be the individual buddhi or the sum total of all buddhis. According to the Samkhya philosophy, mahat is the first stage of creation, which emerges when the equilibrium of the gunas is disturbed in creation. It is also the witness that is part of the individual, which observes but does not participate in action.

Buddhi

Buddhi indicates higher knowledge or intelligence, reasoning, discernment or judgement. It is an important term in early philosophical traditions. In Samkhya philosophy, buddhi is the second of twenty-five tattvas (elements) and emerges in the first stage of evolution from prakriti, known as mahat. Mahat contains all the buddhis of individuals. Ahamkara, the individual sense of Self, is the next to evolve.

Maya (Maayaa)

Maya indicates the illusory nature of the world. Originally, the word meant art or wisdom, secrecy, extraordinary power or magic and sorcery. Maya as a philosophical concept forms an important part of Advaita. The philosophers Gaudapada and later Shankara in the ninth century spoke about the One Reality as the only truth, the world and all creation being illusion or maya, and the word is most commonly used in that sense today. Other philosophical systems do not see the world as totally unreal and maya indicates god's creative power, through which the world came into being. According to Ramanuja, the world is real but is called maya because it attracts people and draws them away from god. Purushottama, a philosopher of Vallabha's school of thought, states that maya is a power of Brahman, and identical with it. Through maya, god becomes many without undergoing any change. That aspect of maya which creates confusion is known as avidya (ignorance). Maya has also been identified with prakriti, the material nature of the universe, the seed from which creation emerges. Among more recent philosophers, Sri Aurobindo stated that though there is One Reality, there are also individual souls. The world is not maya or an illusion, but is real, and needs to be perfected through the spiritual and material evolution of every living being.

Consciousness

Both the Upanishads and other texts provide an analysis of consciousness, and several Upanishads provide details on this. They state that the Self has four parts. The first is Vaishvanara or Vishva, who enjoys the world through Jagrita, or the waking state; the second is Taijasa, whose sphere is Svapna, the dreaming state; the third is Prajna, the state of Sushupti or deep sleep; and the fourth is Nanta Prajnam or Turiya, the state of awareness beyond these. The spiritually advanced person remains in the state of Turiya. A fifth state of Turiyatita is described in some texts, for instance, in the *Turiayatita Avadhuta Upanishad*, which is even beyond all these. Some texts describe three states below normal consciousness. In the state of Turiya or Turiyatita, the individual consciousness is undivided and whole, identified with Brahman or the Paramatman, or closely related to it. Each state is further subdivided into four states. They are also linked with the Pranava, the term for the mantra Om, which has four syllables.

The Body and Its Sheaths

The body, known in Sanskrit as *sharira*, has been extensively analysed in ancient texts, including the Upanishads. The body is seen as more than a physical entity. The *sthula* sharira, or gross body, contains the atman or soul. Within it are also chakras and *nadi*s (subtle centres and channels) that if purified can lead to bliss and perfection. Around it are other subtle bodies. The linga sharira or *sukshma* sharira, the subtle body, does not die with the physical body but retains the impressions and experiences of the physical body, transferring these to another body when the person is reincarnated. The *karana* sharira or para sharira, known as the causal body, retains the record of succeeding births and leads to birth in a particular body, time or place.

Apart from these bodies, there are *kosha*s or sheaths. The *annamaya* kosha or 'food sheath' corresponds with the sthula sharira. The *pranamaya* kosha, *manomaya* kosha and *vijnanamaya* kosha are contained in the linga sharira, while the *anandamaya* kosha is part of the para sharira. The pranamaya kosha is the body created by prana, the breath, and the manomaya kosha by mana, the mind. The vijnanamaya kosha is the wisdom sheath and the anandamaya the sheath of bliss. Among the Upanishads that discuss the koshas is the *Taittiriya Upanishad*. It compares the manomaya kosha with the four Vedic Samhitas (2.3). Within are the *vijnana* and further within the ananda. In other texts, the annamaya is the inner sheath, the rest extending beyond it.

The Senses

Several Upanishads refer to and describe the senses, usually known as Indriya and counted as eleven or sometimes fourteen. The five senses of perception are known as *buddhindriyani* or *jnanendriyani* as they are considered to be under the control of buddhi (higher intelligence). These senses are the eye, ear, nose, tongue and skin. Five more senses are the *karmendriyani*, that is, senses of karma or action. These are the larynx, hand, foot and organs of elimination and generation. Manas (mind) is the eleventh sense, the intermediary between the other senses and the atman or soul.

However, in some systems of Vedanta, there are four inner senses, *antarindriyani*, including manas, buddhi, ahamkara (the ego) and chitta (consciousness). The indriyas thus amount to fourteen and each is presided over by a specific deity, which controls their functioning.

Moksha, the Purpose of Life

Moksha, a term implying liberation or release from the cycle of birth and death, is the final goal of life in Hinduism and is frequently discussed in the Upanishads. Broadly, there are two types of moksha or mukti, one that takes place while the person is still alive and the other that takes place after death. The former is known as jivan-mukti, and the person attaining such a state is a jivan-mukta, a liberated person. Other terms may be used for this state, indicating one who has attained supreme wisdom. Both types have different connotations in the various philosophical schools. Some aspects of the two types of liberation are given below:

Jivan-mukti: Liberation that takes place while still alive and leads to the concept of a person who has ceased to participate in any aspect of life or one who performs actions with total detachment. Shankara, the philosopher of Advaita Vedanta, does not use the term but explains that even after attaining true knowledge the body remains till the fruits of previous deeds have been exhausted. The *sthitha* prajna, a person who has attained wisdom, is described in the Bhagavad Gita. Such a person has no likes or dislikes, fears, sorrows, attachments or desires. He performs good actions but remains unaffected by them. The *Yoga Vasishtha* paints a portrait of a jivan-mukta, a liberated person, who though totally detached at the same time participates fully in life. He appears to be blissful and happy and never has the delusion that he is the doer. Within himself, he is always neutral and beyond desires. In Samkhya philosophy, the *Samkhyakarika* states that the body may still exist for some time after the attainment of true knowledge. Moksha is attained when through right knowledge and discrimination (viveka) the buddhi realizes its difference from Purusha. The Purusha is then finally freed and can never again be bound.

According to the Yoga philosophy of Patanjali, there is a state when a living person has perfect knowledge and thus is *vimukta* or emancipated. But the final stage of *kaivalya* (aloneness, oneness with Brahman) is only when the chitta (mindstuff) merges in prakriti. Vidyaranya wrote a text called *Jivanmuktiviveka*, putting forward various views on jivan-mukti. In this he says that the state can exist when all desires and even the roots of desires are destroyed and simultaneously right knowledge emerges.

Mukti or moksha: Nyaya and Vaisheshika indicate that liberation is possible only after death, when the soul is free of the body. Prabhakara, a philosopher of Mimamsa, has a similar view. However, philosophers are not in agreement on what exactly happens to the individual soul in moksha after death. Four types of moksha are described in the Upanishads. These are *samipya*, or closeness with the divine; *sarupya* or *sadharmya*, similarity of nature with the divine; *salokya*, a conscious coexistence in the same world or plane; and *sayujya*, or union. In Advaita Vedanta, moksha after bodily death implies union with the One Reality, Brahman, where the individuality disappears. According to Ramanuja, moksha is a state where all limitations disappear but the individual soul continues to exist. It attains the nature of Brahman but is not identical with Brahman.

In Vaishnavism and Shaivism, it indicates a close association with the deity of one's choice while individual consciousness is retained. The term moksha is also used in Buddhism and Jainism and is similar to the concept of nirvana in Buddhism. Ancient materialistic schools denied the concept of moksha, while the twentieth-century philosopher Sri Aurobindo believed that the goal of life was not moksha, but evolution to a higher state.[2]

Reincarnation

Transmigration or reincarnation (samsara) is first explained in the Upanishads, though it is mentioned in earlier texts. The beginnings of the concept of reincarnation can be seen in the Vedic Samhitas and Brahmanas, the *Rig Veda* (10.14) has a hymn where the dead go to the world of Yama and, leaving behind all imperfections, return home again. There are other hymns about the spirit departing from the body and going to other worlds. The *Aitareya Upanishad* (Section 2) discusses the three births of a person, the third being when the person enters the womb and is reborn.

The *Kaushitaki Upanishad* (1.2) explains the doctrine of rebirth through the two paths, pitriyana and devayana, and the different stages of devayana (1.4), these being the world of Agni, followed by those of Vayu, Varuna, Aditya, Indra, Prajapati and finally of Brahma. The *Brihadaranyaka Upanishad* (6.2.15–16) states that when a person dies he is offered to the fire (agni), and from this a radiant person (Purusha) emerges. Those who know this truth and who meditate on it with faith go to the light, from the light to the day, from day to the waxing fortnight of the moon, to the six months of the northern course of the sun and then to the world of the gods. From here they reach the sun, then lightning, then, born of the mind (manas), they reach Brahma Loka, the world of Brahma, from which there is no return. Other texts state there is rebirth even from Brahma Loka.

Those who offer sacrifices, charity and austerities go through the smoke of the fire into the night, the fortnight of the waning moon, the six months of the southern course of the sun, to Pitri Loka, the world of the ancestors, and then to the moon. There they become food for the gods and then pass into space, air, rain and the earth. Here again they become food and, offered in the fire of man, are born again in the fire of woman.

Another passage in this Upanishad (5.10.1) states that when a person dies he goes to the air, then upwards to the sun, then to the moon, then to the region where there is no grief or sorrow.

The *Chhandogya Upanishad* (5.10) has similar passages. Here, however, it is further stated that those whose conduct is good will quickly attain a good birth after they return to earth, but those whose conduct is bad get a poor birth. Both mention that there is a category of small creatures who follow neither of these paths but are continuously dying and being reborn.

The two main paths are more clearly described in other Upanishads. Those who offer sacrifices and perform good works go to the world of Brahma but then are reborn. Those who practise austerities and have true knowledge become immortal.

From the time of the Upanishads onwards, reincarnation is accepted by all schools of thought, though there are some differences in the details. Rebirth or reincarnation is said to take place according to one's karma or actions in a previous life. The Bhagavad Gita states that one goes to the region of whatever one worships and then is reborn. Those who follow the true path and do not reach the ultimate goal are reborn with the knowledge they acquired in the previous life.

The Puranas and Shastras go into detail on transmigration and rebirth, various hells and different worlds (lokas) where one can be born as a result of one's deeds. Even the gods die and are reborn in successive *manvantaras* (epochs).

Only moksha, liberation, can free one from the cycle of birth and death. Stories in the epics, Puranas and other texts accept reincarnation and explain good and bad events as the results of past karma. Reincarnation is explained in detail in the Shastras. For instance, the *Manu Smriti* (Chapter 12) states that wrong actions may result in rebirth as a plant or tree, insect or worm, bird or animal, or one of a lower caste. It analyses the types of actions that result in different incarnations. Actions are linked to the three gunas of sattva, rajas and tamas and within each of these are three levels. Actions performed from the highest level of the sattva guna lead to the best type of rebirth. Such people are born as Brahma, Marichi, Prajapati, Dharma or Mahat (12.50). Great sinners (*mahapatakin*), after suffering for a long time in one of the hells, are finally reborn in lower life forms. Brahmana killers, as well as brahmanas who drink wine or steal gold, return in very low forms. One who defiles the preceptor's bed has a hundred incarnations as a plant and animal before regaining human form, while killers of animals are reborn as beasts that eat raw flesh. However, those who steal gems of various kinds don't seem to have a bad fate as they are reborn in the womb of a goldsmith's wife! (12.61). Other minute details are given for the sort of incarnations various acts bring.

The aim of life, however, is to escape from the cycle of rebirth and attain moksha or liberation.

Pitris

The Upanishads mention the *pitri*s and *pitriyana*. Pitri is a term usually used for ancestors or manes, though there are also other types of pitris. Pitriyana is the path after death that leads to the worlds of the pitris, in contrast to the devayana or path of the gods. Those who go to the world of the pitris after death are later reborn. Pitri Loka, the world of the pitris, is said to be different from Svarga Loka or the world of the gods in the Brahmanas. The *Shatapatha Brahmana* states that its door is in the southeast, while that of the gods is in the northeast. The Mahabharata and Puranas also refer to Pitri Loka.

Texts describe different types of pitris. In some texts, even the gods are said to be descended from the pitris. Most pitris, though, are human ancestors who have died and for whom ceremonies have been performed with proper rites. Yama, the god of the dead, is the lord of these ceremonies and performing sacrifices for the pitris brings blessings. The period of *shraddha* or Pitra Paksha is when ancestors are formally revered.

Pitris can be ancestors who are known and remembered or those of the distant past. The *Rig Veda* mentions the two groups as earlier and later ancestors or ancient and recent. The text mentions different groups of pitris, including the Navagvas, Vairupas, Angirasas, Atharvans, Vasishthas and Bhrigus. Of these, the Angirasas and Atharvans were traditionally the composers of the *Atharva Veda* and the Vasishthas and Bhrigus of Mandalas II and VII of the *Rig Veda*. The *Rig Veda* states that all people may not be aware of their pitris but they are known to Agni. The pitris are thirsty for the offerings prepared for them on earth and reach the sacrificial ground in thousands. According to the *Atharva Veda*, pitris live in the air, on earth and heaven and are immortal. Sometimes they are referred to as gods and considered the equal of the gods. The *Taittiriya Brahmana* states that pitris are not the same as humans and were created separately.

The Mahabharata mentions seven groups of pitris. It states that the Vairajas, Agnishvattas and Garhaptyas were three groups of pitris in heaven while the Somapas, Ekasringas, Chaturvedas and Kalas were the pitris worshipped by the four orders of men.

The *Manu Smriti* describes several types of pitris. It says that pitris are free of anger and are pure and virtuous. They are descended from rishis such as Marichi and others, who are descended from Manu, the son of Hiranyagarbha. Pitris include the Somasadas, Agnishvattahs, Barhishadas, Somapas, Havirbhujas or Havishmantas, Ajyapas, Sukalinas, Agnidagdhas, Anagnidaghdas, Saumyas and others. Among them, the Sukalinas are pitris of shudras and are the sons of Vasishtha. It provides other details and says that from the pitris, the devas, or gods, and manavas (people) were descended, and from the devas all other beings.

According to one story in the Puranas, pitris include the sons of the gods. When some of the gods offended the god Brahma, he cursed them and they became fools, but then he allowed them to be reinstructed by their sons, who were therefore called pitris. Most Puranas state that there are seven classes of pitris, three without form, but which can assume any form they like, and four with form.

They are sometimes said to be married to Svadha, a daughter of the rishi Daksha, and in invoking them the term 'svadha' is used, while 'svaha' is used for the gods. There are also other types of pitris, including the ten Prajapatis as well as minor deities or sages who have reached a high level and transcended ordinary life.

Creation

There are a number of different theories of creation in religious texts. Broadly, they can be divided into two types: those that are purely mythical and those based on philosophical enquiry. The Upanishads contain a mixture of myths and philosophy. In a number of passages in the Upanishads, and some in the Brahmanas, all creation arises out of Brahman. This formed the basis for philosophical theories of creation. How does Brahman create and yet remain unchanged, eternal and beyond all action? There are two aspects to creation theories: one is the method and the second is the process. Broadly, Brahman creates through the illusory power known as maya. Brahman is sometimes identified with Viraj or Purusha (the person); at other times Purusha is the first creation. Atman, too, is identified with Brahman as the creator. In fact, the Upanishads have a number of different passages on creation, and it was left to philosophers like Shankara to systematize and analyse these and formulate a coherent theory. Advaita Vedanta states that creation is illusory and arises from Brahman but has no true reality. It accepts Brahman as both the material and instrumental cause of the world. This is known as the *vivarta* view of creation.

Some accounts of creation in the early Upanishads follow.

The *Taittiriya Upanishad* states that in the beginning there was nothing. From non-being, True Being (*sat*) was created. That Being became the Self or atman (2.7.1). According to the *Aitareya Upanishad*, 'In the beginning the Self or atman was alone. Then he thought, Let me create the worlds, and then the four worlds were created, followed by the Purusha, the deities, food, prana and, finally, the atman which entered into these and gave them life (1.1-3). The elements are connected with creation, and in the *Chhandogya Upanishad*, fire, water, etc. desired to multiply, and thus creation arose.

The *Brihadaranyaka Upanishad* (1.1.2) too includes passages on creation. One of them states, 'In the beginning there was nothing here; because the world was covered by death, by hunger, as hunger is death.' The commentators explain that this hunger is not for food, but a cosmic hunger, a desire to know. Then he (Prajapati) created the mind, then the body, then the whole world. He wanted his body to be offered to him in sacrifice and therefore became a horse (*ashva*). That is why one offers the sacrifice to Prajapati (the *ashvamedha* or horse sacrifice).

Another passage in the text on creation says that in the beginning there was only the atman (the Self) (1.4.1–3). Because he was the first, he is called Purusha. As he was alone, he did not feel happy, and he divided his body, creating a man and his wife. She did not want to unite with her creator and turned herself into a cow. He became a bull, and through them other cows were created. She turned herself into other creatures and thus in the same way all were created. Then He knew, 'I am the creation.' This section also introduces Brahman and states that through the knowledge of Brahman one can attain identity with the universe. The creation of the four castes and their associated deities is described. The father (pita, also implying Hiranyagarbha or the god Brahma) created seven kinds of food through meditation and rituals. Following this are references to the Vedas, the body, mind and Prajapati. The text also states that this (the universe) was first unmanifested, but as it came into being it began consisting of name, form and action.

But the *Mandukya Karika* of Gaudapada explains that creation is ultimately unreal. Just as the immortal cannot become mortal, so the mortal cannot become immortal; that is, intrinsic nature does not change (3.21). Though the Vedic texts say there is both real creation and creation through maya, in actuality, Brahman is the only reality. Brahman is never born, does not sleep or dream and has no form or name (3.36). It continues with the theme that the immortal never becomes mortal and what pre-exists is never born. All entities therefore are free from old age and death. In a series of complicated verses, Gaudapada explains how the eternal cannot be born, therefore creation is apparent and unreal to one who knows the truth.

The *Paingala Upanishad* provides a more coherent description in response to Paingala's question to Yajnavalkya. The description has similarities with Samkhya theories. Yajnavalkya describes Brahman, the one without a second (ekam evadvityam), which is of the nature of truth, knowledge and bliss; ever full, eternal. He explains how from Brahman, the witnessing Self (*sakshi*), Ishvara or god, and other aspects of the world come into being, from mula-prakriti, the root principle of matter, through Ishvara leading to the creation of the individual (1.1–12).

The *Vaishnava Maha Upanishad* identifies Brahman with the god Vishnu and has passages on creation. The first chapter states that in the beginning, Narayana (Vishnu) was alone. There was no Brahma, Ishana, water, Agni, Soma, heaven, earth, stars and sun, but only he, Nara (Purusha) alone. By the desire of the Paramatman and the Yajnastoma (hymn), he created fourteen Purushas (Brahma, Vishnu, Rudra, Ishana, Sadashiva and nine Prajapatis); one female (mula prakriti); the ten organs (five of perception and five of action); manas or the mind as the eleventh, tejas or brilliant intellect the twelfth; ahamkara the thirteenth; prana the fourteenth; atma the fifteenth; next, buddhi, kama, karma and tamas; five tanmatras or subtle elements; five gross elements and the atman as the twenty-fifth, even though he remained detached from his creation.

Creation Theories before and after the Upanishads

Creation myths begin in the Vedas and assume a more complex form by the time of the Puranas.

Rig Veda: In the *Rig Veda*, there are references to various theories of creation. According to early hymns, creation was the result of a cosmic battle or the cosmic separation of heaven and earth. Later hymns include the theory that all creation emerged from the sacrifice of Purusha (primeval man), or from some other form of sacrifice. Alternatively, there was creation through Hiranyagarbha, the golden egg or embryo, or through an unknown god (Ka) or Prajapati. A late hymn in the *Rig Veda* (10.129) ponders on creation, introducing an element of philosophical enquiry. One of its verses states:

> No death was there, nor was there life immortal
> Of day and night there was then no distinction
> That One alone breathed windless by itself
> Than that, forsooth, no other thing existed.

In early texts, there is no clear concept of a supreme creator. In some verses in the *Rig Veda*, Indra is seen as the ruler of all, in others it is Varuna. In the late hymns of the *Rig Veda*, there is Prajapati, who is often identified with Brahma. Prajapati was the primeval man or Purusha.

Brahmanas: Some of the myths in the *Rig Veda* are expanded in the Brahmanas. In the *Shatapatha Brahmana*, a myth of creation through sacrifice follows that of the great flood. After the flood, when Manu was the only person existing, he offered a sacrifice, from which Ida was born. From her the human race came into being. In another myth in this Brahmana, Prajapati is responsible for creation, again through the offer of a sacrifice. In a third and probably later myth in the same text, it said that once nothing existed but water. The waters wanted to propagate their kind and practised tapas, from which a golden egg appeared. Prajapati emerged from this and created the earth, the middle regions and the sky. Through further tapas he created the devas (gods) from his mouth, and daylight was associated with them. Then, with the breath of life that is below, he created the asuras and night and darkness came into being. Another myth says that in the beginning there was 'asat' (unreality, non-being). But in this were rishis, who were Prana, and created seven Purushas who then became Prajapati. Then he created Brahman, the three-fold knowledge (*trayi-vidya*). This Veda (meaning knowledge) was the foundation from which Prajapati created water and then an egg, from which Agni, the earth, and other things came.

Puranas: In Puranic myths, usually Brahma is responsible for creation, though the supreme creator may also be Vishnu or Shiva or sometimes Devi. According to the *Garuda Purana*, once there was nothing in the universe except Brahman, the Absolute. The universe became an expanse of water and in that Vishnu was born in a golden egg. He created the god Brahma with four faces. Brahma then created the devas, asuras, pitris and manushas (people). Next, he created rakshasas and yakshas and then gandharvas. Other creatures came from various parts of his body: snakes from his hair; sheep from his chest, goats from his mouth, cows from his stomach and other animals from his feet. His body hair became herbs, the four castes came from his mouth, arms, thighs and feet, and the four Vedas from his four mouths. He created several sons from his mind, as well as Daksha, Daksha's wife, Manu Svayambhuva and his wife Shatarupa, and the rishi Kashyapa. Kashyapa married thirteen of Daksha's daughters and through them all the devas and all creatures were born.

There are several variations of this creation myth in the numerous Puranas. Even Daksha is seen as the creator in some passages.

According to Samkhya philosophy, creation is the result of two principles: Purusha and prakriti. After dissolution or pralaya, components of the world continue to exist in prakriti, in which the three gunas lie dormant in a state of equilibrium. When the equilibrium is disturbed, creation begins anew. Creation evolves for the sake of Purusha, the eternal soul, in order to give it the right experiences so that it may achieve liberation. Mahat or intellect is the first stage of creation, in which all the buddhis (higher minds) are contained. Next comes ahamkara or ego, followed by the various senses and the elements of nature. Samkhya thus believes that material transformation leads to the production of the world. This is known as the *parinama* view.

Yoga philosophy accepts the Samkhya theory but has the concept of god or Ishvara as the creator.

This version of creation also appears in the Puranas. The *Vishnu Purana* states that at first there was neither night nor day, earth or sky, darkness or light. There was only the One, Brahma and Puman (Purusha) and pradhana (prakriti). These two are Vishnu unmodified, and Kala or time is that which connects them. The supreme Brahma, who is the same as Vishnu, brings forth creation. He is both the creator and the essence of pradhana and Purusha. From pradhana, when the equilibrium of the gunas is disturbed, comes mahat, followed by ahamkara, etc.

The *Manu Smriti* states that in the beginning the universe was in darkness, invisible and unknowable. From this emerged the *Svayambhu*, the Self originated. Wishing to create, he first created water and placed his seed there. This formed an egg, golden in colour, with the effulgence of a thousand suns, and in this Brahma himself was born. As water is called *Nara*, the supreme Self is called Narayana, while Brahma is the individual created by the eternal supreme principle. After one year (of Brahma), the egg separated into two, creating heaven and earth. In the middle was the sky, the eight directions, and the sea all around. Through this evolved mahat, followed by ahamkara, manas or the mind, the tanmatras and the other aspects of life.

Other philosophies have their own views on creation. Nyaya and Vaisheshika analyse and classify material substances in their theories of creation. In their later form, these two schools of thought accept god as the instrumental agent, who fashions the world out of atoms, or out of maya, the material force. Various philosophers speculate on the nature of god, the world and individual souls, but in general accept the agency of god as the creator.

Most philosophies and theories accept that creation is cyclic, and thus there are concepts of successive *yuga*s (ages).

The Yugas

The yugas are long periods of time. These, particularly the Kali Yuga, the present age, are mentioned in the Upanishads. Four yugas, the Krita, Treta, Dvapara and Kali, comprise one Mahayuga. The cycle begins with a golden age (Krita or Satya Yuga), succeeded by gradually declining yugas, after which the Satya Yuga begins again. Manvantaras and kalpas are larger periods of cyclical time, and therefore there is creation and re-creation, with intermittent periods of rest. The Krita Yuga is the golden age of truth and righteousness. Negative emotions such as envy, malice, hatred and deceit do not exist. All people are equal and worship the same deity, and there is only one Veda, known as the *Brahma Veda*. Humans live for 4000 years, are the size of giants and have vastly superior mental powers. Children are born through the power of the mind and not through sex. The yuga lasts for 4800 divine years, which is equal to 17,28,000 human years, and is symbolized by the colour white. It is succeeded by the Treta Yuga, in which the righteousness that existed in the first yuga is reduced by one-fourth. Its primary virtue is knowledge. Four Vedas have now appeared, sacrifices and rituals have started and people have begun to seek a reward for their work. Humans live for 3000 years and still have superior powers. Children are born through a simple touch between two people and not through sex. The yuga lasts for 3600 divine years, which are equal to 12,96,000 human years, and is symbolized by the colour red. In the Treta Yuga, Rama Jamadagnya (Parashurama) exterminated the kshatriyas. This was followed by the Dvapara Yuga. At the end of the Treta and beginning of the Dvapara, Rama, son of Dasharatha, lived.

In the Dvapara Yuga the righteousness that existed in the first yuga is reduced by half. Its primary virtue is sacrifice and the sacred texts of this age are the Puranas. Very few follow truth or duty without seeking rewards. Misery, disease and disasters take place and the caste system comes into existence. Human beings live for 2000 years and children are born through sex, which was not the case earlier. A man can have only one wife and marriage can only take place at the time of the first menstruation of the woman. This yuga lasts for 2400 divine years, which are equal to 8,64,000 human years, and is symbolized by the colour yellow. It is succeeded by the Kali Yuga, which marks a general decline and has only one-quarter of the righteousness that existed in the first yuga. Its main scriptures are the Tantras and people focus on the body instead of the mind. It is a time of anger, hatred,

discord and strife. Humans live for various periods of time and
some reach a hundred years. The Kali Yuga is said to have begun
in 3102 BCE and will last for 1200 years of the gods, equal to
4,32,000 human years. It is symbolized by the colour black. After
this, a new cycle of the Mahayuga will begin, starting again with
the Krita or Satya Yuga.

There are even larger periods of time, including manvantaras
and kalpas. Seventy-one Mahayugas form one manvantara and
fourteen manvantaras form one kalpa, which is one day in the life
of Brahma the creator.

One month of Brahma has thirty kalpas, twelve months
equal one year, and 100 such years form the lifetime of Brahma.
However, according to the *Vayu Purana*, 1000 kalpas comprise
one year of Brahma; 8000 such years make one yuga of Brahma.
One thousand of these yugas is known as a *savana*. Two thousand
savanas make a trivrita, which is Brahma's lifetime. We are now
said to be in the fifty-first year of Brahma's life. At the end of each
kalpa, the universe is destroyed and recreated.

Kalpas in theory are infinite, and some Puranas name more
than thirty kalpas. The present kalpa is the Varaha Kalpa, while
the previous one was the Padma.

Jainism and Buddhism also have similar concepts of kalpas or
cycles of time.

The Many Worlds or Lokas

Several Upanishads refer to the lokas or the various worlds in the
universe. These worlds are also described in other texts, including
the Puranas. The number of lokas usually varies from three to
fourteen. The *Aitareya Upanishad* (1.1) describes the worlds as
Ambah, that is, with clouds filled with water; Marichi, the world
of rays of light, Mara, the world of mortals, and Ap, the world
of water. Ambah is above heaven, which is its support. Marichi

is in the *antariksha*, the middle region. Mara is the earth, and
the world of Ap, below the earth. Triloka, or the three worlds,
are commonly mentioned and consist of heaven, earth and hell,
or of heaven, earth and the intermediate space between the two
(Bhuvarloka). The Upanishads also mention the worlds of various
gods, such as Agni, Varuna and Brahma. In some texts, fourteen
worlds are mentioned. These include seven in the upper world
and seven in the lower world or netherworld. The seven upper
worlds are: Bhuloka, the earth; Bhuvarloka, between the earth and
the sun, where *munis*, *siddhas* and perfected ones live; Svarloka,
the heaven of Indra; Maharloka, where saints such as Bhrigu live;
Janarloka, where Brahma's mindborn sons, Sanaka, Sananda and
Sanat Kumara, are; Tapoloka, the home of Vairajas; Satyaloka,
the heaven of Brahma, reaching which one is freed from rebirth.
The seven lower worlds are: Atala, ruled by Mahamaya; Vitala,
ruled by Hatakeshvara, a form of Shiva; Sutala, under Mahabali;
Talatala, under Maya; Mahatala; Rasatala, where the Daityas and
Danavas live; Patala, in which Vasuki is the ruler and the chief
Nagas or serpent gods dwell. The seven lower realms are also
together referred to as Patala. These are not the same as Narakas
or hells. When the rishi Narada visited these worlds, he said they
were wonderful and better than Indra's heaven. There are different
lists of these lokas in various Puranas. In some texts, there are
eight lokas: Brahma Loka, where the higher deities live; Pitri
Loka, where the pitris, rishis and Prajapatis dwell; Soma Loka,
with the moon and other planets; Indra Loka, where there are the
lesser deities; Gandharva Loka, which has Gandharvas and similar
beings; Rakshasa Loka, the world of the *rakshasas*; Yaksha Loka,
of the *yakshas*; Pishacha Loka, of the *pishachas*. Vaikuntha is the
loka of Vishnu, Go Loka of Krishna, Shiva Loka of Shiva.

Naga Loka, the world of the Nagas, is also referred to.
According to the Mahabharata, it extended thousands of *yojanas*
on all sides and had several walls of pure gold. It was decked with

jewels and gems; there were tanks of water with flights of stairs
made of crystal and rivers of clear and transparent water. The trees
here had diverse species of birds and the gate was 100 yojanas wide
and five yojanas high.

In a mystical sense, all the lokas are represented within the
body. The seven upper worlds can be identified with the seven
main chakras and the lower worlds with chakras in the lower part
of the body.

The Hells: Naraka

Naraka is the usual term for a hell, of which there are many,
referred to in various texts. Hells are mentioned in some of the
Upanishads and in the *Brahma Sutra*, but the emphasis in these
texts is not on these.

The concept of hell is not clearly developed in the *Rig Veda*,
though there is said to be a deep place for the evil (4.5) and a
pit of bottomless darkness (7.104). The *Atharva Veda* describes
Naraka Loka as the deepest darkness, where murderers go after
death. The *Shatapatha Brahmana* describes the torments of hell in
detail. According to the *Manu Samhita*, there are twenty-one hells,
while other texts give varying figures. The *Vishnu Purana* describes
twenty-eight hells to which people are assigned by Yama on the
basis of their misdeeds. These include Raurava, Shukara, Rodha,
Tala, Vishasana, Mahajvala, Taptakumbha, Lavana, Vimohana,
Rudhirandha, Vaitarini, Krimisha, Krimibhojana, Asipatravana,
Avichi and others. There are hells for those who have cheated or
robbed others and for those who kill and harm others. Raurava
(the dreadful) is for those who tell lies or bear false witness;
Vatarodham is for those who have harmed creatures of the forest.
The nature of the hells and the reasons for being sent there vary in
different Puranas. Thus, in the *Devi Bhagavata Purana* (skandha
8), Lalabhaksha is for lustful people and consists of a sea of semen.

People here have to eat semen. In the *Vishnu Purana* it is for those who do not offer food to the gods, pitris and guests and can be translated as a hell where people have to eat saliva.

There are, according to the Puranas, hundreds of thousands of other hells. Hell or Naraka is also interpreted as a state of mind that gives pain or sorrow and therefore should be avoided.

Gods and Demons

Devas

The term deva is generally used for deities. Vedic deities continue to be mentioned in the Upanishads and there are many deity Upanishads, where one or the other of the deities are identified with Brahman. Deities are mentioned in other Upanishads too, where they provide instructions on Brahman or are involved in discussions.

In the Rig Veda some hymns indicate that though the gods had different names, they actually represented one reality. This concept is further developed and brought out in the *Brihadaranyaka Upanishad*. In this text (3.9) it says that Vidagdha, son of Shakala, asks Yajnavalkya about the number of gods and he says there are 303 and 3003 as given in the laudatory hymns, but then shows how these can be reduced to one. He also says there are thirty-three gods, the others only being their manifestations. These thirty-three are the eight Vasus, eleven Rudras and twelve Adityas, along with Indra and Prajapati. The Vasus are aspects of nature, the Rudras are aspects of the mortal body or person, the Adityas represent the twelve months of the year, Indra represents the thundercloud and thunderbolt and Prajapati the sacrifice. The thirty-three gods can be reduced to six, which are fire (Agni), earth (Prithivi), air (Vayu), sky (Antariksha), the sun (Aditya) and heaven (Dyaus). He then reduces these to three, which are the three worlds (lokas) in which all these are contained, then to two, matter (annam) and the life force (prana), then to one and a half, which is that (ayam) which blows (pavate), and finally to one, the cosmic prana which is Brahman.

Ishvara, Indra, Surya, Vayu, Varuna, the Ashvins, Maruts, Parjanya, Prithivi, Dyaus and the Sadhyas are among the many Vedic deities mentioned in the Upanishads. Later Upanishads mention other deities including Ganesha and the avataras of Vishnu.

Asuras

Asuras were considered divine beings just like the devas, but later the term came to mean a demon. In the *Rig Veda*, several deities are referred to as asuras, including Agni, Brihaspati, Dyaus, Pushan, Savitri and Varuna, but by the later Vedic period asuras were at war with the devas or gods. In the *Brihadaranyaka Upanishad* the asuras and devas are usually said to be in conflict, though they both originated from Prajapati. One passage (1.3.1) in the text says that there were two classes of descendants from Prajapati and the asuras were the elder. The devas wished to overcome the asuras through the sacred chant but the asuras permeated into each part of the body which chanted. Here, the devas represent right action and the asuras wrong or self-seeking action. Another passage describes the instructions given by Prajapati to the devas, asuras and humans, who were all his children. In later texts, there are mixed references to asuras.

At times, the devas temporarily entered into a pact with them, as when churning the ocean of milk for amrita or divine nectar. In the Mahabharata the asura Maya was a great architect and was well-respected. He built a magnificent palace for the Pandavas at Indraprastha. Shukracharya, the guru of the asuras, was extremely learned and is mentioned with respect in several texts. The rishi Kashyapa was the father both of devas and of daityas and danavas, who were types of asuras.

Various texts give different explanations of the term. The word is said to be derived from the root 'as', 'to be' or from 'asu', breath. According to the Nirukta, those created from higher life energies were 'suras' or gods and from the lower energies 'asuras' or anti-gods. The *Taittiriya Brahmana* states that the asu or breath of Prajapati came to life the asuras. The *Vishnu Purana* says that at the time of the churning of the ocean, the daityas came to be known as asuras because they rejected Varuni, the goddess of *sura* or wine, who emerged from the ocean, while the devas accepted her and were known as suras.

Some Puranas state that the asuras ruled the earth for ten yugas, after which it was returned to the devas. Twelve wars were fought between the asuras and devas and the asuras that died were reborn on earth as people and created problems in the world.

As A. Danielou points out, 'It is significant that it was not for their sins that the antigods had to be destroyed but because of their power, their virtue, their knowledge, which threatened that of the gods—that is, the gods of the Aryas.' Later, however, a mythology was created to show that though the asuras were initially virtuous, their nature gradually changed. They stopped performing sacrifices and violated sacred laws.

Minor Deities

Minor groups of deities include the Gandharvas and the Nagas. Gandharvas are divine musicians while Nagas are snake deities who live in beautiful worlds.

Rituals or Sacrifices: Yajnas

Sacrifices, known in Sanskrit as yajnas, are of many different types. There are cosmic sacrifices, resulting in creation, ritual sacrifices to propitiate a deity or gain some desire, and internal sacrifices, the

offering of oneself for a divine purpose. Though the Upanishads in
general reject rituals, many rituals are mentioned in them.

The *Yajur Veda* as well as the Brahmanas are the earliest
texts describing ritual sacrifices. Later texts include the Grihya
Sutras and Shrauta Sutras. All power and accomplishment was
linked with sacrifice and thus Prajapati the creator was identical
with sacrifice. A sacrifice had to be performed according to the
precise and exact directions laid down by tradition, and only by
the brahmana caste. Among the sacrifices conducted in India in
ancient days were several to increase or assert the power of a king,
such as the ashvamedha or horse sacrifice, the rajasuya, *vajapeya*,
punar abhishekha and *aindra mahabhishekha*. Other sacrifices
included Soma sacrifices, fire sacrifices of the agnihotra and the
daily household sacrifices. Five daily sacrifices for the dvija or
twice-born were known as the pancha-maha-yajna, and consisted
of deva-yajna or deity worship, which may consist of offerings
to the sacred fire in the home; Brahma-yajna, which consists of
studying, reciting and teaching the Vedas; pitri-yajna, or ancestor
worship; bhuta-yajna, which consists of offerings to propitiate
spirits; bhuta is alternatively interpreted as the animal world and
food is kept at appropriate places for animals and birds; manusha-
yajna, a sacrifice for people which includes offerings to brahmanas,
the poor and homeless and guests.

Later, a short form of this sacrifice was devised, which consists
of reciting the Gayatri Mantra five times while focusing on the
five objects of worship. Other types of sacrifice include offering
lights, incense, flowers, etc., along with ritual prayers.

Animal sacrifices were common in ancient days.

The Upanishads point out the symbolism of some of the
sacrifices and state that true sacrifice is one that takes place within
the heart and mind. Such sacrifice can be of one's ego or of one's
negative tendencies. According to the Bhagavad Gita, the best
sacrifice is that done with purity of mind and without seeking a

reward. This also indicates an internal sacrifice, an offering of the Self to the divine.

The *Brihadaranyaka Upanishad* (1.1–2) begins with the symbolism of the ashvamedha or horse sacrifice. It says, 'Dawn is the head of the sacrificial horse, its prana [breath] is the air [vata].' Every part of it is compared with some aspect of the world. Succeeding verses indicate that even in the absence of a real horse, the sacrificial horse should be meditated upon as Prajapati, leading to an identification with that deity.

Jnana and Ajnana

Jnana, which means knowledge, is an important part of the path to Brahman. In fact, the Upanishads are called the jnana *kanda*, the knowledge section of the Vedic texts, in contrast to the karma kanda, that of ritualistic actions. Jnana marga is the path of knowledge leading to the realization of god. Jnana yoga is a similar term, a means of achieving union with the divine through knowledge. To use knowledge to attain divine unity, it is necessary to understand the nature and structure of knowledge. Thus, all the ancient schools of philosophy, the Samkhya, Vaisheshika, Vedanta, Yoga and Mimamsa, analyse knowledge extensively. These analyses differ in detail but in general they distinguish between valid and invalid knowledge and attempt to classify the means of knowledge, or pramanas. Three methods of valid knowledge accepted by most of these schools are perception, inference and scriptural testimony. In addition, most of them add remembrance (smriti) intuitive knowledge (arshajnana), comparison, and tradition. Vidya is a term also used for knowledge and *vijnana* is another term, often translated as wisdom.

Jnana is also contrasted with ajnana.

Ajnana specifically refers to spiritual ignorance. In general, ajnana is a veiling or illusory power that conceals the true nature of reality. Ajnana is also known as avidya, though the two terms are sometimes differentiated. It is only when ajnana is removed that the supreme truth can be realized. To remove it, however, its origin and nature have to be understood. The importance of the concept led to most schools of philosophy also analysing ajnana.

Its relationship with Brahman is variously explained by writers on Advaita. Though in Advaita, Brahman is the only reality, ajnana prevents the soul from realizing its identity with Brahman. Avidya obstructs the pure nature of Brahman, and thus through karma (actions) and earlier impressions of knowledge (purva-prajna-samskara) the individual (jiva) comes into being. However, according to the Advaitic philosophers, ajnana cannot have a separate existence as there is only one reality.

In Samkhya philosophy, ajnana is identified with prakriti. Prakriti, composed of the three gunas of sattva, rajas and tamas, hides the truth of Purusha. In Samkhya, the identification of Purusha with buddhi is another form of avidya. In Yoga philosophy, when the Purusha cannot distinguish between buddhi and itself and attributes the transformations and impermanence of buddhi to itself, that is avidya.

Other philosophers provide various definitions of ajnana or avidya.

According to Madhva (thirteenth century) there are two types of avidya—jivachchhadika and paramachchhadika—and both are forms of prakriti. In the first type, the jiva or individual soul is unable to perceive its spiritual power, while in the second type the Supreme is hidden from the jiva. Nimbarka believed that neither maya nor ajnana or any of its aspects could create the world. Ajnana was a quality of the individual being, associated with the person's own karma.

Karma

Karma comes from the Sanskrit root 'kri', meaning 'to do'. Karma means 'that which is done' or 'action', and actually can refer to any action. It also indicates the results of action and is used as a synonym for fate and destiny. In its latter use, it is the law of cause and effect, the principle that 'as you sow, so shall you reap'. Every action has a result, and good or bad fortune are said to be the result of one's own actions. The Upanishads use karma in both ways, both as the path of action and as the result of action. The path of action consists of performing one's duties and the prescribed Vedic rituals, while the path of knowledge is that prescribed in the Upanishads through which results of actions fall away.

Karma can be changed or modified through right action, and a state beyond the effects of karma is achieved through union with the divine.

Karma is first described in the *Shatapatha Brahmana* and further explained in later texts.

Two Important Mantras: Om and Hamsa

Many mantras are described in the Upanishads. Among them, 'Om' and 'Hamsa' can be considered the most important. Om, the most sacred of mantras, is also spelt Aum. It is a compound of four syllables: 'a' 'u' and 'm' and the half or ardha-matra above. The first three letters traditionally represent the first three Vedas. Om is frequently mentioned in the Upanishads and referred to as the Pranava. The *Mandukya Upanishad*, among others, provides a description of Aum. It states that all that is past, present and future is Aum. Aum represents the nature of Brahman, the Absolute, and is the symbol of the Supreme, the beginning, middle and end of all things. Aum is also the atman and its three letters reflect the waking, dreaming and sleeping states of consciousness. Those who know the Aum that is beyond its individual parts reach Turiya, the fourth state of consciousness. A person with such knowledge is a great sage. Aum is the god (Ishvara) seated in the heart; meditating on this, the Self transcends sorrow. The *Katha*

Upanishad states that Om is Brahman, the highest, and one who has a true knowledge of this word obtains all desires (2.16). Later texts state that its three letters—A, U and M—symbolize the three divine aspects of creation, preservation and destruction, or the three Hindu deities, Brahma, Vishnu and Shiva.

Hamsa is another important mantra, again frequently mentioned in the Upanishads. It represents the breath going in and out. The perfection of this mantra and the constant repetition of it leads to the state of a Hamsa or Paramahamsa yogi or sannyasi (see the Sannyasa and Yoga Upanishads) who meditates on 'Ham-Sah' (I am He, or I am That), signifying identification with the Supreme. Ham-Sah is mentally chanted with every inhalation and exhalation. The technique is also described in other texts.

Literally, Hamsa is a sacred bird, a wild goose or swan. It is also a poetical or mythical bird. In the *Rig Veda*, it is said to be able to separate Soma from water, and in later texts, milk from water, when the two are mixed together. This implies the separation of the pure from the impure. It is the vahana or vehicle of the Vedic Ashvins and of the gods Brahma, Sarasvati and Varuna and is identified with various deities, including Vishnu, Shiva and Surya. Varuna blessed the swan and made it pure white, beautiful like the moon. Hamsa is also the name of a sect of rishis. In the Mahabharata, Krishna is referred to as Hamsa. Hamsa is also a Prajapati and an incarnation of the god Vishnu in the Krita Yuga. He was also known as Yajna (sacrifice) and taught Yoga to Sanaka and other rishis.

The white Hamsa symbolizes the purity of the soul or spirit. It is the atman within the individual and is like the flame of a lamp in a windless place. It is located in the Anahata Chakra and in the Sahasrara Chakra.

Hamsa was the name of several people in ancient texts. In the *Chhandogya Upanishad*, Satyakama Jabala is instructed by various beings including a hamsa (swan).

Hamsa was the first mythical teacher of the philosophy of Dvaita.

According to the *Bhagavata Purana* (11.7.10), in the old days there was only one Veda, one god and one varna or caste. That caste was known as Hamsa. This implies that even after caste developed, the ideal was to have no divisions and this perfect ideal was represented by the term Hamsa.

Prana

Breath is a topic analysed in several Upanishads. Prana, the term used, is more than just breath; it is the life force. It indicates the vital force of every living being or the spirit of life. Prana is celebrated even in the *Atharva Veda*, where there is a hymn to Prana personified. Ten forms of prana are described in the Upanishads and other texts: prana, *apana, vyana, samana, udana,* naga, *kurma, krikara, devadatta* and *dhananjaya.* Of these, prana is the vital function through which air is drawn into the body; apana is the force controlling ejection or elimination; vyana is concerned with the distribution of the force; samana with assimilation; udana is related to the voice and sound. The other five are subsidiary pranas that control belching, eyelid movement, hunger and thirst, yawning and hiccups. In Yogic texts, the pranic body, known as the pranamaya kosha, is said to surround the material or visible body.

Chakras

Chakra, literally 'wheel', is a term for the mystical energy centres within the human body. Chakras are mentioned in the early Upanishads and described in more detail in the Yoga Upanishads as well as in other Yogic and tantric texts. There are seven main chakras through which the Kundalini or divine energy is raised along the Sushumna Nadi located in the spinal cord. These are the Muladhara Chakra at the base of the spine, the Svadhishthana Chakra just below the navel, the Manipura Chakra at the solar plexus, the Anahata Chakra in the centre of the chest, the Vishuddha Chakra in the throat, the Ajna Chakra in the centre of the forehead and the Sahasrara Chakra on the crown of the head. Among other chakras commonly mentioned in texts are the Lalana Chakra, also known as the Kala Chakra, with twelve petals, located above the Vishuddha at the root of the palate; the Soma Chakra, above the Ajna Chakra; the Manas Chakra, with six petals, also located above the Ajna Chakra. In addition, there are several more chakras including chakras in the hands, feet and joints and all parts of the body, as well as five higher chakras within the area of the brain. The crown chakra is also referred to as the Brahma-randhra.

The chakras are linked by energy channels known as nadis.

There are some special texts focusing on the chakras, for instance, the *Shat Chakra Nirupana*.

Kundalini

The Kundalini is described in the Yoga Upanishads as well as in other Upanishads and in tantric and other texts as a coiled serpent located at the base of the spine. It is a hidden source of energy within the human body, which when activated gives the person superhuman powers. Spiritual, breathing and physical techniques are prescribed to arouse the sleeping Kundalini and lead it through the chakras or energy centres to the crown of the head. The *Shat Chakra Nirupana* describes Kundalini, on the Svayambhu (self-created) linga of the god Shiva, in the Muladhara Chakra. It states:

Over it shines the sleeping Kundalini, fine as the fibre of the lotus stalk. She is the world-bewilderer (jagan-mohini,

the creator of Maya), gently covering the mouth of Brahma-
dvara (the head of the linga) by her own. Like the spiral of
the conch-shell, her shining snake-like form goes three-and-
a-half times around Shiva, and her lustre is as that of a strong
flash of young lightning. Her sweet murmur is like the
indistinct hum of swarms of love-mad bees. She produces
melodious poetry and all other compositions in prose or
verse, in Sanskrit, Prakrit, and other languages. It is she who
maintains all the beings of the world by means of inspiration
and expiration, and shines in the cavity of the Mula Chakra
like a chain of brilliant lights.[3]

Nadis

Nadis are hidden channels of energy within the body, said to
be like light waves or sound waves. The nadis are mentioned in
several texts including various Upanishads, particularly the Yoga
Upanishads, other yoga texts, texts on Ayurveda and Tantra and
in other sources. In Ayurvedic texts, they are described as actual
physical channels. In these texts they are alternatively known as
dhamani, shira, shrotas, marga and by other terms.

Shrikanada, in his text *Nadi-vijnana*, states that there are 35
million nadis, of which 72,000 are the channels of the senses and
700 convey the nourishment received by food to all parts of the
body. While in most such texts the nadis are said to originate from
the Muladhara Chakra, he says that they originate from the navel
(nabhi kanda).

The *Brihadaranyaka Upanishad* (2.1.19) states that they
originate from the heart and are as fine as a thousandth part of a
hair. Shankara, in his commentary on this text, states that there are
2,72,000 of them, which spread from the heart to the rest of the
body. The *Chhandogya Upanishad* (8.6.6) says that there are 101
nadis that start from the heart while the *Prashna Upanishad* says

there are 100, each with 2200 branches. Later Yoga Upanishads provide more details. The *Subala Upanishad* says that in the subtle sheath there are ten branches of ten each and out of each of these 72,000 nadis branch out. Within the centre of the heart are nadis known as *hita*, each the size of a thousandth section of a hair. The nadis link the supreme Self with the different spheres of action.

The Upanishads and other texts state that the three most important nadis are the Ida, Pingala and Sushumna. The Sushumna is the central channel, which, according to some texts, runs from the base of the spine, the Muladhara Chakra, along the spinal cord, through the other main chakras up to the crown of the head. It then curves downwards, like the handle of a walking stick, to the nostrils. Within it is the vital essence known as the Vajra Nadi and within that the Chitrini, brilliant and subtle. Inside this is the Brahma Nadi, representing pure intelligence, shining like the minds of sages, revealing pure knowledge. On either side are Ida, to the left, cool and white, representing the moon, and Pingala, to the right, red and hot, representing the sun and fire. There are variant descriptions of these nadis and, according to some, they cross each other like the caduceus and end in the nostrils. Along these central nadis rises the Kundalini, the serpent power or sacred energy. The other nadis pervade the subtle body, bringing consciousness and energy to every cell. Among these are the Gandhari, which connects the corner of the left eye to the left leg; Hasti-jihva, from the left eye to the big toe of the left foot; Kuhu, the pubic nerve of the sacral plexus, on the left; Vishvodara, the lumbar nerves; Sarasvati, to the right of Sushumna, reaching the tongue; Pusha, from the corner of the right eye to the abdomen; Payashvini, the auricular branch of the cervical plexus, located between Pusha and Sarasvati; Shankhini, between Gandhari and Sarasvati; Yashasvini, from the right thumb to the left leg; Varuna, the sacral nerve between Kuhu and Yashasvini; Alambusha. Though physical locations are given for these nadis, they are all etheric energy channels. The nadis are energized and purified in various ways, by yogic and tantric techniques, particularly pranayama, or specific breathing techniques.

When purified, the person becomes happy, peaceful, optimistic and enthusiastic. The body is slim and radiant and the mystic fire is aroused.

Nada

Nada is a Sanskrit word meaning 'sound' or 'tone'. Nada can be both external and internal. External or audible sounds can lead to god, while internal sounds indicate a contact with the divine.

Among internal sounds, Anahata Nada, unstruck or divine sound, can be heard within oneself, particularly in the Anahata Chakra, the hidden energy centre representing the heart.

The *Hamsa Upanishad* describes ten stages of inner nada. At first, a sound like 'chini' is heard, and at the next stage, a sound like 'chini-chini'. In the third stage is the sound of a bell, in the fourth a conch, in the fifth of a *tantiri* (lute), the sixth of *tala* (cymbals), the seventh of a flute, the eighth *bheri* (drum), the ninth *mridangam* (two-sided drum), the tenth of thunder. As one begins to hear these, corresponding changes take place in the body and mind. In the tenth stage, the atman merges with Brahman and all duality disappears (see *Hamsa Upanishad* in Part 2).

Nyasa (Nyaasa)

Nyasa literally means placing, putting down or inserting.

The term is used for an ancient technique which involves activating power in one's own or another's body through touch, accompanied by mantra and meditation or concentration. Nyasa is mentioned in the Upanishads and in other texts.

There are several different types of nyasa. One type involves assigning parts of the body to various deities and activating them by touching the body. Anga Nyasa is touching different parts of the body with the hands or fingers while reciting a mantra to stabilize the body before starting meditation. In Kara Nyasa, the hands and fingers are touched by those of the other hand. Nyasa is also done to activate the chakras or energy centres. The actual process has to be learnt through a guru.

Gunas, Dravyas and Tattvas

The nature of the world is analysed and categorized in philosophy, and these categories are referred to in the Upanishads.

Guna, which means quality, refers to the basic qualities or characteristics according to which people can be classified, and is used in this sense in most texts, including the Upanishads. Most often, three gunas are mentioned. These three are sattva or serenity and purity, rajas or energetic activity and tamas or dullness. Certain foods are associated with these qualities. The theory of the three gunas is also described in the Bhagavad Gita and other texts, though Samkhya provides the most detailed analysis and description of the gunas. According to this, the gunas are contained in prakriti, in a state of equilibrium, and creation begins when this equilibrium is disturbed. All the senses as well as all forms of matter come into being through the action of the gunas. Most people have all the three gunas but one predominates in each individual. Ideally, a person should cultivate sattva (see Chapter 2 for more on Samkhya and the gunas).

According to the Puranas, the gunas reflect the primary qualities of the three deities: Brahma, Vishnu and Shiva. The *Markandeya Purana* states that Brahma has the guna of rajas, Shiva or Rudra of tamas and Vishnu of sattva. However, in a number of Puranas, each of the deities is also considered supreme, containing all three gunas.

In Vaisheshika philosophy, the gunas are qualities that are inherent in substances and twenty-four such gunas are recognized.

Seventeen are listed in Kanada's *Vaisheshika Sutra*. They are: rupa (colour), *rasa* (taste), *gandha* (smell), sparsha (touch), *samkhya* (number), *parimana* (size), *prithaktva* (individuality), *samyoga* (conjunction), *vibhaga* (disjunction), *paratva* (priority), *aparatva* (posteriority), buddhi (knowledge), sukha (pleasure), dukha (pain), ichchha (desire), *dvesha* (aversion) and *prayatna* (effort). In his commentary, Prashastapada contributed seven more: *gurutva* (heaviness), *dravatva* (fluidity), *sneha* (viscidity), dharma (merit), adharma (demerit), *shabda* (sound) and samskara (faculty).

In Madhva's philosophy, the three gunas are classified under dravyas, while other gunas form a separate category. They are similar to those in *Vaisheshika*, while in addition there are mental qualities including kripa (mercy), *titiksha* (endurance), bala (strength), saundarya (beauty) and many more.

Dravya in Sanskrit means a substance, thing or object. In philosophy it indicates the basic substances that comprise the world. According to Nyaya philosophy, there are nine dravyas: the five elements, prithivi, ap, tejas, vayu, akasha; kala (time); dik or disha (direction, space or region); atman (the soul), manas (the mind). The *Vaisheshika Sutra* has a similar list of earth, water, fire, air, ether, time, space, soul and mind.

In Dvaita there are twenty dravyas: Paramatman (god or the supreme Self), Lakshmi, jiva (souls), avyakritakasha (unmanifested space), the three gunas of sattva, rajas and tamas, mahat, ahamkara, buddhi, manas, indriya (the senses), varna (speech sounds), andhakara (darkness), vasana (root impressions or tendencies), kala or time, pratibimba or reflection.

Other philosophies have different categorizations.

Tattva is a term for the principles of prakriti or matter. The term also refers to categories of various phenomena. Tattva is an element or elementary property, the essence or substance of anything. Tattva-jnana indicates the knowledge of truth or the true principles of something.

Tattvas are classified in the early schools of philosophy as well
as in Buddhism and Jainism and are listed in the Upanishads. In
Samkhya philosophy there are twenty-five tattvas or true principles.
These are prakriti or *avyakta*, the unmanifested state; mahat
or buddhi; ahamkara; the five tanmatras; the five mahabhutas
or elements; the eleven organs including manas, five organs of
perception and five of action; and Purusha. According to the
Mahabharata there are twenty-four tattvas, while the *Bhavishya
Purana* lists twenty-three. The Lokayats consider only five, that is,
the five elements. In Vedanta, tattva is said to be a combination of
'tad' and 'tvam' and indicates 'That thou art' and is the mahavakya
by which the identity of the world with Brahman is revealed.

In Shaiva Siddhanta philosophy, there are thirty-six
tattvas. The first five are pure tattvas, consisting of Shiva or the
bindu representing Shiva. The Shiva-tattva pervades all others.
From this comes Shakti, Sadashiva, Ishvara and Vidyeshvara
or Shuddha vidya (pure knowledge). These have the nature of
chit or pure consciousness. The next seven are mixed tattvas:
maya (the material cause), kala (kaala or time), niyati (destiny),
kala (kalaa or creativity, drawing the soul towards pure
knowledge), vidya (limited knowledge), raga (attachment) and
purusha. Purusha, though pure, may appear impure because
of its associations. These are followed by avyakta or prakriti,
buddhi, ahamkara, manas, the five cognitive senses, the five
conative senses or organs of action, the five tanmatras and five
mahabhutas.

In Jainism, there are seven tattvas, while some Upanishads
mention up to ninety-six tattvas.

Padartha

Padartha is a general term indicating a category which includes
the above terms. According to Monier-Williams, padartha is that

which corresponds to a meaning of a word, a material object or a subject. All early philosophical systems used it in the sense of subject or category and attempted to classify the material and non-material world into a variable number of padarthas. The terms tattva and prameya are sometimes used in the same way as padartha. Depending on the context in which it is used, there can be varying classifications of padarthas even within the same philosophy.

Advaita recognizes two padarthas, atma and anatma, the soul and that which is not-soul; Vishishtadvaita has the above two as well as god. However, according to different accounts, Vedanta has seven padarthas. Samkhya sees Purusha and prakriti as padarthas, while it recognizes twenty-five tattvas. Mimamsa describes five padarthas. Nyaya and later Vaisheshika have seven padarthas. These are: substance (dravya), quality (guna), activity (karma), generality (samanya), particularity (vishesha) and inherence (samavaya), to which later a seventh aspect of non-existence (abhava) was added. According to Madhva, reality (padartha) is of two kinds, svatantra or independent, and paratantra or dependent. God is the only independent reality. Elsewhere it is said there are four padarthas: god, prakriti, jiva and jada (matter). In the *Madhvasidhantasara*, ten padarthas are listed, including dravya, guna (quality), karma (action), samanya (class character), vishesha (particularity), vishishta (qualified), amshi (whole), shakti (power), sadriya (similarity) and abhava (negation).

The term is also used in Buddhism and Jainism.

Virat or Viraj

Virat or viraj indicates sovereignty, excellence or splendour. Viraj is often personified as a secondary creator or is associated with creation. Viraj can be either male or female. According to the *Rig*

Veda (10.90.5), Viraj is born from Purusha and Purusha in turn from Viraj. In the *Atharva Veda,* Viraj is a female, identified with a cow, or with prana, the life breath. In the Mahabharata, Viraj is the name of the primeval being, Purusha, and is at times identified with Shiva or with Vishnu.

The *Manu Smriti* (1.32) states that Brahma divided his body into two, one male and one female, and from the female Viraj was born. Viraj then produced Manu Svayambhuva, who in turn created the ten Prajapatis. The *Bhavishya Purana* says that Manu was the male half of Brahma and Shatarupa the female half. According to some Puranas, creation came about through the union of Viraj and Shatarupa. Viraj as a creator is identified with Purusha, Brahma, Agni, Prajapati and in later texts with Vishnu or Krishna. In Vedanta, Viraj is a name of the supreme intellect. Viraj is also the name of several others and of a Vedic metre. Invocations are to be made in this metre, especially when food is prayed for.

Four

The Teachers

WHO COMPOSED THE Upanishads and who were the originators of the new ideas? The Upanishads are anonymous but have some clues within them regarding authorship, location and dates. The names of both rishis and kings are mentioned in the Upanishads. Rishis, rishikas and kings were also composers of Rig Vedic hymns. There is logic in presuming, therefore, that these three groups continued to contribute to evolving philosophical concepts. Based on certain passages in the Upanishads, scholars including the German scholars Richard Garbe (1857–1927) and Maurice Winternitz, and more recent ones such as Paul Horsch, believe that the concept of Brahman originated with the kshatriyas. Kings are mentioned in the Upanishads who teach certain ideas to brahmanas as if these were something new and unknown to the latter. Among these kings are Ajatashatru, Pravahana Jabali, Ashvapati Kaikaya and Janaka. Of them, Ajatashatru (*Brihadaranyaka* 2.1) said it was contrary to the natural order of things for a kshatriya to teach a brahmana (indicating that caste already had a deep hold). If we look at some of the teachings of the kings, not all of them are related to the key concept of Brahman. For instance, in the *Chhandogya Upanishad*, Ashvapati provided brahmanas with the knowledge of Vaishvanara Agni. Pravahana Jabali (*Chhandogya* 5.3 and *Brihadaranyaka* 6.2) explained reincarnation or transmigration of the soul.

There was always a close relationship between kings and their purohitas, who were brahmanas and advised them on matters of state, which may have led to an interchange of ideas. In their support for one another kshatriyas and brahmanas were intertwined and Olivelle[1] feels it is naive to take at face value that kings were the actual authors of Upanishadic doctrines. Was it perhaps advantageous to brahmanas to portray this? The traditional founders of Buddhism and Jainism too were kshatriyas, and so were some of the incarnations of the god Vishnu, such as Rama. Olivelle believes that new thinkers in both groups created the Upanishads. As seen earlier, women too participated in discussions; among them, Gargi and Maitreyi are well-known. But the philosophy expert S. Dasgupta feels that though women and kshatriyas may have contributed, the Upanishads are a natural evolution from the Brahmanas and Aranyakas, and there is no indication that something drastically new was suddenly being taught.[2]

Apart from the kings mentioned above, the noted teachers in the Upanishads include Yajnavalkya (*Brihadaranyaka Upanishad*), Uddalaka Aruni (in the *Chhandogya Upanishad*), Shandilya and Satyakama Jabala, among others. The first three were brahmanas, while Satyakama was of unknown origin. Gods and rishis were also among the teachers, for instance, Prajapati, Brahma and Sanat Kumara. Lists of teachers are mentioned in some Upanishads, particularly the *Brihadaranyaka* (see *Brihadaranyaka Upanishad* in Part 2).

Teaching in the Upanishads is often in the form of dialogue between student and teacher.

It is interesting that even the late Upanishads refer to ancient teachers, perhaps trying to suggest that the text has equal sanctity and antiquity. The Upanishads, however, do not provide many details on them and here we look at some of these teachers as known from other sources.

Agastya is a sage or rishi who is said to have lived in ancient days. He is first mentioned in the *Rig Veda*. Here he is referred to as a Mana or Manya and the son of Mana. In one passage, he is said to be the son of Mitra and Varuna. In the *Aitareya* and *Shankhayani* Aranyakas, Agastya is known as a teacher. In the Mahabharata, Drona states that his guru was Agnivesha, who had been the student of Agastya. There are other references to him in the *Rig Veda*, *Atharva Veda*, Brahmanas and Aranyakas, but legends and stories concerning him are fully developed in the Ramayana, Mahabharata, Puranas and other texts.

Agastya was rather short and has been described as 'dwarfish'. He was said to have been born from a pitcher, into which the gods Mitra and Varuna dropped their semen when they saw the beautiful apsara Urvashi. Thus, he was known as Kumbhayoni (born in a pitcher) or Maitravaruni. He was the brother of Vasishtha, who was born at the same time in a similar way. Agastya was very learned, well-versed in the Vedas and in the use of various magical weapons. Though he was an ascetic, he finally married, as he was told only those with sons to perform their ancestral rites could enter heaven. Out of the essence of all living beings, he created a beautiful girl named Lopamudra and gave her as a daughter to the king of Vidarbha. It was this Lopamudra whom he later married. They had a son named Dridhasyu, also called Idmavaha, who chanted the Vedas at birth. In the Ramayana, Rama visited Agastya's ashrama, which was located near Panchavati.

Agastya is not mentioned often in the Upanishads but the *Tripuratapini Upanishad* refers to Agastya Mantras as well as to his wife Lopamudra.

Aitareya Mahidasa is the traditional author of the *Aitareya Upanishad*, also mentioned in other texts, including the *Chhandogya*.

Ajatashatru, king of Kashi, is mentioned as a teacher of Brahman in several Upanishads, including the *Kaushitaki* and *Brihadaranyaka*. In history, Ajatashatru is known as a king of Magadha but Ajatashatru in the Upanishads is a different and earlier king.

Angirasa, a great rishi, is described in the *Rig Veda* and later texts including the Upanishads. He is the first of the Agnidevas or fire gods, the first sacrificer, associated with fire rituals, and a teacher of divine knowledge (brahma vidya). Angirasas were the descendants of the rishi Angiras or sometimes of the god Agni. In the *Rig Veda*, Angirasas are mentioned as pitris along with Atharvans and Bhrigus and are associated with Yama. They are said to have become immortal through sacrifice and to have gained Indra's friendship. They are closely associated with Indra. Some scholars feel they were priests of the ancient past, dating back to the Indo-Iranian period.

As descendants of Angiras, some of the Angirasas represented various types of agnis or fires.

The Anukramanis attribute several Rig Vedic hymns to members of the Angirasa family. They are said to be authors of hymns in mandalas 1, 5, 8, 9 and 10. Among the Angirasas mentioned are Abhivarta, Amahiyu, Ayasya, Baru, Bhikshu, Bindu, Putadaksha, Brihanmati, Brihaspati, Dharana, Dhruva, Divya, Harimanta, Hiranyastupa, Krishna, Priyamedha, Murdhanvan, Nrimedha, Purushamedha, Pavitra, Prabhuvasa or Prabhuvasu, Pracheta, Rahugana, Samvarta, Saptagu, Savya, Shishu, Shrutakaksha or Sukaksha, Suditi, Purumila, Tiraschi, Uchathya, Vihavya and Virupa. Some of these are also referred to in later texts including the Mahabharata and the Puranas as sons or descendents of Angirasa.

Angirasa or his descendent Ghora Angirasa is associated with
the composition of the *Atharva Veda*. In later texts, he is one of
the mindborn sons of the god Brahma. He is also said to be one
of the sixteen Prajapatis created by Brahma, who then created
the universe. Atharva Angirasa as a name of the *Atharva Veda* is
mentioned several times in the Upanishads.

Ashvalayana was a scholar and composer of Sanskrit texts.
He is said to have been the disciple of Shaunaka and the author
of a Shrauta Sutra, a Grihya Sutra and other texts, as well as the
originator of a *Rig Veda* shakha (branch or school). He is not
mentioned as the author of any Rig Vedic hymn. Ashvalayana
is the author of part of the *Aitareya Aranyaka*. In the *Kaivalya
Upanishad*, he approaches the god Brahma with a request for
supreme knowledge. He appears as a teacher in the *Sarasvatirahasya
Upanishad*.

Atharvan was an ancient priest whose name is found
fourteen times in the *Rig Veda*, three times in plural, and
several times in the *Atharva Veda*, which was once known
as the *Atharvana Veda*. In the *Rig Veda*, Atharvan produced
Agni or fire, who became the messenger of Vivasvat. Atharvan
also brought order through sacrifices and Indra is said to be
his helper. According to the *Atharva Veda*, Atharvan was a
companion of the gods. He gave a cup of Soma to Indra, and
a Kamadhenu (wish-fulfilling cow) was given to him by the
god Varuna. Possibly, he was the head of a family of real or
mythical priests. Atharvan is also used as a generic term for a
priest, while Atharvans in plural are a class of pitris or ancestors
who live in heaven. He was the father of Dadhyanch, a rishi
known for his knowledge. Two people mentioned as composers
of hymns in the *Rig Veda* are Bhishaj or Bhishak Atharvana
(10.97) and Brihaddiva Atharvana (10.120).

Bhishaj Atharvana is also one of the traditional composers
of the *Atharva Veda*. The name Bhishaj refers to his connection

with medicine and healing. Atharvan is mentioned in other texts as well.

In the *Shatapatha Brahmana*, he is an ancient teacher, and is a teacher in the lists of the *Brihadaranyaka* who conveyed knowledge to Dadhyanch. He was obviously very ancient even at this time and belonged to the distant past. The *Mundaka* says that Brahma taught the knowledge of Brahman to his eldest son, Atharvan, who taught it to Angir. Atharva Angirasa is mentioned in the *Prashna Upanishad*. In the *Atharvashikha*, Atharvan instructs other rishis on Om. In the *Shandilya Upanishad* he instructs Shandilya on Yoga.

Atri was an ancient rishi or sage described in the *Rig Veda* and later in the Mahabharata, Puranas and other texts. Atri is mentioned around forty times in the *Rig Veda* and six times in the plural. He is a rishi of the five tribes and, along with Manu, an ancient ancestor. Atri is spoken of with Indra and Agni but is mainly connected with the Ashvins, who are said to have saved him from a deep pit, from darkness and from a demon. The Ashvins prevented him from burning in fire and are said to have made him young again. Atri, or the Atris together, found the sun that was hidden by Svarbhanu and placed it in the sky. This is also referred to in the *Atharva Veda*. In the *Shatapatha Brahmana*, Atri, a priest who removed darkness, was the same as Vach or originated from her. Atri is mentioned in connection with the rishi Saptavadhri, who is connected with the Ashvins and also referred to as Atri Saptavadhri. Mandala 5 of the *Rig Veda* is attributed to Atri and his descendents. In the same text he is one of the ancestors of the human race. In later texts he was one of the sons of the god Brahma and was married to Anasuya. The great rishi Dattatreya was born to them.

Atreya is a collective name for the sons or descendants of the rishi Atri. The Anukramanis mention a number of rishis known as Atreya or Atri, mainly in Mandala 5, but also in 8 and 10.

Atri is mentioned as a rishi in several Upanishads. In the *Jabala Upanishad*, he questions Yajnavalkya on realizing the infinite Self. The Shandilya mentions him as the father of Dattatreya.

Bharadvaja is an ancient rishi to whom several hymns in the *Rig Veda* are attributed. The whole sixth mandala is said to be composed by Bharadvaja or the family of Bharadvajas. He is also known as Bharadvaja Barhaspatya, that is, Bharadvaja, descendant of Brihaspati. According to the *Panchavimsha Brahmana*, Bharadvaja was the purohita or priest of Divodasa, a king mentioned in the *Rig Veda* who was the ancestor of Sudas. He is also mentioned in the Ramayana, Mahabharata, Puranas and other texts. In the Puranas his love for Vedic study is described. One lifetime was not sufficient so he obtained a boon from the god Indra to live for thousands of years in order to continue his study.

Others of the Bharadvaja family mentioned in the *Rig Veda* or Anukramanis include Nara, Payu, Rijishva, Shasa, Shunahotra, Suhotra, Vasu, Garga and Shirimbitha.

Shamyu Barhaspatya is said to be the composer of some hymns in the sixth mandala and Tapumurdha Barhaspatya of one in the tenth mandala (10.182).

Bharadvaja was also the name of other rishis. He is mentioned as a rishi in various Upanishads and as the name of several teachers in the *Brihadaranyaka*. In the *Mundaka* he was the teacher of Angirasa.

Bhrigu is an ancient rishi whose name occurs twenty-one times in the *Rig Veda*. Bhrigu means shining, from the root bhraj, and is thought to have originally been a name of fire.

In the *Rig Veda*, Bhrigu is said to have received Agni (fire) from heaven. In the Brahmanas he is referred to as Varuni, a son of Varuna. The Bhrigus were a family of priests related to the Angirasas, descended from Bhrigu. Even in the *Rig Veda*, the Bhrigus seem to have been priests of olden times. Both the Bhrigus and Matarishvan are connected with fire. Matarishvan brought it as lightning but the Bhrigus kindled the fire on Earth. Bhrigus are mentioned with the Yatis and Praskanva, and in another passage with the Dhruyus and Turvasha, as the enemies of Sudas. Thus, in some passages they seem to be a historic group. In one Rig Vedic hymn (8.35) they are invited to drink soma along with the thirty-three devas, the Maruts, Apah, Ashvins, Ushas and Surya. In the *Atharva* (5.19) Bhrigu is a rishi, a leader of a clan or group, and also in the Brahmanas. In later texts there are several stories relating to Bhrigu.

The Bhargavas are those descended from Bhrigu. The Anukramani lists some Bhargavas as composers of hymns in mandalas 8, 9 and 10. Among them the most important is Jamadagni Bhargava, also known as Rama Jamadagnya. Others include Bharga Pragatha, Bhriguvaruni, Syumarashmi, Ita, Kavi, Nema, Somahuti and Vena. Shukra in later texts is known as Bhrigu and was the priest of the asuras. In the Puranas, Bhrigu is one of the Prajapatis.

He was brought up by Varuna and thus is also known as Varuna's son. These accounts probably relate to two different incarnations. His descendants are known as Bhargavas and include Parashurama, the Rudras and several rishis. He married Puloma (Pulomaa) and became the father of Chyavana. According to some accounts he had seven sons including Chyavana. In the Mahabharata he instructed the rishi Bharadvaja on the nature and origin of the world.

Bhushunda is said to be a rishi named Jabala in the Upanishads.

In other texts, he is a wise crow who lived on a *kalpa-vriksha* (sacred tree) on a peak to the north-east of Mount Meru. When the rishi Vasishtha went to Devaloka, the world of the gods, he heard about this crow and went to meet him. Bhushunda told him that he and his twenty brothers were born from seven swans, the vahanas or vehicles of the goddess Brahmi. These swans had sported with the crow Chanda, who was the vahana of the matrika (goddess) Alambusha. Bhushunda's brothers lived for several kalpas (ages) but then they renounced the world and reached Shiva Loka, the heaven of the god Shiva. Bhushunda himself could remember five pralayas (periods of dissolution), twelve churnings of the ocean of milk for amrita and several other events that take place in each yuga and kalpa.

Bhushundi was a crow who instructed Garuda on the god Rama. His story appears in the *Bhushundi Ramayana* and in the *Ramacharitamanasa* of Tulasidasa.

Dadhyanch, an ancient rishi, is first mentioned in the *Rig Veda*. He was the son of Atharvan and he kindled Agni or fire. The Ashvins wanted the secret knowledge of soma (Madhuvidya) revealed to him by the god Indra. They replaced his head with that of a horse as he had promised not to reveal the knowledge. After the horse's head had told the Ashvins what they wanted to know, his real head was restored to him. The horse head fell on a lake on Mount Sharyanavat and remains there, granting boons to men. Indra used them to kill ninety-nine *vritra*s (demons). Here again the horse, or the horse-head, is symbolic of knowledge. The Upanishads refer to this story.

Dadhicha is often considered the same as Dadhyanch. The Mahabharata states that he was the son of the rishi Bhrigu. The god Indra sent Alambusha, the celestial Apsara, to disturb his penance. Excited by her, his semen fell in the river Sarasvati, which bore him a child named Sarasvat. At another time he gave up his life to help the Devas defeat the Asuras. From his bones, Tvashtr (or Dhatr) created the Vajra, which Indra used to destroy the asura Vritra.

Dattatreya, a teacher in the Upanishads, is considered an incarnation of the Hindu god Vishnu. Dattatreya was born as the son of the rishi Atri and his wife Anasuya. He was mild, gentle and very learned. He was worshipped by the king Kartavirya and gave him a boon of a thousand arms. The *Harivamsha* states that Vishnu came to the world as Dattatreya to revive the knowledge of the Vedas. His main characteristic is kshama, or mercy. He is also the protector of dharma and the teacher of divine knowledge. As a deity, he sometimes represents the three gods Brahma, Vishnu and Shiva together. A Puranic story explains how he came to represent all three deities.

Brahma, Vishnu and Shiva once appeared to Anasuya as brahmanas and asked her to offer them food after removing all her clothes. Anasuya could not refuse them but her purity enabled her to turn the gods into babies. Their wives pleaded with her to restore them to their original forms and in return she asked for a boon—that they be born to her. Thus, Dattatreya was born. In his images, the three gods are depicted together or Vishnu is shown accompanied by the vahanas (vehicles) of the other two. Dattatreya images are often accompanied by a cow and four dogs. Some interpret these as representing Mother Earth and the four Vedas, which came under Dattatreya's protection, though they may also represent his love for animals, for which the sage was known. In several temples Dattatreya is represented only by footprints (*padukas*). From around the eighth century CE, Dattatreya, the ancient sage, seems to have been appropriated by other sects. According to tradition, he composed the *Avadhuta Gita*, probably of the ninth century, as well as other texts. This Gita describes the liberation of an Avadhuta and has Advaitic passages. Dattatreya the ancient sage and Dattatreya the Avadhuta probably belong to two different traditions. Other accounts in later texts state that he loved songs and musical instruments and did not bother about caste. He was the creator of the Soma plant and saved the gods from the demons. The *Markandeya Purana* indicates that he was involved in tantric rites and that he stayed at Mahur, a centre of Shakti worship. The Natha Yogis take Dattatreya as their guru and believe he was a great siddha. The Mahanubhava sect of the thirteenth century also focused on the worship of Dattatreya. Another aspect of Dattatreya is as a protector from evil influences.

Several saints of the Gujarat–Maharashtra region are considered incarnations of Dattatreya. Among them is Sai Baba of Shirdi.

Janaka was a contemporary of Yajnavalkya and there seem to have been several kings known by his name. Janaka in Vedic texts, as has been pointed out by scholars such as Upendra Thakur, is not the same as Janaka, the father of Sita. The Vedic Janaka was a great king with the title Samrat and was particularly renowned as a philosopher. Brahmanas from other kingdoms came to his court for discussions. The *Brihadaranyaka Upanishad* records that Janaka, king of Videha, performed a sacrifice in which there was a profusion of gifts. Brahmanas from Kuru and Panchala were assembled there and Janaka wanted to discover the most learned. He confined a thousand cows with ten *pada*s of gold on each one's horns and promised them to the most learned. Yajnavalkya took the cows and a dialogue between him and other brahmanas began. Convinced finally of his superior knowledge, he asked Yajnavalkya to teach him. The rishi Yajnavalkya then became his priest and adviser. According to the Puranas, Janaka was a king who was the son of Nimi and grandson of Ikshvaku. Cursed by Vasishtha, Nimi lost his body and became 'videha' (without body). As he had no sons, the rishis churned (mathana) his body and obtained a child, who was therefore known as Mithi Janaka (born of churning). His city was then known as Mithila, and the country Videha. According to some accounts, all succeeding kings were known as Janaka, though they had other names as well.

Apart from a description in the Ramayana, there are several stories about Janaka in the Mahabharata and the Puranas, though these may refer to various different Janakas as all scholars agree that there were several.[3]

Janaka was married to Kaushalaya. He was against the role of the brahmanas and performed sacrifices himself. Because of his pure life, he became a brahmana and rishi, though he was born a kshatriya. Janaka is said to have met the sage Ashtavakra and had a dialogue with him, later known as the *Ashtavakra Gita*. Janaka also had several conversations with other rishis or sages. Among the rishis he conversed with were Ashmaka, Mandavya and Parashara.

Janaka was compassionate and pious. A story in the *Padma Purana* states that he visited one of the numerous hells and by his piety saved those who were there from torture.

All the Janakas had great renown as scholars and teachers and conversed with rishis and philosophers.

Kashyapa was one of the seven great rishis, said to be the grandson of the god Brahma and the progenitor of human beings, as he was the father of Vivasvat and grandfather of Manu. He is also called Prajapati.

Some of the Vedic hymns are attributed to him and in Vedic texts he is also a mythical being associated with the sun. In the Mahabharata and the Puranas, he is a rishi who married a number of daughters of Daksha, through whom all beings in the world were descended.

Krishna, though a popular deity and an incarnation of Vishnu, is first mentioned as a rishi, a composer of a hymn (8.74) in the *Rig Veda*, but this may not be the same as the later deity. In the *Chhandogya Upanishad*, Krishna, son of Devaki, is a great scholar, a student of Ghora Angirasa. Krishna as a deity is mentioned in the later Upanishads. In the Mahabharata Anukramani, Krishna is said to have descended from Angirasa. Krishna, son of Devaki, is mentioned in the *Ghata-Jataka*. In a few passages in the Mahabharata, Krishna is described as a ritvij, a priest. He is said to have meditated at Gandhamadana, Pushkara and Badari. At the same time, Krishna was a great warrior.

There are several myths and stories relating to Krishna as an incarnation of Vishnu. Krishna is described in the Mahabharata and in the Bhagavad Gita, which forms part of the Mahabharata, as a divine being, a form of the Supreme. His life is described in more detail in the *Harivamsha*, an appendix to the Mahabharata, and in the Puranas, particularly the *Bhagavata Purana*. Krishna is also described in later bhakti literature, such as the *Gita Govinda* and the poems of Chandidas, Chaitanya Mahaprabhu and others.

Nachiketa was an ancient rishi, the son of Uddalaki. He is well known from the *Katha Upanishad* and is also mentioned in other texts. According to the Mahabharata, Yama communicated the thousand names of Shiva to him and Nachiketa in turn taught them to Markandeya.

Narada, an ancient rishi or sage, is mentioned in the Upanishads and described in the Mahabharata, Puranas and other texts. Narada lived in Svarga or heaven but made frequent trips to Earth. He provided inspiration to Valmiki to compose the Ramayana and, according to the *Chhandogya Upanishad*, gained divine wisdom from Sanat Kumara. According to the Mahabharata, he visited the Pandavas a number of times and advised them on right action and conduct and also tried to persuade Dhritarashtra to get Duryodhana to make peace, but failed. The Mahabharata describes him as having matted locks and being clothed in golden rays. He had a staff made of gold as well as a gold waterpot. Narada was skilled in music and dancing and his beautiful vina brought forth melodious notes.

Narada narrated the *Brihannaradiya Purana* and the *Naradiya Purana* to Suta.

However, in the Puranas, Narada is a complex character. He was one of the seven rishis created by Brahma but had a number of odd births, partly because of his mischievous nature. In one life, he was born as a Gandharva, in another as a worm. After he had persuaded the sons of Daksha to wander the earth, he was reborn as his son or, according to another account, as Kashyapa's son. He was once changed into a monkey and on another occasion into a woman. But Narada continued to wander between heaven and earth, predicting the future and giving advice, both good and bad.

Other stories about him state that it was through him that the vina became the earliest musical instrument of the world. It was originally the instrument of the devas. Narada supported the devas in their struggle against the asuras over obtaining amrita or divine nectar and protected the pot of amrita. He was also known by various other names including Devarishi, Parameshthi and Surarishi.

Parashara is a rishi who is mentioned in the *Rig Veda* along with the rishis Shatayatu and Vasishtha. According to the Anukramani, he composed some of the hymns of the *Rig Veda*, though some feel this is not correct. The *Nirukta* states he was the son of Vasishtha. In the Mahabharata and the Puranas he is described as the son of Shakti and Adrishyanti, the grandson of Vasishtha and the father of Vyasa.

Pippalada is a rishi who founded a school of the *Atharva Veda*, which was named after him. In the *Prashna Upanishad* he guides other rishis on the path to enlightenment.

Sanat Kumara is a mindborn son of the Hindu god Brahma. His other mindborn sons are usually mentioned as Sanaka, Sananda and Sanatana, while some texts list a total of seven. According to Puranic myths, these sons refused to marry as they were created from the pure element of sattva. They remained innocent and celibate eternally and some Puranas state they never grew beyond the age of five. They had mastered all the Vedas and travelled together to Vaikuntha, the heaven of Vishnu.

Shaunaka is said to be the author of the *Aitareya Brahmana* and part of the *Aitareya Aranyaka*. He is mentioned in the Upanishads, and in the *Mundaka Upanishad* he questions Angirasa.

Shuka is the son of the rishi Vyasa, described in ancient texts. According to some accounts, Shuka was born when Vyasa's semen dropped on a fire he had kindled. A story in the Mahabharata states that Vyasa pleased Shiva, who granted his wish that he should have a son. When Vyasa saw the apsara Ghritachi in the form of a female parrot his seed came out and Shuka was born from the firesticks (arani).

Other accounts state that Vyasa married Vatika, daughter of the rishi Jabala, and Shuka was born from them. There are other stories too.

Shvetaketu is the son of the rishi Uddalaka and grandson of Aruna, who is described in ancient texts. In the *Chhandogya Upanishad*, Shvetaketu was instructed by his father on the nature of Brahman. Uddalaka gave him several examples to show that Brahman was the essence of the universe and explained how he too was of the same essence ('Tat tvam asi', or 'That thou art').

In the Mahabharata, Shvetaketu is said to have established the practice of chastity in marriage. According to a story associated with this, one day a brahmana came and caught his mother by the hand and took her away. Uddalaka said this practice was sanctioned but Shvetaketu vowed that it would not happen in future.

There are several other stories of Shvetaketu. He was the uncle of Ashtavakra, who grew up thinking he was his brother.

Uddalaka Aruni is the name of a rishi described in the Upanishads and other texts. He was the father of Shvetaketu. His daughter Sujata was married to his disciple, the rishi Kahoda, and from them Ashtavakra was born. According to one account in the Mahabharata, he caused Shvetaketu to be begotten by a disciple of his. Uddalaka taught Shvetaketu the supreme knowledge of the nature of Brahman.

Uddalaki is a rishi, the father of Nachiketa, described in the *Katha Upanishad* and other texts.

Vamadeva, a rishi, is the composer of a number of hymns in Mandala 4 of the *Rig Veda*. He was also known as Vamadeva Gautama. Brihaduktha Vamadevya, the composer of some hymns in the tenth mandala, seems to have been a member of his family. He is mentioned in the Upanishads.

Vasishtha is a rishi to whom many hymns of the *Rig Veda* are ascribed, including those of the seventh mandala as well as some others. He is said to be one of the seven great rishis and also one of the ten Prajapatis. In one of the hymns of the *Rig Veda*, he and the rishi Agastya are described as the offspring of Mitra and Varuna. When these two gods saw the beautiful apsara Urvashi, their seed fell and the two rishis were born from it. This is explained in the Puranas as his second birth. In another account, Vasishtha was the son of Varuna and associated with the Tritsus, a Rig Vedic clan, and was the priest of King Sudas.

The rivalry between him and the rishi Vishvamitra has often been described, right from the time of the *Rig Veda*. Vasishtha owned Nandini, also known as Shabala, a wish-fulfilling cow who provided him with all he needed. The story of how Vishvamitra, then a king, attempted to take away his cow and after failing practised austerities and became a rishi himself, is described in the Ramayana and other texts. There are several other stories about Vasishtha.

He is described as the family priest of King Harishchandra and of the King Ikshvaku and all his descendants for sixty-one generations. According to the Ramayana, when Rama's coronation was announced, Vasishtha arrived at Ayodhya with his students to conduct the religious rites (Ayodhya Kanda 14).

Vasishtha represented a superhuman person, or one of a line of rishis or priests, all with the same name.

The rishi Vasishtha was one of the mildest and most pious rishis described in texts. He had all powers but never used them to benefit himself. Had he wished he could have brought all his sons to life again or rescued them from Yama's abode, but he did not so. He was capable of killing Vishvamitra but refrained. He had overcome anger, and never sought revenge. He advised others but never imposed his will on them.

Apart from the stories in the epics and Puranas, there are a number of local legends about Vasishtha. Some of these are about a tantric Vasishtha, different from the above.

Vishvamitra is a rishi to whom the hymns of the third mandala of the *Rig Veda* are assigned, and he is said to be the son of Kushika. According to later texts, he was the son of Gadhi, king of Kannauj, a descendent of Puru, and a king himself. According to the Ramayana (Bala Kanda 51), there was once a king, Kusha, son of the god Brahma. Kusha's son was Kushanabha and his son was Gadhi. Vishvamitra was the son of Gadhi. His intense rivalry with the rishi Vasishtha is described in several texts.

Vishvamitra visited the ashrama of Vasishtha and when he attempted to take away Vasishtha's sacred cow, he realized the power of an unarmed rishi and was determined to become one. When Vishvamitra undertook severe austerities to become a rishi, the gods were afraid of his power and sent the Apsara Menaka to seduce him. She succeeded, and a daughter Shakuntala was born. Vishvamitra then realized his error and sent Menaka away. Finally, Vishvamitra received the boon that he would become a brahmana and a rishi. Even after obtaining this, he did not forget his rivalry with Vasishtha.

There are several other stories about Vishvamitra. He became an immensely powerful rishi, but was always prone to anger.

Vyasa is a rishi of the ancient days. According to tradition, he arranged the Vedas, compiled the Mahabharata, and was the author of the Puranas. His life is described in the Mahabharata and other texts. He was the son of the rishi Parashara and Satyavati. He was dark in colour and so was known as Krishna, and being born on an island (dvipa) was known as Dvaipayana. As soon as

he was born, he attained the age of five years. He then told his
mother that he had a lot to accomplish and left her, saying that if
she ever needed him he would come immediately. Satyavati later
married King Shantanu and had two sons, one of whom died in
battle, and the other, Vichitravirya, died leaving two childless
widows. Though he was a rishi, it was his duty to see they had
children, therefore, through Vyasa, Dhritarashtra and Pandu
were born. Before approaching the wives, Vyasa wanted time to
make himself presentable but at Satyavati's insistence he went
to the women unkempt and in his rishi's garb. Ambika, one of
Vichitravirya's wives, was so terrified at the sight of the rishi that
she shut her eyes and so Dhritarashtra was born blind, whereas
the other wife, Ambalika, turned pale out of fright and so Pandu
was born absolutely pale. Only the maid servant was natural and
normal, and through her the wise Vidura was born.

Vyasa later had a role in the birth of the Kauravas, the hundred
sons of Dhritarashtra. Gandhari, Dhritarashtra's wife, prematurely
gave birth to a lump of flesh. Vyasa preserved this and from it were
born a hundred sons and one daughter. He frequently gave advice
to the Pandavas and other characters in the Mahabharata.

According to the Mahabharata, he prayed to Lord Shankara
(Shiva) for a son. As he was kindling the sacred fire, his semen
dropped on it and a boy was born named Shuka. Immediately,
Shuka grew up and was initiated into the brahmacharya stage,
after his Upanayana was performed by Indra. Shuka was instructed
by Vyasa and King Janaka. According to some of the Puranas,
Shuka was born after Vyasa married. The Skanda Purana states
that Vyasa married Vatika, daughter of the rishi Jabala, and Shuka
was their son.

Vyasa was also called Veda Vyasa because he divided the
Vedas, which originally were one, into four smaller texts. Four
pupils, Paila, Sumantu, Jaimini and Vaishampayana, memorized

and narrated one Veda each, while Lomaharshana Suta memorized and transmitted the Puranas.

Vyasa is also listed as an incarnation of Vishnu. Badarayana, who compiled the *Brahma Sutra*, is said to be the same as Vyasa.

Several Vyasas are mentioned in the Puranas as incarnations of Vishnu or Shiva. According to the *Vishnu Purana*, in every Dvapara Yuga, Vishnu, in the form of Vyasa, divides the Veda, which is actually one, into many, to adapt it to the capacities of the people. In the Vaivasvata Manvantara, the present Manvantara, the Vedas have been arranged twenty-eight times in successive Dvapara Yugas and thus in this age there have been twenty-eight Vyasas. The *Linga Purana* says that the twenty-eight Vyasas were actually incarnations of Shiva. There were also others known as Vyasa. Thus, Vyasas are born in successive ages to arrange and propagate the Vedas and other texts. While this is the traditional view, scholars feel Vyasa is a title used by many of the authors and compilers of ancient texts. The names of many of those mentioned as Vyasas appear as authors of some of the Vedic hymns.

Vyasa as a great composer and narrator of sacred literature is still revered. He is also said to have founded the order of sannyasis, and is worshipped on Vyasa Purnima (Guru Purnima), the full moon day of the month of Ashadha (June–July).

Yajnavalkya is a very wise rishi who is prominent as a teacher in the Upanishads. He is said to have composed the *Vajasaneyi Samhita* or *Shukla Yajur Veda*, as well as the *Shatapatha Brahmana*, the *Brihadaranyaka Upanishad* and the *Yajnavalkya Smriti*. It is unlikely that he was the author of all these texts as they are of different dates and it is presumed that there were at least two Yajnavalkyas.

Part II

The Texts

THIS SECTION PROVIDES an idea of each of the 108 Upanishads listed in the *Muktika Upanishad*. This is not a translation of the texts, but a summary and an attempt to understand their main features. The ideas in these Upanishads are far more complex than what is revealed here. Sri Aurobindo, for instance, suggests that dual meanings often exist. He also believes that the opening sentence of each Upanishad provides the essence of the text and sets the tone of the whole Upanishad.[1]

As Swami Veda Bharati says, one cannot look for some logical or coherent sequence. One has to see the Upanishads as tools to meditation or a means to ignite intuition. 'No translation can be perfect, especially from ancient texts of a tradition. [. . .] The inspired texts contain many truths in different layers of their meanings and thus may be translated in such a way that one rendering is totally different from another but both are accurate.'[2] Each word has layers of meaning which are gradually revealed. Sri Aurobindo remarks that the Upanishads are vehicles of illumination and not of instruction, and are for seekers already familiar with Vedic ideas and even with some personal experience of the truths on which they are based.[3] Detailed commentaries are available for the early Upanishads and some of the later ones; while Shri Upanishad Brahmayogin has commented on every one of them. Commentaries have been consulted to understand the complex and multilayered texts. (For an explanation of the main topics in the Upanishads see Chapter 3.)

Many of the Upanishads are divided into sections and subsections, referred to by different terms. They are called kandas,

kandikas, khandas, adhyayas, brahmanas and by other terms.
These are translated as chapters, sections or books. Though the
number of sections and sometimes verses are mentioned, it should
be noted that there were different versions of the texts, particularly
of the later Upanishads.

Among the early Upanishads are the *Aitareya*, *Kaushitaki*,
Taittiriya, *Brihadaranyaka*, *Chhandogya* and *Kena*, while slightly
later are the *Kathaka*, *Shvetashvatara*, *Maha-Narayana*, *Isha*,
Mundaka, *Prashna*, *Maitrayaniya* and *Mandukya*. These fourteen
can be dated to before the third century BCE. Various scholars
differ slightly in the relative dating of these texts though all agree
that the prose Upanishads are the earliest. Patrick Olivelle, based
on a consensus of various views, provides the following sequence:
1. The earliest are the *Brihadaranyaka* and *Chhandogya*, probably
seventh to sixth centuries BCE, though they may include passages
that belong to much earlier times; 2. These are followed by the
Aitareya, *Taittiriya* and *Kaushitaki*, sixth to the fifth centuries BCE
(all these are prose Upanishads); 3. He places the verse *Kena* next;
4. Followed by the *Katha*, *Isha*, *Shvetashvatara* and *Mundaka*;
5. After this are the *Prashna* and *Mandukya*, two prose Upanishads.

Though some of the early Upanishads are in prose, in the
descriptions below, for convenience we have used the term 'verses'
for the shorter passages in each section.

Five

The Earliest Upanishads

Brihadaranyaka Upanishad

THIS UPANISHAD IS one of the earliest available, generally dated to the eighth or seventh century BCE, and also the longest. It is a very complex text and most scholars use Sri Shankara's commentary to get a better understanding of it. His commentary was further explained by the Advaita scholars Anandagiri, Sureshvara and Vidyaranya. There are other commentaries, including that of Madhva from the standpoint of Dvaita.

The *Brihadaranyaka Upanishad* is attached to the *Shukla Yajur Veda* and forms part of the *Shatapatha Brahmana*. The text has six adhyayas (chapters). These chapters form part of the seventeenth section of the *Kanva* recension of the *Shatapatha*, and the fourteenth of the *Madhyandina* recension.

Sri Shankaracharya's commentary follows the *Kanva* text, where the six chapters are chapters three to eight of Section 17.

Each adhyaya has further subdivisions which are called Brahmanas, and each Brahmana has paragraphs known as kandikas.

The chapters are also divided into three kandas or sections of two chapters each, based on the commentary (varttika) of Sureshvara: the first two form the *Madhu Kanda*, chapters three and four consist of the *Yajnavalkya Kanda* or *Muni Kanda*, which describes the teachings of the rishi Yajnavalkya; and chapters five and six are classified as the *Khila Kanda* with additional or supplementary topics. In addition, the first kanda is also classified as *upadesha* (teaching) containing the basic principles of Advaita. The second kanda puts forward logical explanations (*upapatti*) regarding the teaching or upadesha. The third deals with types of meditation (*upasana*). Vidyaranya too agrees with this classification.

Despite this attempt to see it as a unified whole, the *Brihadaranyaka* has many seemingly disparate themes and topics. Paul Deussen[1] feels the three kandas were originally independent texts. This would account for the repetition of Yajnavalkya's conversation with his wives and for the several lists of teachers.

An account of the text and its main themes follows. (The numbers in brackets refer to the adhyaya, Brahmana and verses.)

Adhyaya 1 has six Brahmanas, each with a varying number of kandikas.

The first, known as the *Ashva Brahmana*, begins with the symbolism of the ashvamedha, or the horse sacrifice. The first verse begins by stating: 'Dawn is the head of the sacrificial horse, its eye is Surya (the sun), its prana (breath) is the air (vata)' (translated from the Sanskrit). Every part of it is compared with some aspect of the world. Succeeding verses indicate that even in the absence of a real horse, the sacrificial horse should be meditated upon as Prajapati, leading to identification with that deity (1.1.1–2).

The second Brahmana with seven kandikas continues with the symbolism of the horse sacrifice but begins with passages on creation. It states: 'In the beginning there was nothing here; because the world was covered by death, by hunger, as hunger is death' (1.2.1). First, he (Prajapati) created the mind, then the body, then the whole world. He wanted his body to be offered to him in sacrifice and therefore became a horse (ashva). That is why one offers the sacrifice to Prajapati.

The third Brahmana, with twenty-eight kandikas, mentions the devas and asuras, both decendants of Prajapati, and how the devas used the Udgitha (sacred chant) to defeat the asuras. (There is a similar passage in the *Chhandogya Upanishad*.) The kandikas here refer to the jyotishtoma soma sacrifice, though it is not specifically mentioned, the role of the udgatr priest in it, and the benefits of this.

Following this, there are passages on creation (1.4). It says that in the beginning there was only the atman. Because he was the first, he is called Purusha (the person). This section also introduces Brahman, and states that through the knowledge of Brahman one can attain identity with the universe. The creation of the four castes and their associated deities is described. Pita (the father signifying the god Brahma) created seven kinds of food through meditation and rituals (1.5). Following this are references to the Vedas, the body, mind and Prajapati. Next, the text states that this (the universe) consists of name, form and action. *Vaga* (speech or sound) is the common feature of all names, form in general is the source of all forms, and general action the source of all activities (1.6).

Adhyaya 2 also has six Brahmanas. The sixth Brahmana is the *Vamsha Brahmana*, providing a line of teachers for the first two chapters.

The first Brahmana in this adhyaya begins with Gargya Balaki, who approaches Ajatashatru, king of Kashi, and says that he will tell him about Brahman. The conversation that follows is almost the same as in the *Kaushitaki Upanishad* and concludes with Ajatashatru teaching Balaki (2.1).

The second Brahmana discusses the body and the prana within it, comparing it to a calf (2.2). The seven decay-preventing gods that represent different aspects of the eye are referred to. These are Rudra, Parjanya, Aditya, Agni, Indra, Prithivi and Dyaus. Those that know this are never short of food (that is, they serve the prana or vital force as food). The next verse (2.2.3) states there is a mantra which says there is a bowl; it has its opening below and it bulges above. In it there is knowledge revealed, and seven rishis sit by its side, and speech is the eighth. This refers to the head, and the seven are the organs in it. The following verse (2.2.4) continues with this theme, identifying the eyes, ears, nostrils and tongue with the rishis Gotama, Bharadvaja, Vishvamitra, Jamadagni, Vasishtha, Kashyapa and Atri.

By comparing physical organs with gods and rishis, this Brahmana makes them something sacred.

The third Brahmana (2.3) describes Brahman, which has two forms, gross and subtle, mortal and immortal, limited and unlimited, seen and unseen. Succeeding verses explain this further.

The fourth Brahmana has the story of Yajnavalkya and his two wives (2.4). Yajnavalkya tells his wife Maitreyi that he is going to renounce the world and therefore he would like to make a final settlement with her and his other wife, Katyayani. But Maitreyi asks whether if the whole world and its wealth belonged to her, she would be immortal? If not, what would she do with it? Yajnavalkya responds that she has always been dear to him and now she has said what is dear to his heart. He explains that the wife, as well as other things, are not loved for themselves, but because of the Self that is in them. He concludes (2.4.5) by telling Maitreyi that the Self should be realized by hearing about it, reflecting on it, and meditating on it. The next verse (2.4.6) again refers to Brahman. It says that brahmanas, kshatriyas, worlds and gods reject those who think Brahman is different from the atman, while verses 7 to 9 use a musical analogy, saying that notes can be grasped only by the general effect, not by one particular note. This indirectly refers to Brahman, as only by knowing Brahman can the rest be known. After this (2.4.10), Yajnavalkya's explanation to Maitreyi continues. He says that just as different types of smoke come from a fire so from limitless reality ('mahat bhutasya') come the *Rig Veda*, *Yajur Veda*, *Sama Veda*, *Atharva-Angirasa*, Itihasa, Puranam, Vidya, Upanishads, shlokas, sutras, elucidations and explanations. They are like the breaths or emanations of Brahman. Then (2.4.11–12) Yajnavalkya provides further explanations of Brahman and how everything is part of it, just as all sorts of water merge in the sea, as all sounds merge in the ear, all thoughts in the mind, and as salt in water pervades all of it, in the same way everything is pervaded by Brahman.

But Maitreyi is confused by his statement that after attaining That (Brahman), individual consciousness would not exist (2.4.13). Yajnavalkya explains that when everything is Brahman, there can be no duality.

The fifth Brahmana (2.5) begins with the statement that the earth is *madhu* (honey) to all beings and has further explanations of Brahman, which is the means of becoming all. This is the same madhu that Dadhyach, well-versed in the *Atharva*, conveyed to the Ashvins through the horse's head (2.5.16–19). This story is narrated in the *Shatapatha Brahmana*, and madhu here refers to knowledge. It then explains the Brahman that is everywhere, without beginning or end.

The sixth Brahmana (2.6) has a line of teachers: Pautimashya, it says, received the knowledge from Gaupavana, who received it from another Pautimashya, who received it from another Gaupavana. The line is thus traced through this Gaupavana–Kaushika–Kaundinya–Shandilya–another Kaushika–another Gautama.

Then Gautama received it from Agniveshya who received it from Shandilya and Anabhimlata, Anabhimlata from Gautama, continuing through Saitava and Prachinayogya–Parasharya–Bharadvaja–another Bharadvaja and Gautama–Gautama from another Bharadvaja–this Bharadvaja from another Parasharya–this Parasharya from Baijavapayana–who learnt it from Kaushikayani–Ghritakaushika–Parasharyayana–Parasharya–Jatukarnya–Asurayana and Yaska–Asurayana from Traivani–Aupajandhani–Asuri–Bharadvaja–Atreya–Manti–Gautama–another Gautama–Vatsya–Shandilya–Kaishorya Kapya–Kumaraharita–Galava–Vidarbhikaundinya–Vatsanapat Babhrava–Pathin Saubhara–Ayasya Angirasa–Abhuti Tvashtra–Vishvarupa Tvashtra–Ashvins–Dadhyach Atharvana–Atharvan Daiva–Mrityu Pradhvamsana–Pradhvamsana–Ekarshi–Viprachitti–Vyashti–Sanaru–Sanatana–Sanaga–Parameshthi–Brahman, the eternal.

The knowledge in this is thus very ancient, proceeding from Brahman through a long line of teachers, including both rishis and gods.

Adhyayas 3 and 4 are those associated with Yajnavalkya.

Adhyaya 3 has nine Brahmanas. The first is *Ashvala Brahmana*, followed by the *Artabhaga Brahmana* and the *Bhujyu Brahmana* as the third. The fourth is the *Ushasta Brahmana*, the fifth *Kahola Brahmana*, the sixth *Gargi Brahmana*, the seventh *Antaryami Brahmana*, the eighth again the *Gargi Brahmana*, and the ninth *Shakalya Brahmana*. Each Brahmana is named after a person who questions Yajnavalkya.

Janaka, king of Videha, organized a sacrifice in which many gifts were distributed, and which was attended by brahmanas of Kuru Panchala. Janaka wanted to know who was the most learned among them, and offered a thousand cows, each with ten padas of gold on their horns, to the one who could prove this. He said, let the greatest Vedic scholar drive these cows home. Yajnavalkya told his own student (brahmachari) Samashravas to drive the cows home, and he did so. Others were angry, and Ashvala, Janaka's hotr priest, asked Yajnavalkya, 'Are you the greatest Vedic scholar?'

'I bow to the greatest, I want the cows,' said Yajnavalkya (3.1.1–2).

Ashvala then asked him a series of questions, mainly related to the sacrifice, to which he replied (3.1.3–10).

Then Artabhaga of the line of Jaratkaru questioned him on the same theme (3.2.1–13); he was followed by Bhujyu, grandson of Lahya (3.3), Ushasta, the son of Chakra (3.4.1–2), Kahola, the son of Kushitaka I (3.5.1–2), and Gargi, the daughter of Vachakanu (3.6.1).

After this, Uddalaka, son of Aruna, questioned him and asked him to describe the antaryamin, the inner controller (3.7.1–23). Uddalaka said, 'In Madra we lived in the house of Patanchala Kapya, studying sacrificial scriptures. His wife was possessed by a gandharva. When asked who he was, he said he was Kabandha.' The gandharva asked Patanchala Kapya several questions, including if he knew the antaryamin. Yajnavalkya explained it, ending with the words, 'He is your own self, and immortal. Everything but him is perishable.'

Once again, Gargi, daughter of Vachkanu, questioned him (3.8). She began by saying, 'As a person in Kashi, or the king of Videha, could string his unstrung bow and take two bamboo-tipped arrows painful to his enemies, and approach them closely, in this way I will ask you two questions.' Her first question was: 'What pervades that above heaven and below the earth, as well as between, and which was, is, and will be?'

Yajnavalkya replied that it is the unmanifested akasha (space). Gargi again posed the same question, adding at the end: 'What pervades the unmanifested akasha?' Yajnavalkya said the knowers of Brahman call it the imperishable and then provided a further description of it. It is neither coarse nor fine, neither short nor long, neither red nor oily, not shadow or darkness, not air or

akasha. It is unattached. It has neither taste nor smell, eyes or
ears, tongue or mind. It is non-effulgent, without vital breath or
mouth. It is without measure, exterior or interior. It does not eat,
and no one eats it (3.8.8). He continued with his explanations,
and finally Gargi said, 'None of you will defeat him in arguments
about Brahman.'

In the ninth Brahmana (3.9), Vidaghda, son of Shakala
(Shakalya), asked him about how many gods there were. At
first Yajnavalkya says there were as many as those mentioned
in the Nivid (group of mantras) of the Vishvedevas, that is, 303
and 3003. Then, with further questions, he reduced them from
thirty-three to six, to three, to two, to one and a half and finally
to one. When Shakalya asks which were those 303 and 3003,
Yajnavalkya says there were actually only thirty-three, the eight
Vasus, eleven Rudras, twelve Adityas, Indra and Prajapati. He
then explains who these are and what they represent. The six
are Agni, Prithivi, Vayu, Antariksha, Aditya and Dyaus, and
the thirty-three gods are included in these. The three gods are
the three lokas or worlds; the two are *annam* (food) and prana; the
one and a half is that which blows (pavate), the air. Even though
this is one, it is said to be one and a half, because by it everything
lives. The one is Prana, that is, Brahman. He also describes other
deities including those of different directions and the prana and
other types of breath, and compares a person with a tree. This
section ends by affirming that Brahman is the ultimate goal.

Adhyaya 4 has six Brahmanas.

In the first Brahmana, King Janaka of Videha is seated to
give audience when Yajnavalkya arrived. Janaka asked why he had
come—did he want cattle or answers to some questions? Both,
replied Yajnavalkya. Janaka then asks what others have told him
on Brahman and hears the views of Jitvan, son of Shilina; Udanka,
son of Shulba; Barka, son of Vrishna; Gardabhivipita, descendant
of Bharadvaja; Satyakama, son of Jabala; Vidagdha, son of Shakala;

and further clarifies what they said. Then King Janaka offers him a thousand cows and an elephant-like bull, but Yajnavalkya tells him that his father believed one should not accept anything from a pupil before instruction was complete.

In the second Brahmana, Janaka asks Yajnavalkya to teach him. Yajnavalkya begins his reply with a description of some of Janaka's qualities. He had controlled his mind through the knowledge of secret names (of Brahman), and he was honoured and wealthy. He had studied the Vedas and had been instructed in the Upanishads. But, asks Yajnavalkya, does he know where he will go when released from the body? When Janaka says he does not know, Yajnavalkya begins an explanation with a description of the inner body and the nadis called hita that carry the essence of food and of prana. Then he describes the atman that cannot be described, except as 'Not this, not this'. It cannot be seen, never decays, is unattached, unfettered, never suffers and never perishes. Knowing this, Yajnavalkya says that now Janaka has attained the fearless (abhayam, indicating Brahman). In return, Janaka says that his empire and he himself are at his service.

The third is the *Jyotir Brahmana*. Sureshvara's commentary on this extends to 1975 verses, indicating its importance.

It begins with Yajnavalkya again visiting Janaka, but making a resolve to say nothing. In the past, though, Yajnavalkya and Janaka had discussed the agnihotra and Yajnavalkya had offered him a boon. Janaka chose the right to ask any question. Now Janaka asks, 'What serves as light for a man?' Yajnavalkya says it is the sun, but then there are succeeding questions. When the sun sets, the moon provides light; when there is no moon, fire provides light; if no fire, sound provides light, in the sense that if one hears a sound, one can reach there. If there is no sound, the Self provides light.

Janaka then asks, what is the atma or Self? It is that reflected in the intellect (*vijnanamaya*), says Yajnavalkya, in the prana or vital breath, and as a self-effulgent light within the heart. Simulating the intellect, it roams between the two worlds and transcends this waking world, which represents forms of death (ignorance and its effects). When a person is born, he gets a body which is associated with evils, and when he dies he discards those. There are two states for the person: in this world and in the next. The dream state is between these two, and in this intermediate state one can survey both worlds. When he dreams, he takes away a little of this world, makes the body unconscious and creates a dream body through his own light. In this state a person has self-illumination (4.3.7–9). (In later texts the Turiya state is higher than the dream body.) In the dream state there are no real chariots, animals or roads, but the Self creates them. There are no joys, delights or raptures, but it creates them. There are no pools, tanks or rivers, but it creates them, for it is the karta, the doer (4.3.10). Regarding this are the following shlokas: The Purusha who shines, who travels alone, makes the body unconscious but is itself awake, and wanders wherever he likes (4.3.11). Succeeding verses have more on the dream world and on the world of sleep.

The nadis called hita are described fine as a hair, divided into 1000 parts, and filled with white, blue, red, brown and green fluids, representing the subtle body (4.3.20).

After this is a description of deep sleep, where the person does not hear or see, yet there is something that hears and sees, that is the witness, the one without a second, that is the world of Brahman (4.3.32).

The fourth is the *Shariraka Brahmana*, which describes how the Self or individual atma departs at death, spends some time in the other world and then enters a new body. It has passages on the self and on Brahman.

The fifth Brahmana has a similar theme, and repeats the story of Yajnavalkya and his two wives, Maitreyi and Katyayani, with minor variations. At Maitreyi's request, he instructs her in Brahman.

The sixth Brahmana once again has a line of teachers, almost the same as that given earlier. In three long verses, the teachers are traced from Pautimashya to Brahma, the self-created, the ultimate source of the teaching. Pautimashya received the knowledge from Gaupavana, who received it from another Pautimashya, who received it from another Gaupavana. The line is thus traced through this Gaupavana–Kaushika–Kaundinya–Shandilya–another Kaushika–another Gautama.

Then Gautama received it from Agniveshya who received it from Gargya, Gargya from another Gargya, the other Gargya from Gautama, continuing through Saitava–Parasharyayana–Gargyayana–Uddalakayana–Jabalayana–Madhyandinayana–Shaukarayana–Kaushikayani–Ghritakaushika–Parasharyayana–Jatukarnya–Asurayana and Yaska–Traivani–Aupajandhani–Asuri–Bharadvaja–Atreya–Manti–Gautama–another Gautama–Vatsya–Shandilya–Kaishorya Kapya–Kumaraharita–Galava–Vidarbhikaundinya–Vatsnapat Babhrava–Pathin Saubhara–Ayasya–Angirasya–Abhuti Tvashtra–Vishvarupa Tvashtra–the Ashvins–Dadhyach Atharvana–Atharvan Daiva–Mrityu Pradhvamsana–Pradhvamsana–Ekarshi–Viprachitti–Vyashti–Sanaru–Sanatana–Sanaga–Parameshthin–Brahman, the self-created.

Adhyayas five and six, together known as the *Khila Kanda* or supplementary section, contains some additional information. They can be considered portions to be meditated upon.

Adhyaya 5 has fifteen Brahmanas.

The first Brahmana has only one verse, beginning with the mantra 'Purnamadah Purnamidam', etc. After this it states that Om is Brahman. It is ancient, it is ether containing vayu (air), says the son of Kauravyayani. The seekers of Brahman know that Om is the means of knowledge (veda) to attain Brahman. (Or, according to an alternative interpretation, that Om represents all the Vedas.)

The second Brahmana with three verses says that Prajapati had three kinds of offspring: devas, people (manushya) and asuras.

They lived with their father Prajapati as brahmacharis (students). When their term of study was over, the devas asked him for some instruction. He said, 'da' and then asked if they had understood. Yes, they said, you told us to control yourselves (damyata). He affirmed they had understood him correctly. Similarly, when the people and then the asuras asked him, he again said 'da', which the people correctly understood as 'datta', give, and the asuras as 'dayadhvam', be compassionate.

That same thing is repeated today by the heavenly voice in the form of thunder, 'da, da, da', which means control yourselves, give and have compassion, and these three should be practised. (T.S. Eliot used this in his poem 'The Wasteland'.)

Each Brahmana has different themes, though most provide an explanation of Brahman. Words related to Brahman are broken up into syllables and each syllable explained. Meditating on their statements would lead to an understanding of them. In succeeding Brahmanas, Prajapati is said to be in the heart (*hridayam*), and the same as Satya Brahman (the true Brahman). The syllables 'bhur', 'bhuvar', 'svar' and others are also connected with various aspects of being.

The sixth Brahmana describes the Manomaya Purusha, radiant by nature, seen within the heart. He is the lord of all and rules the universe, while the seventh Brahmana says that lightning is Brahman because it disperses the clouds.

The fourteenth Brahmana explains the importance of the Gayatri Mantra at length in eight verses. In the eighth, Janaka, king of Videha, says to Budila, the son of Ashvatarashva, 'How is it that you, who called yourself a knower of the Gayatri, have come to be an elephant and are carrying me?' He replies that it is because he does not know its mouth. Janaka says that fire is its mouth. It can burn any amount of fuel and in the same way any amount of sins are consumed and purified by the Gayatri.

The fifteenth Brahmana is also found in the *Isha Upanishad*, stating that the face of truth (satya) is covered with a golden vessel.

Adhyaya 6 has five Brahmanas.

The first describes the qualities of the different organs of the body. Then they go to Prajapati asking which one of them was the best (vasishtha) (6.1.7). He says it is that one by whose departure the body would suffer most. Each one departs in turn, and the body stays alive, but when prana is about to depart, like a great Saindhava horse pulls out its tether, they call him back, saying, 'We shall not be able to live without you.' (A Saindhava horse is a horse in the region of the river Sindhu [Indus].)

In the second Brahmana, Shvetaketu, grandson of Aruna, comes to the assembly of the Panchalas and meets King Pravahana, son of Jivala. He and his father are then instructed by the king. (The same passage is in the *Chhandogya Upanishad* 5.3.10.)

The third Brahmana describes various rituals to accomplish certain desires, such as greatness or becoming a king or ruler. The last part of this (6.3.7–12) again has a list of teachers.

Uddalaka, son of Aruna, after imparting the rules for the ritual to his pupil Vajasaneya Yajnavalkya, says, 'Even if one sprinkles it on a dry stump, branches would grow and leaves spring forth.' Each says the same after imparting it to their student.

Vajasaneya Yajnavalkya teaches this to Madhuka, son of Paingi, who imparts it to Chula, son of Bhagavitta, who teaches Janaki, son of Ayasthuna, who teaches Satyakama, son of Jabala, who imparts it to his pupils, and says one should not impart this to anybody except one's son or disciple.

The passage on teachers is followed by a description of four things that should be made out of fig wood (*audumbara*): the ladle, bowl, fuel and two churning sticks. Ten kinds of cultivated grain are mentioned: rice, barley, sesamum, beans, millet, panic seed, wheat, lentils, pulses and khala-kulah, which could be chickpea,

188 The 108 Upanishads

and *Dolichos uniflorus*. These provide an idea of agriculture at the time.

The fourth Brahmana includes the creation of women by Prajapati and the act of procreation. Several details on the right way to do this are provided. Uddalaka Aruni, Naka, son of Mudgala and Kumararahita, says that many men, who are brahmanas only in name, have union without this knowledge, and depart from the world without merit. Most of the passages are for the birth of a son, but there is one for the birth of a daughter 'who will be a scholar and have a long life' (6.4.17). More rituals are prescribed after the son is born. There is also a passage on how to win over a woman (the wife). He should first talk to her, offer her desired objects and if she still does not yield to him, should strike her with a stick or with the hand (6.4.7), and another on how to curse the lover of his wife, who would then have no remaining merit (6.4.12).

Section 5 has a line of teachers in four verses. These are teachers of the whole Upanishad who are named after their mothers.

They are: The son of Pautimashi, who received the teaching from the son of Katyayani, who in turn received it from the son of Gautami, and further from the son of Bharadvaji, from the son of Parashari, from the son of Aupasvasti, from the son of (another) Parashari, from the son of Katyayani, from the son of Kaushiki, from the son of Alambi, from the son of Vaiyaghrapadi, from the son of Kanvi, from the son of Kapi, from the son of Atreyi, from the son of Gautami, from the son of Bharadvaji, from the son of Vatsi, from the son of (another) Parashari, from the son of Varkaruni, from the son of another Varkaruni, from the son of Artabhagi, from the son of Shaungi, from the son of Sankriti, from the son of Alambayani, from the son of Alambi, from the son of Jayanti, from the son of Madukayani, from the son of Manduki, from the son of Shandili, from the son of Rathitari, from the son of Bhaluki, from the two sons of Kraunchiki, from the son of Vaidabhriti, from the son of Karshakeyi, from the son of Prachinayogi, from the son of Sanjivi, from Asurivasin the son of Prashni, from Asurayanga, from Asuri, from Yajnavalkya, from Aruna, from Upaveshi, from Kushri, from Vajashravas, from Jihvavat the son of Badhyoga, from Asita the son of Varshagana, from Harita Kashyapa, from Kashyapa the son of Nidhruva, from Vach, from Ambhini, from Aditya. These Shukla Yajuses received from Aditya (the sun) are explained by Yajnavalkya Vajasaneya.

The fourth verse suggests that there are two lines of teachers which are the same up to Sanjivi from Prajapati and diverge after that. Thus, the fourth verse states that the son of Sanjivi received it from Mandukayani, he from Kautsa, he from Mahitthi, he from Vamakakshayana, he from Shandilya, he from Vatsya, he from Kushri, he from Yajnavachas the son of Rajastamba, he from Tura the son of Kavasha, he from Prajapati, he from Brahman.

Chhandogya Upanishad

This Upanishad is also one of the earliest, dating to before 600 BCE, possibly to the eighth century BCE. It is attached to the *Sama Veda*, consisting of eight out of the ten chapters of the *Chhandogya Brahmana*. It is an important Upanishad and forms the basis for the *Brahma Sutra*. There are many statements in this text on the nature of Brahman and its identity with the atman, which Shankaracharya focused on in his commentary.

The text can be divided into two parts on the basis of its subject matter. The first five sections or prapathakas can be said to form the first part, dealing with upasana, that is, meditation and worship, while the second with prapathakas six to eight explain philosophy, though Part I also has passages on Brahman and the inner light. Worship and the meditation associated with it are a preliminary phase for those who are not ready to follow the path of knowledge (jnana) that leads to Brahman. Shankaracharya says that upasana that is based on the scriptures provides a support for the mind. The philosopher Sadananda supports this view, stating that upasana is an activity of the mind that focuses on Saguna Brahman, Brahman with qualities. Vidyaranya explains it as worship prescribed by a teacher. It can include meditation on a symbol, a deity or a concept. Through it the mind attains an attitude of devotion and becomes calm and purified, ready to focus on Brahman.

The main topic in this Upanishad is the sacred chant. Among other topics, it also describes devayana, the pranas, Brahman, the inner light and the states of consciousness. It looks at the true nature of sacrifice, of the individual and of the world. Symbolically, the whole of a person's life is a sacrifice, divided into three parts. In addition, there are different types of sacrifices: ascetic practices and abstaining from pleasures are considered sacrifices without priests in which non-violence, uprightness and truth are the gifts given. Even eating, drinking, laughing and talking can be considered a sacrifice.

Part I

Prapathaka 1 has thirteen sections. It begins with an explanation of Om, which is the Udgitha, and why it should be meditated upon. The first verse says: 'Om, which is the Udgitha, should be meditated upon, as the Udgitha is sung, beginning with Om.' The Udgitha is a *Sama Veda* verse, a sacred chant. To understand it, one should know something of the sacrificial ritual, which developed into a highly formalized structure with sixteen priests, four representing each of the four Vedas. The main *Sama Veda* priest was the udgatr, and it was he who sang the Sama verse beginning with 'Om', known as the Udgitha. Om is explained in detail in the next few verses. It is used not only by the udgatr but also by the adhvaryu and hotr priests in their rituals. (The latter were the main priests of the *Yajur* and *Rig* Vedas.) A story of the devas and asuras, both the offspring of Prajapati, follows. The devas, it is said, meditated on the Udgitha (Om) as the Prana, as a means to overcome the asuras, but the asuras pierced it with evil. Succeeding verses continue with this theme, until finally the asuras were destroyed (1.2). Among those who meditated on the Udgitha were Angiras, Brihaspati and Ayasya. Baka Dalbhya knew it and became the udgatr of those in the Naimisha forest. (Baka Dalbhya is known in the Mahabharata and other texts.)

The Prana is then praised (1.3), while the next section (1.4) focuses on the Udgitha, Om and chhandas (metre). The gods, afraid of death, began to practise the threefold knowledge (the rituals of the three Vedas), and covered themselves with metrical verses. Because they covered (chhand) themselves with verses, the hymns are called chhandas (1.4.3). Further sections also explain and comment on the udgitha. Sections 6 and 7 equate the *Rig* and *Sama* Vedas with various aspects, including the body, speech, and light. In Section 9 the Udgitha is identified with akasha (space). Section 11 mentions types of priests and the divinities of the sacrifices, while Section 12 is interpreted as a satirical comment on outer sacrifices. It begins with stating that next would be the udgitha of the dogs. Baka Dalbhya or Glava Maitreya (who seem to be the same person) go to study the Vedas. A white dog appears and around it come other dogs. The other dogs ask the white one to obtain food for them by singing. Baka Dalbhya keeps watch and the dogs sing, just like the priests! (In Madhva's commentary, the god Vayu takes the form of a dog.) Finally, Section 13 comments on certain sacred syllables, such as 'hau' and 'hum'.

Several people are mentioned in this chapter, which help to place it in a historical context. Some of them are already referred to. In addition, there is Kaushitaki (of olden times) (1.5.2), who asked his son to meditate on the sun, the prana and the udgitha. In 1.8–9, three people well-versed in the udgitha are referred to: Shilaka, the son of Shalavat, Chaikitayana of the line of Dalbhya, and Pravahana, the son of Jivala, and their discussion on the saman and the udgitha is provided.

Atidhanvan, the son of Shunaka, is also mentioned, who taught the udgitha to Udarashandilya. In 1.10, there is a reference to a time when the crops of the Kurus were destroyed by thunderstorms. At this time, Ushasti, the son of Chakra, lived with his child wife in a poor condition, in the village of a man who owned an elephant. After eating the beans provided by him, he replaced the Sama priests at a sacrifice because of his superior knowledge.

Prapathaka 2 with twenty-four sections deals with different topics, particularly meditation on various chants and sacred syllables under different circumstances. For instance, those who use chants and meditate on water of the clouds or oceans will not die in water; those who use them with animals become rich in animals, that is, goats, sheep, cows and horses (2.6). The Revati chant also centres around animals (2.18). Other chants mentioned along with their benefits include the Gayatra, Rathantara, Vamadevya (for sexual intercourse), the Brihat, Vairupya, Vairaja, Shakvari, Yajnayajniya and Rajana. Different methods of chanting are prescribed, along with the basic ethics for living a virtuous life, which include tapas or religious practices, and brahmacharya, along with the study of sacred wisdom. The last section (24) refers to chants to different deities such as the Adityas and Vishvedevas and the results achieved.

Prapathaka 3 with nineteen sections looks at different aspects of the four Vedas and the secret teachings (Upanishads). It refers to Atharvangirasa as the author of the *Itihasa Purana* (the *Atharva Veda*), and mentions Brahman, as well as several gods including the Vasus, with Agni at their head; the Rudras, with Indra at the head; the Adityas, with Varuna at their head; the Maruts, with Soma at their head; the Sadhyas, with Brahma at their head. The context is the description of various nectars of the sun. For those who know this *Brahma Upanishad*, the sun neither rises nor sets, the day is forever. This doctrine was narrated by Brahma to Prajapati, who revealed it to Manu, who told it to his offspring. It was revealed to Uddalaka Aruni by his father. A father may reveal the doctrine of Brahman to his eldest son or to a worthy disciple, not to anyone else.

The Gayatri is also mentioned as that which contains everything (3.12.1–2). Brahman can be known through the Gayatri. Brahman is described as the akasha (space) within the heart that is omnipresent and unchanging (3.12.7–9) and five aspects of it are five pranas. The light which shines above heaven and above everything is also that which is within a person. The universe comes from Brahman and merges in it. The atman within the Self is described: 'This is my Atman, within the heart, smaller than a grain of rice, a barley seed, a mustard seed, a grain of millet, or even the kernel of a grain of millet. This is my Atman within the heart, greater than the earth, greater than the middle regions and the highest spheres, greater than all the worlds' (3.14.3).

The text goes on to describe the three stages in the life of a person, of twenty-eight-plus-forty-eight-plus-forty-eight years, and the mantras he should recite if anything ails him during this time. Mahidasa knew this and thus lived for 116 years. In another passage (3.17.5), the life of a man is compared to a Soma sacrifice. The following verse states that this truth was taught by Ghora Angirasa to Krishna, son of Devaki. Ghora explains that when death approaches, a person should take refuge in three thoughts, that he is indestructible (akshata), unchanging (aprachyuta) and consisting of the subtle prana.

Following this, there are further descriptions of Brahman and its supreme light.

Prapathaka 4 with seventeen sections narrates several stories. It begins with the story of King Janashruti, the great-grandson of Janashruta, who is known for his generosity. When he is praised by a bird flying overhead (Shankara explains them as rishis or devas that had taken the form of birds), another bird refers to Raikva with the cart. (Raikva with the cart is known from other texts as an enlightened but eccentric person who lived under his cart.) Janashruti overhears this and goes to meet Raikva. He takes a gift of 600 cows, a necklace and a chariot with mules and asks Raikva to teach him. 'O Shudra!' Raikva responds. 'Keep your gift'. (Of course the king is not a Shudra, the implication is that the gift is unworthy.) However, while again calling him a Shudra, he accepts the third gift of 1000 cows, a necklace, a chariot with mules, his daughter as his wife, and a village. The text says that these are the villages named Raikvaparna, in the country of Mahavrisha, where Raikva lived. Raikva explains certain truths to him and mentions Shaunaka of the line of Kapi and Abhipratarin, son of Kakshena, in his stories. Among the stories in this section is the well-known story of Satyakama Jabala, who does not know who his father is but is accepted as a student by Gautama, son of Haridrumata, because of his honesty. Satyakama is asked about his family by Gautama and replies that he does not know. He had asked his mother, says Satyakama, and she had told him she was a maidservant who worked in many houses and he was born from one of them. The rest of the story, though, is not as well-known. He is then given 400 cows to take care of by Gautama; he stays with them (in the forest) until they reach 1000. Later, he is instructed on Brahman by various beings, including one of his bulls, the god Agni, a hamsa (swan) and a madgu (diver bird). By the time he reaches Gautama, he already shone with the light of Brahman, but Gautama too instructs him and Satyakama becomes a teacher himself.

Another story is about Upakoshala, the son of Kamala, who lives as a brahmachari with Satyakama Jabala. After twelve years of study, the other students go home but Satyakama does not allow Upakoshala to leave. Satyakama's wife urges him to teach the boy but instead Satyakama leaves on a journey and the young man begins to fast out of sorrow. Seeing this, as he had sincerely tended the fires, the various agnis including the *garhaptya* (household fire), the *anvaharya* (southern fire) and the *ahavaniya* (eastern fire) teach him part of the knowledge of Brahman. When Satyakama returns, he gives him further instruction on Brahman. The one who knows Brahman travels on devayana, the path of the gods, after death, and never returns.

Prapathaka 5 has twenty-four sections. In the first two, Prajapati explains how prana or the vital breath is the greatest of the organs of the body. Satyakama Jabala also explains this to Goshruti, the son of Vyaghrapada.

The third section states that Shvetaketu Aruneya (the grandson of Aruna) reaches the assembly of the Panchalas. There, the king Pravahana, son of Jivala, asks if his father has instructed him. Shvetaketu replies that he has but then does not have answers to the questions asked by the king. His father too does not have the answers and goes to the king to study. The king asks Gautama (Shvetaketu's father, also known as Uddalaka Aruni) to stay with him to study. He says that this knowledge had not reached any brahmana before him. His teachings continue into Section 10. Among them, Pravahana explains the symbolism of sacrifice. Those who know this, he says, and practise austerities in the forest travel on devayana, the path of the gods. Finally, he reaches lightning, and a person who is not a human being comes and leads him to Brahman. Other paths too are described but those whose conduct has been evil may be born as a dog, a pig or a chandala (5.10.7).

In Section 11, Prachinashala, the son of Upamanyu, Satyayajna, the son of Pulusha, Indradyumna, the grandson of Bhallavi, Jana, the son of Sharkaraksha, and Budila, the son of Ashvatarashva, great householders and great scholars, come together to find out what Brahman is. They go to Uddalaka Aruni (son of Aruna), who feels he would not be able to explain to them, and goes with them to King Ashvapati of Kekaya, who, he says, knows the Vaishvanara self. (Among the four states of consciousness, this is the waking self.)

When they arrive, they stay there the night and the next day the king says: 'In my kingdom, there is no thief, no miser, no wine-drinker, no man without a sacrificial fire, no ignorant person, no adulterer, no adultress.' He then explains the Vaishvanara self to them, which is identical with the universal Self. He mentions various parts of the universal Self as they are represented in the world and the sacrifice to the universal Self within one's own Self. Offerings should be made to the breaths, including the prana, vyana, apana, samana and udana (the five main pranas).

Part II

Prapathaka 6 has sixteen sections, in which there are further discussions on Brahman. There is another story about Uddalaka Aruni, who sends his son Shvetaketu to study. Shvetaketu goes to his teacher's house at the age of twelve and returns at the age of twenty-four, thinking he knows everything. Then his father asks him if he knows that by which one hears what cannot be heard, sees what cannot be seen and knows what cannot be known.

Shvetaketu then realizes that he is ignorant of this and asks for instruction in it. Uddalaka explains through a series of examples, beginning by saying that just as through one clod of clay the nature of clay is known, in the same way all truth can be known. He explains the nature of the world and provides several explanations of Brahman and of the universal nature of life.

In two of the most famous passages, Uddalaka explains to his son Shvetaketu how Brahman pervades everything. In one, he asks Shvetaketu to break the seed of a banyan tree and tell him what he sees. Shvetaketu responds that he sees nothing and Uddalaka says: 'What you cannot see is the essence, and in that essence is the mighty banyan tree. In that essence is the Self of all that is.'

The second is where he asks Shvetaketu to put some salt in water and leave it overnight. In the morning he asks Shvetaketu to bring him the salt, but obviously he cannot as the salt has dissolved. Then Uddalaka asks Shvetaketu to taste the water from the top and all sides and Shvetaketu understands that the salt is still there. In the same way, Uddalaka explains that Sat (Being or Truth) is there throughout the body.

Another example is given of a man blindfolded and taken from the land of Gandhara to a place where there is no one. He wonders where and how to go but then someone comes along who loosens his blindfold and tells him the way to Gandhara. That person is like the teacher who will instruct him in true knowledge.

Prapathaka 7 has twenty-six sections. It begins with the rishi Narada, who approaches Sanat Kumara (one of the mindborn sons of the god Brahma) and asks him to teach him. Sanat Kumara asked Narada to first tell him what he already knows. Narada says he knows the four Vedas, the Puranas (this here implies the epics), Itihasa, the Veda of Vedas (grammar), the rituals to propitiate the pitris, 'the science of portents, the science of time, logic, ethics, etymology, Brahma-vidya, the science of elemental spirits, the science of weapons, astronomy, the science of serpents, and the fine arts'. But he says all that he knows are only words. He does not know the Self and is full of sorrow, and has heard that the knowledge of the Self releases one from sorrow.

Narada's response provides an idea of the type of education imparted to a student at that time.

Sanat Kumara says that all Narada knows are names. Meditating on a name such as Brahman will take him as far as that name reaches. In response to further questions, Sanat Kumara says that meditating on speech as Brahman is higher than meditating on a name and higher than that is meditating on mind as Brahman. Even greater is to meditate on will as Brahman, and beyond that on chitta (consciousness). Dhyana or meditation is greater than chitta, and greater than that is meditating on understanding as Brahman. Next, he speaks of meditating on the following as Brahman, each greater than the former: strength, food, water, fire, akasha, memory, hope, prana. He who knows the prana is an *ativadi*. One must understand the Truth, and for this reflection and faith are required. One should become single-minded through the performance of one's duties. Finally, one attains bliss (ananda), which is the same as the infinite. When one sees, hears and understands nothing but the Infinite, then one has realized it (7.24.1).

Sanat Kumara concludes that people describe possessions such as cows, horses, elephants, gold, slaves, wives, fields and houses as greatness, but the Infinite Self has nothing to do with this. It is everywhere and self-supporting. Everything comes from it, and one who knows this has no death, disease or sorrow.

Thus, Sanat Kumara, who taught Narada, is called Skanda.

Prapathaka 8 has fifteen sections. It directly describes Brahman that is in the lotus within the akasha of the heart. Here there is no old age or death, and all desires are contained within. It goes on to say that whatever he desires from this space comes true. The true Self resides in the heart. Further, it says that Brahman is attained by brahmachari or continence.

Further, in the same section, Prajapati instructs Indra on the real Self.

Thus, in many different ways, the *Chhandogya* discusses the nature of the Self, which lives within the heart and yet contains all the worlds.

Aitareya Upanishad

The *Aitareya Upanishad*, another early Upanishad, can be dated to between the sixth and fifth centuries BCE, according to Patrick

Olivelle and other scholars. It is attached to the *Rig Veda* and the *Aitareya Brahmana* and forms part of the *Aitareya Aranyaka*, consisting of Chapters 4, 5 and 6 of this text. The Upanishad has to be seen in the context of what preceded it in the Aranyaka, which suggests rituals through which Prana can be attained. Prana refers to both breath and the life force, and here Prana is identified with Saguna Brahman, Brahman that has qualities. But as the succeeding Upanishad shows, this cannot be the ultimate goal. Shankara and Madhva are among the commentators on this Upanishad.

The traditional author is Aitareya Mahidasa.

Each of the three sections of the Upanishad deals with important topics. Even though the text is an early one, the concept of Brahman as the source of all, and its identity with the atman, had already developed.

The text deals with Brahman, atman, creation and rebirth. It also describes the four worlds and mentions the rishi Vamadeva.

Brahman is perceived as pervading everything, only after the atman has created the worlds and the different parts of a person, which are finally integrated.

The *Aitareya Upanishad* that follows the chapters on ritual shows that only Nirguna Brahman, the unqualified Brahman, can be the goal. The atman is the only reality, existing before and after creation. Creation spontaneously emerges in the world through the power of maya. The *Aitareya* records first the creation of the worlds, then the Purusha or Virat, representing physical forms, then the devas or deities, next, the elements, followed by individual parts of the body, and then food to sustain them, and describes how these parts cannot exist without the atman, which finally enters them and gives them life. The purpose of the text is to show how with true knowledge the world of duality can be transcended.

The first chapter has three sections. Section 1 describes how everything in the world is created by the atman. It begins with the words 'atma va idam eka evagra asit', meaning 'in the beginning only the atman or soul existed'. The atma then thought, let me create the worlds, and a description of creation follows. The worlds were: Ambah, that is, clouds filled with water; Marichi, the world of rays of light, Mara, the world of mortals, and Ap, the world of water. Ambah is above heaven, which is its support. Marichi is in the antariksha, the middle region. Mara is the earth, and the world of Ap, below the earth. Once the worlds were created, the Atma created world guardians; that is, he made a person, Purusha (representing the cosmic person, Virat), gave him a shape and separated the various parts. In Section 2, the deities were then assigned to the different parts and hunger and thirst was assigned to them, and in Section 3 food was created for them. Each part tried to grasp food but it could only be grasped through the apana (a form of prana, or the breath). Then the atman thought, how could all these exist without me? He entered the person through the end (where the parting of the hair ends), the entrance known as *vidriti*, and then perceived the person as Brahman, pervading everything. The perceiver is known as Idandra, who indirectly is called Indra.

The second chapter contains the theory of the three births of a man. The first birth is when the embryo is formed in a woman; the second is when the baby is born; the third is when the person dies and is reborn. This chapter mentions the rishi Vamadeva, who knew the births of all the gods while still in the womb.

The third chapter has only four verses. It begins with questions on who the Self or the atma is, through which everything is known, by whom one sees, hears and tastes. It goes on to say it is the heart, mind, wisdom, sorrow, memory, purpose and various other attributes, and all these are just names of consciousness (prajnanam). The third verse goes on to say that it is Brahma, Prajapati, Indra, all the gods, the elements, everything that is born, horses, cows, people, elephants, everything that breathes, that moves or flies or even does not move. All this is prajnanam, and prajnanam is Brahman. The fourth verse concludes that He (referring to Vamadeva) has become one with Prajnanam (consciousness or intelligence).

Kaushitaki Upanishad

The *Kaushitaki*, an early Upanishad which can be dated to the sixth or seventh century BCE, is also known as the *Kaushitaki Brahmana Upanishad*. Ian Whicher dates it to the eighth century BCE and Patrick Olivelle to between the sixth and fifth centuries BCE. Commentaries include those of Shankarananda in his Dipika. It is referred to in Shankara's *Brahma Sutra* commentary.

This Upanishad is attached to the *Rig Veda* and forms part of the *Kaushitaki Aranyaka* (also known as the Shankhayana) which is part of the *Kaushitaki Brahmana*.

The text has four chapters or sections. It deals with the path to the other world, prana or life breath, the worship of the sun and the new moon, and the identity of the god Indra with prana, as well as with rebirth and liberation through knowledge. In Chapter 4, Ajatashatru, king of Kashi, explains the nature of Brahman to Gargya Balaki, who was famed for his learning in the scriptures. Brahman exists as the Self in various phenomena and knowledge of the true Self leads to ultimate unity.

Apart from Ajatashatru, among the other teachers mentioned are Kaushitaki himself, Chitra Gangayani, Paingya, Shushka Bhringara and Pratardana.

The world of Brahma and other heavenly worlds are described. Brahman is beyond these worlds, but what exactly is it? The text also refers to the Vedas, sacrificial rituals, the worship of the sun, Pratardana, son of Divodasa, and Indra and his exploits.

Section 1 with seven verses begins with Chitra Gangayani (elsewhere Gargayani) who wants to perform a sacrifice. He

chooses Aruni to perform it for him, but Aruni sends his son
Shvetaketu. When Shvetaketu reaches there, Chitra begins by
asking him a question. 'Is there a hidden place in the world in which
you would place me? Or is there another way, and will you place
me in that world?' Shvetaketu does not know what he is talking
about, and returns to ask Aruni. Aruni does not know either, and
suggests they both study with Chitra. They then go to Chitra and
ask him to teach them (1.1). Chitra then explains the doctrine
of rebirth through the two paths, pitriyana and devayana (1.2).
Through devayana or the path of the gods, the person reaches
the worlds of various gods, first that of Agni, then of Vayu, then
of Varuna, then of Aditya, then of Indra, then of Prajapati and
finally of Brahma. The world of Brahma is elaborately described,
and includes the lake Ara, the moments *yeshtika* (those moments
when desires are subdued) and the river Vijara (the ageless), the
tree Ilya, the city Salajya, the residence Aparajita, the hall Vibhu,
the throne Vichakshana and the seat Amitaujas. There are two
doorkeepers, Indra and Prajapati, and two mothers, Manasi and
Chakshushi, who are called the weavers of the worlds. Brahma
himself welcomes the person reaching here, and says that as he has
reached this timeless river, he will never grow old. As the person
crosses through the different aspects of this Brahma world, each of
which represent certain attributes, he is freed from opposites and
reaches Brahman (1.4, etc.).

Section 2 (fifteen verses) begins by stating that Kaushitaki used
to say that Prana is Brahma. Paingya, too, used to say the same
thing. It goes on to describe how to attain the highest treasure or
even one's beloved. It describes the inner agnihotra (fire sacrifice)
of self-restraint, according to Pratardana, and explains that the
uktha (recitation) is Brahman. This is what Shushka Bhringara
used to say. Therefore, one should meditate on it as the *Rik*,
Yajus and Saman (that is, types of verses and prose passages) as
shri (beauty), yashas (glory) and tejas (splendour). It then refers

to the sacrificial ritual and says the adhvaryu priest 'prepares this self which is related to the sacrifice and which consists of works'.[2] The one who knows the self of three-fold knowledge becomes the self of Indra.

One should worship the sun every day for the removal of sins, as Kaushitaki used to, and the new moon for prosperity. The full moon should be worshipped with the prayer beginning: 'You are King Soma, the wise . . .' The chapter also refers to how Brahman shines when the fire blazes, when the sun is seen and at other times, including when one speaks, hears and sees.

Section 3 has links with the *Rig Veda*. It begins with Pratardana, the son of Divodasa, visiting Indra. The god Indra asks him to choose a boon but Pratardana asked Indra to choose for him. After first refusing, Indra said that the most beneficial boon was that Pradardana should know him, Indra. He, Indra, had killed the three-headed son of Tvashtr and delivered the Arunmukhas, the ascetics, to the wolves. He had killed the Prahladas in the sky, the Paulomas in the atmosphere and the Kalakanjas on the earth, yet not a hair of his was injured. Hence, the one who knows Indra can never be injured.

Next, Indra explains that he is the prana and the wisdom self (prajna-atma). So whoever worships him as life and immortality reaches his full life-span in this world and is indestructible in the heavenly world.

Divodasa is referred to in the *Rig Veda*, while Indra is the most important god in that text. Indra's exploits mentioned here are also referred to in that text.

Section 4, however, leaves behind the *Rig Veda* and instead contains explanations of Brahman as explained by Ajatashatru. It begins with an account of Gargya Balaki, who was learned in the scriptures. He had lived among the Ushinaras, Matsyas and Kashi-Videhas. He comes to Ajatashatru, king of Kashi, and says that he will teach him about Brahman. Ajatashatru says he will give him

1000 cows. Hearing something like this, people start calling for Janaka. (King Janaka was known for his wisdom.)

Balaki successively speaks of meditating on the person in the sun, the moon, thunder, air (vayu), space (akasha), fire (agni), water, the mirror, shadow, the echo, sound, a dream, the body, the right eye and the left eye, but Ajatashatru rejects all these as not leading to the true Self. Ajatashatru then asks who it is through which all that Balaki mentions can be known.

Balaki then approaches Ajatashatru as a teacher. Ajatashatru says that it is contrary to nature that a kshatriya should have a brahmana as a pupil, but begins his lesson by taking him to the sleeping King Soma, whom he wakes up by poking him with a stick. Where was this person while he was asleep? In the channels within the body called hita, extending from the heart, which have a thin essence coloured white, red, yellow or black; there one remains even when a person is in dreamless sleep. Ajatashatru then explains the essential unity of the Self. When Indra understood the unity of the true self, he remained unconquered.

Taittiriya Upanishad

The *Taittiriya*, another early Upanishad, belongs to the Taittiriya school of the *Yajur Veda* and is attached to the *Taittiriya Samhita*, that is, the Krishna or *Black Yajur Veda*. It consists of parts 7–9 of the *Taittiriya Aranayaka*, and this Aranyaka is part of the *Taittiriya Brahmana*. Stephen Phillips dates it chronologically after the *Brihadaranyaka*, *Chhandogya* and *Isha*, probably around the sixth century BCE. Winternitz, Paul Deussen, Olivelle and others generally date the *Isha* later. Among the important commentaries on this ancient text is that of Shankara, who divided it into three sections known as *valli*s. Sayana has also commented on this text and names the first section the Samhita Upanishad as it also refers to Samhita (combination). However, Shankara's commentary has more value.

Taittiriya comes from the word 'tittiri', a partridge, also the name of a Vedic rishi.[3]

Of the three sections, the first is the *Shiksha Valli*, the second *Brahmananda Valli* and the third *Bhrigu Valli*. The first section has a series of prayers and explains various mystic syllables. It ends with instructions to students who have completed their studies to speak the truth, follow the path of virtue and look upon their mothers, fathers, teachers and guests as god. The second section explains the nature of Brahman, who is the source of all. One who knows the bliss of Brahman is free of all fear. In the third section, Bhrigu, the son of Varuna, approaches his father and asks him to teach him the nature of Brahman. In a series of lessons, Varuna explains how everything is Brahman. This Upanishad also contains a description of the pancha-kosha, or five bodies of a person.

The beginning invocation asks for blessings from the Vedic deities Mitra, Varuna, Aryaman, Indra, Brihaspati and Vishnu. It praises the god Brahma and the god Vayu, which it identifies with the visible Brahman. In continuity it says, 'I will speak of Brahman, of ritam, and of satyam.' Finally, it asks for protection and ends like all other invocations, with 'Om, Shanti, Shanti, Shantih'.

Shiksha Valli: The *Shiksha Valli* has twelve *anuvaka*s or topics. Though shiksha is later translated as imparting learning or teaching, in Vedic times shiksha had the specific meaning of phonetics or pronunciation. The second verse or anuvaka states that this section will explain shiksha or pronunciation in the context of sound, pitch, quantity, force, modulation and combination (Samhita). It then explains Samhita or combination in five categories: the worlds, heavenly lights, knowledge, progeny and the human body. Thus, this Upanishad has some diverse topics. Meditating on these five would lead to union with them, including with the light of Brahman (1.3.6). This section also has some beautiful prayers and is closely connected with the Vedic Samhitas.

The text states that Om is the best of the Vedic hymns and
assumes all forms (1.4.1). The composer also prays that Indra may
provide him with wisdom and that he may attain immortality.

Worldly desires, however, are intermixed with the immortal
quest, thus, 1.4.3 starts with the lines:

'May I become famous among men, Svaha!'

'May I become richer than the rich, Svaha!'

The next topic is the four mystical utterances, that is, bhu,
bhuvah, suvah and mahah. These are *vyahritis*, that is, words used
in rituals.

The fourth vyahriti, which is mahah, the text says, became
known to the son of Mahachamanasa.

Maha represents Om, Brahman, the Self and the sun or the
moon. Bhu is the earth, fire and the prana (breath). Bhuvah is the
mid-region, the air and apana (a type of prana). Suvah is the world
beyond, the sun and the vyana (a type of prana).

The next topic is the contemplation of Brahman.

An important verse here describes the space (akasha) within
the heart, where the immortal, luminous Purusha dwells. This
verse also describes the Sushumna, the secret channel in the spine,
which moves upwards to the top of the head. However, it says the
Sushumna is the path to realize Indra, but finally the soul, passing
through the Sushumna, goes through fire, represented by bhu; air,
represented by bhuvah; the sun, represented by suvah; and then
rests in Brahman, represented by mahah. Becoming Brahman, he
attains everything (1.6.1).

Next, categories of five are discussed (1.7.1): five parts of the
universe, five deities of nature, five elements, five pranas, five sense
organs, etc.

Following this, Om is identified with Brahman. Thus, 'when
a Vedic teacher desires to attain Brahman', he says Om (1.8.1).

This section concludes with the basic ethics that should be
practised on this path, which include the learning and teaching of

the Vedas, being devoted to the truth, following the right path and performing social duties. It mentions certain teachers and their views. For instance, Satyavachas of the line of Rathitara says truth alone should be practised, Taponitya, the son of Purushisti, says only austerity (tapas) is required, while Naka, son of Mudgalya, says only the learning and teaching of the Veda is important.

The tenth section refers to Trishanku after he attains the knowledge of Brahman. He then describes himself as an indestructible shining treasure, pure and immortal (1.10.1). The eleventh section provides instructions to the departing student, while the twelfth concludes with an invocation.

Brahmananda Valli: Brahman is certainly the focus of this Upanishad. The second valli begins with the invocation 'sah nau avatu' and states that the one who knows Brahman attains the Supreme. Brahman is reality, knowledge and infinity, hidden in the cave of the heart and in the highest akasha (2.1.3). It also discusses food and explains the five bodies of man and compares the manomaya kosha with the four Vedic Samhitas (2.3.2). Within is the vijnana kosha and further within the ananda kosha.

Brahman (2.7.1) is described as the self-created and as satya (the true), who was one, but became many (2.6.1).

Next, the bliss of Brahman is explained. It is hundreds of times more than anything that can be experienced. The one who knows it loses all fear (2.9.1).

Bhrigu Valli: In the third valli, Bhrigu, son of Varuna, asks his father about Brahman. After practising austerities (tapas) he understands that Brahman is bliss (ananda). Further verses are practical, stating that the knower should not abandon food (3.8.1) and should provide food and lodging to anyone who requires it (3.10.1). Next, various meditations on Brahman are prescribed.

Kena Upanishad

The *Kena Upanishad* belongs to the *Sama Veda* and forms the ninth chapter of the *Talavakra Brahmana*, and therefore is also known as the *Talavakra Upanishad*. The first eight chapters of the *Talavakra Brahmana* include rituals and meditation to purify the Self. These chapters provide the basic training for the individual to understand Brahman, revealed in the Upanishad forming the ninth chapter. The Upanishad is in both verse and prose, and possibly the prose sections are earlier. The text probably belongs to around the fifth century BCE. Based on relative dating, Philips feels it is later than the *Brihadaranyaka*, *Chhandogya*, *Isha*, *Taittiriya* and *Aitareya*, which can be dated before the sixth century BCE. Others, however, place the *Isha* at a later date. The *Kena* has an extensive commentary of Shankara. It gets its name from the first word of the text, that is, 'Kena' (by whom).

This Upanishad describes the nature of Brahman, superior to all the devas or gods, who can be personalized as Ishvara. It explains that Brahman is the source of all life and knowledge. The Upanishad has four khandas or sections. Khanda 1 has nine verses. The first verse puts forward the questions that sets the tone of the Upanishad. It asks, 'By whom [kena] is the mind directed to go towards its objects? By whom does the prana [vital breath], which precedes everything, perform its functions? By whom is the speech that people speak directed? Which deva directs the eyes and ears?'

This Upanishad thus seeks to understand a hidden mystery about the power behind our actions. The commentary explains that these questions are put forward by a sadhak, an aspirant for the truth, who has purified his consciousness through action (karma) and worship (upasana), and sees that there is something behind all this that he does not know. Shankara says that the guru will reveal the answer to the one who is fit to receive and understand it. The second verse explains how He (Brahman) is the power who directs these functions, and those who renounce the world can understand it. Further verses explain that That Reality (Brahman) is different from both the known and the unknown. It cannot be revealed by speech, understood by the mind, seen, heard or smelt, yet it is that by which all these actions take place. Section 2, with five verses, continues with the same theme. It explains that those who think they know Brahman do not really know it; they only know its form as conditioned by people or by gods. But the one who says 'I know, yet I do not know' is on the verge of discovering Brahman as he has recognized that the 'I' cannot know. The third verse has the paradoxical statement 'It is known to whom it is unknown', but Shankara explains this. It can be known only to the one who has no trace of individuality left, who has no sense of duality. At the same time, the fourth verse explains that Brahman is known by the one who understands it as the source of every action. When Brahman pervades consciousness, only That is seen and nothing else. Shankara also refutes the different interpretations of these verses. The fifth verse states that when the atman is realized (its identity as Brahman), then it attains immortality.

As Brahman is difficult to understand, the third section, which has twelve verses, explains it through a story.

It refers to a victory of the devas in the past. They think they have won but actually it is Brahman who has won the victory for them. To reveal himself to them, Brahman then appears in the form of a yaksha (divine spirit), but they do not know who he is. They ask first Agni and then Vayu to find out, but they cannot. When asked about their power, Agni says he can burn the whole world, and Vayu that he can blow off everything on the earth. But neither can burn or blow a single straw presented by the yaksha. Next, Indra is asked to find out who the yaksha is, but when he goes towards it, it vanishes, and Uma, daughter of the Himalayas, appears in its place. Here, Brahman is personified and acts, taking the form of a yaksha and then of Uma.

The fourth section with nine verses begins by Uma telling Indra that Brahman is the yaksha, the great spirit. The gods too do not know Brahman. Since Indra is the first to know Brahman, he is greater than all the other gods. Agni and Vayu are greater than the rest as they are the next to know Brahman. The fourth verse in this section explains that those who cannot experience the formless Brahman can meditate on some aspect of it, while the fifth suggests inner meditation to understand Brahman. The mind, which goes in all directions, is compared with Brahman, which is everywhere. The sixth verse provides Brahman with a mystical name and says that the individual mind communicates with Brahman, who is called Tadvana, adored by all. In the seventh and eighth verses, the teacher affirms he has conveyed the secret knowledge concerning Brahman. He adds that austerities, self-restraint and sacrificial rites are its feet, the Vedas its limbs, truth its abode.

One who knows this Upanishad is established in the highest heaven, says the Upanishad in conclusion.

Six

Early Upanishads: 2

Katha Upanishad

THE *KATHA UPANISHAD*, a verse Upanishad, can be dated between 600 and 400 BCE. It is also known as the *Kathaka Upanishad*. Scholars differ about whether it is pre or post the development of early Buddhism. Deussen believes it is of around the same date as the Kena, while Winternitz and Phillips see it as pre-Buddhist. Richard King,[1] however, places it after the composition of the early Buddhist Pali Canon. The *Katha Upanishad* is usually associated with the Taittiriya shakha of the *Yajur Veda*. The *Taittiriya Brahmana*, attached to the *Taittiriya Samhita (Yajur Veda)*, has a similar story about Nachiketa as is contained in this Upanishad. However, the text is sometimes said to belong to the *Sama Veda* or even to the *Atharva Veda*. The text has two chapters or parts, each with three sections, and numerous commentaries, including that of Shankara, representing Advaita. Ramanuja has not commented on the entire text but on parts of it in his work *Shribhashya*. Madhva too has a commentary on it.

This is one of the most popular Upanishads as it presents its philosophy through a coherent story. As usual, the main theme is Brahman. The explanation here is easier to access because it is presented through the story of Nachiketa, a pious boy. The text also describes the atman, Purusha, which can be identified with Brahman, the nadis or channels of inner energy, and prana, the vital breath.

Chapter 1: Nachiketa's father, the rishi Vajashravasa, performs a sacrificial ritual which involves giving away his wealth. Seeing his father offering old and barren cows to brahmanas, Nachiketa feels this sacrifice has not been performed in the right spirit. He knows he is dear to his father, and so he questions him, saying, 'To whom then will you give me?' He asks again and again till the angry father says, 'I will give you to death (Mrityu)'. The boy dutifully goes to the house of Yama, the god of death, who happens to be away. He waits for him for three days, and when he returns, Yama, in apology for his absence, grants him three boons. For the first boon, Nachiketa asks that his father be pacified. For the second, Nachiketa asks for knowledge of the fire (Agni) that leads to heaven and immortality, and Yama teaches him the fire sacrifice, which is then named after him. For the third boon, Nachiketa says, 'There is that doubt when a man is dead—some say he is, some say he is not—this I should like to know.' Then Yama teaches him the truth about life and death, and about the atman, knowing which all is known and neither grief nor fear remain. In this text, the god of death is referred to as both Mrityu and Yama.

The most important part of the *Katha* is Yama's explanation in response to Nachiketa's question about whether or not a person exists after death (1.1.21). At first, Yama refuses to answer this. Choose another boon, he says, as even the gods used to have doubts about this. He suggests that Nachiketa choose elephants, horses, cattle or gold, or a long life, or rule over the earth. He offers him beautiful women with their chariots and musical instruments that mortals cannot otherwise obtain. But Nachiketa rejects all these offers, saying that these are all temporary. Once again he asks for knowledge 'of the great hereafter about which a man has his doubts' (1.1.29, trans. Swami Nikhilananda).

Yama is pleased. He explains the difference between the good and the pleasant (1.2.1). The calm soul, he says, always chooses the good, but fools choose the pleasant out of greed. They do not even think of the hereafter and there are many who have not heard of the atman. There are others who have heard of it but do not understand it. The one who can explain it is wonderful, and the one who hears and understands it is rare. The atman must be taught by one who has become one with it; it cannot be known by reasoning or argument (1.2.8–9). (Shankara, though, in certain passages says Brahman can be known through reason and discrimination.) Posing the same question in a different way, Nachiketa says: 'That which you see as different from righteousness and unrighteousness, different from cause and effect, different from what has been and what is to be—Tell me That' (1.2.14).

Yama then explains that the syllable Om is the same as Brahman. This is the goal of the Vedas and that desired by those who follow brahmacharya (1.2.16–17).

Three verses follow (1.2.18–20) which are similar to those in the Bhagavad Gita. They state that the atman is not born and does not die. It has not come from anything and nothing arises from it. It is without birth, eternal, ancient, and does not die when the body dies. It cannot be killed and it does not kill. The atman, which is smaller than the smallest and bigger than the biggest, is hidden in the hearts of all living beings. One who has controlled the senses and is free of desires sees it and becomes free from sorrow (The term used is *dhatuprasadat*, which Shankara explains as 'the vision obtained through the tranquility of the senses and the mind'. However, dualists explain it as 'through the grace of the creator'.)

The text continues with the description of the atman. Even when sitting it goes far, and lying it goes everywhere, indicating that the atman is everywhere even without moving. At the same time the atman is within the living being, and only one's own self can know the atman, which both rejoices and does not rejoice (1.2.21). The wise man who has realized the atman does not grieve (1.2.22).

The text goes on to explain who can attain the atman. It cannot be attained by one who studies the Vedas, nor by intelligence, nor by listening to sacred texts. The atman is attained by the one who chooses it above all else. The person seeking the atman should be ethical and tranquil.

Further explanations of the atman follow. The body is like a chariot, the buddhi (intellect) the charioteer, the mind the reins, the horses the senses and various objects the road. The role of each is described, but it is the atman who is the master of the chariot (1.3.3–4).

1.3.9 mentions the supreme place of Vishnu, reached by one who uses his intelligence (vijnana) as the charioteer and the mind as the reins. Here, as the commentary explains, it is not Vishnu's heaven Vaikuntha that is meant, but Vishnu in his aspect as the Paramatman or Supreme soul.

Succeeding verses explain that the great Self, the mahan atman, is beyond the intellect or buddhi. Beyond the great Self, also termed mahat, is the unmanifested (avyakta), beyond that is the Purusha, and beyond the Purusha is nothing. The atman is hidden in all beings but can only be seen by those with a subtle intellect. The atman is eternal. It is without sound, touch, taste or smell; it does not decay. Realizing it, one has transcended death.

Here the term Purusha is used in the same sense as Brahman.

Chapter 2: In the second chapter, Yama explains that the self-created (svayambhu) Supreme lord created the senses with outgoing tendencies, but wise souls do not look outwards. Everything is known and experienced only through the atman, and the one who knows the atman grieves no more. It also states that the one who knows Brahman also knows Aditi, the soul of all devatas (deities), who was born as Prana. (Aditi has been translated as 'the enjoyer or experiencer of all objects' by Shankara; it also means 'the one who is not bound'; and Prana is said to represent Hiranyagarbha. In the *Rig Veda*, Aditi is the mother of the gods.)

Further verses state that Brahman can be realized only by the mind. The Purusha, which is the size of the thumb, is like a flame without smoke. It is always the same, and is the lord of the past, present and future (2.2.13). Those who see Brahman as different from its attributes focus on those and not on the source.

There is more on the atman in Section 2, where, it is said there is a city with eleven gates (the body with eleven apertures), and within is the atman. The one who meditates on it attains liberation. It is the sun in the bright heavens, the air in the mid regions, and fire on earth. Prana and apana cannot alone sustain the body, they depend on the eternal Brahman. The Purusha is also identified with the pure Brahman. It remains awake while the sense organs sleep and all worlds are within it. When the one, eternal reality is realized, there is an indescribable supreme joy. There the sun does not shine, nor the moon or stars, nor lightning, nor fire. Everything is lighted by his shining light (2.2.15).

The third section refers to the eternal Ashvattha tree, with its roots above and its branches below, and how everything comes from Brahman, that is seen everywhere. The senses have their own origin and they are not the same as the atman, and when the individual realizes this, there is no more grief. Beyond the senses is the mind, beyond the mind is the intellect, beyond the intellect is the great atman, higher than the great atman is the unmanifest (2.3.6–7). Beyond the unmanifest is the Purusha, all pervading and imperceptible.

The text also refers to the 101 nadis of the heart, one of which pierces the crown. If the prana rises upward through it at the time of death, a person attains immortality. It refers to the Purusha, no larger than a thumb, which is the inner Self in the hearts of people. That Self is bright and immortal.

Nachiketa understood all that had been taught by Mrityu and attained Brahman. Anyone who understands this and gains a knowledge of the inner Self will also attain Brahman.

Isha Upanishad

The *Isha Upanishad* forms the fortieth chapter and the last of the *Vajasaneyi Samhita* of the *Shukla Yajur Veda*. The *Isha* in this sense is different from other Upanishads, as it forms part of a Samhita, not a Brahmana or Aranyaka. This is the reason for some scholars assigning it a very early date. This verse Upanishad is often dated between about 600 and 300 BCE. Radhakrishnan, however, feels it is one of the earliest, belonging to the eighth to seventh century BCE, and that it is pre-Buddhist in nature. Phillips, too, assigns it an early date. However, even though it is placed within a Samhita, as a verse Upanishad it is likely to be later. This short Upanishad of eighteen verses contains the essence of Upanishadic philosophy. The text has passages that are difficult to interpret and have been variously explained by different schools of philosophy. Shankara's introduction to this states that the atman is not connected to actions, it is not something to be attained through action. But actions are prescribed for people according to their level. Those who want or seek the results of actions in this world or even those who want to enjoy heaven can perform actions. Only those who want to destroy ignorance, remove sorrow and attain supreme bliss are in the right state to read this Upanishad.

Shankarananda, too, among others, has commented on this Upanishad.

Among more recent scholars, Sri Aurobindo has an extensive commentary on this text.[2]

'Ishavasyam', the first word in the text, can be translated as 'covered by Isha' (god). The first verse states that as everything in the world is covered by god, one should not cling to or covet anything. The second verse says that those who wish to act in the world and live for the full lifespan of a 100 years should perform actions according to the scriptures. No work is attached to the person who does this. As the third verse states, those who are ignorant of this have killed their souls. The following verses, 4–8, describe Brahman and the atman. The Supreme, though it stands still and is unmoving, is always ahead, faster than the fastest. It moves and yet it does not move. It is near and yet it is far. It is inside and also outside. And the one who can see all living beings in his own Self, and his own self in all, becomes free from all care and disturbance. He (the supreme spirit) who is radiant, pure, self-existent, all pervading, has no body, yet is in every living being.

Verses 9–11 condemn both ignorance and knowledge. Both avidya or ignorance and vidya or worldly knowledge are inadequate. Transcending both, one reaches immortality. The next two (Verses 12–14) refute both becoming and non-becoming. It is only by transcending both that the supreme can be reached.

The Upanishad also deals with the unity of god and the world, and with the paths of action and contemplation that should be united in one's life. The last few verses contain a prayer that is used even today in funeral rites. It states:

The face of truth is covered with a golden disc. Unveil it, O Pushan, so that I who love the truth may see it.
O Pushan, the sole seer, O Controller, O Sun (Surya), offspring of Prajapati, spread forth your rays and gather up your radiant light that I may behold you of loveliest form. Whosoever is that person (yonder) that also am I.

May this life enter into the immortal breath; then may
this body end in ashes. O Intelligence (kratu), remember,
remember what has been done. Remember, O Intelligence
what has been done, Remember.

O Agni, lead us, along the auspicious path to prosperity,
O god, who knowest all our deeds. Take away from us
deceitful sins. We shall offer many prayers to thee (Verses
15–18, trans. S. Radhakrishnan).

Shvetashvatara Upanishad

The *Shvestashvatara Upanishad* is dated between the sixth and
fourth centuries BCE. This Upanishad is of the Taittiriya school of
the *Krishna Yajur Veda*.

Swami Veda Bharati dates it to somewhere around the time of
the *Katha Upanishad*.

References by Shankara and others indicate that this
Upanishad was actually composed by an individual. The Upanishad
is named after Shvetashvatara, the rishi who taught it. The name
literally means, 'He who owns a white mule.' Paul Deussen feels
that though it has individual characteristics, it was added to by
others. He dates the Upanishad after the *Katha*, which this often
refers to, and provides a comparison of these. In addition, the
Shvetashvatara provides a definite form to some Vedantic ideas
which were incompletely developed earlier. The explanation of the
world as maya also occurs for the first time in this text (4.9–10,
1.10). But at the same time the text quotes from the Vedas and
identifies Brahman with Ishana, Isha or Rudra. The identification
of Rudra with Shiva does not take place in early texts and is not
clear in this one either, though Shiva is mentioned seven times as
an adjective. The relationship of the Upanishad with Samkhya is
another aspect. The *Katha* also has many pre-Samkhya passages.
The *Shvetashvatara* has a number of concepts and terms used

in Samkhya: Purusha, pradhana, avyaktam, vyaktam, the three gunas, lingam (6.9), five-fold bhavas (1.4.5). The words Kapila and Samkhya are used in the text (5.2 and 6.13). But the theism of this Upanishad is in contrast to Samkhya. For instance, pradhana is part of devatma shakti, the power of the divine soul. Did this mean that the *Shvetashvatara* already knew the Samkhya system of Kapila? Deussen thinks not,[3] but that the Samkhya system arose out of the thinking of the times, reflected in this Upanishad. This Upanishad is thus an important source for the Samkhya system.

The text has a commentary by Shankara, though there are some doubts about whether this was really his, though the style is similar. Swami Veda Bharati points out that though the *Muktika Upanishad* implies that the Shanti Mantra is 'sah navavatu . . .', Shankara gives it as 'purnam-adah'. But most traditions agree that it belongs to the *Krishna Yajur Veda*. Like the *Katha*, *Maitrayani* and Bhagavad Gita, the *Shvetashvatara* is syncretic. It can be interpreted to support Samkhya or Vedanta or to see the two schools as part of one. Commenting on this Upanishad, Shankara elaborates on Samkhya philosophy in 1.4.

The language is pre-classical; it is between Vedic and classical. Many of the verses in this are found in the Vedas, Bhagavad Gita and other Upanishads.

The text has six chapters, with 113 verses. It states that Brahman has a three-fold nature, as Ishvara or god, the atma or individual soul, and prakriti or nature. Ishvara is identified with Rudra (later Shiva), who is the creator of the world, as well as its protector and guide. Rudra is described as a dweller in the mountains, with an auspicious (shiva) body. The Supreme person (Ishvara) has the colour of the sun. He is all-pervading, dwells in the heart of all beings, and is Bhagavan (god). He is the whole world, the lord of immortality, and all that was and will be. This could be called a composite Upanishad reconciling different views.

Adhyaya 1 has sixteen verses. The first verse begins with a statement about the questions people ask when discussing Brahman, such as what is the cause? Is it Brahman? From where are we born? Who presides over our pleasures and pains?

The text goes on to ask whether nature, fate, chance, the elements, the womb or the cosmic person (Purusha) could be the cause of existence. This, or their combination, does not seem likely. Nor could it be the individual atma or soul, which is subject to joy and sorrow. But it is through meditation that the non-dual creator, with its luminous creative power that is hidden in its own gunas, the self-power of the divine (devatma-shakti) can be realized. (According to Veda Bharati in the oral tradition, devatma-shakti is the Kundalini, and the related power that can be conveyed through shakti-pata [xiii].)

The next few verses describe the Self in various ways, comparing its different elements with a spoked wheel and a river. The great wheel of Brahman gives life to everything. The ninth verse has been extensively commented upon by Shankara. It states that the knower and the one who does not know, god and non-god, are both eternal. Does this imply dualism? Shankara explains it is not so, but others interpret it as dualistic. Verse 10 says that Pradhana (matter) is perishable but Hara (Shiva) is immortal. Uniting with him, the illusion of the world disappears.

Verses 13–16 describe a meditation with a simile of using Om as the fuel stick, with the body as the lower stick, which then reveals the true Self, just as fire emerges from the fuel sticks. This analogy is found in other Upanishads too.

Adhyaya 2 has seventeen verses. The first five verses begin with a prayer to the god Savitr (Savita). (Also in *Vajasaneyi Samhita* 11.1-5, *Taittiriya Samhita* 4.1.1.) The prayer is an offering that helps to focus the mind and reason on god. Prayer is a force that helps to arouse Shakti or divine power.

Verses 6–7 deal with ritual, stating that when Agni arises from the fuel sticks, Vayu and Soma too make their appearance. Through this, the mind becomes focused. Verses 8–15 deal with aspects of asanas and pranayama that form part of yoga, while the last two verses (16 and 17) describe the all-pervading deva (god). As Shankara makes it clear in his commentary, prayer, ritual, asana and pranayama are only preliminary practices to enable the person to then focus on Brahman.

Adhyaya 3 has twenty-one verses. Verses 1–6 state that Rudra or Isha is the atman residing in all beings. At the same time, he rules the whole world with his sovereign power. Rudra is described in similar terms to Rig 10.181.3. He has eyes, faces, arms and feet on all sides. It is said that all the gods arise from him, and he even created Hiranyagarbha. He is the dweller in the mountains and their protector. He carries an arrow in his hand and the request is that the arrow may not hurt man or beast.

Succeeding verses (7–21) continue with a description of Brahman. Brahman is the highest and greatest, within each being and yet containing the whole universe. Brahman is also identified with Purusha. There are verses here which occur in the *Nilarudra Upanishad* (8.5), the *Maha-Narayana*, the *Rig Veda*, and which have similarities with the *Katha*. In several verses, the text describes the Purusha, that illuminates everything like the sun and is higher than the world. It is without form and without sorrow. It dwells in the heart of all living beings. The twenty-first and last verse is a personal one, beginning, 'I know him, that ancient ageless one.'

The fourth adhyaya with twenty-one verses describes Brahman in different ways. He is equated with Rudra, is the lord of all, unborn and eternal. The last verse again appeals to Rudra not to harm them, their children, cattle and horses. Again there are passages similar or identical to other texts, including the *Chhandogya*, *Katha* and *Maha-Narayana* Upanishads.

The fifth adhyaya with fourteen verses shows how one reaches Brahman by moving from ignorance to knowledge. It describes Brahman as the one who presides over everything and also as the individual soul or atman. The secret of Brahman is hidden in the Veda and Upanishad (5.6). It appears in the heart, the size of a thumb, shining like the sun (5.8).

The sixth adhyaya with twenty-three verses again describes Brahman. It ends with three personal verses, saying that after practising austerities, favoured by Veda or by deva, Shvetashvatara found Brahman and taught it to the group of rishis who had transcended the ashramas (the four stages of life). This highest secret was transmitted in the Vedanta in the ancient past. It should not be taught to one who is not calm, or who is not a son or a pupil.

Mundaka Upanishad

This Upanishad can be dated between the sixth and third centuries BCE and belongs to the *Atharva Veda*. Patrick Olivelle feels it is post-early Buddhism. It has three chapters or sections and is related to the *Prashna Upanishad*. Its commentaries include those of Shankara and Madhva.

The *Mundaka* is also known for the term 'satyameva jayate' (3.1.6) meaning 'truth will prevail'. This forms India's motto and is part of the national emblem.

Chapter 1: This has two parts. The first section with nine verses begins by stating that Brahma, the first of the gods, taught the knowledge of Brahman to his eldest son, Atharvan, who conveyed it to Angir. Angir taught it to Satyavaha of the Bharadvaja clan, who conveyed it to Angiras. Then Shaunaka approaches Angiras. He asks what is that by the knowing of which all things become known. Angiras describes two kinds of knowledge, the lower and the higher, the former of the world and the latter of Brahman. He states that the knowledge of Brahman is greater than the path of the Vedas, which advocates rituals and sacrifices. Brahman is imperishable (aksharam), luminous, subtler than the subtle. It is speech, life and mind, immortality and truth. (Those who worship Brahman go beyond life and death, but those who have desires are reborn.)

The second section with thirteen verses discusses the sacrificial rituals described in the Vedas and how they should be practised to achieve the desired results. The seven flames, Kali, Karali, Manojava, Sulohita, Sudhumravarna, Sphulingini and the luminous Vishvaruchi are mentioned. The good deeds of performing rituals lead to the heaven of Brahma. But even these sacrifices conducted by eighteen persons (sixteen priests, the sacrificer and his wife) can be destroyed, and consist of inferior works. Those who practise these rituals along with humanitarian works get their reward in heaven but then they are reborn.

Other wise men live in the forest and focus on deities such as Hiranyagarbha. They depart by the path of the sun, to the place where the imperishable person dwells (Saguna Brahman). After looking at all these worlds gained by works, a brahmana should focus on freedom from desires. For nothing eternal can be attained by something that is not eternal. Then he should approach a guru, with fuel in hand, who knows the Vedas and has a knowledge of Brahman, and learn from him.

Chapter 2: This chapter also has two sections. The first section, which has ten verses, begins by stating that the truth is that everything comes from Brahman and returns to it again. Brahman is that self-luminous and formless Purusha, uncreated, existing within and without. It has neither prana nor mind and is pure, higher than Saguna Brahman.

It again reiterates that everything comes from Brahman, including the Vedas, the kratus, the worlds, devas, sadhyas, men, cattle, birds, prana and apana, rice, grain, penance, faith, truth, continence and law, as well as the oceans, mountains and rivers, the plants and everything else.

The Purusha alone is the universe, supreme and immortal, hidden in the cave of the heart.

The second section, with twelve verses, continues with the description of Brahman, radiant and seated in the cave of the heart, the supporter of everything. Everything shines by its light and it pervades everything.

Chapter 3: Section 1 begins with the analogy, also found in other texts, of two birds living on the same tree. One eats the sweet fruit, but the other watches. The first is the jiva, bewildered by its own helplessness, but when it sees the other, the Supreme Self, it becomes free from grief (3.1).

This section has some beautiful passages on Brahman. It refers to the atman, resplendent and pure, whom the sinless sannyasis behold residing within the body, which is attained by unceasing practice of truthfulness, austerity, right knowledge and continence (3.1.5). It is seen here dwelling in the cave of the heart of conscious beings (3.1.7).

Section 2 also continues with descriptions of the atman and Brahman. It states that the atman cannot be attained through the study of the Vedas, nor through intelligence, nor through much learning. He who chooses the atman, by him alone is the atman attained (3.2.3). The atman, in addition, cannot be attained by one who is without strength or earnestness or who is without knowledge accompanied by renunciation. But if a wise man strives by means of these aids, his soul enters the abode of Brahman (3.2.4). The last verse states that Angiras declared this truth in olden times.

Prashna Upanishad

The *Prashna Upanishad* belongs to the *Atharva Veda* and is connected with the *Mundaka Upanishad*. The text has six chapters, classified as six prashnas or questions. Brahman, Prana and the nadis are among the topics discussed.

Prashna 1 with sixteen verses begins with a group of rishis devoted to Brahman seeking answers from the rishi Pippalada. (This Brahman is obviously the lower, Saguna Brahman.) The group consists of Sukesha, the son of Bharadvaja; Satyakama, the son of Shibi; Sauryayani, of the family of Garga; Kausalya, the son of Ashvala; Vaidarbhi of the family of Bhrigu; Kabandhi, the son of Katya.

Pippalada asks them to remain with him one year, practising austerities, chastity and faith, and then to question him.

After a year Kabandhi asks the first question, From where are creatures born? Pippalada explains that Prajapati created rayi and prana, that is, matter and life. The sun is identified with prana or life and the moon with rayi or matter. Rayi is also translated as food. This section also describes pitriyana and devayana, the two paths to the other world.

In Prashna 2, Vaidarbhi puts forth the question: How many gods support the body of the created being? How many display their power through it? And which is the highest? He replied that akasha (space) is that deva or god. The others are Vayu, Agni, Ap, Prithivi (wind, fire, water, earth), as well as speech, mind, eye and ear. Then prana shows that with its five divisions it is the main support of the body as nothing can exist without it.

Prana is then described and praised. As spokes in a wheel, all are fixed in prana, including the *Rig Veda*, *Yajur Veda*, *Sama Veda*, kshatriyas and brahmanas (2.6). Prana moves in the womb as Prajapati, and offerings are made to it. It represents the true activities of the rishis and of the Atharva-Angiras. Prana is Indra, Rudra and the Protector. The text says, 'You are the vratya, O Prana, and the Ekarshi fire that consumes the butter. You are the Supreme Lord of all, We are the givers of the butter that you consume, O Matarishva. You are our father (2.11).' Continuing with the same theme it states that everything that exists here and in heaven is under the control of prana.

In Prashna 3, Kausalya asks Pippalada, from where is prana born? How does it come into the body? How does it stay there after it has divided itself? How does it support the external and the internal?

Pippalada begins his reply by saying that Kausalya is asking difficult questions, as he must be extremely devoted to Brahman. He continued by saying that prana is born of atman. It comes into the body through the activity of the mind and employs other pranas in their various places. Apana is involved in excretion and generation; it moves through the mouth and nose and resides in the eye and ear (that is, the two eyes, two ears, two nostrils and the organ of speech). Samana is in the middle and equally distributes what has been offered as food. From this prana fire arise the seven flames.

The atman is in the heart where there are 101 nadis. Each of these has 100 branches and each of these in turn has 72,000. Vyana moves in these. Udana ascends upwards through one of the nadis and takes the departing soul to the other world. The sun (Aditya) is the external prana, for it rises favouring the prana in the eye. The earth deity controls the apana. Akasha is samana; fire is udana. Whatever one is thinking at the time of death, with that one enters into prana. Prana, fire and the soul lead to the next world, fashioned by thought.

In Prashna 4, Sauryayani then asks: what sleeps in a person and what remains awake? What deity sees dreams? In whom is the happiness of deep sleep? And in whom are all these together? Pippalada explains that all these are gathered together in the mind. The prana fires remain awake. Apana is the garhaptya fire, vyana the anvaharyapachana fire, and prana the ahavaniya fire. Samana is the priest and udana the fruit of the sacrifice.

In dreams, the mind sees glory but when the jiva is overcome by light, no dreams are seen, and there is happiness. In fact,

Pippalada goes on to explain, all this rests in the Supreme Atman. This includes the elements, the sense organs, the manas, buddhi, ahamkara, chitta and tejas. Behind all this is the Purusha, established in the imperishable atman. The one who knows that being, bright, without shadow or body, without colour, attains the Supreme, the Purusha. The one who knows the atman enters into all.

In Prashna 5, The next question is put forward by Satyakama. He asks that if someone meditates on Om all his life till he dies, which world would he go to? Pippalada explains that Om is the same as Brahman. Even meditating on a single letter of it has great benefits and meditating on all its four syllables together leads to the highest reality.

In Prashna 6, the last question is posed by Sukesha. He says that Hiranyanabha, a prince of Koshala, once asked him if he knew that person with sixteen parts, and he had to reply that he didn't. Who is that person? Pippalada replies it is the Purusha from whom the sixteen parts arise, like the spokes of a wheel, and knowing him a person becomes free of parts and immortal.

Pippalada ends by saying, 'Thus far I know the Supreme Brahman, there is nothing higher than this.' (Trans. Swami Nikhilananda.)

Mandukya Upanishad

The *Mandukya* is one of the most important Upanishads. Though extremely short, with only twelve verses, its importance lies in its lengthy commentary by Gaudapada, which laid the basis for the philosophy of Advaita. As stated earlier, Gaudapada was the teacher of Govinda, who was the teacher of Shankara. This Upanishad gets its name from the rishi Manduka. It is attached to the *Atharva Veda*. The text has been variously dated from around the fifth century BCE to the first century CE. Those such as Mahony, dating it in the fifth to fourth centuries BCE, place

it along with the *Shvetashvatara*, *Prashna*, and *Maitri*. To Patrick
Olivelle, this and the *Prashna* belong to the first century CE.

It elaborates on the nature of Brahman or the Absolute and
the sacred word Om, which represents Brahman. Shankara also
comments on the text and on Gaudapada's Karika or commentary
and further elucidates the basic Advaitic principles.

The text: The Upanishad begins by stating that everything, past,
present and future, is Om, and that Om is the same as Brahman.
Everything is Brahman, including the atman or Self. It goes on to
say that the Self has four parts. The Vaishvanara Self consists of the
jagrita or waking state. In this waking state, consciousness relates
to external things, which has seven limbs and nineteen mouths,
and enjoys gross objects. The second part or quarter is Taijasa,
the dream state, where consciousness is internal, enjoyment is
of subtle objects, and there are again seven limbs and nineteen
mouths. Deep sleep is where the person sees and knows nothing
and does not dream. This third quarter is Prajna, which is a
blissful state. This one (prajna) is the source of all, the antaryamin
(inner controller), the place where all beings have their origin
and dissolution. The fourth quarter is that which is conscious of
neither the internal nor the external world. It is not consciousness,
nor unconsciousness. It is unseen and cannot be thought of or
described. It is unchanging, non-dual and auspicious, and is the
Self, that which should be known. That Self is Om, which has
three letters: a, u, m. Vaishvanara is represented by the letter
'a', because it is the first, and the one who knows this attains all
desirable things and becomes the foremost. Taijasa is represented
by the second letter, 'u', as it is intermediate, and the intermediate
is similar to excellence. The knowledge of those who know this is
heightened and the person becomes equal to all. Everyone born
in this line is a knower of Brahman. Prajna is represented by 'm',
because of 'measuring or because of absorption'. He who knows

this measures all this (the universe) and becomes the place of absorption (that is, the Self). Om, without any parts, represents Turiya, the state beyond all, which is non-dual and auspicious. Om is thus the Self, the atma. The one who knows this enters the (universal) Self through his own self.

This is the brief summary of the twelve verses. Why did Gaudapada choose this to write his Karika or commentary consisting of 253 verses? By commenting on and explaining it, Gaudapada delineates his own philosophy, that of Advaita.

The Karika: Gaudapada's commentary has four parts. The first is the *Agama* with twenty-nine verses which explains the *Mandukya Upanishad* and provides an extensive commentary on the four states of consciousness that are also known and described in other Upanishads.

Gaudapada says that both waking and dreaming states are similar as the objects seen in both are unreal. Only the subject, the constant witness Self, can be real. That which is complete in itself, inborn, and never ceases to be itself, is the only reality, as something subject to change cannot be real. He explains that vishva or the Vaishvanara self enjoys what is gross, Taijasa what is subtle, and Prajna enjoys bliss. When the enjoyer knows these three aspects of enjoyment, he remains beyond them and is not caught in them. While non-perception of duality is common to both Prajna and Turiya, in Turiya there is neither dream not sleep. When the jiva or individual, sleeping under the influence of maya awakes, he realizes Turiya, a state that is non-dual, unborn, beyond sleep or dreams. The three letters of Om lead to Vishva, Taijasa and Prajna, but when one is free from letters, there is nothing to attain. One should concentrate on Om, for Om is Brahman. It is without cause, without inside and outside, without effect. It is beyond measure and infinite. It is Ishvara, seated in the hearts of all. The one who knows Om is the real sage (muni).

The second section, *Vaitathya-prakarana*, has thirty-eight verses. It explains unreality and the phenomenal nature of the world. Just as dream objects are unreal, the objects in the waking state too are unreal (2.4). Anything that has a beginning and an end is unreal. But if all these objects are unreal, who sees them and who is the creator? (2.11). The response is that the shining atma imagines them through its own maya. This is the definite conclusion of Vedanta (2.12). There are things that exist internally as long as the thought of them lasts, and things that exist externally between two points of time. Both are imaginary (2.14). First the jiva is imagined and then other objects. The commentary goes on to say, depending on what people know, they consider various things real—those who know prana think it is real, the same with those who know the Vedas, etc. Some consider time to be real, some the directions, and others have various theories. Some think the mind is real, some dharma and adharma. Some say twenty-five tattvas (principles) are real, some twenty-six or thirty-one, some an infinite number. (These are references to materialists, Buddhists, Mimamsakas, Samkhya, Patanjali, Pashupatas.) Others too think various things are real. If a teacher shows you something, you think that is real. Just as dream and magic are seen to be real, or a city in the sky, so by Vedanta, the whole universe is known to be unreal (2.31). 'There is no dissolution, no origination, none in bondage, none striving or aspiring for salvation, and none liberated. This is the highest truth' (2.32). This verse is found in other Upanishads and is the key to this section as it indicates the total unreality of the world. The next few verses provide methods to realize this. One should continuously fix one's mind on non-duality. In addition, the mendicant (yati) who has renounced the world should have no relationship with others and should not perform any rituals, but should depend only on reality (tattva).

The third section, the *Advaita-prakarana*, has forty-eight verses and lays down the main principles of Advaita. It begins by stating that one who practices upasana or various types of worship reaches the conditioned Brahman. The text goes on to describe the unconditioned Brahman, which is beyond any limitation, using the analogy of spaces within a jar. In his commentary on Gaudapada, Shankara refutes the Samkhya and Vaisheshika views, explaining that a space within a jar is not a transformation of space, and nor really a part of space. In the same way an individual is neither a transformation of nor a part of the Supreme Self. Jars have different shapes, thus so does the space within them, but in reality the space in each one is the same. Similarly in the living being, the soul that is contained within the koshas (sheaths or bodies), as explained in the *Taittiriya Upanishad*, is none other than the Supreme Self (3.11). Further passages explain how all multiplicity is unreal. There is also a reference to the views of dvaitinah, the dualists (3.17). Shankara explains dualist views as those of Kapila, Kanada, Buddha, Arhat (Jain) and others and confirms that Advaita is the highest reality (3.18). Further, the text goes on to reiterate that though the Self may seem different in various individual entities, in reality it is not so.

In addition, it says that just as the immortal cannot become mortal so the mortal cannot become immortal, that is, intrinsic nature does not change (3.21). Though Vedic texts say there is both real creation and creation through maya, in actuality, Brahman is the only reality. Brahman is never born, does not sleep or dream, and has no form or name. It shines with an eternal light, contains everything, and has complete knowledge (3.36). To remove sorrow, misery and fear and to attain self-knowledge and peace, control of the mind is essential (3.40), as the highest bliss is found in one's Self (3.47). The section ends by stating that the highest truth is that no individual is ever born (3.48).

Section 4, *Alatashanti-prakarana* with 100 verses, develops these principles further. This section gets its name from the nature of a burning stick circled in the air, which creates the illusion of a circle of fire, *alatachakra*. The world with its various forms is said to be a similar illusion. It continues with the theme that the immortal never becomes mortal, and what pre-exists is never born. All entities therefore are free from old age and death. In a series of complicated verses, Guadapada explains how the eternal cannot be born. He discusses theories of cause and effect to refute other philosophies. Nothing can be born that exists, does not exist, or both exists and does not exist. Shankara further explains this. The objection raised is 'is not a jar produced from earth and a son born of a father?' This is refuted in the commentary that states that these notions are just words. 'If a thing already exists, then just because it exists, it does not pass into birth like earth or a father. If a thing does not exist, then by the very fact of non-existence, it does not undergo birth like the horn of a hare, etc. If it is both existent and non-existent, then also it does not take birth as it is impossible to have a thing that is self-contradictory. Hence, it is established that nothing whatever takes birth' (commentary on 4.22). The text ends with the following verse: 'After realizing that state (of reality) that is inscrutable, profound, birthless, uniform, holy, and non-dual, we make obeisance to it to the best of our ability.' Shankara adds three verses of salutations to Brahman, which though birthless, appears to be born through its inscrutable power.

Maitrayaniya Upanishad

The *Maitrayaniya* or *Maitri Upanishad* is usually considered to be of the Maitrayaniya shakha of the *Krishna* or *Black Yajur Veda*, but is sometimes said to belong to the *Sama Veda* as in the *Muktika Upanishad*.

The text is found in different versions, varying from one to seven prapathakas, and there seem to be several additions to the text made at a later date. Its commentaries include those of Vidyaranya, the seventeenth-century Ramatirtha, as well as

Upanishad Brahmayogin. Because of the different versions, van Buitenen has attempted a critical edition of the text. Maitri is mentioned as a teacher in the text.

It contains elements of Samkhya and Buddhist philosophy and has been variously dated from between the fourth century BCE to the first century CE. It is certainly later than the early Upanishads as it has quotations from many of them, including the *Brihadaranyaka*, *Chhandogya*, *Katha*, *Shvetashvatara* and *Prashna*. Among other topics, it describes the atman that is different from the body but identical with Brahman, and differentiates between a great or immortal self, and the individual soul or elemental self. It refers to various types of prana and to meditation on Om.

Prapathaka 1 begins by describing the merits of a sacrifice to Brahman and continues with the story of King Brihadratha, who installs his eldest son on the throne and goes into the forest, where he performs tapas for 1000 days (or years). Then, like a fire without smoke, the sage Shakayanya appears and asks him to choose a boon. Brihadratha requests an explanation of the atman. At first, Shakayanya asks Aikshvaka (the Ikshvaku king Brihadratha) to ask another question as this is difficult to explain. The king, describing the impermanence of life and referring to many other kings and warriors who renounced the world, persuades him to respond.

In Prapathaka 2, Shakayanya explains how to reach the ultimate goal by purifying the mind and turning it towards Brahman, revealing the teaching provided by the revered Maitri. The Valakhilyas had posed a question to Kratu Prajapati (a rishi who had 60,000 children the size of a thumb, who were known as Valakhilyas). They questioned Kratu about the body, which was like a cart when intelligence was absent. What was it that gave it this intelligence? Kratu responded by describing the one who stands alone, pure and clean, eternal, without breath or mind. This invisible, subtle Purusha, was called Vishva by Prajapati. The story of Prajapati follows. In the beginning he was alone but he created many offspring and entered them as the five Pranas. The body is the chariot and the mind the charioteer, and the body revolves in the world like the potter's wheel.

In Prapathaka 3, a question is raised (by the Valakhilyas to Prajapati Kratu) about the two selves, only one of which performs actions and enters a body. But the body emerges from the darkness of the womb and is full of diseases, one should not identify with it. The body has so many aspects like ignorance, jealousy and stupidity.

In Prapathaka 4, they (the Valakhilyas) continue with their questions. How would the elemental self (bhutatman) unite with the true self (hitvatman)? Kratu begins by saying that whatever has happened cannot be reversed. Passion and illusion lead to false delights but the elemental self is attached to them and does not recall its true higher state. The elemental self should study the Vedas and perform its duty according to the four ashramas or stages of life. Along with this he should practice austerities (tapas) and through this attain sattva (the quality of goodness). From this understanding is reached, and through understanding a knowledge of the atma. The one who knows the atman does not return.

The one who has Brahma-vidya or knowledge of Brahman affirms that Brahman exists. Om is a reflection of Brahman. The one who meditates on Om and practices tapas attains Brahman, going beyond the god Brahma, and then the ruler of the chariot unites with the atman. Even after this, the Valakhilyas ask about the gods. Some meditate on one god, some on another—such as Vayu, Agni, Brahma, Rudra, Vishnu and others; which one is best for them? Kratu replies that all these are forms of Brahman. Worshipping any one of them leads to the world of that deity. Gradually, one moves to higher worlds and finally attains unity with Purusha.

Prapathaka 5 begins with a song of praise by Kutsayana to the One, who is every god, Brahma, Vishnu, Rudra, etc. In the beginning, the world was in darkness (tamas). Then with the power of rajas or passion, it moves on to sattva (the form of goodness). Its essence is Prajapati, called Vishva (implying everyone). The three gunas represent the three gods Rudra, Brahma and Vishnu. That one is threefold, who developed the eightfold, elevenfold, and twelvefold one. (These are interpreted as referring to the different components of the individual.) Then this Self enters all created beings.

Prapathakas 6 and 7 are considered supplementary to the main text. These emphasize that there is only one Supreme Self and provide methods of meditation and worship. S. Radhakrishnan states that these last two sections are 'comparatively modern'.[4] Signe Cohen sees prapathakas 5 and 6 as later than the others.[5]

Seven

The Samanya Vedanta Upanishads

TWENTY-ONE UPANISHADS ARE usually classified as Samanya
Vedanta texts, that is, general Upanishads dealing with Vedanta.
These are: *Akshaya, Adhyatma, Annapurna, Atma, Atmabodha,
Ekakshara, Garbha, Maha, Mantrika, Muktika, Mudgala,
Niralamba, Paingala, Shariraka, Shukarahasya, Sarvasara,
Savitraya, Subala, Surya, Skanda, Vajrasuchika.* Mahony dates
these and other minor Upanishads between 100 BCE to CE 1100.[1]
Out of these, the *Mantrika* and *Sarvasara* are relatively early texts.

There are some variations in this classification. Sometimes
three ancient Upanishads are added to these, thus reaching
twenty-four; that is, the *Shvetashvatara, Maitrayani, Kaushitaki*.
The list of twenty-four also varies. Upanishad Brahmayogin
includes the *Annapurna, Maitri* and *Kaushitaki*. These Samanya
Vedanta Upanishads have the same themes as the early Upanishads,
and therefore most of them are explained briefly.

Adhyatma Upanishad

The *Adhyatma Upanishad* belongs to the *White* or *Shukla Yajur
Veda*. It discusses the nature of Brahman and the path of liberation.

It states that one should always focus on Brahman and meditate on the true Self within. One should not identify with the body or the senses or be attached to the world. One should know that 'I am Brahman' and constantly remember this. Brahman is beyond beginning and end, beyond all actions and all worldly forces. It is subtle, certain and unblemished, beyond thought, mind and words. Brahman is the only truth, the only reality, there is no other.

Akshaya or *Akshi Upanishad*

The *Akshi Upanishad* belongs to the *Taittiriya Samhita* of the *Krishna Yajur Veda* and has two parts. The first part consists of prayers and salutations to the sun and light. In the second part, Samkriti requests the sun to teach him Brahma-vidya, the knowledge of Brahman. The sun describes the nature of Brahman, the stages towards non-attachment and liberation and the significance of Om. It explains how to reach the true Self, which is knowledge and bliss, free from all impurities.

The text begins with Samkriti visiting Aditya Loka, the world of the sun god. There he worships him through the Chakshushmati Vidya, the science related to seeing. He reveres him as the god Surya, the sky-wanderer, the leader of the army, of energy and light, and asks him to lead him from darkness to light. (Here, the famous mantra beginning 'tamaso ma jyotirgamaya' is used.) The god Surya Narayana is pleased with this. He says that no one would become blind in the family of a brahmana who studies this vidya.

Samkriti then asks Surya to teach him about Brahman. Surya says he will explain the true knowledge by which a person attains liberation. Only One exists, tranquil, without beginning or end. A person on this path, says Surya, avoids wrong actions and sense gratification and performs only noble deeds. The person speaks in a gentle and loving way and sees the good points of others, not the bad. Along with this, he studies the Shastras. Then, when thoughts of transmigration touch the mind, the first stage of yoga is reached. After this, the second stage of vichara or analysis is attained. In the third stage, detachment grows and the aspirant begins to perceive Reality. In the fourth stage, non-duality is established. All duality is dissolved.

The text then compares the first three states to the waking consciousness and the fourth to the dream state (though this does not correspond with a state of non-duality). The fifth is like deep sleep, where the outer world no longer affects one, and the sixth state corresponds with the fourth state of consciousness, Turiya. Then, he reaches the seventh state, liberation beyond the body.

The text next describes the importance of focusing on Om and on Brahman.

Annapurna Upanishad

The *Annapurna Upanishad* is attached to the *Atharva Veda*. It is a long Upanishad with five sections. Section 1 has fifty-seven verses. In this, a yogi named Nidagha asks Ribhu, a knower of Brahman, to teach him about it. Ribhu explains how he obtained this knowledge by propitiating the goddess Annapurna, using her mantra of twenty-seven syllables. He then explains to Nidagha, how to attain the knowledge of Reality. For this, everything in life should be renounced, including the mind. The mind becomes unattached. Such a person may act in the world or may not, but he is never an agent or experiencer.

In Section 2, which has forty-four verses, Nidagha asks about the reasons for attachment and bondage, and how to gain liberation. Ribhu explains how to control the mind and be united with Brahman. The jivan-mukta, the liberated one, does not crave anything in the future, does not count on whatever is in the present and does not think of the past. Nevertheless, he never ceases to work.

In Section 3, which has twenty-four verses, Nidagha asks Ribhu about any sage who was liberated while still living. Ribhu replies that in Sumeru lived the sage Mandavya, who had been instructed by Kaundinya. Mandavya had been a jivan-mukta, liberated while living. Ribhu describes the process of how Mandavya attained this, by first sitting in meditation and controlling his mind.

In Sections 4 and 5, the nature of a jivan-mukta is described as one who no longer has desires or attachments. He is silent and yet active and knows his Self to be identical with Brahman.

Atma Upanishad

The *Atma Upanishad* belongs to the *Atharva Veda* and has two sections. In Section 1, which has four verses, the rishi Angiras explains the three types of Self: the Self that constitutes the external Self or body, the inner Self, and the Supreme Self. For the external Self, different parts of the body, that is, skin, eyes, ears, etc., are listed. The internal Self includes the elements, emotions and the consciousness of oneself as Purusha. The highest self is the eternal atman, free from the bonds of action.

Section 2 has thirty-one verses and describes the pure, non-dual atman and its identity with Brahman. The one who knows Brahman has no sense of 'mine' or 'I' and no desires. Even though he has a body, he lives beyond the body and is nothing but Brahman.

Atmabodha Upanishad

The *Atmabodha Upanishad* belongs to the *Rig Veda* and has two sections. It has a few lines praising the god Vishnu, but goes on to describe the state of knowledge of the inner self (atmabodha). In one of its verses, the person who has achieved this state says: 'I have no bondage, no liberation, no shastra, no guru. I have gone beyond maya; whatever happens, I have no misery, I am filled with joy; I know myself, all ignorance has gone. I have no actions to perform, no duty, no kula [lineage or family], and no gotra.' Such a person knows that Brahman pervades the whole world, just as sugarcane is sweet in all its parts. When clouds block the sun, the person without knowledge thinks it does not exist, in the same way, the ignorant lack knowledge of the shining Brahman.

Ekakshara Upanishad

The *Ekakshara Upanishad* belongs to the *Krishna Yajur Veda, Taittiriya Samhita*. It sees the god Vishnu as creator, lord of all, and source of the world, seen through the Sushumna. He is Parjanya, Hiranyagarbha, Subrahmanya, Arishtanemi, Indra and Soma. The Vedas proceed from him, and he is the Vasus, Agni and the Rudras. He is Varuna, Aryaman and other gods, the eternal dweller in the cave of the heart, the ancient, golden lord, the supreme goal of the wise.

Garbha Upanishad

The *Garbha Upanishad* belongs to the *Krishna Yajur Veda, Taittiriya Samhita*. This provides a description of the body and its constituents. It explains the stages of growth in the womb (garbha). The baby remembers its past lives in the ninth month, but after being born, forgets it. Still, it always yearns for liberation.

Maha Upanishad

There are different versions of this text. Deussen calls it a short Upanishad[2] and classifies it as a *Vaishnava Upanishad*, but it is actually known in a very long form.

This long text has six sections or chapters. Section 1 with thirteen verses states that in the beginning Narayana was alone. There was no Brahma, Ishana, water, Agni, Soma, heaven, earth, stars and sun, but only he, Nara (Purusha) alone). By the desire of the Paramatman and the Yajnastoma (hymn), he created fourteen Purushas (Brahman, Vishnu, Rudra, Ishana, Sadashiva and nine Prajapatis), one maiden (Mula-Prakriti), the ten organs (five of perception and five of action), manas or mind as the eleventh, tejas or brilliant intellect the twelfth, ahamkara the thirteenth, Prana the fourteenth, atma the fifteenth, next buddhi, kama, karma and tamas, five tanmatras or subtle elements, five gross elements with the Being or Sutratman as the twenty-fifth. The Supreme Being remained detached.

Narayana continued his creation, producing a person with three eyes and a trident, a golden egg from which came Brahma, as well as other deities, the metres and the Vedas. The text then states that one should meditate on the eternal Narayana, who has 1000 heads and eyes and is the source of all. He is Brahma, Shiva and Indra, and is present everywhere (1.10–13).

Section 2 with seventy-seven verses begins by stating that Shuka realized the truth at birth and, similarly, a person can gain knowledge of the Self through his own Self. Shuka knew the truth through his subtle intellect and then remained rapt in it. He did not conceive that the atman is real, his mind merely turned away from worldly temptations. Once he asked his father, the rishi Vyasa, seated alone on Mount Meru, about the origin and dissolution of the world. Vyasa provided this knowledge, but Shuka was already aware of everything he said. Vyasa understood this and asked him to enquire from Janaka, king of Mithila. Shuka goes to Janaka's city of Videha and Janaka explains that when the mind realizes that nothing seen is real, there is liberation. Janaka continues with explanations similar to the Bhagavad Gita—one who has equanimity, who does not rejoice or feel sorrow when things go well or badly, who is silent, without ego, fear or pride, who has given up all dharma and adharma, who eats any food, and does not have thoughts or desires, who has a mind, yet is mindless.

Section 3 has fifty-seven verses. In this, Nidagha, while still a young boy, is permitted by his father to go on pilgrimage. After visiting three and a half crore sacred places, he goes to Ribhu and explains at length that he is troubled in his mind and has lost the taste for various things. Everything in the world is born only to die and then be reborn. While describing the ephemeral nature of the world, he also (39–48) describes women as the flame of sin. They are pleasing to the eye, yet not to be touched or they burn man like grass. They are the basket of all defects, the chain of misery. He goes on to say that everything in the world perishes, even the yogis, siddhas, the unborn Vishnu, Shiva, Brahma, Rudra, nothing was permanent. Wealth, birth and death are only for a moment, everything dies.

Section 4 has 131 verses. Ribhu responds to him. He says, Nidagha, there is nothing more to be known by you, you already know everything by your intellect and God's grace. Then Ribhu goes on to tell him how to remove the error caused by impurity of the mind. One must control the inner and outer senses, maintain contentment, continue with enquiry and have contact with good people. He advises him to remain like a dumb, blind and deaf person, giving up with his mind the thought of all things as the Self. The wise person should enquire, who am I? The contented person gives up longing for anything. The text also comments on schools of thought. It says that schools from the Trinachiketa to the Yoga depend on Ishvara's illusion, from the Lokayata to Samkhya on jiva's illusion—aspirants to liberation should not consider these schools but only the truth about Brahman (4.73–75).

Ribhu goes on to say that the auspicious path cannot be obtained without subduing the mind and giving up desires through one's own efforts. One should forget about what is mine and not-mine, give up involvement. It is strange that Brahman is forgotten by people.

Section 5 has 186 verses; Ribhu describes the seven steps of ignorance and the seven steps of wisdom. Each of these has hundreds of variations and intermediate steps. Liberation follows after the seven stages of knowledge: auspicious desire, reflection, thinning of the mind, attainment of sattva, detachment, reflection on objects and Turiya. Ribhu then explains these further. Reaching the seventh stage, even animals are liberated. Ribhu also looks at the different types of life and rebirth.

Section 6 has eighty-three verses. Ribhu continues with this theme, that nothing exists but Brahman. The text ends with the merits of studying this Upanishad. It is a valuable Upanishad on attaining Brahman.

Mantrika Upanishad

The *Mantrika Upanishad* of the *Vajasaneyi* or *Shukla Yajur Veda* probably dates to the first century BCE or earlier. It has twenty-one verses and discusses the nature of Brahman, Maya and the individual and includes elements of different philosophies, Vedanta, Samkhya and Yoga. It begins with the mystical statement: The eight-footed pure Swan (Hamsa), bound with three cords, subtle and imperishable, to whom three ways lead, is seen by all yet cannot be seen.

This verse indicates that though the atman, represented by the Hamsa, is visible, it cannot be seen. The text goes on to say that living beings exist in darkness but those who are established in the sattva guna are able to see the supreme. The common metaphor of two birds, one who eats the fruit and one who looks on, is mentioned. The tattvas of the Samkhya system are referred to, but finally the text affirms that those who know Brahman are dissolved in avyakta, that is, they become Brahman.

Mudgala Upanishad

The *Mudgala Upanishad* belongs to the *Sama Veda*. It identifies the god Narayana (Vishnu) with Brahman. Jan Gonda believes it is a medieval text but Klaus Witz places it as post-Vedic but early Vaishnava.

The text has four chapters or sections. The first presents an explanation of the first nine verses of the Purusha-sukta (10.90) of the *Rig Veda*. In this Upanishad, Purusha is identified with Vishnu, who sacrificed himself. The Mudgala explains that 1000 heads indicates a number that cannot be counted, while ten fingers suggests an infinite distance. The entire Purusha-sukta thus indicates that it is the god Vishnu that pervades all space. The second chapter says that Vasudeva provided a knowledge of Bhagavan to Indra, and also of the two parts of the Purusha-sukta. It was difficult for people to understand the Purusha that is beyond name and form, therefore he took on a form with 1000 parts. This Narayana provides moksha to all. Three parts of him are in heaven, while the fourth, Aniruddha-Narayana, created all the worlds. Chapter 3 states that thus the single god became many, and is worshipped in different forms, while Chapter 4 says that those who study this text will become Purusha in this birth.

Muktika Upanishad

For information on this particular Upanishad, see the introduction of this book.

Niralamba Upanishad

The *Niralamba Upanishad* belongs to the *Shukla Yajur Veda*. This text raises and answers forty-one questions that must be known to remove ignorance. Next, the Niralamba provides the answers to these questions.

The forty-one questions are: (1) What is Brahman? (2) Who is Ishvara? (3) Who is a jiva (living being)? (4) What is Prakriti? (5) Who is the Paramatma (Supreme Self)? (6) Who is Brahma? (7) Who is Vishnu? (8) Who is Rudra? (9) Who is Indra? (10) Who is Yama (the god of death)? (11) Who is Surya? (12) Who is Chandra? (13) Who are the Suras? (14) Who are the asuras? (15) Who are the pishachas? (16) Who are men? (17) Who are women? (18) Who are animals, etc.? (19) What is the immobile (sthavaram)? (20) Who are brahmanas, etc.? (21) What is a jati (caste)? (22) What is action? (23) What is non-action? (24) What is jnana or knowledge? (25) What is ajnana or ignorance? (26) What is sukha or pleasure? (27) What is dukha or sorrow? (28) What is svarga (heaven)? (29) What is naraka (hell)? (30) What is bandha (bondage)? (31) What is moksha (liberation)? (32) What is upasya (to be adored)? (33) Who is the disciple? (34) Who is the vidvan (learned one)? (35) Who is the deluded? (36) What is the asuram (demoniac)? (37) What is tapas (austerity)? (38) Which is the supreme abode? (39) What is to be sought after? (40) What is to be rejected? (41) Who is the renouncer (sannyasin)? The responses to the questions state that Brahman is the Supreme Spirit, who through mahat, the ego, the elements, and other aspects of life, remains non-dual, pure and unqualified. God too is Brahman, who through the power of prakriti brings forth creation. All the deities and others mentioned in questions 6–20 are also Brahman. It goes on to say that caste really doesn't exist, for bones, flesh and blood have no caste. It responds to the other questions too, and ends by stating that the sannyasi is the liberated one, who is the same as Brahman.

Paingala Upanishad

This Upanishad belongs to the *Shukla Yajur Veda* and has four
sections or chapters. A shorter version of it is attached to the
Atharva Veda. It is classified as a *Samanya Vedanta Upanishad*. The
date is uncertain but it may be of the sixth century CE. Shankara
refers to it in his commentary on the *Brahma Sutra*.

It consists of a dialogue between the rishi Yajnavalkya and his
pupil Paingala (son of Pingala).

Chapter 1 with twelve verses begins with the verse 'Then
(atha) Paingala, after serving his teacher for twelve years,
asked Yajnavalkya to tell him the great secret (paramarahasya)
of aloneness (kaivalya). In response Yajnavalkya describes
Brahman, the one without a second (ekam evadvityam), which
is eternal and has the nature of truth, knowledge and bliss, ever
full, eternal. He explains how from Brahman, the witnessing
self (sakshi), Ishvara or god, and other aspects of the world
come into being. When mula-prakriti, the root principle of
matter, changes because of the quality of sattva in it, it develops
a veiling power. Ishvara is reflected in it and through the power
of maya it becomes the first cause of creation, sustenance and
dissolution. From this veiling power in Ishvara comes mahat,
the power of projection, because of the quality of rajas. What
is reflected in it becomes the Hiranyagarbha consciousness
from which comes the power of creating matter through tamas.
Virat consciousness is reflected in it and conceives the sense
of Self, and its form manifests as the god Vishnu. From Virat
rose the five elements which contain the three gunas. These
root elements were further subdivided using the gunas and the
various functions and organs were created. Still they could not
function on their own. To provide them with consciousness,
he pierced through the microcosm, the caverns of the cranium
and the crowns of individuals and entered them. Though

non-conscious by nature, they now began to function as if they were conscious. 'The omniscient Lord, together with a streak of Maya, on entering the individual bodies, and deluded by it, became the jiva; due to self-identification with the three bodies (he) became both agent and reaper (of action's fruits). Possessing the attributes of wakefulness, dream, deep sleep, fainting and death, like a chain of buckets (attached to a water wheel) he is born and dies, revolving like a potter's wheel' (12).

Chapter 2 also has twelve verses. In the first verse, Paingala asks Yajnavalkya, 'How does Isha, the all-pervading lord, the cause of the creation, maintenance and dissolution of all the worlds, assume the state of the jiva, the individual soul?'

Yajnavalkya replies that he will explain the difference between the jiva and the divine. He describes the aspects of the gross body, including its different parts such as the skin, bones, etc., the emotions and functions. Then god creates Prana, the principle of life, its modifications, prana, apana, samana, vyana and udana, and its subordinate functions, naga, kurma, krikara, devadatta and dhananjaya. Next he creates the organs of action and the inner senses and their modifications. The deities presiding over them are the directions as well as vata (air), arka (the sun), Prachetas, the Ashvins, fire (vahni), Indra, Upendra, Mrityu, Chandra, Vishnu, the four-faced (Brahma) and Shambhu. The five kosha or body sheaths are described. These are the annamaya, pranamaya, manomaya, vijnanamaya and anandamaya. The annamaya or food body comes into being and grows through food and rests in the earth. The pranamaya kosha consists of the five pranas and the organ of action. The manomaya kosha consists of the mind and the organs of perception. The vijnanamaya kosha consists of the intellect and the organs of perception. These three sheaths of life, mind and intelligence form the subtle body. The anandamaya kosha consists of knowledge of one's own form and is the causal body.

Next it discusses the states of consciousness, vishva, taijasa and prajna, that is, of waking, dreaming and sleeping, and also refers to death, bondage and release.

Chapter 3 with six verses begins with Paingala asking Yajnavalkya to narrate a detailed account of the mahavakyas or great statements. Yajnavalkya provides the classic statements of the Upanishads: 'Tat tvam asi', that is, 'That you are', and also 'You are the seat of Brahman', 'I am Brahman'. It goes on to provide further explanations of Brahman who should be meditated upon. The knower of Brahman becomes liberated in this life. Meditation should be on the unchanging, imperishable being within who manifests diverse aspects. The one who is liberated when alive is blessed, and all his duties have been fulfilled. He attains that state that is without sound, touch, form and desire.

Chapter 4 with twenty-four verses begins with another question as Paingala asks Yajnavalkya about the qualities and actions of a knower. Such a person, says Yajnavalkya, has both humility and all other good qualities. It describes how a person with a pure mind and consciousness attains the state of Brahman. It ends by stating that the one who studies this Upanishad attains the highest state of Vishnu.

Sarvasara Upanishad

The *Sarvasara Upanishad* belongs to the *Taittiriya Samhita* of the *Krishna Yajur Veda*. Like the *Niralamba*, it asks a number of questions, though not quite as many. Questions include those on bondage, moksha or liberation, ignorance and knowledge (avidya and vidya), states of consciousness, of Jagrat (waking), Svapna (dreaming), Sushupti (dreamless sleep), and the fourth, Turiya (the state beyond these three). Other questions include on the five bodies of a person: annamaya, pranamaya, manomaya, vijnanamaya and anandamaya koshas; the karta, or agent of action;

the jiva or individual Self; the kshetrajna (knower of the body); the sakshi (witness); the kutastha; the antaryamin (internal ruler); pratyagatman (inner self); the Paramatman (Supreme Self); the atman and maya. These are then explained.

Savitri Upanishad

The *Savitri Upanishad* is attached to the *Sama Veda*. It begins by asking, 'Who is Savitar, who is Savitri?' The reply is that Agni is Savitar, Prithivi or earth is Savitri, and Varuna is Savitar, water is Savitri. It continues with other identifications of Savitar and Savitri, the masculine and feminine representatives of sun and light. The pairs are Vayu–Akasha, Yajna–Chhandas, Stanayitnu (thundercloud)–Vidyut (lightning), Aditya–Dyaus, Chandra– Nakshatra, Manas–Vach, Purusha–Stri, and connects the Gayatri Mantra with these pairs. These nine pairs correspond with bhur–bhuvar–svar, that is, the earth, mid-regions and heaven, and are equal to atman and Brahman. This is the Savitri-vidya, says the text. Next, the mantras Bala and Atibala are explained, as well as benefits of meditation on the goddess Savitri and the Savitri-vidya.

Shariraka Upanishad

The *Shariraka Upanishad* belongs to the *Taittiriya Samhita* of the *Krishna Yajur Veda*.

This Upanishad describes the body and its different aspects, along with the three gunas and their qualities and the four states of consciousness. It states that the body is a combination of five elements: earth, water, fire, air and ether or space (akasha). The hard elements in the body are related to earth, the liquid to water, and what is hot to fire. Movement relates to air and that which is porous to space. It further relates the elements to different parts of the body, including the senses and the mind. As for the gunas, rajas is reflected in the belief that 'I am the doer and the enjoyer', tamas is present in sleep, laziness, delusion, attachment, sex and theft, and sattva is above these. Right knowledge is sattva, the practice of rituals is rajas and tamas is blindness. As for the states of consciousness, this Upanishad states that the waking state uses the five sense organs, five of action, and four inner senses. The dream state uses the four inner senses. In dreamless sleep, the mind is active, and in the fourth or Turiya state, only the soul or atma remains.

The knower is the empirical Self, different from the Supreme. The twenty-five tattvas are mentioned, with Purusha as the twenty-fifth and Avyakta as the twenty-fourth.

Shukarahasya Upanishad

The *Shukarahasya* is attached to the *Taittiriya Samhita* of the *Krishna Yajur Veda.*

In this Upanishad, Shiva instructs Shuka, son of the rishi Vyasa, on the Rahasya or secret Upanishad. It is Vyasa who requests Shiva to instruct his son. After obtaining the knowledge of the supreme Brahman, inherent in Om, Shuka asks for more knowledge. Shiva then conveys this secret Upanishad to him, along with the four mahavakyas (Verses 22–24). It explains each word of the mahavakyas, and adds methods of meditating on them. Shuka, after being instructed by Shiva, gives up all possessions. He renounces the world and is one with the Supreme. As a renunciate he begins to leave the place and though Vyasa is happy he calls after him, and the whole world echoes him. The Upanishad ends by stating that the one who studies will attain moksha through the grace of the guru.

Skanda Upanishad

The *Skanda Upanishad* is attached to the *Taittiriya Samhita* of the *Krishna Yajur Veda.*

In this Upanishad, Skanda (the god Karttikeya) states that through compassion of the great god, he identifies himself with Brahman. In the text, Shiva and Vishnu are also identified. Shiva is the jiva and the body is a temple. Knowledge arises when non-difference is understood, meditation is the mind without any object. To bathe is to remove mental impurity, and cleanliness implies the control of the senses. Living by oneself without duality, one attains liberation.

Subala Upanishad

The *Subala Upanishad* belongs to the *Shukla Yajur Veda* and has sixteen sections.

It consists mainly of a discussion between the rishi Subala and Brahma, the creator. It begins with an account of creation by the Supreme person (Purusha) and by Brahma. It describes the attainment of Brahman by the six means of truthfulness, charity, austerity, fasting, chastity and detachment from worldly objects. Simultaneously, self-control and compassion should be practised. It describes the different types of prana (breath) and the centre within the heart from where the various nadis branch out. This Upanishad identifies Brahman, the Supreme reality, with Narayana (Vishnu).

Surya Upanishad

The *Surya Upanishad* belongs to the *Atharva Veda*. It begins with a reference to Atharva-Angirasa, a name of the *Atharva Veda*, and states that it will explain the Surya Mantra according to the *Atharva*.

Surya, the sun or Sun God, is identified with the manifest Brahman. All creatures are born from him, protected by him and dissolve in him. It prescribes various meditations and mantras for

Surya worship and provides different names of Surya, including
Bhanu, Mitra, Savitr and Aditya. Surya is also identified with the
golden Narayana, who propels the chakra or wheel of time, and
who is seated in the chariot of the sun.

Vajrasuchika Upanishad

The *Vajrasuchika Upanishad* belongs to the *Sama Veda* and can be
dated to medieval times.

    This text discusses the four castes and their basis. The second
verse raises the question of why a brahmana is so identified. Is it
because of his jiva or individual soul, his body, his birth, his actions,
or the rituals he performs? The question is answered in succeeding
verses. It cannot be the jiva as this transmigrates and is reborn; nor
are there any distinguishing marks on the body because everybody
has the same elements. It can't be birth, as great rishis are born in
different ways, for instance, Vyasa from Satyavati, daughter of a
fisherman, Gautama from a hare, Jambuka from a jackal, Agastya
from a vessel and Vasishtha from an apsara. Many kshatriyas have
great knowledge, actions are performed by all, and therefore the
only criteria for recognizing someone as a brahmana is one who
has realized Brahman, who knows that the atman is eternal, one
without a second, and the same as Brahman that pervades the
whole world.

    There is also a Buddhist text known as the *Vajrasuchi*, which
some assigned to Ashvaghosha, a Buddhist scholar of the second
century. The general conclusion is that this is much later and not
composed by Ashvaghosha.

Eight

The Deity Upanishads

THE DEITY UPANISHADS are classified into Shaiva, Vaishnava and Shakta.

Shaiva Upanishads

The Shaiva Upanishads are fifteen: *Akshamalika, Atharvashikha, Atharvashira, Kalagnirudra, Kaivalya, Ganapatya, Jabalya* or *Jabali, Dakshinamurti, Panchabrahma, Brihad-jabala, Bhasma-jabala, Rudrahridaya, Rudraksha-jabala, Sharabha, Shvetashvatara*. Among these, *Kaivalya, Shvetashvatara, Atharvashiras, Atharvashikha* and *Kalagnirudra* are relatively early. As the *Shvetashavatara* is considered a major Upanishad, it is in Chapter 6. Among the others, Klaus Klostermaier groups the *Akshamalika, Brihad-jabala, Bhasma-jabala, Rudraksha-jabala* and *Kalagnirudra* together as those that explain the rites and symbols of Shaiva worship. These are related to rituals of the Pashupata sect.

The *Nilarudra* is another early Shaiva Upanishad, but is not included here as it is not part of the *Muktika* list.

Akshamalika Upanishad

The *Akshamalika Upanishad* is attached to the *Rig Veda*, and has sixteen long verses. It is believed to have been composed after the twelfth century CE. It discusses the varieties of aksha-malas (rosaries), how they should be made and consecrated, and their symbolism. This is considered a Shaiva Upanishad because in it Guha (a name of Karttikeya, a son of Shiva), provides instruction on the value of worship with a rosary of aksha beads for the ordinary people who do not know the atman or Brahman. Prajapati approaches Guha and says that such people would benefit by reciting mantras and using an aksha-mala. He requests Guha to explain the right way of using this mala. He says that an impure mind cannot know the atman which is no different from Brahman. If a practitioner wishes to use an aksha-mala to purify himself, having established the fifty Sanskrit letters on its beads, he should conform to the rules relating to this. Prajapati wants to know the rules for the types of malas, the number of threads, the presiding deity, the way the letters should be recited and the benefits (1).

Guha explains that a mala can be made of coral, pearl, crystal, conch, sandalwood, silver, gold, Putranjiva fruits, lotus seeds or rudraksha beads. The letters of the alphabet from 'a' to 'ksha' should be established in the beads. It should be strung with three threads of gold, silver and copper, with gold in the middle. The mukha or main bead representing 'ksha' is at the apex, while the other beads represent the fifty ordinary letters from 'a' to 'ha'. More details follow on how each bead and thread should be understood. The three threads represent the gods Brahma, Vishnu and Shiva, while the mukha bead should be thought of as Sarasvati. The text further explains how the beads and the knots separating them should be conceived and how the aksha-mala should be purified. Next it explains how each of the letters should be invoked in the relevant beads with mantras, beginning with the first and going on to the last. Two examples are given here of a vowel and a consonant: 'Om! O, Umkara! [the letter u] that bestows all kinds of strength and is possessed of great excellence, be firmly established in the fifth bead' and 'Om! O Ghamkara [the letter gh], you who bestow prosperity and cause firmness, be established in the twentieth bead'. Finally one comes to the last letter, ksha. The mantra for this is: 'Om! O Kshamkara, that reminds one of the difference between the Para and Apara [undifferentiated Brahman and qualified Brahman], that are of the form of transcendent radiance, be firmly established in the shikhamani [the head], the mukha [mouth] of the mala.'

After establishing the letters with purificatory rites, further mantras are prescribed while touching the beads. Various powers and deities are invoked and asked to reside in the beads and to provide their blessing. The ninety-six tattvas of the Samkhyas, and the Shaivas, Shaktas and Vaishnavas are among those invoked. The latter indicates the late date of this Upanishad. Further instructions are provided on how to touch the beads 108 times and how to worship the mala with specific mantras. Through this the delusion that the universe is different from Brahman will be removed. It goes on to provide descriptions of Brahman, who dwells in the hearts of all, who is the goddess Sarasvati in her Para form in the Muladhara, along with other descriptions. The aksha-mala has the character of the tattvas (eternal principles), the vidyas (mystical knowledge) and the devas, and is adored by the rishi Vasishtha and served by the rishi Vishvamitra.

The Upanishad concludes by saying that reciting the aksha-mala in the morning and evening frees one from sins.

Atharvashikha Upanishad

The *Atharvashikha* is attached to the *Atharva Veda* and has three khandas or chapters. It was composed sometime in the

first millennium BCE. The text has a commentary attributed to
Shankara, but it is not believed to be his.

In this Upanishad, Atharvan or Atharva maharishi instructs
the rishis on 'Om', known as the dhyanamantra, the best mantra for
dhyana or meditation. It looks at the four states of consciousness
and identifies the Turiya, or fourth state, beyond waking, sleeping
and dreaming, with taraka, the means of crossing over to the other
world. It includes a meditation on the god Shiva.

Chapter 1 has ten verses. The Upanishad begins with the
rishi Angiras, Paippalada (the son of Pippalada) and the rishi
Sanat Kumara asking Atharvan about the best form of meditation
(dhyana). They approach him after first purifying their minds.
Atharvan explains that meditating on Om is the best form
of meditation as it is both the Para and the Apara Brahman
(the limited and unlimited Brahman). Its four components or
syllables are the four Vedas. The Upanishad further connects
each syllable with a Veda and with deities. The syllable 'a' is
connected with the *Rig Veda*, through the riks (verses). Its
region is the earth (Prithivi), the presiding deity is Brahma, the
subsidiary deities are the Vasus, the metre is Gayatri, Agni or
fire is the Garhaptya. For the second syllable, 'u', its region is the
mid-ethereal (Antariksha), its Veda is the *Yajur*, through
the yajus, its deity is Vishnu, with the Rudras as subsidiaries, the
metre is trishtubh, the Agni or fire is the Dakshina. For the third
syllable, 'm', the region is celestial (Dyaus), the Veda is the *Sama*
through its samans, the deity is Rudra, the subsidiary the twelve
Adityas, the metre jagati, the Agni Ahavaniya. The fourth is
the ardha-matra, the region is that of the moon (Soma Loka),
the Veda is the *Atharva*, through the Atharvana Mantras; the
Samvarta Agni is the presiding deity, the Maruts the subsidiaries,
Virat is the metre, Ekarshi is the fire; it is reputed as Bhasvati
(the radiant one) in all systems of Vedanta, and represents the
state of consciousness known as Turiya (3–6).

Succeeding verses provide more information on each. The colour of 'a' is a mixture of red and yellow; Brahma is the deity; the colour of 'u' is a mixture of lightning and krishna (blue-black), Vishnu is the deity; 'm' is shining white, the deity is Rudra, as Ishvara has the attribute of bright white; the ardha-matra is again like lightning along with all colours, the deity is Purusha, who through his Turiya form fills all matras (accents) and all the world.

Providing further explanations of the inner meaning of Om, the text and commentary says the four syllables are represented by Vishva, Virat, Otr and Turiya, each further subdivided (1.8). It goes into more descriptions and methods of meditation. Om is also said to raise the prana from the Muladhara to the Brahma-randhra (from the base of the spine to the top of the head). Om is often referred to as the Pranava, in this and other texts. The first khanda and commentary clearly identifies Om with Brahman.

Chapter 2 describes the Turiya-omkara. It states that Om enables one to cross over to the other shore and thus become one with Brahman. This is known as its Taraka character, from Tara, a boat. It shines within everything and pervades the whole world.

Chapter 3 equates the four syllables of Om with the four states of consciousness, the ardha-matra being the Turiya state, and provides more instructions on how to meditate on the syllables of Om to reach that state. Meditation creates identity with Vishnu, Rudra or Ishana. It also states that Brahma, Vishnu, Rudra and Indra, the creator, sustainer, destroyer and leader of the gods, cause the whole world to come into being, but the prime cause is Brahman known as Ishvara (3.4). Constantly meditating on Brahman, if the atman in the space of the heart is seen even for a fragment of a second, one attains the highest fruit.

The Upanishad concludes by stating that the twice-born (Dvija) who studies this becomes a jivan-mukta and then a videha-mukta.

Atharvashira Upanishad

The *Atharvashira Upanishad* belongs to the *Atharva Veda*. This Upanishad has seventy sections (here termed verses for convenience) and is believed to be composed around the fifth century BCE. This text sees Rudra as the Supreme Being and Rudra explains Brahman to the devas.

It states that the devas go to Mahakailasha in Svarga Loka and ask Rudra, 'Who are you?' Rudra replies that he is the innermost atman, existing before creation. He is the Parameshvara, the Supreme Lord, and nothing exists apart from him. Rudra reveals himself in his divine form and explains that he is Brahman and all that emanates from Brahman, he is the antaryamin, the atman and the anatman, both male and female, the four Vedas, and everything else in the world. The passages here are similar to those proclaimed in the Bhagavad Gita by Krishna. For instance, Rudra says, 'I am the three sources of energy, the Gayatri, the Savitri, the Sarasvati, I am the three Vedic metres . . . I am the most excellent in quality, I am the most excellent in knowledge', etc. (Verse 4) After this the devas worship Rudra, who is Brahman, Om, bhur bhuvar suvar and everything else. They pray that they may become immortal through the Soma sacrifice, attain the radiance of Rudra through offering him the fruits of the sacrifice and see the radiance of all the deities within them, who were all part of Rudra. Rudra is the one absolute existence (Verse 44).

The Upanishad goes on to explain Om and its uses, and various terms that also describe Om, the Pranava, as well as Rudra. The terms include Sarvavyapi (the all-pervasive one); Ananta, the one without end; Tara (boat), a term that takes one beyond fear as it implies crossing beyond this world in a boat; Sukshma, the subtle one; Shukla, the one that manifests itself; Vaityota, which reveals the non-existent; Para Brahman, which expands, containing everything; Eka, the one; eko Rudra, the one

Rudra, because he alone is all, and the root or cause of everything; Ishana, who controls (ishate) all worlds; Bhagavat, because he looks at all beings as part of himself (bhaga=part); Maheshvara, because he absorbs all beings as the destroyer and then regenerates them; Mahadeva, because he is glorified (mahiyate). The Srirudra Paramatman forms the self-luminous substratum of being.

It should be grasped as all Vedantic texts say that Brahman is the same as the atman and all should move towards that end (Verses 63–65). Rudra is identical with the Paramatman (Verse 66).

The Mahapashupata vrata is described, which consists of meditating on Brahman as Rudra. This leads to the attainment of kaivalya (aloneness). The pashus (jivas) bound by the pashas (cords) (of delusion) attain identity with Pati (Rudra) and gain freedom. It goes on to say that Agni and all the elements, the world and even the avyakta from which they originate are ashes. Applying the fire of Brahman and taking the ashes, using the mantra of Agni, one should smear the limbs with them; this is the Pashupata vrata. Any brahmana who studies this text attains all fruits as well as kaivalya. This was explained by the exalted Atharvashiras.

Two prayers follow. The first is in praise of Rudra, the second asks for protection when the mukhyaprana (main breath) in the Anahata Chakra rises to the Sahasrara (see Chapter 3 for the chakras), to the vessel of the Turiya and the self-luminous god there is broken to pieces and nirvikalpa samadhi (undifferentiated samadhi) is attained. It also asks for sustenance and knowledge as long as the body exists, and finally for union with Brahman.

Bhasma-jabala Upanishad

The *Bhasma-jabala Upanishad* belongs to the *Atharva Veda*. In this Shiva instructs Bhushunda on the sacred bhasma and rudraksha. Its composition is probably after the twelfth century CE.

Chapter 1 has eleven verses. The rishi Jabala, also known as Bhushunda, visits Shiva on Mount Kailasha. A description follows of the god, who transcends Brahma, Vishnu and Rudra. Jabala asks him about the tripundra mark (the three lines on the forehead) and bhasma (sacred ash). Parameshvara (Shiva) explains the homa ritual, the mantras to be used and the rules and mantras for wearing bhasma. If the seeker does not follow these, he becomes a fallen man. Without wearing bhasma no task should be done, not even water should be drunk. If a day is missed, the sannyasi should fast and repeat the Pranava 12,000 times (according to another version of the text, 1000 times).

Chapter 2 has thirty verses. In this, Mahadeva explains the daily duties of brahmanas, which include wearing the tripundra mark, reciting Rudra-suktas (verses to Rudra) and wearing rudraksha beads. At the three Sandhyas (junctions of the day: dawn, noon, sunset), Shiva should be worshipped as the Purusha that releases pashus (souls) from their pasha (bonds). Shiva also states that 'I along with Uma am Brahman.' He describes the benefits of living and dying at Kashi (Varanasi) and of following his precepts. Those who do so find there is no better place for liberation than Avimukta (Varanasi). Worshipping the jyotirlinga known as Vishveshvara yields the best results as it is the highest of these lingas. The method of worshipping the linga is also prescribed.

Brihad-jabala Upanishad

The *Brihad-jabala Upanishad* is attached to the *Atharva Veda* and was probably composed after the twelfth century CE. This Upanishad has eight sections known as Brahmanas. In this, Kalagni Rudra, a form of the god Shiva, describes the benefits of vibhuti and other forms of sacred ash. This Upanishad contains a number of dialogues between Kalagni Rudra and Bhushunda,

Janaka, Yajnavalkya and others. Brahman created the world but
turned it into ashes to show that everything else is unreal. Other
aspects of this Upanishad are explanations of vibhuti, rudraksha,
brihad-jabala-vidya, Shiva and Shakti and the attainment of
kaivalya.

Brahmana 1 with fifteen verses begins with the creation of the
world by Prajapati (Brahma) after pralaya (dissolution). Creation
begins with an intense desire which then takes form. The creative
intellect (manisha) of poets and seers lies deeply in the hearts. The
one who seeks it there attains Prajapati.

Prajapati then meditates and takes the form of Bhushunda,
the crow. As Bhushunda he approaches Kalagnirudra and asks him
about the greatness of vibhuti and rudraksha and the brihad-jabala-
vidya, which grants liberation. Kalagni described the five faces of
the god Shiva, and their relationship with other aspects. From the
Sadyojata face comes the earth, and then nivritti (detachment),
from which is born the tawny-coloured cow, Nanda. From its
dung vibhuti is prepared. From the Vamadeva face comes water
and then pratishtha (accomplishment), the dark-coloured cow,
Bhadra, and from its dung bhasita (ash) is produced. From the
Aghora face comes vidya (learning), fire and the red cow, Surabhi,
whose dung produces bhasma. From the Tatpurusha face comes
air, the power of peace, the white cow, Sushila, and from its dung
kshara (ash) is produced. From the Ishana face comes akasha
(space or ether), the power of shantyatita (transcending peace) and
the multi-coloured cow, Sumana. Its dung produces raksha (ash).
The powers of these five types of ash are next described. Vibhuti
gives power and prosperity, bhasma consumes sins, bhasita shines
brightly, kshara removes troubles, raksha provides protection.

The second Brahmana has nineteen verses. Bhushunda asks
Kalagnirudra about the bhasma bath, which has the characteristics
of Agni and Soma (the moon). He describes the heat and radiance
of fire and the soft nectar of the moon that produce the world.

The concept of Shiva and Shakti are explained. The one whose body is burned by the fire of Shiva and drenched by the nectar of Soma enters the deathless world of yoga. Shiva has two Shaktis, one above, located between the Ajna Chakra and Sahasrara in the Brahma-randhra (top of the head), and one below, in the Muladhara. When these Shaktis or powers of Shiva join together through the upward and downward movement, Brahman is attained. The world becomes bhasma as there is no world other than Brahman. This is a process with many complex aspects, explained in more detail in the Upanishad.

In the third Brahmana, which has thirty-eight verses, Bhushunda asks Kalagnirudra more about vibhuti. He describes in detail how bhasma is to be prepared, the types of cows and the mantras to be used. There are also substitutes or different ways of preparing bhasma.

The fourth Brahmana with forty-one verses has further explanations of the bhasma-snana or bathing in ashes; using various Shaiva Mantras one should sprinkle the ashes on the angas or body parts. The brahmana sprinkles ashes over the entire body but the kshatriya avoids the face, representing Tatpurusha. Bhasma should be sprinkled in the morning and evening twilights, at the dead of night, before and after sleeping, eating and drinking water, after performing essential duties, and after coming in contact with women, eunuchs, cats, eagles, cranes, mice and others of that kind to expiate the sin. He should not sprinkle ashes over his body when near the gods, fire, the guru or old men, or when one of the lowest caste is within sight.

Before noon, ashes mixed with water from a conch should be applied.

Next, methods of applying the tripundra are prescribed. The brahmana should sprinkle ashes over the face and the kshatriya over the head, then the tripundra is applied to thirty-two places or half that number, that is, sixteen, eight or five. The best is thirty-two places, which are then listed, together with the mantras to be used and the deities to be focused on. Next, the sixteen, eight and five places are described along with mantras and deities.

The fifth Brahmana with twenty verses equates the tripundra with the three Vedas. The types of ashes to be worn by the different castes and for the different stages of life is described, and shudras too are mentioned. The different types of ascetics mentioned are yatis, vanaprasthas, ativarnashramis and Shivayogis. Shiva yogis can use ashes from a Shiva temple or those associated with Shiva. Even those who do nothing else will be blessed by wearing the tripundra, while those who give up wearing it can never get liberation. Those who are against the bhasma mark are tainted by great sin. Next, the further merits of a bhasma-snana (ash bath) are described. It also describes the bhasmanishtha, one who wears the tripundra, lies on ashes and is covered in ash.

In the sixth Brahmana with eighteen verses, Bhushunda asks Kalagnirudra about the virtues of the five-named bhasma. Kalagnirudra tells him the story of Karuna. He was descended from Vasishtha and the son of Dhananjaya, from his senior-most wife. Dhananjaya had a hundred wives. Karuna's wife was Shuchismita. As his brothers troubled him, he visited the shrine of the god Nrisimha on the banks of the river Bhavani. There he inadvertently smelled a lime fruit that had been offered to the god and was cursed by the others there to become a fly for a hundred years. His wife protected him (as a fly), but his brothers caused him to be drowned in oil. His wife took his fly body to Arundhati, who revived him with vibhuti created from the agnihotra, along with the Mrityunjaya Mantra. After a hundred years a brother again caused his death, and once again bhasma revived him. Arundhati explained that in the city of Kashi there were five such revivals and in earlier days bhasma had revived several of the gods. After his second revival by Arundhati he was also relieved from the curse and assumed his prior form under the name Dadhichi and reached his own ashram.

Another story about bhasma is related to Gautama's marriage to Ahalya. Seeing her beauty, all the gods lust for her and their spiritual development is arrested. They go to the rishi Durvasa who frees them from the sin by using bhasma and the Shatarudriya Mantra. Additional qualities of bhasma are described—it provides the knowledge of Hari and Shankara and destroys all sins, including of the murder of a brahmana. It is the bhasma of Shiva which transforms Hari and gives Vasudeva a white lustre. Hari then glorifies Shiva.

It is further explained that bhuti (ashes) generates all power. In the body, the Vasus are in front, the Rudras to the right, the Vishvedevas to the left. Brahma, Vishnu and Maheshvara are in the navel, with the sun and moon on either side.

The riks (verses) of all the Vedas rest in Brahman, in which all the gods find dissolution. The fire of Brahman turns everything into ash. Those who know the Vedas know that the holy ash is the akasha in which all gods and worlds are contained. (Thus, dissolution into Brahman is related to being consumed and turned into ash.) Those who know Brahman are absorbed in it. The wisdom or vidya known as brihad-jabala is found in the four Vedas, which bestows immortality. The one who knows it becomes a guru. The guru who imparts this requires a dakshina (gift) such as that of a cow.

In the seventh Brahmana, which has seventeen verses, King Janaka of Videha asks rishi Yajnavalkya to describe the rules for wearing the tripundra mark. Yajnavalkya describes the application of bhasma with the mantras of the Panchabrahmas, Sadyojata, etc. He next explains the fruits of bhasma-dharana. By this, one comes to realize that everything except Brahman is bhasma and thus one attains union with Shiva. Several Paramahamsas (high-level sannyasis) such as Samvartaka, Aruni, Shvetaketu, Durvasa, Ribhu, Nidagha, Jadabharata, Dattatreya, Raivataka, Bhushunda and others were liberated through vibhuti-dharana.

Next, Yajnavalkya explains that whether one is a brahmana, kshatriya, vaishya or shudra, the one who wears bhasma will attain Shiva. With bhasma ash, the hairs on the body will turn into Shiva lingas.

Janaka and Paippalada then go to Brahma Loka and ask Prajapati about the tripundra mark, and he replies that it is as great as Ishvara. Then Paippalada goes to Vaikuntha and questions Vishnu, who says the same. Next, Paippalada approaches Kalagnirudra, who explains that one who wears the bhasma and tripundra in the correct way attains identity with Shiva as well as immortality and identity with Brahman.

Sanat Kumara then asks Kalagnirudra about the rules for wearing the rudraksha. He explains that the rudraksha originates from the eyes of Rudra. When Sadashiva destroys the world and closes his eye of destruction, rudrakshas are generated. There are huge benefits to be attained by wearing the rudraksha; for instance, if worn on the head, it is equal to the fruit of a gift of 1000 cows.

The eighth Brahmana with ten verses deals with the fruit obtained by studying this Upanishad, as explained by Kalagnirudra. Among other things, it surmounts death (mrityu) and leads to freedom from sin, the conquest of all worlds and the knowledge of all the shastras. The teacher of the Brihad-jabala-vidya is superior to all others.

Dakshinamurti Upanishad

The *Dakshinamurti Upanishad* belongs to the *Krishna Yajur Veda* and is of uncertain date. This Upanishad has thirty-three verses. It describes the secret philosophy of Shiva as Dakshinamurti, the south-facing one. It has mantras relating to Shiva and methods to reach the knowledge of the Shivatattva. The rishi Markandeya explains this knowledge to Shaunaka and others. The setting is the region between the Sarasvati and Drishadvati rivers known as Brahmavarta, where Shaunaka and other rishis are assembled under a great banyan tree. They approach Chiranjivi Markandeya and ask him how he has lived for such a long time in perpetual bliss. He explains that it is through the experience of Shivatattva (Shiva as the supreme) that he has attained the bliss of Brahman. Shaunaka then asks him nine questions concerning Shivatattva to which Markandeya replies. Markandeya explains the nature of Shiva Paramatman as Dakshinamurti, who bestows kaivalya on all on whom his gaze falls.

He describes the different secret mantras through which Dakshinamurti should be worshipped, and his forms and attributes for meditation. Anga-nyasa (touching the body parts to invoke a deity) is prescribed, using the mantras. Some chakras and the light within are also mentioned, and the method of meditating to generate the inner light. The story of Markandeya being saved by Shiva from Yama is referred to. Various descriptions of Dakshinamurti are provided, including that he is bright white, like crystal and silver. He is surrounded by Shuka and other rishis. The Sahasrara Chakra and Anahata Chakra are where the Parmatman can be seen. The Ajna Chakra is also mentioned.

Ganapatya Upanishad

The *Ganapati* or *Ganapatya Upanishad* is attached to the *Atharva Veda* and has nineteen verses. This late Upanishad is perhaps of the sixteenth century CE.[1] It identifies the god Ganesha, also known as Ganapati, with Brahman and the supreme creator. The Upanishad begins with an invocation of praise to the deity, whose seed syllable (Bija Mantra) is 'Lam'. He is of the form of Turiya and Omkara, and the Kutasthatman (all controller). He is the Pradhana-purusha in the mula-prakriti, the jiva and atman in all, and has the character of Vishnu and Rudra and is identical with Brahman. It asks for protection and knowledge. As Brahman, Ganapati is both knowledge and intelligence, the creator and sustainer of the world. The text goes on to say that located in the Muladhara (chakra), Ganesha is meditated upon by Yogis and is beyond Brahma, Vishnu, Rudra and other gods. He is eternal, beyond the three gunas, and beyond the past, present and future. Other seed syllables too are described, including 'gam'. The symbolism of the Ganesha Mantra (Om Ganapataye Namah) is given, as well as the Ganapati Gayatri and a meditation on the deity:

> Let us think of the one-toothed, let us meditate on his crooked trunk, may it direct us;
> With one tusk and four arms, carrying noose and goad, with his hands dispelling fear and granting boons, with a mouse as his vehicle;
> Red, with a large belly, and ears like winnowing baskets; wearing red, limbs smeared with red paste, worshipped with red flowers;
> A merciful god to his devotees, creator of the world, and the primary cause of creation.[2]

All aims are said to be attained by 1000 repetitions of this Upanishad, and worshipping Ganesha leads to intelligence, fame and freedom from obstacles. Though he is the beloved son of Shiva, he is also the supreme Brahman.

Jabali Upanishad

The *Jabali* or *Jabalya Upanishad* is attached to the *Sama Veda* and has twenty-three verses. *Jabali* explains the nature of Pashupati (the Lord Shiva) and the jiva (the individual soul).

In this, Paippaladi (the son of Paippalada, Paippalada meaning a son or descendant of Pippalada) asks the rishi Jabali to explain the knowledge of Para Brahman. At first, Jabali remains silent and

Paippaladi understands that silence indicates the profound truth of Brahman. Paippaladi then asks Jabali shorter questions on tattva (Brahman), the jiva, pashu and Ishvara. When Jabali responds that he will explain all this, Paippaladi wants to know how he gained this knowledge. Jabali says he has received this from Shadanana (the six-faced, a name of Karttikeya, son of Shiva), who received the knowledge from Ishana (Shiva) through upasana (worship and meditation). Jabali explains the identity of the jiva or pashu with Shiva, also known as Isha and Pashupati Parameshvara. Jabali explains that Pashupati is attained through the wearing of vibhuti marks, the tripundra and the process of wearing them, which is termed Shambhavavrata (the vow of Shambhu) that has been explained in the Vedas.

Then, Sanat Kumara enquires about the size of the tripundra mark, and the three lines, their relationship with Om and with the various agnis and deities and this is explained. Wearing this has many benefits, including ultimate union with the supreme Shiva.

Kaivalya Upanishad

The *Kaivalya* is a short Upanishad that deals with the nature of Brahman. This Upanishad is attached to the *Krishna Yajur Veda* or according to other sources to the *Atharva Veda* and has two different though similar versions. The version used here is attached to the *Atharva Veda*. The *Kaivalya* is considered a minor Upanishad and is classified as a Shaiva text. In date it is close to the *Shvetashvatara*, *Manduka* and *Maha-Narayana*. Osho best explains the concept of *Kaivalya*. It is when one is alone but not lonely, when one has no need for another and instead has a sense of wholeness. He explains that this ultimate freedom has been called moksha, nirvana and kaivalya.

The Upanishad begins with a request from Ashvalayana, an ancient rishi, to the god Brahma, to reveal to him the highest state.

Brahma says that immortality (amritatattvam) is not attained by work (karma), children or wealth, but only by renunciation (tyaga). It describes the method of meditation on the inner Self, through which the truth of Brahman can be known.

The text begins with the words 'Then Ashvalayana approached the Lord Parameshti (Brahma).' Then, or *atha*, is the way many scriptures begin, indicating that there are certain prerequisites the student has already undergone or practised, making this enquiry possible. Ashvalayana is a teacher (rishi) in the *Rig Veda*. Ashvalayana next asks the lord to teach him the Brahmavidya, the highest knowledge that is a secret to most people, by which the Purusha or Self can be reached. To him, Pitamaha (the god Brahma) says, 'Know this by shraddha, bhakti and dhyana, i.e., faith, devotion and meditation (2). It cannot be attained by work, children, wealth, or renunciation. Self-controlled sages attain immortality, higher than heaven [nakam], when they enter the cave [of the heart] where it shines.'

Further, he says, it can be attained by those who are pure in mind and on the path of renunciation (4). (The same verse is in *Mundaka* 3.2.6).

It then describes how to sit in a comfortable posture (sukhasana) in an undisturbed place that is clean and pure, in an attitude of sannyasa, having controlled the senses, and then meditate on the lotus of the heart (hridaya-pundarika) that is untainted, clear, pure and free from sorrow (5). The Upanishad continues to describe the formless one seated within the heart. It is unthinkable, unmanifest, has endless forms, is auspicious (shivam), is peaceful, immortal, the origin of Brahma, the creator, without beginning, middle or end, the One, all-pervading, of knowledge and bliss (chidananda), formless, wonderful.

After explaining the formless Brahman, the text suggests worship on a form of the blue-necked Parameshvara, the consort of Uma (7), that is, Shiva. Both Shiva and Uma are worshipped together. Here, Shiva is seen as the Supreme, he is Brahma, Indra and Shiva, he is Vishnu, Prana, Kala, Agni and the moon, self-luminous, immutable, the Supreme.

More descriptions of the Supreme and how to attain it follow.

The importance of the *Kaivalya* lies in it being a straightforward and poetic description of Brahman. Several similar verses are found in the major Upanishads and in the Bhagavad Gita, but this text is concise, with just twenty-four verses. Two verses of this poetic description are given below:

> That which illumines the states of waking, dreaming and sleeping, that Brahman am I. Knowing this, one is free from all bonds (17).
> I am smaller than the smallest, and larger than the largest. I am the varied universe. I am ancient, the Purusha, the supreme ruler (Isha), effulgent and auspicious in form (Shiva-rupa) (20).

Verse 18 uses the term Sadashiva (I am Sadashiva), which could be used as a name of Shiva or translated as 'ever auspicious' (as by Swami Chinmayananda).

There are two more verses after Verse 24, considered Part II of the text. It states that one who has not seen Brahman can study the Shatarudriya every day, which will provide a number of benefits including the fruit of Avimukta (Avimukta is either Varanasi or the Ajna Chakra). One who is a sannyasi and chants the Shatarudriya reaches Brahman and kaivalya (The Shatarudriya is a passage in the *Yajur Veda*).

Kalagnirudra Upanishad

The *Kalagnirudra Upanishad* belongs to the *Krishna Yajur Veda* and has ten prose passages. This Upanishad is a dialogue between

Sanat Kumara and Kalagnirudra (Shiva). It deals with the rules for bhasmadharana, that is, wearing the tripundram (three-line mark) with ashes in order to attain Brahman. This Upanishad helps the upasaka (worshipper or devotee) to attain the state of Kalagnirudra through removing the ignorance of the atman. The rishi of the mantra for this Upanishad is Samvartagni, the metre is anushtubh.

Sanat Kumara, the mindborn son of Brahma, meditates on Kalagnirudra, who then appears before him. Sanat Kumara through his meditation realized that to tell an ordinary person 'all this is Brahman' is useless. But if the person first purifies himself, then it would be possible to know Brahman. With this in mind, Sanat Kumara asks Kalagnirudra for the rules for the tripundram. Following these rules would purify the mind and thus later lead the person to Brahman. Kalagnirudra then explains the rules, known as the Shambhavavrata, as well as the mantras to be used. Sanat Kumara then asks about the measurement of the lines, the deities associated with them and other aspects. The three lines are connected to the Vedas, deities, various agnis, the syllables of Om, among other things. Understanding this and practising correctly, one will reach kaivalya. If someone cannot practise it, he should study this Upanishad and even this will lead him to Brahman, shining at the topmost part of the Pranava as the Turiya. (The Pranava is Om, and the ardha-matra or crescent and dot above it represents Turiya, the fourth state of consciousness.)

Panchabrahma Upanishad

The *Panchabrahma Upanishad* belongs to the *Krishna Yajur Veda* and has forty-two verses. The date of composition is around the seventh century CE according to Stella Kramrisch[3] as she places it earlier than the Vishnudharmottara Purana that she assigns to this date. In this text, Panchabrahma, the five Brahmas, are identified

with five aspects of the god Shiva. The text begins with Shakala
asking Paippalada (the son or descendant of Pippalada) what came
first and Paippalada lists the Panchabrahma: Sadyojata, Aghora,
Vamadeva, Tatpurusha and Ishana, which are aspects of the
god Shiva.[4] The text describes the nature of each of these, while
the commentator explains them as the five faces of Sadashiva.
Tatpurusha transcends the state of Turiya, that is, it is Turiyatita,
while Ishana is of the character of avyakta (the unmanifest) and
akasha (space), transcending the seven svara or notes of music, and
even the shanti svara beyond them. Ishana is the Pancha-brahma
which it hides within itself and is the source of all creation. It is
the Para Brahman, containing all. Shiva is the same as Brahman,
and the five Brahmas are contained within. The text advocates
the chanting of the five-syllable Shiva mantra, 'Namah Shivayah'.
Once, Mahadeva (Shiva) instructs the rishi Galava on this, and
blesses him, vanishing into himself. Everything is contained in
the Pancha-brahma, which is the non-dual Shiva, the same as
Brahman, the prime cause of all.

In the Brahmapura (the body of Brahman in the microcosm)
is the white lotus known as the dahara, and in the middle is the
daharakasha. That akasha is Shiva, of non-dual consciousness, and
total bliss. This Shiva, existing in the heart of all beings, is the
liberator from the bonds of the world.

Rudrahridaya Upanishad

The *Rudrahridaya Upanishad* belongs to the *Krishna Yajur Veda*
and has fifty-seven verses. It emphasizes that Rudra (Shiva) is the
essence of all. The text begins by Shuka asking his father Vyasa
about the greatest god. Vyasa replies that Rudra has the character
of the god of all gods. Uma has the nature of Vishnu and those
who worship Hari (Vishnu) are actually worshipping Rudra. Uma,
along with Shankara, is known as Vishnu (10). Uma represents all

goddesses, and Rudra all aspects of creation. It is he who created the trimurti, splitting one into three.

Brahman, who is sat-chit-ananda, is the support of all. The aim is to unite with Brahman, who is the same as Shiva. There is an artificial difference between jiva and Isha (god). There are two suparnas (birds) in the body, the jiva eats the fruit and Ishvara does not, but the difference between them is unreal (41–46). The sage who realizes that Brahman is his own atman has reached sat-chit-ananda (being-consciousness-bliss).

Rudraksha-jabala Upanishad

The *Rudraksha-jabala Upanishad* belongs to the *Sama Veda* and has forty-nine verses. The Upanishad is of the tenth century CE or later and focuses on the sacredness of Rudraksha beads. Bhushunda, who is also known as Jabala, asks Kalagnirudra about the benefits of rudraksha. Kalagni explains how they were created. When he destroyed the Tripura (the three cities), he closed his eyes. Drops of water that fell from them became rudrakshas. Even uttering its name brings great merit of the gift of ten cows, and looking at and touching them even more. Rudraksha trees sprang from the drops of water (aksha=eye).

The different types of rudrakshas are explained, and it is said that there are four types to be used by the four castes: white for brahmanas, red for kshatriyas, tawny for vaishyas, black for shudras.

Next, the good and bad types of rudrakshas are explained and the best type described. The text also indicates the large number of aksha beads that should be worn, for instance, 500 over each shoulder, 108 like a sacred thread from shoulder to hip, and more on the head, neck, wrist, arms, ears, waist, etc. It is said that rudrakshas should always be worn, the minimum being 300 and the maximum 1000 (though if they are worn as earlier described, the number would exceed 1000).

While wearing them, various mantras are to be uttered. The *Akshamalika Upanishad* is mentioned to learn the right way of consecrating the beads.

Bhushunda further questions Kalagnirudra on the benefits of wearing beads with varying numbers of facets. Kalagni explains that the one with a single facet is the real form of the Paratattva (Supreme), that with two represents Ardhanarishvara, three represents the three Agnis, four, the god Brahma with four faces, five, the Pancha-brahma, that is, the five-faced Shiva, and six, the god Karttikeya. More types of beads are described, with facets up to fourteen. The one wearing rudraksha should not drink alcohol or eat meat, garlic, onions, radish and the fruit of the shleshmataka (tamarind) and vidvaraha trees. Those who want spiritual powers should not eat these. Special days for wearing rudraksha are also explained.

Then, Sanat Kumara asks Kalagnirudra for more rules for wearing rudraksha. Other rishis too approach him, including Nidagha, Jadabharata, Dattatreya, Katyayana, Bharadvaja, Kapila, Vasishtha and Pippalada. Kalagni again explains that rudrakshas come from the eyes of Rudra. When Sadashiva closes his eyes at the time of pralaya (dissolution), rudrakshas drop from them. Finally, it is said that the one who studies the Rudraksha-jabala vidya becomes a guru and can initiate others. He is purified from all kinds of heinous crimes and sins and becomes one with Shiva, the Paramatman, and does not incarnate again.

(Rudrakshas are also described in other texts, including texts on ayurveda and various Puranas such as the *Shiva Purana*, *Padma Purana* and *Bhagavata Purana*. The different types of rudrakshas have between one and thirty-eight mukhis or facets.)

Sharabha Upanishad

The *Sharabha Upanishad* belongs to the *Atharva Veda*. It praises the god Shiva, particularly in the form of Sharabha.

The rishi Paippalada (descendant of Pippalada) and the god Brahma begin to discuss Parameshvara, the supreme god. Paippalada asks Brahma about the highest god among the trinity of Brahma, Vishnu and Shiva. Brahma explains that he and all other gods emanate from Isha (Shiva), the father of the gods.

He describes how Maheshvara took the form of Sharabha, the fabulous beast, and defeated Nrisimha (the god Vishnu in his man-lion form). The other gods asked him to spare Vishnu. Then Rudra became the hero Virabhadra after piercing Vishnu. Many other conquests of his are described. He had also created the avataras of Vishnu, that is, Matsya, Kurma, Adivaraha, Nrisimha, Vamana, as well as Manmatha (Kama) and Yama. The gods pray to him and Parameshvara removes all their afflictions that arise through birth, death and old age. The blissful state of Brahman, of the atman in the recess of the heart, is attained through Rudra, the Paramatman, the Lord Ishana. He is worshipped as Brahman by Vasishtha, Vyasika (Shuka, son of Vyasa), Vamadeva, Virinchi and other rishis and glorified by Sanatsujata, Sanatana and other sons of Brahma.

There is also a mention of Maya, of illusions that can be surmounted only through knowledge of Shiva Paramatman. Vishnu is praised and said to be the same as Rudra (verses 25–30). The gods thought that Brahma, Vishnu and Shiva were different, but they were all a part of the Paramatman. Isha or Shiva is the eternal, Supreme Paramatman.

This great shastra (text) should only be revealed to a pious and good man, a devotee of god and guru, and of his own atman, and one who performs the austerities of the Vedas. Studying this text, it is said, has tremendous benefits, releases one from all sins and leads to oneness with Shiva.

Shakta Upanishads

The Shakta Upanishads are eight: *Bahvricha, Bhavana, Devi, Sarasvatirahasya, Saubhagyalakshmi, Sita, Tripura, Tripuratapini.*

The Shakta Upanishads can be dated between the twelfth and fifteenth centuries. Farquhar dates them to the thirteenth century or later. There are also even later *Shrividya* and *Shrichakra* Upanishads.

They appear at a time when Devi (goddess) worship was prominent, and equate the supreme atman or Brahman with Devi or one of her forms. These Upanishads combine tantric elements with references to the Vedas and a focus on Brahman. They see the goddess in one of her forms as the Supreme Brahman. Certain practices described in these texts are different from those in other Upanishads, but the end result aimed at is the same, that is, Brahman, the ultimate reality.

The Shakta Upanishads correspond with the Shrividya tradition, which looks at the goddess as Supreme. The worship of the *Shrichakra*, a complex mandala, which represents the goddess, particularly the deity Lalita–Tripurasundari, forms part of this.

Arthur Avalon explains that all Upanishads are shruti (revealed texts), and that tantric is largely a Western term. He points out that the *Suta Samhita* 1.5.4 uses the term 'tantriki' for a way of worship different from Vaidiki. It states that Para Shakti (Supreme Shakti) can be worshipped according to Vedic or tantric methods based on the preference of the person. According to him, 'The tantra shastra in its Shakta form has a special affinity with the Atharva Veda.'[5] He also says that Trayi Vidya does not refer to three Vedas but to three kandas (methods), karma, upasana and jnana (action, worship and knowledge).

It does not mean, he adds, that the Upanishads not commented on by Shankaracharya are without authority. He may not have had the time or considered it necessary, but Appayya Dikshitar, Narayana and Shankarananda have commented on others. Bhaskaraya has commented on the *Kaula*, *Bhavana* and

Tripuramaha Upanishads and Appayya Dikshitar on the *Bhavana* and *Tripuramaha*. Lakshmidhara has commented on the *Aruna* (the *Kaula Upanishad*, not discussed here, forms the basis of the Kaula doctrine.)

Lakshmidhara provides a tika (gloss) on the *Aruni Upanishad* that appears in the Lakshmidhari in Verse 11 of the *Saundaryalahiri*. The *Tripura, Tripuratapini, Bhavana* and *Devi* Upanishads, along with the Shri-sukta of the *Rig Veda* are recited in Shrividya rituals.

Bahvricha Upanishad

The *Bahvricha Upanishad* is attached to the *Rig Veda* and has nine verses. It is referred to by the Advaita scholar Madhava, hence it should be before the fourteenth century when Madhava lived. A part of the early *Aitareya Upanishad* is sometimes called the *Bahvricha*, but this text is entirely different. The *Bahvricha* has the commentary of Appayya Dikshitar.

The Bahvricha means 'one who knows the Rik' or the *Rig Veda*.

The text states that in the beginning, only Devi existed. She created the world, and is known as a part of Kama and of Shringara (Love and Beauty). Through her, Brahma, Vishnu and Rudra were born, as well as the Maruts, Gandharvas, Kinnaras, and all kinds of other beings including people. She is the Para Shakti (Supreme power) and the Shambhavi-vidya, established as the secret Om. The Upanishad goes on to affirm that she is the atman, the only reality, equal to Brahman. She illumines the inner and outer worlds and is described as Maha-Tripurasundari.

She is also known as Shodashi, Shrividya, Panchadashakshari, Shri-mahatripura-sundari, Bala, Ambika, Bagala, Svayam-vara-kalyani, Bhuvaneshvari, Chamunda, Chanda, Varahi, Tiraskarini, Raja-Matangi, Shuka-shyamala, Laghu-shymala, Ashva-rudha,

Pratya-angira (opposed to Angira), Dhumavati, Savitri, Sarasvati, Gayatri, Brahma-nanda-kala.

Bhavana Upanishad

The *Bhavana Upanishad* is attached to the *Atharva Veda* and focuses on Para Shakti and the inner body. The *Bhavana* was commented on by Bhaskaraya of the eighteenth century as well as by Upanishad Brahmayogin, the two versions used being slightly different. There is also a third, longer version with sixty-seven sections, while that used by Bhaskaraya has thirty-six. Bhaskaraya's commentary provides ritual practices and is used by Shrividya practitioners.

Para Shakti, the higher Shakti (feminine power), is seen as supreme in this text. Its philosophy can be called Shaktadvaita.

The text begins by stating that the guru is Para Shakti and is the cause or creator of all. The form of this Shakti is within the body and is represented by the Shrichakra with its nine aspects. The offerings are received by Varahi, the father, and Kurukulla, the mother. There are further descriptions of the inner body, the ten pranas and the fourteen main nadis. The inner self is also compared to various goddesses; the unmanifest, the great, and the sense of 'I' are represented by the inner triangle, with the three deities, Kameshvari, Bhagamalini and Vajreshvari. Absolute awareness is Kameshvara, while the supreme deity is Lalita, identical with the Self.

Worship occurs when all distinctions such as you, I, existence, non-existence, the sense of duty and non-duty have been removed. Meditation on the inner chakra is described here, based on Shakta elements.

This text is thus a combination of tantric ideas, goddess worship and elements of Advaita. The commentator Bhaskaraya emphasizes the tantric aspects, whereas Upanishad Brahmayogin focuses on its Advaitic aspects.

Devi Upanishad

The *Devi Upanishad* is attached to the *Atharva Veda* and focuses on the glory of the goddess Devi. It begins with the gods asking Mahadevi, 'Who are you?' Devi replies that she is the Supreme Being, identical with Brahman, including all that is born and unborn. In the fourth and fifth verses, Devi mentions other deities, saying that she moves with the Rudras, Vasus, with Adityas and Vishvedevas, supports Mitra, Varuna, Indra, Agni and the two Ashvins, and upholds Soma, Tvashtr, Pushan, Bhaga, the wide-stepping Vishnu, Brahma and Prajapati. Though this Upanishad is attached to the *Atharva Veda*, these verses are very similar to the *Rig Veda* (10.25.1–2), while the succeeding verses (8–12) are also found in the Devi Gita (1.44–48).

She, here, is the eight Vasus, the eleven Rudras, the twelve Adityas. She is the Vishvedevas (those) who drink Soma and (those) who do not; she is the yatus, asuras, rakshasas, pishachas, yakshas and siddhas (18). She is sattva, rajas and tamas. She is Prajapati, Indra and Manu. She is the grahas (planets), nakshatras and other luminous bodies. She is the divisions of time, and the form of Kala (Time). In one verse she is described as seated in the lotus of the heart, resplendent as the morning sun, holding a hook and noose, with hands in the abhaya and varada mudras, three-eyed and red-robed, tender-hearted and granting all desires.

She is unknowable, without end, incomprehensible and unborn. She alone is present everywhere, yet she has all forms. Beyond her there is nothing (Verses 26–28).

These verses indicate her elevation to the supreme status of Brahman.

Sarasvatirahasya Upanishad

The *Sarasvatirahasya Upanishad* is attached to the *Taittiriya Samhita* of the *Krishna Yajur Veda* and is known in two or more

versions. In one it has sixty-eight verses in a single section, while
in another the text is divided into two chapters. It focuses on the
goddess Sarasvati as the supreme deity (Shanti Mantra 'Van me
manasi'). This summary is based on Upanishad Brahmayogin's
text and commentary.

Some of its verses are found in the *Vakya-sudha*, an Advaita
text. Based on this, Winternitz and Louis Renou dated it to before
1000 CE, with a possible composition by Shankara. The early
German scholar Windischmann feels the Balabodhini attributed
to Shankara was also known as the *Vakya-sudha* and *Drigdrishya-
viveka*, but many texts attributed to Shankara may not have been
composed by him. The text has elements of Advaita, bhakti and
goddess worship.

In this Upanishad, some rishis ask Ashvalayana to explain to
them how the knowledge of 'tat' or 'that', signifying the supreme
Brahman, can be gained. By what meditation would they know
the truth? He says he has attained it through the ten-verse mantra
praising the goddess, as well as the seed syllables related to her
worship. Both these are revealed in this Upanishad. Sarasvati is
described as shining like pearls, camphor and the moon, wearing
garlands of golden champaka flowers (5). In addition, she is referred
to as the Supreme ruler and the essence of Vedanta (Verse 7). The
seed syllables include mystical sounds such as 'hrim' or 'srim'.

Various rishis apart from Ashvalayana are mentioned in
connection with the mantras, including Bharadvaja, Atri,
Madhuchhandas, Uchathyaputra, Bhargava, Brihaspati and
Gritsamada, most of whom are known from the *Rig Veda*.

Sarasvati is identified with the goddess Sharada, 'dwelling in
Kashmir's city' (Verse 37).

In other verses, she is called the spouse of Brahma and is also
known as Bhavani. In one of the verses (46), Sarasvati explains
that even the god Brahma gained self-knowledge through her.
Truth, knowledge, bliss and Brahmanhood are her nature. The

next few verses state that through the equilibrium of the three gunas, sattva, rajas and tamas, Prakriti was created in her, and she is also Purusha. Creation caused by Maya too is described, as well as the appearance of the jiva and the veiling power of Brahman.

Three important verses (60–63) describe two types of concentration in the heart, that with aspects and without. Concentrating without aspects is like a flame in a windless spot, bringing the joy of deep experience. When the Supreme Self is realized, immortality awaits the mind wherever it goes (Verse 66).

Saubhagyalakshmi Upanishad

The *Saubhagyalakshmi Upanishad* is attached to the *Rig Veda*. It describes the goddess Lakshmi and the path of yoga.

The *Saubhagyalakshmi* has three parts. In the first part, with twelve verses, the devas ask the Lord Narayana to explain to them about Shri, the goddess of prosperity. Narayana explains the method of meditation on her through fifteen verses that begin with the word 'hiranyavarnam' or golden. The rishis of this hymn are mentioned as Ananda, Kardama, Chiklita and Indirasuta. The verses of the Shri-sukta are used to consecrate the body. The verses, as well as some seed syllables, are also to be placed in the chakras. The goddess is extensively described in a number of verses. She shines like burnished gold. She is bathed in water contained in jars, poured on her by elephants through their trunks. Her symbolic seat and nine powers and methods of worship are explained. She is the spouse of Vishnu, golden in form, and holds a lotus. She has a garland of gold, a chaplet of silver and is adorned with pearls. She is the moon goddess and the sun goddess and is fond of bilva leaves. This section ends with the statement that the science of the goddess Shri is only for those free from desires. This statement is made even though she is actually worshipped for prosperity and wealth.

The second section, with nineteen verses, explains the path of yoga. The yogi is alert and eats little. Practising pranayama in a secluded place, seated in a firm posture, the yogis see the inner light while meditating on Om. When the Sushumna channel is cleared, divine sounds are heard in the Anahata Chakra, the yogi's body becomes sacred and filled with splendour. After the knots of Vishnu and Rudra too are pierced, the prana moves upward to the space of perfection. The all-pervading sound is then heard and one becomes like Sanaka and other sages. The finite is then identified with the infinite, the fragments with the whole, and, meditating on the vast source, one becomes immortal. Renouncing the sense of I, the sage is rooted in truth and never again has sorrow. Like salt melted in water, the self and mind are fused, leading to bliss. The lower and higher selves are joined, wakefulness, dreams and sleep vanish, along with sorrow, and Brahman is attained, that is the same everywhere.

In the third section, with ten verses, the devas ask the lord about the nine chakras, which are then described. At the base (Muladhara) is the Brahma Chakra shaped like three waves, which grants all desires. The next is the Svadhishthana, with the power to attract the world. The third is the navel chakra called Manipuraka. It can grant all siddhis. The Hridaya (heart) Chakra with eight petals and the lingam of light is next, with hamsa as the symbol. The person becomes beloved of all and attracts the whole world. Upanishad Brahmayogin comments that this is the Turiya Chakra that leads to the state of Turiya, beyond waking, dreaming and sleeping.

The fifth is the Kantha (throat) Chakra, with a width of four fingers. The Ida Nadi is to the left, Pingala to the right, and Sushumna in the middle. Meditating on this, one attains the knowledge of Anahata (the unstruck note). The sixth is the Talu (palate) Chakra. Amrita flows there and it also has the tenth opening (uvula) which one should meditate on. There, the chitta or mindstuff is dissolved. The seventh is the Bhru (brow) Chakra. This is the Ajna Chakra which gives power over words. The eighth is the Brahma-randhra, the Nirvana Chakra. One should meditate on the opening there, like a thread of smoke. It is the chakra of Para Brahman, which provides moksha. The ninth is the Akasha (space) Chakra. It is upturned and one should meditate on the centre of it, leading to the supreme void. All desires are fulfilled here.

The Upanishad ends with a list of the benefits to be gained by reading it. The person is purified, has all types of knowledge, and wealth and possessions. He never returns, that is, he has attained immortality.

Sita Upanishad

The *Sita Upanishad* is attached to the *Atharva Veda* and has thirty-seven verses. The goddess Sita is seen as the first cause and the Supreme being.

The first twenty verses discuss Sita and her different forms. The Upanishad begins by the devas asking Prajapati, 'Who is Sita?' Prajapati replies that Sita is the first cause, she is prakriti and the Pranava (Om). The 'i' in her name represents maya, who is unmanifested; 'sa' stands for satya or truth, and 'ta' is the goddess of speech. In manifested form she is beautiful like the moon, with faultless limbs, adorned with ornaments. She sustains all embodied beings by Shri Rama's presence. Verse 8 again says that she is Om, the Supreme cause, while Verse 9 begins with the same verse as the *Brahma Sutra*, 'Now, therefore, an enquiry into Brahman.' The text then goes on to describe Sita. She is the Vedas, all the gods, all the worlds, all forms and a lot more, including all activities and attributes. She can assume all forms including those of devas, people, gandharvas, the elements, organs of sense, the mind and prana. Her power is threefold, the power of desire, of knowledge, and of action. There are three Iccha Shaktis (powers of desire) represented by the goddesses Shri, Bhumi and Nila. Auspiciousness is the form of Shri, holiness is the form of Bhumi, Nila represents the sun, moon and fire. As the moon, she is the mistress of herbs, of the tree of plenty, of plants of all kinds and of amrita, or divine nectar, the drink of immortality. She satisfies the gods with amrita and the animals with grass. As the sun, she illuminates all the worlds and revolves as the wheel of time. As fire she is the food and drink of all beings. She is the sacrifice of the gods and dwells inside and outside fuel as coolness and warmth and is both eternal and fleeting.

The goddess Shri assumes this threefold form for the protection of the world. She is known as Shri and Lakshmi. Bhumi or Bhudevi sustains the earth, and her essence is the Pranava. Nila is adorned with lightning. She nourishes all living beings and assumes all forms. As the root of the worlds, she takes the form of water. The form of kriya-shakti, that is, the power of action, emanates as sound from the mouth of Hari. This becomes a drop, which then becomes Om. From Om comes the Rama–Vaikhanasa mountain. On that mountain are many branches (shakhas) of action and knowledge. Succeeding verses (from 21 onwards) discuss the four Vedas and the Vaikhanasa philosophy. The *Atharva* is considered the same in essence as the other three Vedas, but slightly different as it has aspects of magic. The number of shakhas in each Veda are given, after which it (Verse 26) describes the Vaikhanasa philosophy. Vaikhanasa looks at the pratyaksha darshana, and munis (sages) are always engaged in this philosophy. Next, the six Vedangas are listed. The Upangas, Nyaya and Mimamsa works on dharma and the Vedas are mentioned, as well as all branches of Nibandha, on conduct or ethics (achara), the Dharma Shastras upheld by great rishis, itihasa and Purana. This is followed by a list of other auxiliary branches of knowledge, vastuveda, dhanurveda, gandharvaveda (music), daivika (occult) and ayurveda, referred to here as the five Upavedas. Danda, niti, varta (commentary), vidya, conquest of vayu (the breath), these are the twenty-one known through the light of the self (as self-evident).

Once again, the Vaikhanasas are referred to (Verses 32–33) which state that the word of Vishnu was revealed through Vaikhanasa as the three Vedas. Vaikhanasa, the rishi of olden days, brought forth these three.

The text goes on to describe the power to act, which has a Brahma form (Brahma-mayam rupam). The power is then described as the memory of the Lord. The power has many aspects, including that of manifestation and evolution, constriction and expansion. It contains everything, including faces, limbs and colours. It is at the same time both different and non-different. As the consort of the Lord, Sita is dependent on him, containing latent power that manifests itself. Just by closing and opening her eyes, she creates, sustains and destroys. When she retracts her power, she rests on the Lord's chest as the srivatsa. Further verses (36–37) describe her numerous powers. In the last verse (Verse 37), she is clearly identified with the goddess Lakshmi, seated on a throne in padmasana, though indirectly the identification has already been made with the reference to the srivatsa.

Tripura Upanishad

The *Tripura Upanishad* is attached to the *Rig Veda* and has seventeen verses. It focuses on three mystical paths of the goddess and links tantric practices with the Vedas.

Brooks actually questions why this text is classified as an Upanishad, that is, is it Vedic or tantric? Scholars differ, but the eighteenth-century commentator Bhaskaraya says it is both. The text belongs to the Shrikula, that is of beneficent goddesses, rather than Kalikula, which has terrible images.[6] This Upanishad is first mentioned by Kaivalyashrama, who comments on the Saundarya Lahiri. He is after Lakshmidhara (circa 1500), considered an authority on Shrividya, and before Bhaskaraya, but only Bhaskaraya and Upanishad Brahmayogin look at the complete text. Though it uses Vedic language, Brooks feels it belongs to the post–fifteenth century.[7] There is also a commentary attributed to Appayya Dikshitar, though it may not be his, and another commentary by Gangacharana Vedantavagisha that is Advaitic like that of Upanishad Brahmayogin. Yet another is assigned to Ramananta tirtha or Vachaspati.[8] The *Tripura* is a companion to the Bhavana, which prescribes internal worship, while this is external. According to Brooks, 'As a Kaula-oriented text advocating the ritual use of wine, meat, sexual intercourse and erotic meditation, Tripura Upanishad deals with Tantrism's most radical doctrines and practices'.[9]

In just a few verses, the *Tripura* deals with all the important topics of Shakta tantrism. The text begins with a reference to Tripura, the three cities, and the three pathways. Like all tantric texts, it is difficult to understand without a commentary.

In the first verse, the Binduchakra is said to contain three letters—a, ka, tha—forming a triangle. In the next few verses, other triangles are referred to, thus providing a description in five verses of the Shrichakra of Tripurasundari. The sixth verse says that all devis are actually Tripura, while the next (Verse 7) says by knowing her the sadhak attains the light of Tripura. Verse 14 says that both male and female elements of the universe are equal. Bhaskaraya comments on this by quoting an agamic verse that says Shiva without Kundalini is no better than a shava (corpse). The text also describes nirguna dhyana, and therefore can be interpreted as an Advaitic text.

Tripuratapini Upanishad

The *Tripuratapini Upanishad* belongs to the *Atharva Veda* and has five parts. Among its commentaries is one by Vachaspati. The *Tripuratapini* is similar to the *Tripura Upanishad* but much longer.

Part I has thirty-nine verses. It begins by stating that the Lord (Sadashiva), disguised as Prajapati, Vishnu and Rudra, came to be known as the goddess Tripura. Succeeding verses praise both the god Shiva and the goddess Tripura and state that everything including the Vedas was created by the union of Shiva and Shakti (Verse 6). Next the text provides a mystical explanation of the Gayatri Mantra. It repeatedly focuses on the divine union of Shiva and Shakti, bringing forth all creation. It also explains other mantras, including some seed syllables. The mantras include those of Agastya, Vagbhava, Kama and Shanmukha. The methods in which the mantras should be repeated are described. By repeating the Agastya Mantra after that of Shanmukha, one reaches the supreme Shiva. Various ways to use the mantras given in the text are provided, which are quite complicated. In the last verse, Sadashiva affirms that all is really Brahman. It also speaks of meditation of various divinities in the heart.

The second part too, with thirty-four verses, contains the mysteries of the seed syllables and mantras, an explanation of the Shrichakra, and methods of worshipping the goddess. The third part with fifteen verses deals with mystical marks and sacred and powerful triangles. It explains the hand mudras for these and the Chakra Kamakala (3.13). There are also explanations for performing nyasa (internalizing the gods through touch).

In Part IV, with twenty-two verses, the devas, being satisfied with the description of the Gayatri Mantra, ask the Lord about the Mrityunjaya Mantra, and the Tryambaka hymn in anushtubh metre is explained. Tryambaka is so called as he is the master of the three cities. After this is expounded, the devas ask for explanations of the mantras of Shiva, Vishnu, Surya and Ganesha, through which Bhagavati (the goddess) herself will be revealed. In addition, the importance of Om, the Gayatri, Savitri, unuttered mantra (Ajapa), the Sarasvati and the matrika (alphabet) are explained. The text further mentions the mantras of the goddess of speech and explains when the Gayatri, Savitri, Sarasvati and Ajapa Hamsa are to be chanted (4.21). The matrika, it is said (21) pervades all words, shastras and Vedas, while the goddess pervades everything.

In Part V with twenty-eight verses, the devas ask the Lord, who had explained everything about Tripura, to now explain Brahman. The Lord then explains that through the fourth and final maya (avidya, jnana, vijnana and samyagjnana), Brahman is indicated, who is the Supreme person, the supreme Self, whose essence is consciousness (2). In That there are no seen or unseen worlds, devas or asuras, beasts or non-beasts, ascetics or non-ascetics, outcastes or non-outcastes, brahmanas or non-brahmanas. There is only the Supreme Brahman, single and quiet (5.3). The seeker needs to be detached and to centre the mind in the heart. Further verses say Brahman has no parts and is beyond concepts, without beginning or end, immeasurable. Certain verses are similar to other Upanishads, for instance, 'there is no restriction, no origin, none in bondage, none who strives; none seeks liberation and none are liberated, That is the truth (5.13).' Other verses continue to explain Brahman. Whether waking, dreaming or sleeping, there is only one Self, but differences exist as long as the illusion of words encompasses us (Verse 18). The following verse (19) says the lower Brahman is the word, while 5.23 says that focusing the eye of knowledge one must invoke the thought: I am Brahman. The last verse (28) says whoever knows this fourth (wisdom) as the imperishable Brahman attains that state.

Vaishnava Upanishads

The Vaishnava Upanishads are fourteen: *Avyakta, Kalisantarana, Krishna, Garuda, Gopaltapaniya-Purva* and *Uttara, Tarasara, Tripadvibhuti-Maha-Narayana, Dattatreya, Narayana, Nrisimhatapini-Purva* and *Uttara, Ramatapini-Purva* and *Uttara, Ramarahasya,*

Vasudeva, Hayagriva. These texts exist in different versions. The *Maha-Narayana* is considered the earliest.

These texts see Vishnu or one of his forms as the Supreme Brahman.

Avyakta Upanishad

The *Avyakta Upanishad* belongs to the *Sama Veda*. As it is mentioned in Gaudapada's commentary, the date is before the seventh century. The text has several versions.

The Upanishad begins with a prayer, followed by seven chapters. It includes some verses from the *Rig Veda* and other Upanishads and has a mixture of different ideas.

The srishti, or introduction to the text, containing three verses, has a prayer to Narasimha, an incarnation of Vishnu, to 'make me Brahmamatra', that is, of the nature of Brahman. It goes on to say that that there are three stages of the universe— the first is avyakta, or unmanifested; the second is mahatattva, or partially manifested; and the third is ahamkara, that is, the fully manifest or the ego. These three correspond with three hymns of the *Rig Veda*, the Nasadiya-sukta, Hiranyagarbha-sukta and Purusha-sukta.

Chapter 1 has three verses. It begins with a verse similar to the Nasadiya-sukta, stating that in the beginning there was nothing, only knowledge and bliss. Then the one became two, red was the unchanging aspect (Purusha), and yellow Maya (This represents the Samkhya theory of Purusha and prakriti). They united and produced an egg. This became Prajapati. As Prajapati pondered on his origin, he was told by Vach (the goddess of speech) that he came from Avyakta, the unmanifested, and his purpose was to create. Prajapati then practises tapas (austerities) for a thousand years, remaining a brahmachari (celibate student).

Chapter 2 also has three verses. It states that Prajapati sees a verse in the Anushtubh metre which has great power. Using the mantra, he enquires into the meaning of the Red One and sees a Light (Vishnu) along with Shri, on the chariot of Suparna, with Shesha's hood spread above, with eyes being the atma of Shashi, Surya and Havya. (Mrigamukham, naravapusham) Prajapati worships Maha Vishnu, the lord of the whole world.

In Chapter 3 with two verses, Prajapati asks Vishnu how to create the world. Vishnu replies that he should meditate on his own Self, while reciting the Anushtubh verse.

Chapter 4 has five verses and explains how Prajapati meditates and gains the powers of creation.

Chapters 5 and 6, with three and two verses respectively, continue with creation. Using the thirty-two syllables, Prajapati creates the three worlds, thirty-two gods, the Rudras, Adityas, Vasus, people assigned to the four castes (brahmana and shudra are mentioned), the Vedas and the Gayatri, Trishtubh and Jagati metres. Next he creates Ardhanarishvara and divides them to create women and men.

Chapter 7 has a concluding verse in praise of Vasudeva and this Upanishad.

Dattatreya Upanishad

The *Dattatreya Upanishad* is, according to some sources, attached to the *Vajasaneyi Samhita* of the *Shukla Yajur Veda* and, according to others, to the *Atharva Veda*.

It describes the various mantras for worshipping Dattatreya, a form of Vishnu. It begins by Brahma asking Narayana the method of transcending the world.

These mantras include those with one, six, eight, twelve and sixteen syllables as well as longer mantras for specific purposes.

The sixteen-syllable mantra is 'Om aim krom kleem hram hreem hraum sauh dattatreya svaha.'

Garuda Upanishad

The *Garuda Upanishad* is attached to the *Atharva Veda* and has twenty-five verses. It is a late Upanishad that reveres Garuda, the vehicle of Vishnu. It describes Garuda as having claws, a beak and wings of steel. It provides a method for protection against poisons, particularly from the bite of snakes. Brahma is said to have taught this science to Narada, who conveyed it to Brihatsena, through whom it was passed on to Indra, and then to Bharadvaja, who taught it to his pupils. The science is referred to as the science of Brahman.

The text mentions the divine snakes Anantaka, Vasuki, Takshaka, Karkotaka, Padmaka, Maha Padmaka, Elapatraka, Mahailapatraka, Kalika and Kambalasvatara. Those who hear this on a moonlit night and wear it (as an amulet) are free of snakebite for twelve years.

There are several myths and stories about Garuda and his enmity with snakes, though Garuda also has other aspects. In the *Garuda Purana*, his body symbolizes the Vedas.

Gopaltapaniya-Purva and Uttara Upanishad

The *Gopalatapaniya Upanishad* is attached to the *Atharva Veda* and dates to around the seventh century CE. It has two parts. In the first or Purva section, Gopala (the god Krishna) is seen as the Supreme being and creator of the world. Bhakti or devotion to Gopala or Krishna, who is also Govinda, is the method of release from bondage. In the second part, the beautiful city of Mathura is described. It is worshipped by Brahma and Rudra, among others, and is protected by the chakra, gada, bow and mace. Here, Krishna lives, along with Shakti, other women, Balarama, Aniruddha, Pradyumna and Rukmini.

The *Purva-tapaniya* has 49–54 verses in different versions.

The Upanishad begins with a verse in praise of Krishna, who is sat-chit-ananda, who has the knowledge of Vedanta and is both guru and witness.

The second verse states that some munis (sages) ask Brahma: Who is the supreme god? Other questions are: Whom is death afraid of? By knowing whom does everything else become known? Who has created the worlds? To all these questions the answer is Krishna or one of his forms. Both Govinda and Gopijanavallabha are mentioned. All these are names of the Supreme. Liberation is attained by meditating, glorifying and worshipping him (Verse 6).

Brahma describes Gopala as one with a complexion like a monsoon cloud, clothes of lightning, two arms and the knower of transcendental knowledge, supreme controller, decorated with ornaments, surrounded by gopas and gopis (male and female cowherds) and surabhi cows. He rests under a sura-druma tree, and stands on a red lotus flower. Breezes from the Yamuna touch him and those who know him are freed from birth and death. By chanting his mantra 'klim krishnaya govindaya gopijanavallabhaya svaha' one attains the Supreme (Verses 11–12). The text continues with beautiful and poetic descriptions of Krishna, episodes from his life and of methods of worshipping him.

The *Uttara-tapaniya* has 68–118 verses in different versions. It begins with the gopis asking Krishna which brahmana they should give charity to. Krishna replies that they should give it to the rishi Durvasa. He tells them the method of crossing the Yamuna to approach him: they should just say, 'Krishna the brahmachari' and the Yamuna would provide a path. The gopis cross the Yamuna with these words and go to the ashrama of Durvasa, worship him and provide him with delicious food made from milk and ghi and in return he blesses them.

How should they return, they ask him. He asks them to meditate on him as one who only ate durva grass, and the Yamuna would give them a path.

But Gandharvi (Radha) is thinking about the contradictions in these statements. How is Krishna a brahmachari? And how is it said that Durvasa only eats durva grass? Through various examples, Durvasa explains that he is in essence spirit and therefore not an enjoyer of material things. Similarly, Krishna is the Supreme and the creator of two kinds of bodies like the two birds in a tree. One eats while the other is the witness. Krishna has true knowledge and is free from birth and death. He cannot be an enjoyer of the world.

Gandharvi further asks about Krishna, why he was born in the womb of Devaki, how to worship him, and about who his elder brother Balarama really is.

Durvasa replies that in the beginning there was only the Lord Narayana. The god Brahma was born from the lotus of his heart, and was granted a boon. Brahma used the boon to ask the Lord a question: Which was the best of his incarnations?

The Lord then explained that there are seven sacred cities on earth and the most sacred of these is Gopala-puri, that is, Mathura. He then provides an extensive description of Mathura, its forests and its deities, of the supreme god, Gopala or Krishna, and of Balarama, Aniruddha, Pradyumna and Rukmini.

Other deities mentioned and offered obeisance include Rudra, Aditya, Vinayaka, Surya, Vidya-devi, Indra, Agni, Yama, Nirriti, Varuna, Vayu, Kubera and Ishana.

Hayagriva Upanishad

The *Hayagriva Upanishad* is attached to the *Atharva Veda*. It describes the Hayagriva form of Vishnu. In this Upanishad he is the teacher of knowledge. Hayagriva is literally 'horse-necked'

and in this form Vishnu has the head of a horse. According to
one story in the Puranas, Brahma is said to have cursed Vishnu
because in a test he proved to be the greatest of the gods. Thus,
Vishnu lost his head and attended a yajna of the devas wearing a
horse's head. After that he meditated and with the blessings of
Shiva regained his original head. In another story, Vishnu took the
form of Hayagriva to restore the Vedas, which had been stolen by
two asuras, to Brahma.

In this Upanishad, the rishi Narada asks the god Brahma
to teach him the knowledge of Brahman. Brahma tells him that
whoever gains the knowledge of the mantras known by Hayagriva
attains everything. The Upanishad then goes on to provide various
mantras of Hayagriva. One who knows these would gain liberation
and the knowledge of Brahman as Hayagriva can be identified
with Brahman. His form transcends the universe and consists of
knowledge and bliss. He has restored the Vedas and within him
are the Rik, Yajus and Saman. His body consists of Om and the
Sama chant.

Kalisantarana Upanishad

The *Kalisantarana Upanishad* is attached to the *Krishna Yajur
Veda*. It is a short text of three verses, probably of the fifteenth
century. It contains the famous verse 'Hare Krishna, Hare Rama'.
Kali refers to the Kali Yuga, while 'santarana' indicates crossing
over, that is, it provides liberation in this Kali Yuga.

After the shanti mantra 'Om sah navavatu . . .' the text begins
by Narada approaching the god Brahma at the end of the Dvapara
Yuga. He asked him how he, Narada, who kept roaming the earth,
would be able to transcend the Kali Yuga. Brahma responds that
he will reveal to him that which the shruti (revealed texts) keep
secret, through which one can cross the samsara (ordinary life) of
the Kali Yuga. The secret is to constantly repeat the name of the

Lord Narayana, who is the first person, the Adi Purusha. When questioned further about this, Hiranyagarbha reveals this mantra: 'Hare Rama Hare Rama Rama Rama Hare Hare Hare Krishna Hare Krishna Krishna Krishna Hare Hare' (Verse 2).

This sixteen words would remove all the evil effects of the Kali Yuga. There are no rules or regulations regarding this mantra; it can be chanted at anytime, anywhere. After chanting it three and a half crore times, the person is purified, all sins are destroyed and he is released from bondage.

(This mantra was promoted by Gaudiya Vaishnavism and later by the Hare Krishna movement.)

Krishna Upanishad

The *Krishna Upanishad* belongs to the *Atharva Veda*, and is a late text. The text has twenty-six verses in Part I and a prose section in Part II.

The sages see Shri Rama in the forest; he looks ravishingly beautiful and they realize he is the great god Vishnu. He is of the essence of truth, knowledge and bliss. They ask if they can embrace him. They are told that will be possible when he takes the incarnation of Krishna. Then they will be born as the gopis and can embrace him.

When Krishna is incarnated, their wishes are fulfilled. Everything in Gokula is divine, and his lila or divine play creates an enchanted world. Those who had performed austerities became trees in the forest. Those with negative characteristics became the asuras. The Kali Yuga was approaching, but it was postponed as long as Krishna was on the earth. Aspects of the Vedas and Upanishads were incarnated as 16,108 young women. The quality of mercy became his birth mother, Rohini, the earth mother was Satyabhama. His friend Sudama was an incarnation of humility, Uddhava of 'control of the senses' and Akrura of 'truth'. The rishi

Kashyapa was the mortar in Yashoda's house and the rope with
which she tied him to it was Aditi, mother of the gods. Everything,
thus, was an aspect of the divine, and Vaikuntha (heaven) had
come down to earth.

Narayana Upanishad

The *Narayana Upanishad* is attached to the *Taittiriya Samhita* of
the *Krishna Yajur Veda*. In this Upanishad, Narayana is described as
the ultimate source of all gods and everything that exists. Reciting
and meditating on the Narayana mantra 'Om Namo Narayana'
leads to the highest goal. The text goes on to say that the son of
Devaki (that is, Krishna) and the destroyer of Madhu is the same
as Brahman. Narayana, abiding in all beings, is Brahman.

The *Narayana Upanishad* begins with an introductory verse that
the knowledge of the Narayana principle with three aspects will be
revealed. Through this, maya or illusion will totally disappear. The
first chapter then states that Narayana wanted to create living beings.
He created Prana, manas or mind, the senses, elements, the earth,
followed by Brahma, Rudra, Prajapati, Indra, the eight Vasus, eleven
Rudras and twelve Adityas, all the gods, rishis and metres. In fact, all
beings are born from Narayana and all return to him.

The text goes on to say that Narayana is eternal, the one god.
He is Brahma, Shiva, Shakra (Indra), Kala (time), the Adityas,
Vasus, Ashvins, all rishis, directions and quarters and in fact the
whole universe. He is beyond change and there is no one like him.
Taking Rudra as the charioteer and Manas as the reigns, one goes
only to the eternal abode of Vishnu.

The third chapter seems to end the text, stating that this is the
Upanishad of Narayana, but the fourth then provides an explanation
of the mantra 'Om Namo Narayana'. The fifth continues by saying
that Narayana has merged into bliss, Brahman, the Purusha and
Om. He is the highest Brahman, and any yogi who has seen this

is freed from the bondage of the world. Whoever studies this text will reach Narayana.

Nrisimhatapini-Purva and Uttara Upanishad

The *Nrisimhatapini Upanishad* is attached to the *Atharva Veda* and dates to before the seventh century CE. It has two parts. This long text includes explanations of the Nrisimha mantra, how to recite it and the results.

The *Purva-tapini* has five sections, each termed an Upanishad. In the first Upanishad, Prajapati, born alone on a lotus leaf, has a desire to create the world. After practising austerities (tapas) he sees a mantra-raja (king of mantras) of Nrisimha, composed in the Anushtubh metre. The next few verses describe the mantra-raja at length. It deals with the four regions of the universe, the four Vedas, and other mantras. The Anga-mantras, the limbs or branches of the mantra-raja, are referred to, and include the Pranava Om, the Savitr mantra and the Lakshmi mantra. However, the text states that these mantras cannot be taught to women or shudras, and if anyone does so they go downwards after death.[10] It should only be taught to one's son, if he wishes to hear it, or to a disciple. The one who knows this mantra-raja becomes Prajapati, and whoever knows this Upanishad becomes Maha Vishnu.

The second Upanishad further explains the benefits of this raja-mantra. It begins by stating that the devas were afraid of death, sins and worldly life (samsara), and sought refuge in Prajapati. He informed them of the mantra-raja of Narasimha in the Anushtubh metre and through this they overcame death, sins and worldly life.

The mantra-raja is: 'Ugram viram, maha Vishnum/Javalantam sarvatamukham/Nrisimham bhishanam bhadram/mrityu-mrityum namami aham.'

This has been translated by Deussen as: 'The terrible, mighty, great, Vishnu/Burning in all directions/As man-lion, fearful and gracious/As the death of deaths, I adore him.'[11] Succeeding verses further describe and explain this mantra.

The third Upanishad begins with the devas asking Prajapati the Shakti or power and the vijam or seed of the mantra. Prajapati proceeds to explain that Maya is its creative power and akasha or space is the seed of the world.

In the fourth Upanishad, the devas ask Prajapati to explain to them the Anga-mantras, the subsidiary mantras, also composed in the Anushtubh metre. Prajapati then recites and explains the Pranava (Om), the Savitr, the Yajur-lakshmi and Nrisimha-gayatri.

The fifth Upanishad begins with the devas asking Prajapati for an explanation of the Maha Chakra, the great chakra which the yogis say fulfils all wishes and provides liberation. Prajapati describes and explains the Sudarshana Chakra, the disc of Vishnu, as well as associated chakras which together form the Maha Chakra. The one who knows this is a great teacher and instructor of mantras. This Maha Chakra kills evil spirits and protects from death and should be worn as an amulet. Studying these mantras is equivalent to numerous rituals, sacrifices, the Vedas and other texts, and superior to all other mantras.

The *Uttara-tapani* has nine sections known as khandas. In the first section, the devas request Prajapati to explain to them Om, which is the same as the atman. He explains that Om is the whole world, the past, present and future. Through Om, one experiences that One, which is ageless, immortal and beyond fear.

The second khanda explains the four states of consciousness, represented by the atman and Om. One who knows the state of Turiya through the Nrisimha mantra attains the highest atman, full of bliss, and one without a second, while the third describes how the four lines of the Nrisimha mantra correspond with the four syllables of Om. Again, the fourth khanda explains how the atman, Para Brahman and Om correspond with the Nrisimha

mantra. The same theme is continued in the fifth khanda. The
sixth khanda looks at the lower and higher atman and indicates
how the higher atman is attained, through detachment and the
Nrisimha mantra. The seventh explains how the atman and
Brahman are identical and how they are linked with Om and
Nrisimha. The eighth khanda shows how the identity of atman
and Om are attained in the state of Turiya. In the ninth khanda
the devas ask Prajapati more about the atman. He provides
a full description of the atman, which is the only reality, the
self-luminous highest self. It is Vishnu, Ishana and Brahma, one
without a second, beyond duality. The atman is Brahman, and
Brahman is the atman. It is the only reality, and everything else
is unreal.

Maha-Narayana Upanishad

The *Maha-Narayana Upanishad* is different from the *Narayana*,
and has three variants. One, known as *Tripadvibhuti-Maha-
Narayana* is attached to the *Atharva Veda* and has twenty-five
chapters. In this, Narayana is identified with the Supreme.
Liberation is attained through both knowledge and devotion.

Another *Maha-Narayana* with sixty-four or eighty chapters is
attached to the *Krishna Yajur Veda*. The date could be fairly early,
between 500 BCE and the first century CE. It is included in both
Dara Shikoh's and Colebrooke's collections.

The longer text is also known as the *Yajniki Upanishad*.
According to Sayana, the *Taittiriya Aranyaka* has ten prapathakas
and this Upanishad forms the last. Bhattabhaskara, who is earlier
than Sayana, commented on this along with the whole *Yajur* and
called the *Taittiriya Aranyaka* divisions, prashnas, with this as the
last. This tenth portion is recognized as a khila or supplement,
both by Bhattabhaskara and by Sayana. Bhattabhaskara noted that
it has sixty-four sections.

Shankaracharya refers to it in his commentary on the *Brahma Sutra*, while Sayana affirms that it consists of several topics on karma, upasana and jnana, so far not mentioned in the Samhitas and Brahmanas. Sayana also notes a recension with ninety sections. Swami Vimalananada has provided a translation of this diverse text in eighty sections.

The text begins with praise of Prajapati, the Lord of creation, who enters every being in seed form. It goes on to include descriptions of deities, various mantras, prayers and the merits of sannyasa, among various other topics.

Ramarahasya Upanishad

The *Ramarahasya Upanishad* is attached to the *Atharva Veda* and can be dated to around the sixteenth century CE. It includes Rama mantras, explains how to recite them and describes their results. It is said that Mudgala, Shandilya, Paingala, Bhikshu, Sanaka and other sages approached the god Hanuman and asked him about the greatest among the Vedas, Puranas, other texts and all else. Hanuman replied that it was the Brahma-taraka, that is, Om, and that the god Rama who is equal to Para Brahman, the highest. Then they enquired about the angas (limbs or parts) of the god Rama and Hanuman explained that the deities Ganesha, Sarasvati, Durga, the Kshetrapalas, the Sun, Moon, Narayana, Narasimha, Vasudeva, Varaha, Lakshmana, Shatrughna, Bharata, Vibhishana, Sugriva, Angada, Jambavanta and Pranava are the angas or limbs of Lord Rama.

The rest of the text deals with Rama mantras and methods of worshipping Rama. Rama is to be meditated upon in various forms, blue-complexioned, seated under a canopy, decorated with gems. Reciting the mantras with anga-nyasa, that is, placing Rama within the body through touch, is also described.

Ramatapini–Purva and *Uttara Upanishad*

The *Ramatapini Upanishad* is attached to the *Atharva Veda* and is dated to around the sixteenth century CE. It has two parts, Purva and Uttara, though the first seems complete in itself. The Upanishad describes the mantras of Shri Rama and says that both Sita and Rama should be worshipped. The *Ramapurva-tapini* contains ninety-four verses. Verses 1–6 describe how Maha Vishnu grew up in Dasharatha's house and why he came to be called Rama. Succeeding verses state that Rama is the same as Brahman and then provides the Rama mantra, 'Rama-Ramaya-namah'. In Verse 6 it says that the mantra of Shri Rama has more effect than any other, whether of Shakti, Ganapati, Surya or even of other Vishnu mantras.

The first word, Rama, contains the whole world, as it includes both Prakriti and Purusha, that is, Rama and Sita. The next two words, Ramaya-namah, indicate Rama's identity with the highest (Verse 19). The mantra should be worn on the chest. The text then provides a description of Rama, Sita and Lakshmana. The devas and sages praise and glorify him. Rama is also described as seated on a throne, surrounded by six heroes, around them being other devas and rishis.

The text continues with the construction of a mandala for the worship of Rama, while its last few verses convey the right methods for worshipping Rama. Whoever worships Rama enjoys the fulfilment of all desires and attains liberation.

The *Ramauttara-tapini* has seven sections. It begins with the first few verses of the *Jabala Upanishad*, and Section 4 continues with these. Section 2 has the *Taraka Upanishad*, known from the Oupnekhat. Section 3 identifies the four components of Om, with Lakshmana, Shatrughna, Bharata and Rama and the whole Pranava with Sita. Verses from the *Mandukya Upanishad* follow, after which there is an identity of Rama with Brahman,

thus ensuring that Rama is greater than Sita. Section 5 states that
Rama is the highest, the essence of all gods and other beings, of all
worlds and elements. He is the indivisible atman, the one without
a second.

Tarasara Upanishad

The *Tarasara Upanishad* is attached to the *Shukla Yajur Veda*.
It may be of the fourteenth century CE. The text is available in
different versions with a varying numbers of verses.

This Upanishad praises Shri Rama, who is identified with
Vishnu, and explains the mantra 'Om Namo Narayanaya' used in
his worship. This mantra must be worshipped as knowledge as it
helps one to transcend the world. Om represents the Self, whereas
Namah represents the world. The five syllables of Narayanaya
represent Brahman.

The *Tarasara* has three chapters. Chapter 1 begins with
Brihaspati asking Yajnavalkya about Kurukshetra, the place where
the devas sacrifice, and the seat of spirituality. Where should
one go in order to know Kurukshetra? Yajnavalkya replies that
Avimukta is Kurukshetra, where Rudra initiates one into Taraka
Brahman. One should never leave Avimukta. Taraka is that which
enables one to cross over from this world. 'Om Namo Narayanaya'
is the Taraka. It goes on to explain that Om represents the atman,
Namah has the nature of prakriti (matter), and Narayanaya of
Para Brahman. Each syllable of this mantra also produces various
deities, Brahma, Vishnu, Rudra, Ishvara, the Anda-Virat (or Virat
of the universe), Purusha, Bhagavan (Lord) and Paramatman. The
eight syllables together represent the supreme and the highest
Purusha.

This chapter is the same as that in the *Jabala Upanishad*. It has
six verses.

Chapter 2 with seven verses explains that Om actually has eight subtle syllables. It not only represents the gods Brahma and Shiva, but the supreme god Rama and his associates, Jambavan, Hanuman, Sita, Lakshmana, Shatrughna and Bharata.

Chapter 3 with thirteen verses further explains the mantra, which represents the Lord Narayana and his form as Rama.

Vasudeva Upanishad

The *Vasudeva Upanishad* belongs to the *Sama Veda*.

This is a short Upanishad of five verses. In this, the rishi Narada asks the god Vasudeva (Vishnu) about the Urdhva Pundra or religious marks of the Vaishnavas. Vasudeva replies that after a prayer for protection to the god who holds the wheel, mace and conch (chakra, gada and shankha), who is also Achyuta living in Dvaraka, as well as Govinda, the brahmachari and householder, should apply Urdhva Pundra with his pure finger (next to the little finger) on his forehead and twelve other places, while reciting the Vishnu Gayatri or the twelve names of the god: Keshava, Narayana, Madhava, Govinda, Vishnu, Madhusudana, Trivikrama, Vamana, Shridhara, Hrishikesha, Padmanabha and Damodara (Verse 2). The next verse (Verse 3) says the sannyasi should apply the Urdhva Pundra with his fourth finger on the head, forehead and chest, while chanting the Pranava (Om). Two more verses explain the benefits of this.

Nine

The Sannyasa Upanishads

SEVENTEEN UPANISHADS ARE classified as Sannyasa Upanishads by Upanishad Brahmayogin, and this classification is accepted by several others. Some add two to three more Upanishads in this group.

The seventeen are: *Aruni, Avadhuta, Bhikshu, Brahma, Jabala, Katharudra, Kundika, Maitreya, Narada-parivrajaka, Nirvana, Parabrahma, Paramahamsa, Paramahamsa-Parivrajaka, Sannyasa, Shatyayaniya, Turiyatita Avadhuta* and *Yajnavalkya*.

F.O. Schrader identified earlier and later texts among these. The earliest were: *Aruni, Brahma, Jabala, Katha-shruti* (that is, *Katharudra*), *Kundika* and *Paramahamsa*. Following this, he places the *Ashrama* and slightly later the *Bhikshu, Avadhuta, Sannyasa, Maitreya, Narada-parivrajaka, Nirvana, Parabrahma, Paramahamsa-parivrajaka, Shatyayaniya, Turiyatita Avadhuta* and *Yajnavalkya*. Sprockhoff, a student of Schrader, has done a more detailed study. He assigns the first group to before 1 CE, the *Ashrama* to around 300 CE, the *Narada Parivrajaka* to circa 1150, the *Shatyayaniya* to circa 1200, and the rest to the fourteenth and fifteenth centuries. The later Upanishads include passages from smritis and earlier texts. Through these texts, one can see the historical development of ideas concerning sannyasa. But in the Upanishads, sannyasa is only a means to reach Brahman. Patrick Olivelle feels that none of these is before the first century CE.

Aruni Upanishad

The *Aruni Upanishad* is attached to the *Sama Veda* and sometimes to the *Atharva Veda*. In this, the god Brahma instructs the rishi Aruni (the son of Aruna) on the highest type of sannyasi, the Paramahamsa Parivrajaka. The text has eight verses. In this text, Aruna's son visits the world (loka) of Prajapati and asks how to give up all work (action). Prajapati explains that he must abandon everything: family, friends, sacred thread, scriptures and all the worlds (all fourteen worlds are mentioned here). Whether he is a brahmachari, grihastha or vanaprastha, he should discard everything, including the Gayatri Mantra and the sacred thread.

It goes on to explain that the first stage of being a sannyasi, that is, the Kutichaka living a brahmachari's life, should give up his relatives, the begging bowl, straining cloth, triple staff and the lighting of the fires that lead to particular spheres. He should practice concentration to unite with his atman and of all Vedic texts should focus on the Upanishads. The person who realizes himself as Brahman needs no outer support, but even so should strictly follow the five yamas of brahmachari, ahimsa, aparigraha, asteya and satya.

The highest class of sannyasis, the Paramahamsa Parivrajakas, should live even more simply, sitting or lying only on the ground, using one bowl, following the vow of brahmacharya and giving up all emotions. They should stay in one place in the rainy season, otherwise they should wander, either alone or with a single companion. The one who has truly understood the Vedas should give up everything: father, son, wife, even the begging bowl, the staff and the sacred thread. Such sannyasis should place the mantra Om on various parts of the body. They should have awakened from ignorance and should not have anger.

Avadhuta Upanishad

The *Avadhuta Upanishad* belongs to the *Krishna Yajur Veda*. In this Dattatreya describes the nature of the avadhuta. Such a person is immortal, has discarded all worldly ties and is always full of bliss. An avadhuta is a liberated soul, one who has renounced the world. Totally beyond all that is, an avadhuta follows no rules or practices and has no need to follow conventional norms.

In this Upanishad of thirty-six verses, Samkriti approaches the avadhuta Dattatreya and asks him about the characteristics of an avadhuta. Dattatreya replies that an avadhuta is one who is immortal (akshara), the best (varenya), who has discarded all worldly ties (dhutasamsarabandhana) and who is reflected in the words 'tat tvam asi' (that thou art).

He has nothing to do with caste or with stages of life (the varnas and ashramas), is full of bliss and can be identified with Brahman. A person does not attain immortality by children, rituals or wealth, but by renunciation (tyaga). An avadhuta moves about freely with or without clothes and does not consider anything good or bad, holy or unholy. He performs the ashvamedha sacrifice within himself, which is the greatest sacrifice and the great Yoga (7). He is not affected by anything he does.

The text affirms that there is neither death nor birth; none is bound, none aspires. There is neither seeker after liberation nor any liberated; this indeed is the ultimate Truth (11). The avadhuta lives in a state of bliss and contentment. He has no need to study, concentrate, meditate or teach. However, the body could continue to worship gods, bathe, beg for food—these tasks, though unnecessary, would not affect him. He should repeat the Tara Mantra or recite passages from the Upanishads (27).

One verse states: Let thought contemplate Vishnu or let it be dissolved in the bliss of Brahman. I am the witness. I neither do nor cause anything to be done (Verse 28). An avadhuta is always full of joy, free of all actions and all sins.

The commentator explains that a-va-dhu-ta stands for akshara, varenya, dhutasamsarabandhana and tat tvam asi.

(The term avadhuta can apply to any liberated person, but it also specifically refers to a sannyasi sect. The *Avadhuta Gita* has similar descriptions. The *Uddhava Gita*, forming part of the *Bhagavata Purana*, describes an avadhuta who learns from all aspects of life and who is at home anywhere in the world.)

Bhikshu Upanishad

The *Bhikshu Upanishad* belongs to the *Shukla Yajur Veda*. This short Upanishad has five verses. It describes four types of bhikshus or sannyasis: Kutichaka, Bahudaka, Hamsa and Paramahamsa. The Kutichaka, hut-dwelling sannyasis, live on eight mouthfuls of food and seek moksha through the path of yoga. Past examples of such ascetics include Gautama, Bharadvaja, Yajnavalkya and Vasishtha.

The Bahudaka also live on eight mouthfuls of food, given to them from houses of brahma-rishis. They carry the *tridanda* or threefold staff, the *kamandalu* or water pot, and wear a shikha or tuft of hair, a sutra or sacred thread and a *kashaya vastra* or ochre-coloured garment. They are not allowed alcohol or meat. The Hamsa sannyasis keep travelling and do not stay long in one place. They live on gomutra and gomaya (cow's urine and dung—not to be taken literally, implying products obtained from the cow). They follow the *chandrayana* vow, where food is gradually increased and decreased according to the phases of the moon (chandra), and seek liberation through the path of yoga.

The Paramahamsa shelter at the foot of a tree, a deserted house or cremation ground or a temple, river bank or elsewhere. They may or may not wear clothes and have gone beyond righteousness or unrighteousness. They see the atman in all, receive food from anyone, and with purified minds contemplate Brahman. They have rejected the dualities of pure and impure (shuddha–ashuddha–dvaita–varjita). The commentator relates these to a rejection of the philosophies of Ramanuja and Madhva, which would make this a late text. Examples of Paramahamsa sannyasis are Samvartaka, Aruni, Shvetaketu, Jadabharata, Dattatreya, Shuka, Vamadeva and Harita.

Brahma Upanishad

The *Brahma Upanishad* belongs to the *Krishna Yajur Veda* or to the *Atharva Veda*.

Among the commentators on this text are Narayana and Shankarananda.

In this Upanishad, Pippalada instructs Shaunaka on Brahman. Shaunaka approaches him with a question on Brahmapura, the city of Brahman, located in the body. Pippalada explains Brahman, identifying it with prana and the atman. The text refers to the nadis through which prana is distributed in the body and the four states of consciousness. It also relates these states with the four places in the body in which Purusha is seated: the navel, heart, throat and head. It goes on to state that in the Jagrata or waking state He is Brahma, in the Svapna or dreaming state He is Vishnu, in the Sushupti or deep sleep state he is Rudra and in the Turiya state beyond these, he is Paramakshara, the indestructible. The Supreme is also everything else, including Aditya, Vishnu, Ishvara, the Purusha, the jiva, prana and Agni. It is the indestructible Brahman that shines by itself and in reality nothing exists but this. There are no worlds or devas or Vedas, no sacrifices, no Chandala's son or Pulkasa's son, but within the recess of the heart is the akasha of consciousness, with many openings, the aim of knowledge and the container of the universe. There, neither devas, rishis or pitris have any control, as the one who is fully awakened knows all. They don't control the person, yet the devas, pranas, supreme light and the mahat principle exist within the heart.

Jabala Upanishad

The *Jabala Upanishad* is attached to the *Shukla Yajur Veda* or to the *Atharva Veda*. It explains renunciation and the nature of a Paramahamsa, a type of rishi who has an unmanifested (avyakta) nature, and is considered among the highest ascetics. In this text, Avimukta is used in two ways. It is a name of ancient Varanasi and the name of the god Shiva. The caste system is well-established at this time.

The Upanishad has six short khandas or sections. In the first khanda, the deity Brihaspati approaches the rishi Yajnavalkya and asks him which is Kurukshetra, where the gods perform sacrifices and where Brahman is known. Yajnavalkya replies that it is Avimukta where Brahman resides within all beings. Here, Rudra reveals the mantra through which Brahman can be attained.

In the second khanda, the rishi Atri asks Yajnavalkya how to realize the unmanifest and infinite Self, and Yajnavalkya replies that it can be attained by worshipping Avimukta. The infinite and unmanifest Self is established in Avimukta. Avimukta is established between Varana and Nasi. Varana wards off all faults committed by the senses and Nasi destroys all sins. This is located between the eyebrows, at the top of the nose. This is the true Avimukta.

In the third khanda the brahmacharis or students of Yajnavalkya ask him which mantra leads to immortality and he replies that reciting the Shatarudriya would do so.

In the fourth khanda, King Janaka of Videha approaches Yajnavalkya and asks him to explain the basics of sannyasa. Yajnavalkya responds that one can become a sannyasi after being a student, householder and forest dweller, or alternatively one can make that choice at any point. A person can become a sannyasi whether or not he maintains the sacred fires. Some say (law-givers) that he should first perform the prajapatya sacrifice. This, however, is not necessary, but he should perform a sacrifice to Agni as Agni represents prana. He should perform the traidhataviya sacrifice by which sattva, rajas and tamas are strengthened in him. Then he should inhale the smoke of the fire while reciting a mantra to Agni (provided in the text). Those who do not maintain the sacred fire themselves should obtain one from the home of a Vedic scholar and then perform the rituals. In case he cannot obtain such a fire, offerings of water can be made in the prescribed rituals. He explains that it is Brahman that is to be worshipped, and Janaka agrees.

In the fifth khanda, Atri poses another question. He asks how a person without a sacred thread can be a brahmana. Yajnavalkya replies that the conviction that I am the Self constitutes the sacred thread. But only brahmanas are entitled to take sannyasa, others may attain liberation through dying in battle, or in water or fire, or undertaking an endless journey. But those entitled to take sannyasa must renounce the world and live on alms. Brahman is attained by following this path.

The sixth khanda describes the type of sannyasi known as Paramahamsa. In the past, such sannyasais included Samvartaka, Aruni, Dattatreya, Shvetaketu, Durvasa, Ribhu, Raivataka, Nidagha and Jadabharata. They had no distinguishing marks and though perfectly sane they behaved as if they were out of their

senses. There are two types of Paramahamsas: those who wear
clothes and those who do not. Even those who wear clothes must
discard in water the threefold staff, water pot, alms bowl, sling (to
carry possessions), cloth for purifying water, tuft of hair and sacred
thread.

The second category do not wear clothes and do not bother
about whether or not they receive alms, but take the bare minimum
to sustain the body; they are indifferent to pairs of opposites such
as heat and cold, have no abode but sleep anywhere, have no sense
of 'I' and ultimately obtain liberation.

Katharudra Upanishad

The *Katharudra Upanishad*, also known as the *Kathashruti*, is
attached to the *Krishna Yajur Veda*. In this, the devas ask Prajapati
to explain to them brahmavidya or the knowledge of Brahman.
Attaining brahmavidya, says Prajapati, begins with renunciation.
After removing one's hair, hair tuft and sacred thread, there is a
formal parting from the son. Then the renouncer circumambulates
the village clockwise and departs. The procedure of becoming
an ascetic is further explained. Once he becomes an ascetic, he
gives up the agnihotra or fire sacrifice and renounces everything.
He sleeps on the sand near a river or in a temple. To reach the
self-effulgent light that illumines the whole world, there can be
no compromise on brahmacharya. However, Brahman is only
reached by gaining knowledge of it, not by any other action.

Brahman is sat-chit-ananda and One without a second. The
one who understands that 'I am Brahman' becomes Brahman. The
Self, which is the same as Brahman, has maya or illusory power,
through which akasha (ether or space) and other aspects of the
world emerge.

The five bodies or kosha are referred to, and the anandamaya
kosha or body of bliss is pervaded by Brahman, the innermost

Self. Without this supreme bliss which is the self of all beings, no human being can be alive or perform any actions. This shining Self makes the individual happy, who otherwise is full of sorrow. The ascetic who realizes unity with Brahman is also free from fear. This transcendent Brahman is supreme immortality, existing beyond time.

Kundika Upanishad

The *Kundika Upanishad* is attached to the *Sama Veda*. It begins by explaining the duties of a person before renunciation. It goes on to describe the importance of renunciation, yoga and the ultimate realization of Brahman. After a period of study as a student, that is, of brahmachari, the person should marry a suitable wife with the permission of his teacher. Then living as a grihastha or householder for many years, he should renounce it, divide his property among his sons and enter the third stage of his life, that of vanaprastha. He should live on air, water and approved roots and fruits and should have no regrets for the comforts he has left behind. At this stage he has total self-control and has renounced the fruits of his actions. He is accompanied by his wife, though he follows strict brahmacharya, that is, sex is out of the question. After some time he proceeds as a sannyasi, a total renunciate. Renunciation is essential for escaping rebirth. As he has renounced the sacred fire, he should not even think of it or recite its mantras. However, he can repeat Om, and other mantras related to Self-realization, and also ponder over the texts that describe Brahman.

Further rules for the spiritual path are prescribed. He should wear ochre clothes, live on alms and wander from place to place. He should meditate and possess pure knowledge for the protection of all living beings (Verse 12). He should give up all possessions except a water pot, a bowl for receiving alms, a loin cloth, upper garment and patched clothing to keep out the cold, a pair of sandals, a towel and a ring of sacred grass. He should sleep on a sandy riverbed or outside a temple. Neither praise nor blame should affect him. He should understand the identity of the individual Self with the Supreme.

The text goes on to describe how the five elements arose from Brahman and the state of mind of the wandering vanaprastha. Gradually, the person gains identity with Brahman and loses identification with the body and the sense of 'I'. Certain practices are then prescribed to unite the prana and apana in the body, and to further control the senses. Then, as the prana passes through the Sushumna and reaches the Sahasrara Chakra, he attains Brahman. First, he attains the qualified and then the unqualified Brahman. At this stage he remains untouched by anything around him or anything that happens or does not happen. He sees the Self everywhere, knows that it is One without a second and has perfect bliss. No matter what he is doing, he finds delight in the atman and on leaving the body gains liberation or moksha.

Maitreya Upanishad

The *Maitreya Upanishad* is attached to the *Sama Veda*.

The text has three chapters or sections. Chapter 1 begins with the story of King Brihadratha, who installs his eldest son on the throne and goes into the forest, where he performs tapas for 1000 years. Then, the sun god in the form of the sage Shakayanya asks him to choose a boon and Brihadratha requests an explanation of the atman. At first, Shakayanya does not answer, but the king, describing the impermanence of life, persuades him.

Shakayanya explains how to reach the ultimate goal by purifying the mind and turning it towards Brahman. One should see Brahman present in the lotus of the heart, a witness to the thoughts of the intellect. This is the abode of supreme love, beyond mind and speech, immobile, steady and deep, neither light nor dark, free from all doubts. It is eternal, pure and beyond duality. The ignorant who stick to caste rules and ways of life attain the fruit of that, but only freedom from attachment provides supreme happiness.

In Section 2, with thirty-one verses, the sage Maitreya visits Mount Kailasha and asks the Lord (Shiva) to convey to him the secret of the supreme truth. The great god replies that the body is a temple and the jiva or individual self is Shiva. One should worship him, understanding that 'He and I are one'. He describes the impurity of the body and the need to move towards liberation. The inborn tendencies of the mind need to be destroyed and renunciation should be desired, only after the mind becomes dispassionate. The wisest people then contemplate Brahman; the middling ones contemplate scripture; below them are those who use mantras; and the lowest believe in visiting holy places (2.22). Even those who are learned may not have wisdom and one should contemplate Brahman enshrined in the heart to attain identity with it.

Section 3 with twenty-four verses begins by affirming that I am Brahman and then tries to convey this in different ways, for instance, I am the Guru of all the worlds, I am all the worlds, I have attained perfection, I am pure, I am the Supreme, I remain always, I am He, I am eternal, I am pure, I am free from sorrow, I am consciousness, I am beyond speech, I am the auspicious and the inauspicious, etc.

Narada–Parivrajaka Upanishad

The *Narada-Parivrajaka* is a long Upanishad attached to the *Atharva Veda*. It deals with the stages of sannyasa and is divided into nine sections known as upadeshas.

In the first upadesha, which has two verses, the rishi Narada, known as a musician and a wanderer through the three worlds, reaches the Naimisha forest, where other rishis are gathered for a twelve-year sacrifice. Among them are Shaunaka and others. As Narada arrives there, they ask him a question on attaining liberation. Narada replies that the seeker should be of a good family, wear the sacred thread, have studied the Vedas and performed the forty Vedic rituals and been a brahmachari for twelve years, followed by twenty-five years as a householder and then twenty-five years as a vanaprastha. In addition, he should have studied the duties of four types of brahmachari, six types of householders and four types of vanaprasthas, and should know the four disciplines. He should have given up desires and be self-controlled.

In the second upadesha, Shaunaka and others request Narada to explain the method of renunciation. He said that this is best explained by Pitamaha (Brahma). After completing the sacrifice they all go to the world of Brahma and, after propitiating him, request him to tell them. Brahma then says he will convey the secret taught by the Virat Purusha in the form of the Purusha-sukta and the Upanishads. He again repeats what Narada said were the qualifications, with a few more details.

In the third upadesha, Narada describes those who are not worthy to renounce worldly life: a eunuch, one who does not have right conduct, a deformed person, women and children, the blind, deaf and dumb, the heretic, an emperor, a religious student, a Vaikhanasa sannyasi and a Haradvija, a hired teacher, a man without prepuce and one who does not maintain the sacred fire, even though they are dispassionate. If they become renunciates, they cannot receive the highest knowledge. But someone who is already a sannyasi can advance further to become a Paramahamsa. Certain people can become renunciates only just before death. Even here, renunciation should take place in the prescribed way with correct mantras. A householder can also renounce the world with the right rituals and so can a wise man and a brahmachari.

The text then describes the essential prerequisites for a sannyasi, as given in other texts, and the nature of the true sannyasi and their daily life.

Upadesha 4 continues with this theme. The sannyasi has abandoned the worlds, all objects, the Vedas and rituals, and is established in the atman. He must take care never to speak with a woman or remember one, or even look at a picture of one. There are many more things an ascetic should avoid. Among them, he should not have greed, anger, and passion, he should not use mantras, herbs or medicines, and should not bless others or receive gifts of any kind. He should follow the basic yamas and niyamas. More rules for the life of a Paramahamsa ascetic are prescribed, as well as the manner of renunciation.

The fifth upadesha with sixty-six verses continues to explain the method and type of renunciation. The eleventh verse (5.11) states that there are six stages of renunciation: Kutichaka, Bahudaka, Hamsa, Paramahamsa, Turiyatita and Avadhuta. Succeeding verses explain the characteristics of each. The sixth, the Avadhuta, follows no norms and like a python accepts any food that he receives. More rules are provided for each stage.

The sixth upadesha with forty-two verses refers to the states of consciousness and the tattvas and continues with rules and descriptions of the various stages of the ascetic life.

The seventh with eleven verses expands on the same theme, emphasizing what is forbidden—for instance, the ascetic should see women as snakes, gold as poison, an assembly hall as a cemetery and a capital city as a dreadful (kumbhipaka) hell. The eighth upadesha with twenty-three verses provides further rules and descriptions of each stage. It includes certain mantras to be used for taking sannyasa and different types of Pranavas (Om), with the Brahma Pranava having 128 matras (parts). It further explains states of consciousness. The ninth upadesha with twenty-three verses describes Brahman and all it contains.

Nirvana Upanishad

The *Nirvana Upanishad* is attached to the *Rig Veda* and has sixty-one verses. It has a sutra style and explains the characteristics of the Paramahamsa ascetic. The descriptions are similar to those in other Upanishads. Such ascetics are imperishable and unconditioned. However, unlike other Upanishads, this states that their role is to teach Brahman to various disciples. They have no duties to perform and do not establish monastic centres, but they teach only to benefit others. Compassion is their sport, and they wear the garland of bliss. They are absorbed in Brahman and by their behaviour they reveal that they see Brahman in all beings (Verse 24). The text also refers to them raising the Kundalini through the practise of Hatha Yoga and mentions the khechari mudra. It refers to meditation on the Gayatri through the Ajapa Mantra (the mantra hamsa used while breathing in and out). It also describes Brahmavidya, the supreme knowledge, attained through yoga practice and detachment. The Paramahamsa-parivrajaka, through these practices, realizes Brahman and attains nirvana (ultimate liberation or moksha).

Parabrahma Upanishad

The *Parabrahma Upanishad* is attached to the *Atharva Veda* and has twenty verses. It begins with Shaunaka approaching Pippalada and asking him about Brahman. Everything is present in Brahman, he says, but how did creation and so many different species emerge? Also, what is the nature of Brahman? Pippalada then explains the true nature of Brahman that has no parts and is pure and indestructible. Brahman remains in its own self, does no work and yet brings forth everything that exists. The text also explains how to realize the tripad (threefold) Brahman. The four states of consciousness and the nadis are referred to, as well as yoga with eight parts (Raja Yoga, described in Patanjali's Yoga Sutra). The deities presiding over prana are Vishva, Viraj, Otr and Turiya. The nadis related to these are also four. In deep sleep the jiva rests in the golden sheath in the heart. To realize the inner jiva-Brahman who consists of four padas, there are four places within the body: the eyes, throat, heart and head. These correspond with waking, dreaming, deep sleep and Turiya. The jiva-atman can also be compared to the sacred fires, the ahavaniya, garhaptya, dakshina and sabhya. The deities presiding over the four states of consciousness are Brahma, Vishnu, Rudra and finally the Supreme indestructible one. The four states can be considered to be covered by four fingers. The extent of the sacred thread is ninety-six times four fingers, hence, the tattvas in the inner brahmasutra (the inner sacred thread) are ninety-six. The sacred thread has three threads so the inner brahmasutra has three gunas each with thirty-two tattvas.

The triad purified by wisdom are known as the three gods and the nine Brahmans (five panchapada Brahman and four chatushpada Brahman). Further esoteric details of the internal brahmasutra are provided. For instance, internally the hamsa (mantra) is the tuft, the pranava the sacred thread, and nada the connecting link (5). Further, it is said that jnana (wisdom) represents the tuft and sacred thread (12), while the external sacred thread of cotton is worn only by the ignorant.

Paramahamsa Upanishad

The *Paramahamsa Upanishad* is attached to the *Shukla Yajur Veda* or to the *Atharva Veda*, and goes into details on the Paramahamsa type of rishi.

The text begins with the rishi Narada asking the Lord (Bhagavanta) about the path and duties of the Paramahamsa yogis. Bhagavan explains that it is a very difficult path and one that very few follow. Such a yogi is always one with Brahman. He has renounced all relationships as well as the shikha (tuft), the sacred thread, Vedic study and all actions and everything in the universe. He uses Kaupina, the staff, and the bare minimum of clothes and food. In a further stage, he drops even the staff and uses no covering. He is beyond cold and heat, happiness and misery, and all other emotions. He does not identify with the body and is always identified with Brahman. He has realized that jnana or true knowledge is his shikha and his holy thread. Uniting the jiva with the Paramatman, there is no distinction between them, and this union is his Sandhya ceremony.

The true Ekadandi is one who carries the staff of knowledge and is united with Brahman. Merely carrying a wooden staff but being attracted to sense objects and being without jnana leads to hells such as the Maharauravas. The one who knows the difference between these two is a Paramahamsa.

A Paramahamsa blames none, praises none and bows to no one. He does not invoke god, recite mantras or meditate. He perceives neither duality nor unity, neither you nor I. He does not accept gold or wealth and has no disciples. If he does any of these, he becomes a killer of the atman. Instead, the Paramahamsa always resides in the atman and has realized his identity with Brahman.

Paramahamsa-Parivrajaka Upanishad

The *Paramahamsa-Parivrajaka Upanishad* is attached to the *Atharva Veda* and has more information on the Paramahamsa ascetic.

The text has five long verses and begins with the god Brahma approaching his father Adinarayana (Vishnu), the Supreme Being, and asking him about the characteristics of the Paramahamsa sannyasi. The Lord explains that after completing the three stages of brahmachari, grihastha and vanaprastha, the person can renounce worldly life or can even do so at an earlier stage. He adds that some state that the prajapatya ritual should be practised before renouncing the world, but actually only the Agneyi ritual, to the god Agni, is required, as Agni is Prana. Further details of the rituals are provided. The text states that kshatriyas and others not entitled to renunciation have to attain liberation in different ways, by death in the battlefield, entering water or fire, or undertaking an endless journey. A person who is ill can make a mental renunciation while a healthy person should perform the shraddha and Agni rituals. Then he should pull out his tuft and snap the sacred thread with certain prescribed mantras and a meditation on Om. He should focus on the mahavakyas such as 'I am Brahman' and 'You Are That. He also has to recite: 'Freedom from fear to all from me, Svaha.'

Those not entitled to this method of renunciation recite the householder's prayer, followed by the prayer regarding 'Freedom from fear to all beings'. He should ponder over the truths of the Upanishads and give up all negative emotions, passions and possessions. He maintains the basic ethical principles of the yamas and accepts alms from all the four castes, except those accursed or fallen. He remains unmoved in gain or loss and wanders alone for eight months of the year (avoiding the rainy season). At this point he wears some patched garment, but later he can become a Kutichaka or a Bahudaka or a Hamsa or a Paramahamsa ascetic and discard even his loin-cloth, staff and water vessel. He now has no fixed abode, sleeps on the floor and discards all rituals, only meditating on Brahman as the Pranava.

Next, Brahma asks about the Brahma-Pranava and Narayana explains its sixteen parts, corresponding with the four states of consciousness, each of which also have four states. The fourth verse explains this clearly as it shows each state of consciousness can have four sub-states, one when it is pure and the other three when it assumes some of the characteristics of another state of consciousness. For instance, one can be fully awake or partly awake.

These states are also associated with the syllables of the mantra Om, which form the Brahma Pranava. The four parts of Jagrat are reflected in 'a', the four parts of Svapna in 'u', the four parts of Sushupti in 'm', and the four parts of Turiya in the ardha-matra. This should be worshipped by the Paramahamsa, Turiyatita and Avadhuta ascetics, which will lead to liberation.

Vishnu then provides further descriptions of the Paramahamsa ascetic, who uses no outer props, is always the same, does not feel hunger or thirst or any other of the usual emotions, does not worship any deities and remains focused on Om.

As Om is the Brahma-Pranava, he is one with Brahman.

Sannyasa Upanishad

The *Sannyasa Upanishad* belongs to the *Sama Veda* and has two adhyayas or parts. It explains the methods of renouncing the world and describes the six kinds of ascetics. There are different versions of this text.

Adhyaya 1 has only one verse. It begins by stating that this Upanishad specifically explains aspects of renunciation. A person wishing to renounce the world should get the approval of family and kin, bring together his priests and perform the Vaishvanara sacrifice, giving away all wealth to the officiating priests. Then the five pranas—prana, apana, vyana, udana and samana—should be symbolically placed in the vessels of the five sacred fires, the ahavaniya, garhaptya, anvaharyapachana, sabhya and avasthaya. Then, shaving his head along with his tuft, snapping his sacred thread and seeing his son (if he has one), he consecrates himself with the mantra stating 'You are the god Brahma, the sacrifice and everything.'

The remaining instructions are similar to those provided in other texts. He can receive alms from all the four castes and should eat with his hands as a bowl, just enough to maintain himself. He can stay in a village for one night and in a town for five, and in one place during the rainy season. If he feels too cold or hot he can wear a bark garment or a tattered or patched one. Now his sacred thread is meditation on the atman and Brahmavidya is his tuft. He knows neither night nor day, all is the same to him.

The second adhyaya is a long one with 123 verses. It states that only one who has performed the forty samskaras is entitled to take sannyasa. In addition, such a person should be detached from the world, have given up all desires, be free of emotions and should follow the four disciplines (sadhanas). It also explains that if you decide to renounce the world and do not do so, you can resume this path after the prajapatya sacrifice. Next, three types of people are criticized: one who denounces renunciation, one who supports a fallen ascetic and one who places obstacles in the path of one who wishes to renounce the world (2.3).

The next few verses list those who cannot become renunciates, again similar to that in other Upanishads: a eunuch, a fallen man, a maimed person, women, a deaf person, a child, a dumb person, a heretic, an informer, a student, a Vaikhanasa ascetic, a Haradvija (Shiva worshipper), a salaried teacher, a man without prepuce, one who does not keep the ritual fire. Even if such people renounce the world they are not entitled to be taught the great texts (such as 'That Thou Art'). In addition, those who cannot become sannyasis include: the son of a sannyasi who has fallen from grace, one with a disease of the nails, one who is brown-toothed, a consumptive and a deformed person.

Renunciation should also be banned to recent householders, those who have committed great sins, those who have lost caste, those who do not practise prescribed rituals and those who do not maintain truth and purity. But all these can be set aside for one who is seriously ill or on his deathbed (2.5–7).

Following this, the method of renunciation is prescribed. The tuft should be discarded while reciting 'Om Bhuh Svaha'. The sacred thread should be snapped and left in the water along with his clothes and waistband while reciting the appropriate mantras. There are great benefits to renunciation; in fact, it affects sixty generations of his family before him and sixty after him (2.10). After this, again with appropriate mantras, he should accept a smooth and whole bamboo staff, a water vessel and a yogic garment. He gives up dharma and adharma, truth and untruth, and lives his life with dispassion and wisdom (jnana).

The Upanishad explains that there are four reasons for renunciation. Some are motivated by dispassion, some by spiritual wisdom, some by both these together, while the fourth category renounces the world in order to follow the traditional four stages of life.

Six kinds of sannyasis, along with their characteristics, are described: Kutichaka, Bahudaka, Hamsa, Paramahamsa, Turiyatita and Avadhuta. The Kutichaka sannyasi wears the tuft and sacred thread and holds the tridanda (staff) and water vessel. He has a sling (for carrying his items) and a spade. His clothes include a loin-cloth and patched garment. He eats his food at one place and serves his father, mother and guru. On his forehead, he wears a perpendicular mark of white sandal paste.

The Bahudaka sannyasi is on the whole similar, but wears three (horizontal) lines of holy ash on his forehead. He eats only eight mouthfuls of food given in alms by eight different houses. The Hamsa ascetic has matted hair; the mark on his forehead can be either of those worn by the Kutichaka or Bahudaka; he eats food obtained in alms from anywhere and wears a loin-cloth. The Paramahamsa ascetic has given up the tuft and sacred thread; he receives food in his own hands and wears a loin cloth. He may also wear a patched garment or can be unclad, smeared in ashes. He holds a bamboo staff and has discarded all attachments. The Turiyatita sannyasi lives on fruits and receives them in his mouth like a cow; if he eats cooked rice, he receives them from three houses. He wears no clothes, has no possessions or attachments and disregards his body. The Avadhuta sannyasi follows no rules. He eats food like a python, that is, not regularly, but whenever he gets it. He accepts food from all castes except those who are fallen from the path or accursed. He continuously meditates on the Self, knowing that he is the Supreme Being, and does not identify with the body or with anything in the world.

He has no ego, understands without the mind, is free of desires and is pure consciousness and bliss. He aims to be in such deep samadhi that birds of the forest would build their nests on his head. He contemplates the true nature of his Self: purity, strength, reality, truth, knowledge, bliss, tranquillity and oneness.

Further instructions too are provided. If one who is seriously ill recovers, he should become a renunciate in the prescribed order. Sannyasis should not talk to low-caste women, to those without virtue and a woman during her period. Sannyasis do not worship gods or attend festivals. Depending on the level and nature of the sannyasi, they attain different goals. Those who become sannyasis after illness or affliction gain the world or Bhuh; the Kutichaka sannyasis obtain Bhuva. The Bahudaka sannyasi reaches heaven (Svarga). The Hamsa sannyasi goes to Satya Loka, the world of truth. The Turiyatita and the Avadhuta sannyasis attain supreme bliss by the realization of their true Selves.

This Upanishad provides further instructions on what sannyasis should and should not do, and is almost like a guidebook for them. It ends by praising the Pranava, Om. If the sannyasi repeats it 12,000 times a day, Brahman is attained within twelve months.

Shatyayaniya Upanishad

The *Shatyayaniya Upanishad* belongs to the *Shukla Yajur Veda* and has forty verses. It looks at the four types of ascetics and their

duties and roles in life, as well as the four types of disciplines
such as the Yogayajna. The text begins by stating that the chitta,
the conscious mind, is the cause of bondage and liberation, and
should be controlled and purified. Those brahmanas who know
the Veda and have no desires reach Brahman, following the ascetic
path. It mentions four types of ascetics: Kutichaka, Bahudaka,
Hamsa and Paramahamsa. This text states they possess the signs
of Vishnu and are identified with Vishnu. The devotional acts to
be performed are explained and the Paramahamsas are described
as having jnana (wisdom) as their tuft and sacred thread. They
are beyond passion, greed and other emotions. Most of this
Upanishad is similar to other Sannyasa Upanishads, but here
devotion to Vishnu, identified with Brahman, is prescribed. The
last few verses emphasize the importance of a guru.

Turiyatita Avadhuta Upanishad

The *Turiyatita Avadhuta Upanishad* contains a description of the
Avadhuta who has reached the state of consciousness beyond
Turiya. The text begins as Pitamaha (grandfather, a name of the
god Brahma) approaches Adinarayana (Vishnu) and asks about
the Turiyatita Avadhuta. Narayana says that such an avadhuta is
rare and unique. In this state, a person is pure, the embodiment
of dispassion and totally free. The stages leading up to this are
described: first, that of the Kutichaka (hut-dwelling ascetic),
then a Bahudaka ascetic (wandering mendicant), next the Hamsa
ascetic. Higher than this is the Paramahamsa ascetic and, finally,
the Turiyatita Avadhuta. An Avadhuta who has reached this level
does not chant mantras or practise rituals, wears no caste marks
and has terminated all religious and secular duties. He wears no
clothes and eats anything that comes his way. He wanders alone,
observing silence, and is totally absorbed in non-duality. In some
texts, however, the Paramahamsa and the Avadhuta are considered

the same, while in others there are six types of sannyasis, of which the Turiyatita is the fifth and the Avadhuta the sixth.

Yajnavalkya Upanishad

The *Yajnavalkya Upanishad* belongs to the *Shukla Yajur Veda*. This Upanishad with thirty-two verses also focuses on the Paramahamsa ascetic. The text begins with Janaka, king of videha, approaching the rishi Yajnavalkya and asking him about renunciation. Yajnavalkya explains who can become a renunciate and the methods for this, repeating what occurs in other Sannyasi Upanishads. There is not much unique or different in this text, but a few points are given here. He names the Paramahamsas of the past, including Samvartaka, Aruni, Shvetaketu, Durvasa, Ribhu, Nidagha, Dattatreya, Shuka, Vamadeva and Harita. The text states that the ascetic who is always absorbed in Brahman should not bow down or pay obeisance to anyone. However, if he feels the Supreme is in the atman of any living being he can even bow before an outcaste, a cow, a dog or a donkey (Verse 13). Several verses (14–23) criticize women and warn the ascetic not to be ensnared by them. They are the seeds of evil and the path to hell fires. Discarding women is the same as discarding worldly life and is essential on the ascetic path. Having a son, too, only leads to worries and troubles (Verses 24–26). Further verses explain the need to conquer the senses and refrain from anger. It describes the self-controlled man, who is awake even while others sleep, who knows consciousness.

Ten

The Yoga Upanishads

TWENTY UPANISHADS ARE classified as the Yoga Upanishads. They are: *Advaya-taraka, Amrita-bindu Upanishad, Amrita-nada, Brahmavidya, Darshana/Jabala Darshana, Dhyana-bindu, Hamsa, Kshurika, Mahavakya, Mandala-Brahmana, Nada-bindu, Pashupata-Brahma, Shandilya, Tejo-bindu, Trishikha-brahmana* or *Trishikhi-brahmana, Varaha, Yoga-chudamani, Yoga-kundalini, Yoga-shikha* and *Yogatattva*. The Yoga Upanishads seek to reach Brahman through methods prescribed by yoga. Gavin Flood dates the Yoga Upanishads between 100 BCE and 300 CE, but some of them may be later.

Advaya-taraka Upanishad

The *Advaya-taraka Upanishad* belongs to the *Shukla Yajur Veda*. It explains some aspects of Raja Yoga and has nineteen passages in prose and verse.

Advaya means non-dual, while taraka, literally star, also means to cross over, that is, something that helps the individual

327

Brahman

cross over to Brahman. In addition, it indicates the light between the eyebrows that can be seen through meditation.

This Upanishad enables one to transcend the world and attain Brahman through Taraka Yoga. It is for the Yati (ascetic) who has controlled his senses and established the six qualities: shama, self-control of the mind; dama, subjugation or self-control in action; uparati, cessation or tolerance; titiksha, endurance, cheerfulness; samadhana, intentness, one-pointedness; shraddha, faith.

It explains that the light of Brahman can be seen between the eyebrows. The Sushumna Nadi, which has the form of the sun and the light of the moon, rises from the Muladhara to the Brahma-randhra. The Kundalini is within the Sushumna, radiant and delicate like the thread of a lotus stalk. Seeing it with the mind's eye brings release.

The yogi may see light in front of the forehead and a blue radiant space between his eyes. Externally too, the yogi may see blue, verging on indigo and then changing colour, and other radiant beams, as well as a vast disc like the sun and fire. There is a twofold yoga: taraka and amanasaka (beyond mind). One can see a radiance between the eyebrows and also above the root of the palate. Meditating on the latter brings supernatural power. Both external and internal viewing will reveal the white light of Brahman.

The text states that when the eyes are neither shut nor open (that is, half open), Shambhavi mudra is attained. Wherever an expert in this mudra lives, the place becomes holy.

The inner radiance can be seen through the help of a great teacher. It may be in the Sahasrara Chakra or the light of chit (consciousness), buddhi (intelligence) or Turiya, abiding in the shodashanta (a spot sixteen digits above).

The acharya, well-versed in the Vedas, a devotee of Vishnu, who has no envy, who knows yoga, who is always in yoga, who knows the

Purusha, can be called a guru. 'Gu' indicates darkness and 'ru' the dispeller of darkness. The guru is Brahman, wisdom and the supreme goal. Because he teaches That, the guru is greater than anyone else.

The text ends by saying that whoever reads this is released from the cycle of birth and death.

Amrita-bindu Upanishad

The *Amrita-bindu Upanishad* belongs to the *Krishna Yajur Veda* and has twenty-two verses. It discusses Brahman as the only reality and the means of uniting with it. The text states that the mind is the cause of both liberation and bondage. Those desiring liberation should constantly free the mind from objects of desire. Then, focusing on the heart, one transcends the individual self. Focusing on Brahman, unqualified and as itself, one becomes That. Combining the yoga of qualified Brahman with the mystic syllable Om, one reaches Brahman after transcending Om, and the yogi is then liberated. There is then no dissolution, no creation, no one bound, no one liberated. This is the ultimate truth. For those who see the atman as one in the waking, dreaming and sleeping states and transcend them, there is no rebirth. The Bhutatman found in every being seems to be an individual self, but is only one, though seen singly and in many ways, just as the reflection of the moon in water. The space within a pot is not really carried from place to place, nor does it disintegrate when the pot does. Similarly, the jiva enters into various forms but does not disintegrate with that form. When the oneness of Brahman is seen, the diversity of name and form dissolves. The Shabdakshara (Om) is the transcendent Brahman.

When Om is dissolved, the eternal akshara is revealed. The peace of the atman is attained by meditating on the akshara. The two vidyas are the shabda or qualified Brahman and the transcendent Brahman. One well-versed in the Shabda-Brahman is then able to transcend it. After thoroughly studying books on Brahman, the books should be dropped, just like the husk from grain.

Milk has a single colour even though cows are of different colours, and Brahman is like the milk, the same everywhere even though people are different. Vijnana (knowledge) exists in every being, even as butter is hidden in milk. The churning stick of the mind should be used to find the butter of knowledge.

Knowledge should be used to extract as sacrificial fire, the transcendent Brahman, non-fragile, motionless and tranquil, considered the 'I'. The Upanishad ends by identifying Vasudeva with Brahman.

Amrita-nada Upanishad

The *Amrita-nada Upanishad* belongs to the *Krishna Yajur Veda* and has thirty-eight verses. It discusses yoga with six steps and its ultimate aim of kaivalya. The pure-minded can attain Brahman through shravana (study) and manana (reflection), while those with an impure mind should meditate on Brahman and practice Shadanga Yoga (yoga of six stages).

After studying the Shastras and meditating on them, the wise person leaves them behind. While worshipping Rudra, with Om as the chariot and Vishnu as the charioteer, he drives ahead until he leaves the chariot behind.

The sixfold Yoga is described as pratyahara, dhyana, pranayama, dharana, tarka and samadhi. There are descriptions of pranayama and its parts, of breathing in and out, holding the breath, and kumbhaka, where the breath remains outside the body. Dharana is merging in one's atman and contemplation of Brahman. Inference according to the scriptures is tarka. Finally, attaining the supreme Self is samadhi. Instructions are provided for attaining samadhi, including the posture to be seated in and the type of pranayama and meditation to be performed. Practice of yoga should be constant. The seven doors leading to the atman are explained, including the door of the heart and the head. As explained in other texts, it is said that the yogi should maintain a balance in everything, in sleeping, waking, food and fasting and should avoid fear, anger and laziness. Through this he will progress steadily and by the sixth month attain the kaivalya of his desire. There is more on meditation, the types of prana and the colours associated with pranas. The first prana is in the heart, apana in the anus, samana in the navel, udana in the throat, while vyana pervades the whole body. Prana vayu is the colour of a blood-red gem, apana in the middle of the body is the colour of the indra-kopa insect, samana between them is milk-white and shining, udana is pale white and vyana is bright like a flame. When the pranas reach the head, such a person is not born again.

Brahmavidya Upanishad

The *Brahmavidya Upanishad* belongs to the *Krishna Yajur Veda*. It has 111 verses and looks at Brahman, the Pranava and the nadis.

The text states that Brahmavidya, the knowledge of Brahman, can be attained through Om as Om is Brahman. Om contains the three worlds, the three gods, the three Vedas, the three agnis or fires, the three matras and the half matra representing Shiva, which has three letters. Further explanations follow of the matras of the Pranava, Om. The transcendent nadi, the Sushumna, breaks through the 72,000 nadis and stands in the head. She is the giver of boons to all (10–11). The Pranava of sixteen matras and the real form of the jiva is also described. The jiva that constantly mutters 'So-ham' (I am He) attains the form of the Pranava. The

jiva becomes one with the Paramatman through the practice of
yoga techniques. The various chakras are mentioned and the
Sushumna that pierces through them. The Hamsa-vidya is the
prime method of attaining the Paramatman. The Paramatman can
also be attained through the Vedas and the guidance of a guru as
the guru is Hari incarnate. The jiva is finite, but the atman, which
is Brahman, is infinite. The yoga described here should be kept
a secret from those unqualified to attain it. Further instructions
are provided on how to attain Brahman within the body, through
the practice of pranayama and the recitation of and meditation on
the mantras Om and Hamsa. Nadis, asanas and bandhas are also
described.

Darshana or Jabala Darshana Upanishad

The *Darshana* or *Jabala Darshana Upanishad* belongs to the
Sama Veda and has seven sections. In this Upanishad, Dattatreya
describes the basics of ashtanga or eightfold yoga as a method of
identifying with Brahman.

Section 1 with twenty-five verses states that Dattatreya,
the four-armed Maha Vishnu,, is the lord of yoga. His disciple,
rishi Samkriti, asks him to explain ashtanga yoga. He describes
the traditional eight stages of yama, niyama, asana, pranayama,
pratyahara, dharana, dhyana and samadhi. The ten yamas are given
as ahimsa, satya, asteya, brahmachari (non-violence, truthfulness,
non-stealing, celibacy), daya (compassion), arjavam (rectitude),
kshama (forgiveness), dhriti (firmness), mitahara (temperance in
food) and cleanliness (1.6). The first four of these are also in the
Yoga Sutra, while all ten are found in other texts. The text goes on to
provide an explanation for each of these. Among the explanations,
it states that celibacy is to abstain from contact with women, even
one's own wife, except immediately after menstruation, while
cleanliness refers to internal purity.

After realizing that the atman is the Brahman, there is nothing more to be done.

Section 2 describes the ten niyamas: tapas, santosha, astikyam, dana, Ishvara-pujanam, siddhanta, shravanam, hri, mati, japa (austerities, contentment, belief in the existence of the supreme Truth, generosity, worship of Ishvara, study of the established Truth, modesty, faith, prayer and chanting). The text explains each of these. It states that that tapas is not emaciation of the body but right enquiry, and that prayers can include mantras.

In Section 3, nine asanas are explained: Svastika, Go-mukha, Padma, Vira, Simhasana, Bhadra, Muktasana, Mayurasana and Sukhasana (3.1–2). (Though the Simhasana description was not in the original, it has been added.) Sukhasana, it is said, is for a weak person. After the asanas, one should practice pranayama.

Section 4 explains the chakras and the nadis. It states that in the middle of the body is the fire centre that shines like liquid gold. Taking the body of a man to be ninety-six digits tall, it says that this centre is two digits above the anus and two digits below the genitals and triangular in shape. Then the knot (of the navel) is nine digits from the Muladhara, extending over four digits, shaped like a hen's egg. The nadi located here is known as the Sushumna. Around this are 72,000 nadis, the main ones being fourteen. These fourteen are the Sushumna, Pingala, Ida, Sarasvati, Pusha, Varuna, Hasti-jihva, Yashasvini, Alambusha, Kuhu, Vishvodara, Payasvini, Shankhini and Gandhara. The most important of these is the Sushumna, also known as the Brahma Nadi. This is attached to the spinal cord. Two digits below the knot of the navel is the Kundali (Kundalini) which has eight parts and regulates prana and digestion. Ida is to the left of the Sushumna, Pingala to the right, Sarasvati and Kuhu at the sides of the Sushumna. Gandhara and Hasti-jihva are to the back and front of the Ida, Pusha and Yashasvini to the back and front of the Pingala. The Vishvodhara is between the Kuhu and Hasti-jihva; the Varuna between the Yashasvini and Kuhu. The Yashasvini is between the Pusha and Sarasvati and the Shankhini between the Gandhara and Sarasvati. The Alambusha reaches the navel from the anus. The text continues with further details of these.

After this, the flow of the ten vital airs, prana, apana etc., is described, as in other texts. The location of each of them and their actions are described (30–34).

Next, the deities presiding over the nadis are mentioned, and how the air moves between the nadis. Shiva is the deity of the Sushumna, Hari of Ida, Brahma of Pingala, Viraj of Sarasvati, Pushan of Pusha, Vayu of the Varuna Nadi, and the god Varuna of Hasti-jihva, of Yashasvini, the Sun, of Alambusha again Varuna, and of Kuhu, hunger. The deity of Gandhari and Shankhini is the moon, Prajapati of Payasvini (35–39). Further details on the passage of prana in the bodies is provided. The tirthas (sacred centres of pilgrimage) such as Kurukshetra are placed within the body. For instance, Prayaga is in the centre of the heart. These are more important than the external tirthas, and it is said that yogis do not go to tirthas filled with water or offer prayers to gods made of wood. The tirtha of the atman is the greatest.

Though Shiva is within the atman, the ignorant look for him outside, in wood and stone, streams and prayers. Images are made only to help the ignorant conceive of the Supreme. The one who sees the non-dual Brahman becomes That.

Section 5 with fourteen verses deals with the purification of the nadis. The nadis can be purified after one's conduct is properly regulated, and the body and mind stabilized through the eight steps of yoga, including the yamas and niyamas. After this, methods of drawing the prana through the nadis are prescribed. This will lead to lightness of the body, fire glowing in the mid-region and clarity of sound. The next step is the purification of the atman, leading to bliss.

The sixth section with fifty-one verses describes pranayama and its three parts: rechaka, puraka and kumbhaka. Puraka implies taking in air, kumbhaka holding it and rechaka expelling it. Prana can be drawn into the nadis and also purifies the mind. There is lightness in the body, fatigue is removed and immunity to diseases is attained. Various asanas and mudras are also described. When prana enters the Brahma-randhra, a sound is heard like a conch shell, followed by the sound of thunder and of a mountain torrent. Finally, the atman is realized. The Muladhara and Sushumna are also mentioned.

Section 7 with fourteen verses describes pratyahara, the withdrawal of the senses, such that everything is seen as Brahman. The pratyahara of Vedanta is to recognize the atman as Brahman.

Section 8 with nine verses explains five kinds of dharana (concentration), focusing on the elements, as well as dharana on the atman.

Section 9 with six verses goes to the next step, dhyana or meditation, on Ishvara, the truth (satya) or on Brahman. Through this, non-duality is attained.

Finally, Section 10 (thirteen verses) describes the ultimate goal of samadhi. After Dattatreya had explained all this to Samkriti, he understood the atman and became free from fear.

Dhyana-bindu Upanishad

The *Dhyana-bindu Upanishad* is attached to the *Krishna Yajur Veda*, the thirty-ninth in the list. It has 106 verses and looks at various types of meditation, including meditation on Brahman, on the Pranava, and on deities. It also discusses yoga, the nadis and the chakras. It states that through dhyana, sins accumulated over hundreds of births can be shattered. It describes the Pranava Om and the subtle nature of Brahman that pervades everything. The atman too is all pervasive. Each syllable of the Pranava is described and related to colours, states of consciousness, the three gunas and other aspects of existence. The Pranava is the bow, the atman (here implying manas, the mind) is the arrow and Brahman is the target that can be reached by taking aim. It states that the Ishvara of Omkara is in the middle of the lotus of the heart, like the steady flame of a lamp, the size of a thumb. Methods of using pranayama to meditate on this are explained (19–21). Other aspects of meditation on the Pranava are also described, including meditation on the qualified Brahman, on Vishnu and on the trinity of Brahma, Vishnu and Shiva. The lotus of the heart has its stem above and opens downward, but right meditation causes it to burst into flower upwards.

Next, the sixfold yoga is described, consisting of asana, pranayama, withdrawal of breath, steadiness of breath, concentration and meditation. Though there are as many asanas as there are living beings, the text lists the four main ones as siddha, bhadra, simha and padma (42–43). Next, it describes the chakras—the Muladhara, Svadhishthana, Manipura, Anahata, Vishuddha and Ajna—and refers to the 72,000 nadis. Out of these, seventy-two are important and out of the seventy-two, ten. The ten are then listed similar to other texts: Ida, Pingala, Sushumna, Gandhari, Hasti-jihva, Pusha, Yashasvini, Alambusha, Kuhu and Shankhini. There are descriptions of these, followed by descriptions of the ten pranas which flow through the nadis. The thousands of nadis form the jiva, which is dependent on the prana and apana. The prana moves in and out with the sound 'Ham-sa'. The Upanishad then describes how to arouse the Kundalini using prana and apana. It asserts that celibacy is essential for this (70–73). It also describes certain bandhas, the mula bandha, uddiyana bandha and jalandhara bandha, as well as mudras, including the khechari mudra and maha-mudra, along with methods of discovering the atman in the lotus of the heart.

This Upanishad thus provides many esoteric and yogic means of uniting with Brahman.

Hamsa Upanishad

The *Hamsa Upanishad* has different versions containing similar ideas. The version consulted (of Upanishad Brahmayogin) has twenty-one verses and is attached to the *Shukla Yajur Veda*. The text begins by Gautama approaching Sanat Kumara and asking about Brahman. In response, Sanat Kumara says he will reveal what was taught to him by Parvati, who received the knowledge from the god Shiva. This knowledge is not to be revealed to everyone but is only for the yogi. The text then discusses the method of raising the Kundalini through the chakras, leading to the Paramahamsa (supreme) state. Aspects of the Hamsa Mantra are described in detail and should be meditated on in the lotus of the heart. Hamsa coordinates with the breath as 'Ham-sa So-ham' and therefore is termed Ajapa. Through the Ajapa Hamsa Mantra, nada (divine sounds) is experienced in ten different ways. The tenth is the sound of thunder and this should be focused on, ignoring the other nine. Each sound has a benefit but with the tenth the yogi will merge with Para Brahman. When the mind is dissolved in the mind and when good and evil disappear, then Sadashiva, self-created, effulgent, identical with Brahman, is known.

Kshurika Upanishad

The *Kshurika Upanishad* belongs to the *Krishna Yajur Veda*.

It describes how to use yoga as a kshurika (knife) to cut the obstacles to reach Brahman. The kshurika of dharana (concentration) can be used to attain yoga, after which there is no rebirth. This is recognized as the true teaching of the Veda as told by Svayambhu (the self-created).

A yogic method is then described to attain Brahman. After going to a secluded and silent place, withdrawing the senses and placing the mind in the heart, one should fill the body with the yoga of twelve matras, the pranava (Om) of four matras, with a total of forty-eight matras of Vayu, hold the breath in and then gradually release it. Then one should focus and withdraw, using the thumb, on the ankles, thighs, knees, etc., moving up the body to the first two chakras and then the navel, where he should fix the three (the eyes, mind and vital breath) till mastery. There is the white Sushumna Nadi, surrounded by ten nadis which are black, brown, red, yellow, copper-coloured, etc. The three should be moved up the Sushumna as a spider moves along its web and withdrawn into the heart shining like a blood-red lotus known as *Dahara-pundarika* (the Anahata Chakra) in Vedanta scriptures. Having broken through that lotus, the three reach the throat (Vishuddhi), and so on to the Ajna and Sahasrara Chakras. He should meditate on that form identical with that of the *marman* (vital region) which is in the big toe of the foot.

Mahavakya Upanishad

The *Mahavakya Upanishad* is attached to the *Atharva Veda* and has twelve verses. It discusses the bliss of the atman and the radiant Pranava Hamsa.

The text begins with the god Brahma stating that he will explain the Upanishad (secret teaching) based on his own experience. The chitaditya (sun of consciousness) can be attained by chanting the mantra 'Hamsa-Soham'. In addition, prana and apana should be controlled and the mind concentrated on Brahman. The seeker acquires the knowledge of the atman through three stages of knowledge: jnana, vijnana, and samyak-jnana. Then, meditating on the threefold aspects of the atman (the three states of consciousness), finally, the Paramatman is revealed as sat-chit-ananda (true being, consciousness and bliss). It shines like 1000 suns and is neither samadhi nor yoga but the identity with Brahman. The text continues that even the devas use the yajna of

knowledge to attain the Supreme. The gods Brahma and Shakra
(Indra) know the oneness of Brahman and the Sadhyas, gods of
the past, are jivan-muktas (liberated). Those who experience this
know that they are chid-arka, the sun of consciousness, and the
brilliant radiance of Shiva, and the light of Om. The text ends
with the statement that the one who studies this Upanishad gains
the same benefits as reading the entire Vedas and reaches the
abode of Maha Vishnu.

Mandala-Brahmana Upanishad

The *Mandala-Brahmana Upanishad* is attached to the *Shukla Yajur
Veda*. This is an important Upanishad with a complete description
of many esoteric yogic practices. The text has five main divisions
known as Brahmanas, each with several sections.

The first Brahmana: The first section has eleven verses. The
Upanishad begins with the visit of the rishi Yajnavalkya to Aditya
Loka, the world of the sun god, who asks the Lord how to attain
the atman. The god Surya Narayana responds that the method
to be followed is the eightfold yoga, beginning with the yamas.
The god then describes four yamas, slightly different from the
usual list: 1. The conquest of heat and cold and of desires for
food and sleep; 2. Maintaining tranquillity in all circumstances;
3. Focusing the mind on its main aim; 4. Controlling the senses.
Next, nine niyamas are mentioned that include devotion to the
guru and attachment to the path of truth followed by descriptions
of the next six angas or steps on the path of asana, pranayama,
pratyahara, dharana, dhyana and samadhi.

The second section, with fourteen verses looks at the five
defects inherent in a person, which include desire, anger, fear,
sleep and the breathing out of the vital air. The taraka, or means
of transcending the world, is then described. The Sushumna Nadi,

extending from the Muladhara to the Brahma-randhra, shines like the sun and within it is the Kundalini like streaks of lightning. As the practitioner proceeds, a blue radiance can be seen in the middle of the eyes and in the heart centre. Lights and colours will also be seen outside the body.

In Section 3 with six verses, two types of yoga are described: Taraka and Amanasaka. Taraka, too, is of two types: Murti (image-based) and Amurti (without an image). Murti Taraka is that which focuses on the six chakras from the Muladhara to Ajna, and Amurti that which is above and beyond that (that is, the seventh chakra and others in the brain). Shambhavi mudra, internal introspection with the eyes half open and unblinking, is the last step of the two Tarakas.

Section 4 with four verses, looks at the controversies among those with different beliefs. The yogis say that with internal introspection they see the radiance of the Sahasrara Chakra. Others say they view the divine and radiant Purusha; Shaivites see the blue-necked Shiva; still others see the Purusha of the size of a thumb. But the true reality is the atman, and the one who focuses on that is united with Brahman. The atman is the twenty-sixth tattva, beyond the jiva, which is the twenty-fifth.

The second Brahmana: In Section 1 with ten verses, in response to another question by Yajnavalkya, the lord of Aditya Loka further describes the radiant inner atman, in which the fourth state of consciousness, Turiya, can be seen. Further instructions are provided on how to attain the knowledge of the atman and the fruits of such attainment.

Section 2 with five verses continues with this theme, describing how internal radiance of different types is seen as marks of progress on this path. The one who knows the Pranava has gone beyond duality and reaches the amanasaka (beyond mind) state. No religious rites are required to be performed by such a person.

Section 3 with seven verses states that through the contemplation of Brahman, the state of kaivalya (aloneness) is attained. It goes on to explain the difference between Sushupti, or deep sleep, and samadhi. Unlike deep sleep, samadhi does not consist of inertia, but of a conscious state of being a witness. Through meditating on Brahman, the person becomes Brahman, attaining the state of jivan-mukta. Section 4 with six verses looks at the five states of consciousness, with Turiyatita, the state beyond Turiya, as the fifth. When the yogi realizes the atman as Brahman, everything is attained. In Section 5, with four verses, nirvikalpa samadhi, undifferentiated samadhi, the highest state is described. The Parama yogi (Supreme yogi) then basks in the infinite bliss of Brahman.

The third Brahmana: In Section 1 with six verses, once again Yajnavalkya questions the Purusha (person) of Aditya Loka, who again explains to him the state beyond mind associated with Shambhavi mudra. In this state, the Paramatman, the transcendent Brahman, is seen.

Section 2 with two verses continues with this theme.

The fourth Brahmana: This starts with a different theme and Section 1 with five verses describes five types of akasha (ether or space). Of these, akasha is dark in nature, parakasha has a delusory nature, mahakasha is radiant, suryakasha resembles the sun and paramakasha creates bliss. Following this, the basic requisites for Raja Yoga are summarized. This includes the knowledge of nine chakras (from Muladhara to Ajna, along with Talu, Akasha and Bhru Chakra), the six adharas or areas that support them, three kinds of introspection and the five akashas mentioned above.

The fifth Brahmana: The text continues with the fifth Brahmana (nine verses) which describes how when the chitta, the conscious mind, is silent, the ideal state is achieved. The amanasaka state (that beyond mind) leads to nirvikalpa (undifferentiated) samadhi.

Nada-bindu Upanishad

The *Nada-bindu Upanishad* is attached to the *Rig Veda* and has fifty-one verses. It looks at various aspects of the Vairaja Pranava, the Vairaja vidya as well as nada and the power of sound. The Vairaja Pranava is Om, the various parts of which are in this Upanishad, associated with Viraj, the Supreme person. The text explains twelve different matras of Om. After knowledge is gained, all karma is destroyed. Past actions recede and the nada, the divine sound of the union of Brahman and the Pranava, is heard. Sitting in siddhasana, with eyes in Vaishnavi mudra (wide open), the yogi should listen for the sounds in his right ear. With practice, the sounds will become increasingly subtle, drown all outer sounds and lead to Turiya, the fourth state of consciousness. Sound has the power to captivate the mind. Brahman is contained in the nada of the Pranava and is self-luminous. Nada is the means but not the end as the transcendent atman has no sound and is known as the Paramatman. Through nada, the yogi attains videha-mukti.

Pashupata-Brahma Upanishad

The *Pashupata-Brahma Upanishad* is attached to the *Atharva Veda*. It has two sections: the Purva-kanda and Uttara-kanda. The Upanishad includes seven questions related to the Supreme ruler.

The *Purva-kanda* with thirty-two verses begins with Brahman, the self-created, desiring to create. Then, Kameshvara and Vaishravana are born. Vaishravana, the Valakhilya, asks Brahman seven questions about the world and creation, which are answered by Svayambhu, that is, the self-created Brahman. The questions include those on the vidya (knowledge) of the worlds, the deity, the devas of the Jagrata and Turiya states, time, the planetary bodies and the sky. Svayambhu replies that the vidya of the worlds is the alphabet, the deity is Om. I am the ruler of the three worlds, he says, as well as the controller of the yugas, cycles of time, the sun, moon and planets, the sky and all that exists. He then explains the characteristics of Rudra, Vishnu, Brahma and Indra and states that the real form of the Paramatman is the Hamsa. Next, he explains the similarity between the Yajnasutra, the sacrificial thread, and the brahmasutra, which in this context implies the inner, unseen sacred thread. The Yajnasutra has ninety-six units of thread, each of four digits, while the brahmasutra has ninety-six tattvas, which are then described. In addition, the Pranava, and the Hamsa contained in it, is said to be both the brahmasutra and the brahmayajna (17). The Hamsa, Pranava and states of consciousness are further described. The Hamsa has ninety-six threads, equivalent to the Paramatman. Various yajnas are explained as inner sacrifices, including the vajapeya and the ashvamedha.

The *Uttarakanda* with forty-six verses continues with the description of how Brahman can be attained. Brahman is of the form of Hamsa and is indicated by Om. It is the internal Pranava which brings about knowledge. It refers to the Hamsarka Pranava-dhyana, meditation on Brahman as the Self. It goes on to say that it is Ishvara or Shiva Pashupati that allows the mind and all senses to function. But the atman is the only reality, and whatever is not of it is created by maya. The one who attains the Paramatman is neither the jiva nor Brahman, nor does he belong to any varna or any of the ashramas or stages of life. Dharma and adharma, difference and non-difference, no longer exist. The one who knows the Paramatman sees only Brahman everywhere in all the multitude of forms. Brahman and its bliss have permeated everywhere. Truth and the right path are essential to attain

Brahman. Once the yogi has become Brahman, there is nowhere
to go and nothing more to attain.

Shandilya Upanishad

The *Shandilya Upanishad* forms part of the *Atharva Veda*. In
Section 1, khanda 1 with fourteen verses, Shandilya questions
Atharvan on the eight stages of yoga, which are then described
by him, beginning with the yamas. In khanda 2 (eleven verses),
the niyamas are explained. Khanda 3 with fifteen verses explains
eight types of asanas: the svastika, gomukha, padma, vira, simha,
bhadra, mukta and mayura. Once these are perfected, pranayama
should be taken up for the purification of the nadis. In khanda
4 with fourteen verses, Atharvan describes the nadis, chakras,
pranas and the Kundalini and methods of raising it. Khanda 5
with four verses expounds on those worthy to practice yoga, the
best place of practice, and how to begin. Khanda 6 (five verses)
and khanda 7 (forty-four verses) continue with explanations of
right practice. Khanda 8 (two verses) focuses on five kinds of
pratyahara and khanda 9 (one verse) on five types of dharana,
while khanda 10 (one verse) on two types of dhyana. Khanda
11 (one verse) explains samadhi, the state of union between the
atman and Paramatman.

In Section 2 (six verses), it is stated that even after all these
explanations Shandilya had not realized Brahman and asked
for further instruction on Brahmavidya. Atharvan then explains
Brahman, which is beyond all, and from which all things come
and can be known through knowledge.

In Section 3, khanda 1 (six verses), Shandilya asks how the
world can come into being when Para Brahman is only One.
Atharvan explains that there are three types of Brahman, the
indivisible Para Brahman, the divisible, and the partly divisible
and partly indivisible. Maheshvara, in whom mula prakriti, maya

and the gunas exist, can be called the divisible Brahman. After
Maheshvara practised austerities, many aspects of the world
emerged from him, even though he is one with Brahman. This
is the partly divisible and partly indivisible form. This Lord is
Brahma, Vishnu, Rudra and Indra, with the form of Dattatreya.
Khanda 2 (fifteen verses) explains this further and describes Atri
and Anasuya's son, Dattatreya, auspicious and tranquil, and like
the Indranila gem. He is the Lord of the universe, worshipped by
all yogis, always compassionate, and the eternal witness.

Tejo-bindu Upanishad

The *Tejo-bindu Upanishad* belongs to the *Krishna Yajur Veda*, and
is again on the realization of Brahman through Yoga. The section
on yoga is not very long, the rest of the text being devoted to
explaining Brahman, both by what it is and what it is not.

Chapter 1, with fifty-one verses, seeks to provide the means of
reaching tejo-bindu, the spark of radiance within the heart. The
person who seeks this should be balanced in all aspects of life. A
fifteen-stage process is prescribed for reaching tejo-bindu, which
is the same as Brahman. Though some of the same terms are used
as in other Yoga texts, the explanations provided here are different.
The fifteen angas, parts or stages are: yama, niyama, tyaga, mauna,
desha, kala, asana, mula-bandha, deha-samya, drik-sthithi,
prana-samyama, pratyahara, dharana, atma-dhyana and samadhi.

Succeeding verses provide explanations of each of these.

Yama: Controlling all senses through the realization that all
is Brahman.

Niyama: Focusing consciousness on intrinsic categories and
rejecting the external.

Tyaga: Renouncing the outer world as a result of introspection.

Mauna: Not just maintaining silence, in this context, but a
recognition that Brahman is beyond words.

Desha (place): The right place, that which is secluded and without people.

Kala (time): The right duration is indicated here, or the method of measuring a unit of time, of that which is immeasurable.

Asana: When those accomplished in asana reach the non-dual base of the universe, that is known as siddha-asana.

Mula-bandha: Raja Yogis should adopt mula-bandha, the root of all worlds, attained through restraining the mind.

Deha-samya (equilibrium of the body): There should be equilibrium between the gross, subtle and causal bodies, which would enable their dissolution in Brahman.

Drik-sthithi (stability of perception): This is not about fixing the gaze, but seeing the world filled with Brahman.

Prana-samyama (control of prana): The suppression of all vital function is known as pranayama. Avoidance of contact with the world is rechaka. The attitude 'I am only Brahman' is puraka, and the steadiness of that attitude is kumbhaka.

Pratyahara: When the mind finds the atman (Brahman) in the objects of desire, this is pratyahara.

Dharana: When the mind is abstracted because it sees Brahman everywhere, this is dharana.

Atma-dhyana (meditation on the atma): Dhyana is that state when the mind rests only on Brahman and has no other support.

Samadhi: When the mind reaches the form of Brahman, it is samadhi.

The seeker should practise all this until Brahman spontaneously arises in oneself.

When the world is seen as Brahman, beyond speech and mind, the siddha becomes the king of yogis.

Next, the obstacles to samadhi are pointed out. They include apathy, laziness, desire for enjoyment and absent-mindedness. Those who have an understanding of Brahman but still lack correct knowledge will continue to be reborn. They cannot remain in Brahman, as do Sanaka, Shuka and other knowers of Brahman.

In Chapter 2, Kumara (the god Karttikeya, son of Shiva) asks Shiva to tell him about the essence of the indivisible one. Paramashiva replies that it is the world, it is existence, it is atman, it is mantra, it is action, it is knowledge, it is water, it is earth, it is ether (akasha), it is science, the triple Veda, the austere vow, that which has no origin, Brahman (and a lot more), the mother, the father, Om, etc. (1–23). A number of other aspects are given, and then it is stated that it is consciousness. It is consciousness beyond birth. 'Ether, the Earth, Water, Air, Fire, Brahman, Hari, Shiva, what is little and what is not little, all these are only consciousness. Whatever is only consciousness is the indivisible one essence. The past, the present and future are all consciousness, as well as matter, time, knowledge and the object of knowledge, etc. Apart from this consciousness, the indivisible one essence, there is no Brahman (2.24–41).

In Chapter 3, Kumara asks his father to tell him about the realization of the atman. Parameshvara replies, 'I am the form of the transcendent Brahman, I am exquisite bliss, I am absolute knowledge, I am the absolute transcendent being . . . I am absolute goodness. Having renounced the I, I am the I. I am the I that is devoid of all, I am Turiya and what is beyond Turiya, I am consciousness and bliss . . . I am absolute love, I am without desire, I am the Atman, I am Sadashiva . . . I am served by the Vedas, I am revealed by the Shastra, I am firmly planted in the chitta . . . I am the Adi-shesha, I am the Shesha . . .'

He goes on to say: 'The form of the mind is false. The form of the intellect is false. I am eternal, perpetual and originless . . . the three bodies are false, the three gunas are false, all scriptures are false, the Vedas are false, all Shastras are false, I, the Atman of consciousness, am true. The triad of murtis are false, all beings are false, all truth is false. I am Sadashiva, pervading all existing things.

The preceptor and pupil are false, the mantra of the preceptor is false. Whatever is seen is false, what is conceivable is false . . . all living creatures are false, all enjoyments are false, right and wrong action is false, what is lost and obtained is false, grief and delight are false, good and bad conduct is false. All form, taste, smell, cognition is false, every result of human existence is false, I alone am the absolute truth.'

A passage follows on the mantra 'I am Brahman' that supersedes all others and destroys all duality, all diseases of the mind and all bonds. This mantra alone should be used.

In Chapter 4 (eighty-one verses), Kumara now asks Parameshvara about the jivan-mukta and videha-mukta. The supreme Shiva replies that the jivan-mukta is one who realizes the identity with Brahman. He has absolute consciousness and bliss and no awareness of the body. He understands that nothing is mine, neither the intellect, nor the body, nor the emotions. Even the Turiya is not mine as I am the transcendent Brahman.

The text continues to explain what is 'not mine'. Not mine Brahman, not mine the moon, not mine Rudra, not mine Vishnu, etc. Not mine you, not mine I, not mine childhood, not mine adolescence, not mine old age, I am only Brahman, I am only consciousness, he who realizes this is the pure Hamsa. 'One who has become the Brahman; who has tranquillized his own atman; who is full of the Bliss of the Brahman; who is happy; who is crystal-like in form; who is profoundly silent; he alone is the videha-mukti' (33). Such a person has even abandoned the conviction of being Brahman. He ends by saying, 'One who is within one's own atman, O Shadanana, is videha mukti.'

Chapter 5 (107 verses) is a long chapter, explaining that as there is only Brahman, everything else is unreal. It says that Nidagha asked the rishi Ribhu about the distinction between the atman and the anatman. Ribhu explained the nature of Brahman as the furthest limit of all speech and thought; who is the cause of effects, but Himself being without causes and effects; who is movement of any kind; and who consists of nada, the divine sound. Brahman is absolute consciousness, transcendent and full of bliss, luminous and even beyond the mahavakyas. The one who has realized Brahman is the Sanatana Atman, that is, the eternal atman. For such a person there is no existence or non-existence, no worlds of devas or asuras, no mantras or absence of mantras, no learning or ignorance, no person who sees and nothing that is seen (5.1–15). As everything is Brahman, there is no anatman.

The text continues its theme of negation. There is no world, as it was never created (5.1.23). There is no Ganga, no Gaya, no Setu, no elements, no yoga or yogi, no day or night, no anatman. There is only Brahman. Brahman, which is located in the atman, is meditated upon by Vishnu and other gods. The Upanishad then identifies Brahman with Vasudeva but goes on to say that nothing exists. It is thought and the mind that create problems. Even the Vasus, Rudras and Adityas do not exist as they are only products of the mind.

In Chapter 6 (111 verses), Ribhu continues by saying that the only reality is existence, consciousness and bliss. None of the functions of the mind—intellect, individuality or thought—have any reality. Once again, there is a long list and explanation of what is not. There is no brahmana, kshatriya or vaishya, no bird, animal or anything else, nor women, nor shudras, no lokas, no thinness or fatness, no monism of the great texts, no mystic powers, only existence, consciousness and bliss (3–30). All is Brahman, only the eternal Brahman is real. An equally long list follows of what is Brahman. Brahman alone is the three worlds. The Vedas are Brahman, etc. But everything else in the world, including all perceived differences, including those of time, space, substance, victory or defeat, the senses, prana, the seasons, are all unreal. It continues to emphasize that Brahman is everything. If there is anything else, it is like a mirage in a desert. It goes on to speak of imaginary worlds which have as much reality as this. In short, they are equally unreal.

Having firmly resolved 'I am Brahman', everything else will fade away (5.103–07).

The Upanishad ends with the statement that this great text, explained by Shankara, should not be given to anyone who has no faith in the Veda. Giving up the study of all other Upanishads, one should study only the *Tejo-bindu*, through which, even by studying it only once, one will realize Brahman.

Trishikha-brahmana or *Trishikhi-brahmana Upanishad*

The *Trishikha-brahmana Upanishad* is attached to the *Vajasaneyi Samhita* of the *Yajur Veda*. The text has different versions.

It states that a trishikhi brahmana (a brahmana with three tufts) went to Aditya Loka and asked the lord, 'What is the body? What is prana? What is the cause? What is the atma?'

He replied that all this is Shiva though it looks divided because of Brahman tinged with maya. From Brahman came avyakta, then mahat, the ahamkara, the five tanmatras followed by the five mahabhutas and the world. The Upanishad then looks at the various elements and their relationship with the aspects of a person. For instance, from ether (akasha) emerges the antahkarana, manas, buddhi, chitta and ahamkara (5). From the other elements emerge prana, the senses and various parts of the body. Next, it discusses the twelve divisions of the body and their relationship with the elements and the deities. The deities mentioned are the Moon, the Four-faced One (Brahma), Disha (guardians of the cardinal points), Vata, Arka, Varuna, the Ashvins, Agni, Indra, Upendra, Prajapati and Yama. These have entered the twelve nadis as the presiding deities of the senses. There are further explanations of the elements and how they relate to the different aspects of a person and to the world. The text also explains sixteen parts of Brahman relevant in the creation of the world and the four states of consciousness, with Turiya as the fourth.

It states that the jiva can attain peace by renouncing its karma and it then becomes unchanging and identical to Shiva. But Vishnu and his power of maya also find a place in the text.

The text continues with explanations of yoga, through which the yogi obtains knowledge. Yoga includes both Jnana and Karma Yoga. Fixing the mind on moksha at all times is Jnana Yoga.

Next, the eight stages of yoga are explained, the ten yamas and niyamas. It gives the ten yamas as non-violence (ahimsa), truth (satya), abstinence from stealing (aparigraha), celibacy (brahmacharya), compassion, rectitude, forbearance, fortitude, temperance in food and cleanliness, and the ten niyamas as penance (tapas), contentment, belief in the existence of the Supreme Being, munificence, the adoration of (the all-pervading) Vishnu, the study of the Vedanta (systems of philosophy), modesty, determination, silent prayer and austerity (32, 33).

The text goes on to describe various asanas: svastika, virasana, yogasana, padmasana, baddha-padmasana, kukkutasana, uttana-kurmaka asana, dhanurasana, simha-rupakasana, bhadrasana, muktasana, mayur-asana, matsya-pithaka-asana, siddhasana and paschimottana-asana. Sukhasana is for those not strong enough for other postures. It is any comfortable posture which can be maintained. Those who have mastered asana have conquered the three worlds (34–52). After the yamas, niyamas and asanas have purified the nadis, one should practice pranayama. Descriptions of pranayama follow (53–55).

Next, there are descriptions of various chakras, the Kundalini, the Sushumna and other nadis. For instance, the text states that in the middle of the body is the Agni mandala (seat of fire), which shines like molten gold. It goes on to say that it is triangular in bipeds (humans), quadrangular in quadrupeds, circular in birds, hexagonal in snakes (and other crawling creatures) and octagonal in insects. It is bright like a lamp (56–57).

The text does not quite follow the *Shat Chakra Nirupana*, but its significance is that it indicates that these inner centres of power exist in all living beings, including insects.

The ten types of prana are explained, which circulate in the nadis. These are prana, apana, samana, udana, vyana, naga, kurma, krikara, devadatta and dhananjaya. Prana should be used to purify the nadis.

The person who practises pranayama will be ever alert, with a quick intellect and a vision that sees the past, present and future. Dharana should be performed on the knot of the navel, tip of the nose and big toe. The yogi will then be free of disease and fatigue. Methods of tranquillizing the mind through pranayama are also prescribed. After this it moves on to pratyahara, stating that holding the prana in the eighteen different seats of Marman and moving it from one to the other is pratyahara. The eighteen seats are described (129–33) and then dharana of the five elements in the body is recommended. It mentions the earth goddess, yellow and in the shape of a square, with the emblem of the vajra, the seat of the earth being from the knee to the sole of the foot. The water element is crescent-shaped, white and silver, and extends from the knee to the hip. The middle of the body to the hip is the seat of fire and from the navel to the nose that of air, which is smoky grey. From the nose to the cavern of Brahman is the seat of ether (akasha), the colour and brightness of collyrium. Next, meditations on Aniruddha, Pradyumna, Samkarshana and Vasudeva are prescribed. One can meditate on the qualified or unqualified Brahman. The latter can be seen in the centre of the heart in the shape of a cluster of kadamba flowers, lustrous like a gem, like a lamp in a windless place. Through meditation on Brahman, the jiva will be destroyed and only the atman, identical with Brahman, will exist.

Varaha Upanishad

The *Varaha Upanishad* belongs to the *Krishna Yajur Veda* and has five sections. The first section with seventeen verses begins with the rishi Ribhu, who, after performing tapas for twelve years of the gods (much longer than human years), sees the god Vishnu in his Varaha (boar) form. Varaha asks Ribhu to choose a boon and he requests an explanation of the Brahmavidya, that is, of how to attain the knowledge of Brahman. Varaha begins by explaining and listing the tattvas in three categories. Some say there are twenty-four tattvas, others count them as thirty-six and still others as ninety-six, and all these categories are explained.

The second section has eighty-three verses. Varaha explains that the aspirant should gain detachment by following the practices of one's own varna (caste) and ashrama (stage in life), along with tapas (austerities) and devotion to a guru. He should learn to distinguish between the real and the unreal and be firm in the six basic ethical qualities (shama). These include tranquillity, self-control, continence, endurance, sincerity and meditation. After reaching this point, the person should think of himself as the Supreme consciousness. Then one goes beyond varna and ashrama and realizes the only reality, which is the atman that is identical with Brahman. When the atman is realized, maya and the world no longer exist. All karma is destroyed and there is no attachment to worldly pleasures. The jiva is born into the world but its aim is liberation. When the jiva performs spiritual practices beginning with the trinachiketa vrata (a method to overcome three obstacles) and ending with yoga, these are based on illusions related to the nature of Ishvara. Schools of philosophy beginning with the Lokayat and ending with the Samkhya are based on illusion regarding the jiva. But the truth relating to Brahman is permanent and transcends all states. The one who understands that all is one is Shiva, Hari, and Brahman. Existence, consciousness and bliss is the nature of Brahman. The atman and the mind can be united through yoga and this is the state of samadhi. The yogi can reach this state by raising the Kundalini and by other methods.

Section 3 has thirty verses. It states that Brahman is eternal and non-dual, the indivisible consciousness. There is no birth and death and one should constantly meditate on the eternal Brahman. Brahman can also be identified with Shiva or with Vishnu. Through the power of maya, everything emerges out of Brahman. The chandala and everything from animal to mineral are also no different from Brahman. When superior wisdom dawns, the world is known to be non-existent. The cycle of birth and death emerges from the mind. When the atman is known, all desires, even for psychic powers, disappear.

Section 4 has forty-four verses. It begins with Nidagha asking Ribhu about the nature of a jivan-mukta. Ribhu explains the seven stages, beginning with the right desire, the seventh being the attainment of the state of Turiya. Next, he explains the Pranava. Each of its four syllables has four types: sthula, sukshma, bija and sakshi, which are gross, subtle, seed and witness. The four states of consciousness also correspond with these. The Turiya forms the witness in all cases. The seven stages of the jivan-mukta are related to the Pranava. The four types of the syllable 'a' form the first three stages, of 'u' the fourth stage, of 'm' the fifth stage. The sixth stage is represented by the first three types of the ardha-matra, that is, its sthula, sukshma and bija aspects; the seventh stage is the fourth, the sakshi or witness aspect, and corresponds with the attainment of Turiya. Further descriptions of the seven stages are provided. Two paths are also described, that of the bird and of the ant, represented by Shuka and Vamadeva. Shuka attains liberation immediately by understanding the nature of the atman through samadhi, while Vamadeva, after several births, does so through the practice of yoga.

Section 5 has seventy-seven verses. Ribhu explains the benefits and methods of yoga to Nidagha. He describes the eightfold yoga, similar to descriptions in other texts, as well as the chakras and nadis.

Yoga-chudamani Upanishad

The *Yoga-chudamani Upanishad* belongs to the *Sama Veda* and has 121 verses.. It describes the path of yoga, which will lead to the state of kaivalya. This includes the sixfold yoga, which it states consists of asana, pranayama, withdrawal of breath, holding the breath and concentration leading to samadhi. To succeed in yoga, one must also know the six chakras, the six supports for these, the three types of visions and the five types of akasha. The Upanishad then describes the chakras, the nadis and the types of prana as given in other texts, though with a few extra details. The merits of the Gayatri Ajapa, that is, the Hamsa Mantra, and its methods of practice and benefits are explained next. Following this are passages on awakening the Kundalini. Sitting in padmasana and using pranayama and various bandhas, the Kundalini should be forced upwards, leading to the realization of Brahman. The one who is on this path should eat a limited quantity of bland and sweet food and remain celibate. The three main bandhas are then described, followed by a description of the khechari mudra. Using the yoni mudra to send the semen upwards is also part of the practice. When the network of nadis have been purified, the maha-mudra can be practised, which destroys all diseases, and this mudra is described in detail (65–70).

Seated in padmasana, one should meditate on the Pranava Om. Om is unborn and eternal, it is the Turiya and the transcendent Brahman. Through this, all the tattvas, worlds, gods and living beings came into existence. Om and its various parts and implications are described in detail, along with the Hamsa

Mantra. There are also further details on pranayama, the chakras and the purification of the nadis.

The text summarizes the benefits of yoga, stating that the yogi kills diseases through asanas; through pranayama sin is removed; pratyahara prevents further mental transformations; dharana leads to mental fortitude; while in samadhi, consciousness is transformed (109–13). Nada, the inner sound produced by yoga practices, is also described. The text ends with comments on the necessity of pranayama, that is, of regulating the breath. Pranayama should be practised in gradual stages, and while doing so, pratyahara, the withdrawal of the senses, should also be observed. Finally, there should be a focus on Brahman, as all these practices lead to that ultimate goal.

Yoga-kundalini Upanishad

The *Yoga-kundalini Upanishad*, also known as the *Yoga Kundali Upanishad*, is attached to the *Krishna Yajur Veda*. This is a lengthy and detailed text that deals with various advanced and esoteric yoga practices. Chapter 1 with eighty-seven verses focuses on the rousing of the Kundalini. The first steps are eating the right food in the right quantity and practicing padmasana and vajrasana. Then, first, the Sarasvati Nadi is aroused, and next the Kundalini is drawn to the mouth of the Sushumna through advanced pranayama and various bandhas or locks. All diseases of the middle of the body are destroyed by arousing the Sarasvati. Next, various types of pranayama are described along with four types of kumbhaka (retaining the breath): the surya, ujjayi, shitali and bhastri. The mula, uddiyana and jalandhara bandhas should also be practised. There are several obstacles to the practising of yoga and these should be overcome and the Sushumna cleared of impurities. The Kundalini can then be raised to the Sahasrara Chakra. The yogi then realizes the state of pure Brahman.

Chapter 2 with forty-nine verses focuses on khechari vidya and the Khechari Mantra, which is 'Hrim, Bham, Sam, Mam, Pam, Sam Ksham' (2.20). Muttering it continuously for twelve days, 5,00,000 times a day, leads to Khechari Yoga in which all obstacles are removed and wrinkles and grey hair disappear. Khechari also consists of the gradual lengthening of the tongue over a period of several years. Physical methods are prescribed for this and finally the tongue will lengthen enough to even reach the top of the head. Using the tongue along with prescribed mantras and nyasa, one reaches the Brahma-randhra through the external path, opening the door leading to Brahman.

Chapter 3 with thirty-five verses looks at various meditative practices performed with the eyes shut, half open or fully open. The six main chakras are described and the raising of the Kundalini through the Sushumna, passing through the chakras and leading to liberation and identity with Brahman. All sorrow, the mind and knowledge are destroyed, and only the shining Paramatman remains. The person is then a jivan-mukta, attaining final liberation or videha-mukti when the body dies.

Yoga-shikha Upanishad

The *Yoga-shikha Upanishad* is attached to the *Krishna Yajur Veda*.

The Upanishad has six sections. Section 1 with 178 verses begins with Hiranyagarbha (Brahma) asking Lord Shankara (Shiva) how to escape from maya, the net of illusion. Maheshvara (Shiva) replies that this can only be attained through knowledge of Brahman. Brahman, in the form of knowledge, is supreme and unattached, but through gradual stages assumes the character of the jiva. Through jnana (knowledge) and yoga, the jiva can free itself of defects and become one with the Paramatman. Both knowledge and yoga have to be used together in the right way to attain liberation. The real form of Brahman, which is kaivalya, must be known. The jiva should have right knowledge and should become detached because it is tired of the world. But when the jiva knows 'I am Brahman', everything is attained. Through yoga, the body is transformed and death transcended. The person can then go anywhere and assume any form. Thus, through knowledge and yoga he becomes a jivan-mukta, unaffected by previous karma. Those who have knowledge but remain full of passion cannot gain liberation, but the jiva perfected through yoga, with the knowledge 'I am Brahman', becomes immortal.

The text insists that the practice of yoga is the first duty of the jiva. Asana, pranayama and other aspects of yoga, including the contemplation of Om, must be practised in the right way. After controlling the body, he must focus on the solar disc in his heart centre, within which the eternal flame can be seen. Another method is to arouse the Kundalini through the Sushumna Nadi.

It is best if pranayama is practised under the guidance of a guru. Methods of arousing the Kundalini are prescribed, beginning with a focus on the Sarasvati Nadi, as well as the four kinds of kumbhaka and the three bandhas. Dispelling the darkness of the Sushumna are twenty-one bright nodules, leading to the Brahma-randhra or Sahasrara Chakra. A jiva who has dissolved body and mind through raising the Kundalini reaches identity with Brahman.

Maha Yoga is said to be one, but has four names, which can also be seen as four steps or stages. Mantra Yoga is the constant uttering of the mantra 'Ham-sa'. Hatha Yoga is the union of the aspects of the sun and moon within the body. Then, when the body and the atman are united, Laya Yoga arises. In the last stage, Raja Yoga is attained by the union of the male and female principles. Psychic powers are then gained (136–38). In all types of yoga, prana and apana merge. If the yogi does not attain liberation in one life, he can resume the practices in the next. Final liberation is certain through the right practices. The text includes descriptions of the six chakras and other internal energy centres. The four pithas (sacred sites) in the body are: the Kama Rupa, related to the Muladhara Chakra, the Purna-giri, associated with the Anahata Chakra, the Jalandhara, associated with the Vishuddha Chakra, and the Uddiyana, associated with the Ajna Chakra.

In Section 2, with twenty-two verses, Brahma asks Shankara (Shiva) about the path of yoga, and the Lord replies. The student should first serve his guru for twelve years and gain an understanding of the Mula Mantra. This mantra is the union of Shiva and Shakti arising from the Muladhara. It is the basic pitha and the nada-linga, the emblem of sound. Knowing Om as the Mula Mantra, the jiva is liberated. The nature of the Pranava Om is then further analysed, and there are explanations of uniting Pranava–Prakriti and Bindu, representing the world and the mind. Several esoteric descriptions are provided in this section.

Section 3 with twenty-five verses looks at forms of the nada Brahman. This can also be said to be shabda Brahman and is a means to attaining the state of the imperishable and supreme Brahman. The divine nada unites with prana to become words and music and is known as the Vaikhari. All mantras, sacred and other texts, all languages and types of music are formed from this, presided over by the goddess Sarasvati. The Paramatman or Para Brahman can be attained through meditation on shabda Brahman. Understanding the Vaikhari leads to speech of great power.

Section 4 with twenty-four verses explains the false nature of the jiva, even though it appears to be real. As true knowledge dawns, the jivatman and Brahman have a single identity. The world, too, is then known as false.

Section 5 with sixty-two verses states that the body is like a city with ten gateways. The ten main nadis are the highways along which ten pranas flow, covered by ten senses. There are six inner chakras and a forest fit for practising the six kinds of yoga (Mantra, Laya, Hatha, Raja, Bhavana and Sahaja). There are four pithas shining with the lamps of the four Vedas. In the body are

the bindu, the nada, the linga, Vishnu and Lakshmi. In fact, the
body is the temple of Vishnu. A description of the six chakras and
four pithas and the nadis follow, along with methods of arousing
the Kundalini. Oneness with Narayana as well as certain siddhis or
powers, can be attained through concentration. The importance of
the guru is emphasized, and the greatness of the secret teachings
of the Yoga-shikha.

Section 6 with seventy-nine verses further describes the
Kundalini and the Sushumna Nadi, the other chakras and nadis,
along with meditation on Hamsa as the Paramatman. Nothing
can compare with the Sushumna; meditating on it has more
merit than thousands of ashvamedhas and hundreds of vajapeyas,
as well as pilgrimages to holy sites, the Ganga and the oceans.
Using various yogic techniques to raise the Kundalini through the
Sushumna, Brahman is attained.

Yogatattva Upanishad

The *Yogatattva Upanishad* is attached to the *Krishna Yajur Veda*
and has 142 verses. (Another brief version with only fifteen verses
is attached to the *Atharva Veda*.) It explains various types of yoga,
including the eightfold yoga, Mantra Yoga, Laya Yoga and Hatha
Yoga.

The Upanishad begins with Pitamaha (the god Brahma)
approaching the god Vishnu and asking him to explain the eightfold
yoga. Hrishikesha (Vishnu) then responds. He says that all jivas
are ensnared in maya, but attaining Brahman they gain liberation.
As Brahman is self-manifested, it cannot be known by the Shastras
and Vedas, which, in fact, come from it. He then explains the
stages by which the Paramatman creates the jiva, which is a part
of it. The jiva can attain the state of the Paramatman through
yoga and knowledge. There are four kinds of yoga, Mantra Yoga,
Laya Yoga, Hatha Yoga and Raja Yoga. Mantra Yoga is for the

inferior type of person. Repeating mantras for twelve years, he will gradually gain knowledge and wisdom (21–22). Laya Yoga is the dissolution of the mind through meditation on Ishvara at all times while performing various activities such as walking, eating and standing (23–24). Hatha Yoga is explained next and it has eight stages and twelve subdivisions. The eight stages are the usual ones described elsewhere, with minor variations: yama, niyama, asana, prana-samyama, pratyahara, dharana, dhyana of Hari between the eyebrows and samadhi. The twelve subdivisions are mahamudra, mahabandha, mahavedha, khechari; the three bandhas, mula, uddiyana and jalandhara; dirgha-pranava samdhana; siddhanta shravana; vajroli, amroli and sahajoli.

He describes temperate food as the most important of the yamas, and ahimsa, usually the first of the yamas, as the most important niyama. The siddha, padma, simha and bhadra are the most important asanas. The obstacles on the path of yoga are next pointed out, followed by a description of the right type of mathas (monasteries) for the practice of the steps of yoga. Pranayama is to be used for the purification of the nadis and many restrictions are placed on food. Cooked wheat, green gram, rice, milk and ghi should form part of the food. Salty and spicy food, along with vegetables, are to be avoided. The person should not undertake any fasts or undue exertion and should avoid early morning baths and sex (46–49). The practice of holding the breath is important. Gradually, siddhis (superhuman powers) will develop. Strangely, despite the emphasis on ahimsa, the text also states that such a yogi can wander freely over the earth as he has the power to kill any wild animal with a blow of his hand!

During the practice, the Pranava Mantra (that is, Om) should be used. After some time the ghata stage is reached, that of great effort in the regulation of the breath. At this time, the aspiring yogi unites prana, apana, manas, buddhi, the jivatman and the Paramatman. This practice should then be reduced and higher

practices should begin. Kumbhaka, the holding of the breath, is
a type of pratyahara. Proceeding to dharana, the yogi should view
everything he hears or sees as the atman. More psychic powers
will be attained, but these must be kept secret. As the practice
proceeds, there should be a focus on the chakras and the elements,
using the appropriate mantras, which will finally lead to samadhi.
The yogi can now either give up his body or retain it, roaming
through the world assuming any form as he likes; he can become a
yaksha, a lion or an elephant in an instant. He can attain the state
of Maheshvara or be a celestial being in the celestial world.

The text continues to describe various practices, including the
maha-bandha, the maha-vedha, and the real form of the khechari,
followed by the benefits of the three bandhas: mula, uddiyana and
jalandhara. The viparita-karani asana (upside-down pose), vajroli
and amaroli are also described along with their benefits. Thus, the
twenty stages of Hatha Yoga have been described, leading to Raja
Yoga (131).

The yogi should remain detached from all relationships
and worship the Pranava in the lotus of the heart. As the nadis
are purified and the Sushumna flows upwards, videha-mukti is
achieved.

Eleven

The Brahma Sutra

THE UPANISHADS HAVE several different topics and themes, even though their main focus is Brahman. The *Brahma Sutra*, a Sanskrit text, focuses on their main topic, summarizing the teachings of the Upanishads on this theme. This text, written by Badarayana, and also known as the *Vedanta Sutra*, has been assigned to various dates from 500 BCE to the first century CE. According to tradition, Badarayana is identified with the rishi Vyasa. However, Badarayana is also said to be the teacher of Jaimini, who composed the Mimamsa Sutras. Among the various scholars, S. Radhakrishnan places its date in the second century BCE as it mentions most other philosophical systems prevailing at the time.[1] S. Dasgupta also takes the date to be around the second century BCE. Andrew Nicholson, reviewing the previous estimates, feels the *Brahma Sutra* was composed by 450–400 BCE[2] and that it is the work of not one but several authors. George C. Adams looks at the various estimates and points out that Jacobi is among those who places it at a later date, between CE 200 and 450. He adds that despite the disagreements, all are agreed that it is one of the earliest attempts 'at systematizing the unsystematic contents of a body of scripture'.[3]

The *Brahma Sutra* uses the following Upanishads: *Aitareya*, *Taittiriya*, *Chhandogya*, *Brihadaranyaka*, *Kaushitaki*, *Katha*, *Shvetashvatara*, *Mundaka* and *Prashna*. There are also hints of the *Jabala Upanishad* being used, but the main text is the *Chhandogya*.

The *Brahma Sutra* contains four adhyayas or chapters. Within this are sixteen padas (sections), 223 adhikaranas or topics and a total of 555 sutras (aphorisms). As its name suggests, the text has 'sutras' or short, terse aphorisms. These cannot be understood correctly without explanation and therefore have given rise to a number of commentaries and interpretations. Only scholars familiar with the Upanishads and with the various systems of philosophy can understand these sutras. An adhikarana, which can contain several sutras, has five parts: the subject or vishaya; the doubt or samsaya; the opposite view or purvapaksha; the conclusion or siddhanta; and sangati or agreement with other parts of the text. Each adhikarana is in some way connected to the last. As Sri Aurobindo says, 'the monumental aphorisms of the Vedantasutra are meant rather for the master than the learner.'

The first chapter, 'Samanvaya', unifies the different views of Brahman. Brahman, the infinite creator, develops into the world, but remains itself, unchanged and pure. It also describes the atman or individual soul and its relationship with Brahman. The chapter contains four padas and eleven adhikaranas.

The second, 'Avirodha', provides a refutation of other philosophies including Samkhya, Vaisheshika, Jainism and Buddhism. The third, 'Sadhana', provides methods of sadhana or practice for attaining Brahman. The fourth, 'Phala', describes the benefits or fruits of attaining the knowledge of Brahman. Each chapter has four padas or sections, within which are adhikaranas or topics. The first five adhikaranas of the first chapter are the most important. Thus, though the text is the basis for all schools of Vedanta, it has been interpreted differently by each of them.

Badarayana was not the first to attempt to provide a systematic summary of the main principles of the Upanishads, but his is the earliest that is available. Among earlier writers he mentions are Audolomi and Kashakrishna.

Some of the earliest commentaries are no longer available, but among the important ones are those of Shankara, who explains the philosophy of Advaita; Ramanuja, who interprets it in the context of Vishishtadvaita; Madhva, with the philosophy of Dvaita; Nimbaraka, with Dvaitadvaita; Vallabha, with Shuddhadvaita. Other commentators include Bhaskara, Yadavaprakasha, Keshava, Nilakantha, Baladeva Vidyabhushana and Vijnanabhikshu, as well as many more who elucidate the various commentaries and add their own interpretations.

The variant and extensive interpretations of this text can be indicated by just a few comments on the very first sutra, which also forms the first adhikarana. This sutra (1.1) reads 'Athato brahmajijnasa'. Separating the conjoined words, we get: 'atha', which has different meanings, including now, then, or afterwards; atah, meaning 'therefore'; brahmajijnasa, meaning 'desire for the knowledge of Brahman'. The sentence is translated as 'Now, therefore, the inquiry into Brahman' or 'Then, therefore, the inquiry into Brahman'. Briefly, it means that this text will now inquire into the nature of Brahman. However, the commentators write reams on each word. For instance, what does 'atha', meaning 'now' or 'then', coupled with 'therefore', signify? Most Vedanta commentators agree that 'atha' indicates that there are some prerequisites, that is, antecedent conditions, before which this enquiry into the nature of Brahman can begin.

Shankara puts forward four preliminary spiritual qualifications for the person wishing to enquire into the nature of Brahman. These are: (1) The ability to discriminate between the real and the unreal; (2) An indifference to all pleasures, whether on earth or in heaven, and also an indifference to the fruits of one's actions; (3)

Firmly established in the six virtues (shatsampat), which are shama: equanimity, control of the mind; dama: control of the senses; uparati: not thinking of sense objects and discontinuing religious ceremonies; titiksha: enduring the opposites of pleasure and pain, heat and cold; shraddha: faith in the guru and the Upanishads; samadhana: deep concentration; (4) A desire for liberation. Thus, several qualities are required before a person can begin to study Brahman. But, according to Shankara, the performance of Vedic rituals (karmakanda), or even a knowledge of them, is not required.

However, Bhaskara, Ramanuja and Nimbarka believe that 'now' means that a knowledge and study of the Vedas is an essential prerequisite. It indicates that only when an individual has practised and seen the limited results arising from Vedic knowledge does it lead him to study Brahman. It is a combination of work and knowledge of the Purva Mimamsa that makes a person fit to study Brahman.

Madhva begins by classifying people into three types: the ordinary, middling and the highest or best. The best is fit to enquire into Brahman. Such a person has studied the Vedas but has renounced all work and achieved a dispassionate state of mind. Prescribed actions are helpful in the attainment of knowledge but once one has knowledge no action is required.

To Vallabha, 'now' introduces a new topic; hence there are no prerequisites. But quoting the *Brihadaranyaka* (4.4.5–6), he feels that work without a desire for results, knowledge and devotion is required if anyone wishes for liberation. But for those who follow Pushti-marga, nothing is required as god's grace provides everything.

Next, we come to the word 'therefore'. Shankara says this indicates a reason. It means that because the results obtained by works (sacrifices) do not last, whereas the knowledge of Brahman leads to the eternal, therefore, Brahman should be enquired into. Bhaskara and Ramanuja say that results obtained only by works (not by works and knowledge combined) do not last; therefore,

Brahman should be inquired into. Madhya says that 'therefore' indicates the reason for inquiring into Brahman. Without Brahman, the grace of the Lord cannot be attained.

Finally, we come to the interpretations of the word Brahman. Every commentator quotes extensively from the Upanishads to support his viewpoint. Shankara affirms that Brahman is eternal, unborn and without any attributes. It is infinite bliss, existence and knowledge and the origin of the world. It is formless and the only reality that can be experienced only in deep meditation (samadhi). The world, therefore, is unreal (maya). Bhaskara, however, believes that though Brahman is the eternal, unchanging cause of the world, the world is real. Ramanuja says that Brahman is not without attributes. Existence, knowledge and bliss or infinity are its qualities or attributes.

There are several other interpretations of this single sutra, but only a brief summary is provided here. Ramanuja's bhashya (commentary) on this single sutra runs into eighty pages.

Without going into extensive commentaries, three more sutras are given below to indicate their complexity and the knowledge required to interpret them. Each commentator quotes the relevant Upanishad passages in their explanation and also refutes the theories of contrary philosophies. Without these passages, the concise sutras, which merely hint at the topic, cannot be understood.

Adhikarana 2 contains the second sutra, which reads 'Janmadhyasya yatah'. This is explained as Brahman being that from which everything originates and to which everything returns (1.1.2).

Adhikarana 3 consists of the third sutra, 'Shastra-yonitvat', that is, the scriptures are the source of right knowledge.

Adhikarana 4 has the fourth sutra, 'Tat-tu-samanvayat' (But that is the main purpose). 'That' here refers to the scriptures or sacred texts. Their main purpose is to reveal Brahman.

Chapter 1

Chapter 1 continues with further sutras and adhikaranas.

Pada 1: Sutras 5–31

Adhikarana 5 contains sutras 5–11. It states that Brahman is the only cause of the world. Vedantic commentators refute the Samkhya theories that Pradhana is the first principle. Pradhana consists of the three gunas. These sutras show that shruti, that is, revealed texts, show that Brahman, the intelligent principle, is the cause of the world, and not Pradhana. Pradhana is not an intelligent principle.

Adhikarana 6, sutras 12–19, looks at the nature of Anandamaya, described in the *Taittiriya Upanishad*. Is this an individual self or is this the Supreme Brahman? The conclusion is that Anandamaya is the same as Brahman.

Adhikarana 7, sutras 20–21, show that the golden person seen in the sun and the person seen within the eye (*Chhandogya* 1.6) are again the same as the Supreme Brahman.

Adhikarana 8, sutra 22, shows that akasha, from which everything originates (*Chhandogya* 1.9), is not the physical akasha or ether but is to be understood as Brahman.

Adhikaranas 9–11 (sutras 23–31) show that both prana and light, mentioned in the *Chhandogya* (1.2.15 and 3.13.7) and in the *Kaushitaki* (3.2), are nothing but Brahman.

This pada thus shows that even those passages in the Upanishads that contain other terms, such as Anandamaya and prana, actually refer to Brahman.

Pada 2

The second pada continues with adhikaranas or topics on Brahman, explained by commentators through the relevant quotes from the

Upanishads. This pada looks at those aspects and passages in the Upanishads that are connected with Brahman even though they may not seem to be. The topics are:

1. Sutras 1–8: The first sutra states that everything is Brahman. The discussions on this and the next few sutras conclude that the being that consists of the mind, the manomaya, is also Brahman. This explains *Chhandogya* (3.14.1–2), as well as other Upanishadic passages.
2. Sutras 9–10: This mentions 'the eater', and it can be concluded that the eater is Brahman. There is a passage in the *Katha*, 1.2.25, which says he to whom brahmanas and kshatriyas are food and this actually refers to Brahman.

Further, topics 3–7, with sutras 11–32, identify the Antaryamin, the atman, the Vaishvanara and 'the person in the eye' as Brahman.

Pada 3

The third Pada looks at the nirguna aspect of Brahman which pervades everything and is immortal.

1. Sutras 1–7: The *Mundaka Upanishad* (2.2.5) refers to something with which the heaven and earth are woven, and according to the commentators, this too is Brahman.
2. Sutras 8–9: The Bhuma mentioned in *Chhandogya* 7.23 is the same as Brahman.
3. Sutras 10–12: Akshara, which is part of akasha, mentioned in *Brihadaranyaka* (3.8.8) is Brahman. Akshara can be translated as imperishable and akasha as space.
4. Sutra 13: The Highest Person who is to be meditated upon with the syllable Om (Prashna 5.5) is not the lower but the higher Brahman.

5. Sutras 14–21: The daharakasha (small space) within the lotus of the heart mentioned in *Chhandogya* 8.1 is Brahman.

6. Sutras 22–23: This comments on the *Katha Upanishad* 2.2.15—that by which everything shines and by whose light all lights are illuminated is Brahman.

7. Sutras 24–25: These explain that the person the size of a thumb mentioned in the *Katha* 2.1.12 is Brahman.

8. Sutras 26–33: These are not directly about Brahman. They explain that the Vedas are eternal and the devas too can practise Brahmavidya, as described in them.

9. Sutras 34–38: This topic deals with whether a shudra can practise Brahmavidya. After a lengthy debate the text and commentaries conclude that this is not possible as shudras are not even permitted to listen to the Vedas. However, they can gain knowledge from other texts such as the Puranas. In his commentary, Swami Sivananda feels this passage is a late interpolation. The arguments in the text begin with a reference to Janashruti approaching Raikva and being called a shudra by him when he presented inadequate gifts (*Chhandogya* 4.2.5). But he did not mean that he was literally a shudra, as Janashruti was known to be a kshatriya. Janashruti was grieving as he did not have the knowledge of Brahman and 'shudra' etymologically means 'one who grieves'. The Upanishads also say that only those who have undergone purificatory rites can study the Vedas (*Chhandogya* 4.4.5) and these are only for the upper castes. Next, the story of Satyakama Jabala is taken up (*Chhandogya* 4.4.5). It is said that only when Gautama was convinced that Satyakama was a brahmana did he agree to teach him. The smritis too prohibit imparting Vedic knowledge to a shudra; hence, the conclusion is that they are not allowed to even hear the Vedas. But there were shudras like Vidura and the hunter

Dharma Vyadha who had gained knowledge through their previous births.

10. Sutra 39: The prana mentioned in the *Katha Upanishad* (2.3.2) is Brahman. Some of the sutras consist of single words; thus, this sutra merely states 'kampanat' (trembles). It indicates that the whole world that trembles in prana, referred to in the Upanishads, is actually Brahman.

11. Sutra 40: The 'light' (jyoti) in *Chhandogya* 8.12.3 is the Highest Brahman.

12. Sutra 41: The akasha through which one knows names and forms (*Chhandogya* 8.14) is Brahman.

13. Sutras 42–43: Vijnanamaya, the wisdom kosha or sheath, as mentioned in *Brihadaranyaka* 4.3.7 is Brahman.

Pada 4

The Upanishads use terms that are also used in Samkhya philosophy. This pada explains that though some of the same terms are used, the meanings in them are different in the Upanishads. Thus, terms such as mahat, avyakta and pradhana mean something different in Samkhya philosophy. The twenty-five tattvas of Samkhya are referred to, to see whether they form part of shruti, but this is refuted. The text conclusively shows that pradhana cannot be a cause of the world and that Brahman is the sole cause.

Chapter 2

This chapter refutes different philosophies.

Pada 1

In Pada 1, the first adhikarana takes up the question of whether Smritis (remembered texts) that are not based on shruti (revelation) can be rejected. Should Kapila's text on Samkhya be taken to support Vedantic texts? But the conclusion is that Brahman being the source of all cannot be rejected to accommodate the Samkhya Smriti. Shankara's commentary also explains that 5.2 in the *Shvetashvatara*, which mentions Kapila, is not referring to the Kapila who composed the Samkhya Sutras but here it means 'golden-coloured' and is another name for Hiranyagarbha or Brahma. Samkhya can be rejected mainly because of its theory that pradhana is the cause of the world but also because other aspects do not agree with the shrutis. It does not accept a Supreme Self, affirms that individual souls are pure consciousness and that bondage and freedom are part of prakriti. As for other Smritis, such as the *Manu Smriti*, Ramanuja says their total rejection is not necessary as they deal with ritualistic worship, and such worship can be used to propitiate Brahman.

The second adhikarana refutes the Yoga philosophy of Patanjali. Though it is partly authoritative, it too recognizes pradhana as the first cause of the world. The *Shvetashvatara* mentions some aspects of Yoga, but Patanjali's Sutra does not acknowledge Brahman as Supreme. The *Shvetashvatara* 6.13 praises Samkhya and Yoga, yet in 3.8 it says that only the one who knows Brahman crosses over death. Both systems of philosophy promote duality, but some of their aspects are correct, for instance, in Samkhya it says the soul has no qualities, while Yoga prescribes withdrawal from the world for the wandering sannyasi, which is supported by the *Jabala Upanishad*.

Topic 3, sutras 4–11, says that Brahman can be a cause of the world even though its nature is different from the world. The objections to this are refuted at length. Final emancipation comes from perfect knowledge, which is always the same. Yet, the Samkhyas say pradhana is the cause of the universe and the Nyayikas say it is paramanus or atoms. Who should one believe? Reasoning cannot lead to the truth without the support of shruti. Brahman is the cause and substratum of the universe, both on the basis of shruti and reasoning subordinate to shruti.

Topic 4 refutes other theories that don't fit with the Vedas, that is, those of Kanada and Gautama, referred to here as shishta-aparigraha. Shishta refers to remaining systems, and in this context aparigraha means those that do not accept the Vedas. Just as Samkhya cannot be accepted, so also Kanada, Gautama, Akshapada and Buddhist theories cannot be accepted.

These groups have different views on the nature of the atom. Kanada and Gautama see the atom as permanent, while Vaibhashika Buddhists, Madhyamikas and Yogacharas see it as unreal. Jains see it as both real and unreal.

Topic 5 indicates that distinctions between the enjoyer and the enjoyed can exist in the world (sutra 13), though at the same time they are not different from Brahman, while Topic 6 (14–20) shows that cause and effect are not really different, and Topic 7 (21–23) explains that Brahman cannot create evil. Topic 8 (24–25) shows that Brahman, who has no materials or agents, is nevertheless the cause of the world. Topic 9 (26–29) explains that Brahman is the material cause of the universe even though it has no parts and Topic 10 (30–31) says that Brahman has all powers. Brahman is perfect and has no desires, says Topic 11 (32–33), and therefore does not create the world out of any motive. Emotions such as partiality and cruelty cannot be ascribed to Brahman (Topic 12, 34–36), because pleasure and pain are based on the person's karma. Brahman is like rain through which seeds grow depending on their nature and can be compared with Parjanya. The conclusion in Topic 13 (37) is that only Brahman is the cause of the universe, and it undergoes no change at any time.

Pada 2

This Pada further refutes contrary philosophies. Topic 1 (Sutras 1–10) again is directed against Samkhya beliefs, particularly on how pradhana, which is inert matter, can start creating through

Purusha, who is also inactive. Samkhyas say that pradhana has the three gunas of sattva, rajas and tamas, and when the equilibrium of these is stirred creation starts on its own. But who brings about this imbalance? It can't be Purusha, which is passive and inactive. Topics 2 and 3 (11–17) refute the Vaisheshika theory of creation from indivisible and minute atoms. Atoms, according to them, join together due to a principle known as adrishta, which exists in the soul, but the text shows that the soul cannot cause the atoms to move or combine. Though Manu and other authorities accept some aspects of Samkhya, they do not accept the atomic theory and, therefore, it should be discarded. The theories related to the six padarthas of Vaisheshika can also be rejected. Topics 4 and 5 (18–32) refute the schools of Buddhist philosophy, beginning with the ideas of the Vaibhashikas or realists. The commentary identifies them with Sarvastivadins, though they are only one of their branches. Vaibhashikas, says the commentary, hold that both the outer and inner worlds are real. The external world consists of four types of atoms and the internal and external worlds also consist of five skandhas or groups. Vedantists say this is untenable as there is no intelligent principle or controller. Other Buddhist theories of the Vijnanavadins, Yogacharas and Madhyamikas or Shunyavadins are also refuted, while Topic 6 (33–36) refutes Jaina doctrines. Next, Topics 7 and 8 (37–45) refute the doctrines of the Pashupatas (Shaivites) and Bhagavatas or Pancharatras (Vaishnavites).

Pada 3

Having refuted the doctrines of other schools of philosophy, Pada 3 deals with apparent contradictions in Vedantic thought. Topics 1–9 (sutras 1–15) look at the five elements: akasha, air, fire, water and earth. Beginning with akasha, each apparently originate from the other, but the text and commentary show how all the elements actually emanate from Brahman and are reabsorbed into Brahman. Brahman itself has no origin. Topics 10–17 (sutras 16–50) look at the individual soul and its relationship with Brahman. These topics affirm that there is neither birth nor death, but that the individual soul is permanent and eternal. The jiva is actually identical with Brahman, but is limited by the mind, body and senses. Intelligence is its very nature. Is it anu that is minute, or is it all-pervading? It is actually both but remains anu or tiny when it is connected with samsara, the affairs of the world. Another question arises as to whether the soul is an agent or not and once again the conclusion is that it is both. It is an agent when connected with the instruments of action such as buddhi or the intelligent mind, but at other times it is not. The individual soul can be understood as an amsha or part of Brahman because of its limitations, even though Brahman is actually indivisible and has no parts. When the soul remains in a body, it must follow the ethics and rules prescribed in the sacred texts. The individual soul, says Sutra 50, is a reflection of the supreme soul.

Pada 4

Pada 4 examines the connection between Brahman, the individual and the various pranas and senses. Topic 1 (Sutras 1–4) is on the pranas originating in Brahman. While the first sutra merely states 'tatah pranah' (thus, or likewise, the pranas), the commentary goes on to explain this as the two types of pranas and their origin in Brahman. The primary pranas, that is, types of breath, are prana, apana, vyana, samana and udana, while the secondary pranas are the eleven senses. The opposite or purvapaksha view is that these were eternal, but this is refuted here. Topic 2 (Sutras 5–6) concludes that there are eleven pranas or senses, five organs of knowledge, five of action and the mind as the eleventh, while Topic 3 shows that the senses are minute in size. Topics 4–6 are on the pranas as breath.

The main prana is different from the others and this too is minute in size. Topic 7 (Sutras 14–16) explains that though the senses are presided over by deities, their enjoyer is the individual soul. Topic 8 points out the difference between the pranas as breath and as indriyas or senses. They are separate yet have similar functions, in that both groups support life and nourish the body. Finally, Topic 9 concludes that it is the Supreme Lord or Brahman that creates all names and forms.

Chapter 3

Pada 1

The first pada in this chapter looks at theories of reincarnation. In Topics 1–2 (Sutras 1–11), it is explained that after the body is dissolved the soul that has not merged with Brahman travels to another world. Accompanying the jiva or individual soul are subtle material elements (bhuta sukshma), the pranas and the indriyas (senses). Thus, *Brihadaranyaka* 4.4.2 says, When the soul departs, the prana follows. When the prana departs, the other senses follow. The good soul goes to Chandra Loka, the heavenly world of the moon, enjoys the fruits of its good deeds and returns to earth to fulfil the rest of its karma. The commentary quotes both shruti and smriti in support of this, which brings up the question of caste, as it states that the good are born in the three higher castes and the evil as a dog or pig. Smriti texts have quoted the Upanishads (*Chhandogya* 5.10.7), which say that those who follow the path prescribed for them by their caste enjoy the fruits of their work in heaven and are then reborn in distinguished castes and families with beauty, knowledge, longevity, comfort and property.

What is this residue of karma that brings the soul back to earth? The commentary explains that it is not about good and bad karma but that some actions come to fruition in one type of world and some in another. The Purvapaksha says that death exhausts all karmas but this is not the case. They also say that those who have good conduct get a good birth. To refute this, in Verse 9, the views of the sage Karshnajini are mentioned, and in Verse 11 those of Badari. Karshnajini says that conduct (charana) stands for good karmas remaining after enjoyment in the other world. Badari says that charana or conduct refers to both good and evil works, which can be distinguished as ramaniya-charana and kapuya-charana respectively. Topic 3 (Sutras 12–21) refer to those who are not entitled to go to Chandra Loka. Verse 12 says that those who do not perform sacrifices also go to Chandra Loka, but this is the Purvapaksha view which is refuted.

The text affirms that sinners actually go to Yama Loka, the world of the god Yama, and return to earth after they have suffered for their evil deeds. The Smritis (*Manu Smriti*) are used to support this, and seven hells found there are mentioned in Sutra 15, which are named in the commentary. Five are temporary and two are permanent, and the god Yama supervises all, along with his assistants Chitragupta and others. The shruti, particularly the *Chhandogya*, also describes two paths to two different heavens, those of knowledge and of work. The path of knowledge or vidya leads to Brahma Loka via devayana, or the way of the gods, while the path of work or karma leads to Chandra Loka via pitriyana or the way of the fathers (ancestors). Now, it is said, the sinners go to the third place, like worms and flies that are constantly dying and being reborn.

The fifth oblation is not necessary for those who go to the third place, nor for those born in a different way, such as Sita, Draupadi, Drona and Drishtadyumna. Four classes of beings are also mentioned that are born in different ways: from an egg, a living being and those that germinate from earth or water. Topics 4–6 (Sutras 22–27) explain how the soul descends from Chandra Loka and is finally reborn. This (somewhat fanciful) explanation says that souls cling to rice or other grains and edible plants. The passages also state that killing animals in sacrifices is not wrong as it is sanctioned by the scriptures, though in other cases non-injury to animals should be observed, again as said in the texts. The soul attached to the plant retains its separate self, and when it is eaten it is connected to the person who eats it and enters the womb when that person engages in sex. Finally, the last sutra repeats that it is one's conduct and the remnants of one's karma that lead to birth in a particular family. The commentary quotes *Chhandogya* 5.10.7 that a good birth is in the family of a brahmana, kshatriya or vaishya, bad conduct leads one to be born as a dog or a chandala.

Most important is to avoid rebirth by uniting with Brahman, says the last sutra. This pada, while describing rebirth, also emphasizes this point.

Pada 2

This pada deals with the different states of waking, dreaming and sleeping that are explained in many of the Upanishads. Understanding these is essential in Vedanta.

Topic 1 (Sutras 1–6) looks at the soul in the dreaming state, here referred to as sandhya or the intermediate state. While dreaming, one seems to have creative powers, but are these real? The conclusion is that dreams are created by the jiva and not by Brahman or the Lord. However, dreams can at times provide a message; for instance, the god Shiva taught the mantra Ramaraksha to Vishvamitra in a dream. True reality is concealed from the jiva because of ignorance. As vasanas or impressions of the waking state lead to dreams, both waking and dreaming are unreal.

Topic 2 (Sutras 7–8) looks at the soul in dreamless sleep. Shruti, that is, various Upanishads, says that it rests in the nadis or in the heart or in Brahman while in deep sleep. The conclusion is that it goes through the nadis into the centre of the heart and rests there in Brahman. Topic 3 (Sutra 9) shows that when the soul or atman wakes, it is the same as that which went to sleep, while Topic 4 (Sutra 10) explains the nature of fainting, that is, half death and half deep sleep. If a remnant of karma remains, he returns to consciousness, otherwise he dies. Topic 5 (Sutras 11–21) continues with the nature of Brahman in which the soul is merged in deep sleep. Texts describe Brahman in two ways, as both with and without attributes. The reality is that Brahman has no attributes and no form. Brahman is everything and all are identical with it. However, for purposes of worship or meditation, it can be described with attributes or form. Topic 6 (Sutras 22–30) explains how the term 'neti, neti' (not this, not this) in *Brihadaranyaka* 2.3.6 is not a denial of Brahman itself but of its forms. In fact, it denies everything except Brahman. Brahman, it adds, has no distinguishing attributes.

Brahman is also described as 'satyasya satyam', the 'Truth of Truth', indicating it is the highest. This topic also examines and refutes the views of the Bhedabhedavadas, which affirm both difference and non-difference of the individual soul and Brahman as shruti denies any differences. Both terms 'tat tvam asi' and 'Aham Brahmasmi' in shruti texts show that there are no differences between Brahman and the atman or individual soul. When one attains identification with Brahman, one becomes the infinite Brahman. The ignorance that creates the jiva is then destroyed. Topic 7 (Sutras 31–37) affirms that Brahman is 'one without a second'. It takes up many statements that might seem to imply that either there is something higher than Brahman or that Brahman has a form and shows their true import, which is that Brahman has no equal and no form. Brahman can be compared to light within a room, and light outside, both being the same light. (Anyone who wants to look at the different statements on Brahman should go through these sutras.) Topic 8 (Sutras 38-41) refutes the views of Jaimini on the results of actions. It states that results do not appear automatically, but all takes place through the all-pervading Lord.

Pada 3

Pada 3 looks at the vidyas or meditations by which the jiva or atman can merge with Brahman. Topics 1 and 2 (Sutras 1–5) try to understand why there are different vidyas or upasanas (methods of worship) for the one Brahman and whether similar vidyas, mentioned in different shakhas, are the same or different. Commentaries say that in essence all vidyas are the same as they lead to the same end, that is, Brahman. Some shrutis describe Brahman as Vaishvanara, others as Prana, but there is only one Brahman. Beyond this basic premise, it also says that similar vidyas from different shakhas can be combined in one meditation. Topic 3 (Sutras 6–8) holds that sometimes meditation topics that seem to be the same have subtle differences. For instance, both the *Chhandogya* (1.1.3) and the *Brihadaranyaka* (1.3.1) suggest meditation on the Udgitha, and identify the Udgitha with Prana. But while the *Chhandogya* focuses only on Om of the Udgitha, the *Brihadaranyaka* refers to the entire Udgitha. Topic 4 affirms that Om is mentioned in all Shrutis, but the Udgitha is a special aspect of Om. Topic 5 (Sutra 10) says that the prana vidya explained in the *Chhandogya*, *Brihadadranyaka* and *Kaushitaki* are aspects of the same and prana-vidyas together form one meditation. Topic 6 (Sutras 11–13) says that knowledge and bliss, the essential attributes of Brahman, should always be kept in mind, whereas other aspects are for special meditations. Topic 7 looks at *Katha Upanishad* (3.10–11) which says that the Self or atman is the highest, that is, the same as Brahman, and therefore this should be meditated upon, while Topic 8 (Sutras 16–17) affirms that the Self referred to in the *Aitareya Upanishad* (1.1) is the Supreme Self, and not some other self such as Hiranyagarbha. Topic 9 (Sutra 18) takes up a minor point in prana meditation, while Topic 10 (Sutra 19) again speaks of combining similar vidyas. But Topic 11 (Sutras 20–22), states that when we come to two abodes of Brahman in the *Brihadaranyaka* (5.5), in the sun and in the right eye, specified by the terms 'ahar' and 'aham', these should not be combined for meditation. Even though Satya Brahman is one, the secret names and abodes of these two are distinct. Topics 12 and 13 (Sutras 23 and 24) also refer to vidyas that should not be combined, when Brahman is ostensibly located in different places, as in the sky, the cavity of the heart, or the eye, or when two Purusha Vidyas, though they have the same name, are actually different as in the *Chhandogya* and *Taittiriya*. Topic 14 (Sutra 25) says that rituals such as the Mahavrata mentioned in certain Upanishads are not part of Brahmavidya as these are sacrifices.

What happens to the good and evil deeds of a person who dies after attaining true knowledge? Topic 15 (Sutra 26) agrees with passages in the Upanishads that say these go to the friends and enemies of the person, and this, says Topic 16 (Sutras 27–28), takes place at the time of death, and not, as the *Kaushitaki Upanishad* states, on the way to Brahma Loka or Brahman. Topic 15 also affirms that when shrutis provide incomplete information, they can be combined with other verses. This has also been mentioned by Jaimini. By what path does the soul reach god? Topic 17 (Sutras 29–30) says that the soul of the person who knows Saguna Brahman travels by devayana or the path of the gods, but the one who knows Nirguna Brahman has no path; he becomes one with Brahman without going anywhere. The practice of any vidyas of Saguna Brahman lead to the same path (Topic 18, Sutra 31). A perfected soul, though, can yet be reborn if there is some divine mission to fulfil (Topic 19, Sutra 32). Examples given here include those of Vyasa and Vasishtha. Further, Topic 20, Sutra 33 points out that the negative terms for Brahman, such as it not being gross, can be combined in one vidya. Topic 21 (Sutra 34) refers to passages in *Katha* 3.1 and *Mundaka* 3.1 as the same vidya as they refer to the highest Brahman, and Topic 22 (Sutras 35–36) say that *Brihadaranyaka* 3.4 and 3.5 are one vidya, as in both these Brahman is seen as the inner self. Topics 23–25 (Sutras 37-39) similarly deal with various meditations. Succeeding topics look at the Pranagnihotra, other vidyas, the connection between sacrifices and meditations and similar topics. There are thirty-six topics and sixty-six sutras in this pada.

Pada 4

Is the knowledge of Brahman related to ritual acts, or is this path of knowledge entirely independent? The pada concludes that no such acts are required. Topic 1 (Sutras 1–17) explains that no sacrificial acts are required to gain the knowledge of Brahman. Topic 2 (Sutras 18–20) continues with this theme and states that for sannyasis, only Brahmavidya is required, while Topic 3 (Sutras 21–22) explains that certain parts of vidyas form a meditation in themselves. Topic 4 (Sutras 23–24) state that stories in the Upanishads glorify or expand on the vidyas taught in them. Examples are those about Janashruti, Pratardana and Yajnavalkya and Maitreyi. Once again, Topic 5 (Sutra 25) affirms that sannyasis only need knowledge and not rituals. But as Topic 6 (Sutras 26–27) says, rituals can have a purpose as they indirectly lead to knowledge. On a different tack, Topic 7 (Sutras 28–31) refers to restrictions prescribed in texts regarding food. Only in an emergency can these be ignored. The example of Chakrayana (Ushasti) who ate leftover beans when he was dying of hunger is mentioned here. Though texts assert that the sannyasi can eat any type of food, he should not generally eat what is considered unlawful food. Similarly, Topics 8–9, Sutras 32–39 state that it is important to perform the requisite duties for the four ashramas or stages in life but those who for some reason cannot do so still have a right to knowledge. Further topics deal with the sannyasi, who, once having taken a vow of celibacy should never stray from it, and different types of meditations, that of mauna or silence, balya or attaining a child-like state of innocence, and panditya, the state of scholarly knowledge. But no matter which path one chooses, liberation is of only one type: the realization of Brahman. This pada has seventeen topics and fifty-two sutras.

Chapter 4

Chapter 4 is known as the Phala-adhyaya as it deals with the phala (fruits) of attaining Brahman.

Pada 1

The first pada has fourteen topics with nineteen sutras, mostly dealing with meditation, for which certain guidelines are provided. Meditation is not something that is to be done only once but is to be repeated till the desired result is attained. Only a very rare soul can attain immediate results. There can be meditation on the atman or on Brahman viewed as identical to the atman. Symbols should not be viewed as identical to Brahman. On the whole, meditation should be practised in a sitting posture at any convenient time and place. Attaining knowledge of Brahman frees one from all past karmas, and neither good nor evil affect one. Rituals, however, can be performed, as they help to promote knowledge. When complete knowledge is obtained, the individual is not reborn.

Pada 2

The second pada with eleven topics and twenty-one sutras explains how the soul leaves the body at the time of death, the process being the same for those without knowledge and for those with the knowledge of Saguna Brahman. First, the functions of various organs such as speech are merged in the mind, and next, the mind is merged in prana and prana with the individual soul or jiva. *Chhandogya* 6.6.1 says that when a man departs, speech merges in mind, mind in prana, prana in fire and fire in the highest deity. The commentary explains that this statement is not contradictory, as a further sutra says that the prana merges with subtle elements. The subtle body is not destroyed at the time of death. The life of both the ordinary person and the knower of Saguna Brahman enter the nadis, and that of the knower passes through the heart to the Sushumna Nadi and proceeds to devayana, the path of the devas or gods, while that of the ordinary man exits through another nadi. It is also said that the soul of the knower of Saguna Brahman follows the rays of the sun to proceed to Brahma Loka, whether it is night or day, and even reaches Brahma Loka during the Dakshinayana or southern course of the sun. On the other hand, the knower of Nirguna Brahman immediately merges with it at the time of death.

Pada 3

This pada, with six topics and sixteen sutras, describes the journey of the soul. Devayana or the path of the gods is one of light and is the only way to Brahma Loka. Though various Upanishads describe this path differently, the *Brahma Sutra* affirms that there is only one path and these texts are only describing various aspects or stages on the path. Putting together the information in various Upanishads, Sutras 2 and 3 enumerate the stages on devayana in sequence: first, the soul reaches the deity of fire (Agni) or of archis or rays of light, then the deity of the day, third, the deity of Shukla-paksha or the bright half of the month, fourth the deity of the year, fifth the deity of the world of the gods, sixth the deity of air (Vayu), seventh the sun (Aditya or Surya), eighth the moon, ninth the deity of lightning, tenth the world of Varuna, eleventh the world of Indra, twelfth the world of Prajapati, and finally Brahma Loka. The various deities mentioned guide the soul along this path, leading to Karya Brahma or Hiranyagarbha or Saguna Brahman. The *Chhandogya* and *Brihadaranyaka* mention a guide to Brahman as a being who is not a man (Amanava Purusha). This is a reference to Saguna Brahman. In Sutras 12–14, the opposing view of Jaimini is mentioned, that this is the Para Brahman or Supreme Brahman, but Badari denies this interpretation. It is only when Brahma Loka is dissolved that the souls there reach the Supreme Brahman. Finally, it is said that the soul can be guided to Brahma Loka, only if symbols have not been used in meditation on Brahman. The meditation of the upasaka (worshipper) should be fixed on Brahman, not on a symbol.

Pada 4

This pada looks at how the Supreme Brahman is attained, and the nature of the individual soul in identity with it. It has seven topics and twenty-two sutras. The soul does not gain anything new, but its true nature is revealed as it unites with Brahman. Does this nature have some special characteristics? Jaimini refers to *Chhandogya* 8.7.1 and other passages in the Upanishads to show that characteristics of Brahman described in texts include freedom from sinful actions (apahatapapmatva), true or right determination (satyasankalpatva) and aishvarya (omniscience). Audulomi, however, says the only characteristic is chaitanya or intelligence. Badari points out that these are two different views of the soul, and what Jaimini is referring to is the relative and not the transcendental soul.

If the soul has merged with Saguna Brahman, then every wish of it is fulfilled. A soul in Brahma Loka can take on one or more bodies as it likes and has every power except that of creation.

Conclusion

THE PROFOUND PHILOSOPHY of the Upanishads has inspired people over the ages, both in India and the world. While passages from the Vedic Samhitas are referred to and quoted in the Upanishads, we find both characters and ideas from the Upanishads in several other texts of ancient India, including the Mahabharata, the Bhagavad Gita, which forms part of it, the Puranas, and in those of other systems of philosophy. Similar stories and characters also appear in Buddhist and Jain texts, and the same terms such as atma and karma are used, though their connotations may be different. Ideas reminiscent of the Upanishads are also seen in Greek philosophy; for instance, in the writings of Pythagoras, Empedocles and Plato, among others. Were these drawn from a knowledge of the Upanishads or were these parallel developments?

In addition, the vast number of commentators on the Upanishads, of whom several are mentioned in this book, indicate their importance in the history of Indian philosophy. Their ideas, crystallized in the philosophy of Vedanta, seeped into other philosophical systems and other sects in India, even though the Upanishads themselves became relatively unknown—the preserve of certain groups of brahmanas and philosophers, who continued to comment on and analyse these texts. Their influence can be seen in a number of medieval bhakti and other sects, some of which have been mentioned earlier. The significant idea that Brahman is One without a second probably contributed to the concept of equality among castes, put forward by many of the bhakti saints, along with medieval sects such as the Mahanubhava (see Feldhaus). One can see an even more direct influence in later sects such as those of the Panchasikhas and the Mahima Dharma.

The medieval translations into Persian by the Mughal prince Dara Shikoh probably influenced some of the Sufi sects within India. The concept of asceticism and the search for the divine within the heart are well known in some of these sects. Dara Shikoh's *Fifty Upanishads* reached the Western world before British and German scholars had begun their translations. As noted earlier, the German philosopher Arthur Schopenhauer fell under their influence. Even though Antequil Duperron's Latin translation was very difficult to comprehend, Schopenhauer managed to grasp the basic philosophy, which, along with Buddhism and the work of Western philosophers such as Plato and Emmanuel Kant, influenced his own work. Friedrich Nietzsche, Georg Hegel and Karl Gustav Jung were also affected by Upanishadic philosophy.

Once translations in English were available, others in the Western world, including the poets T.S. Eliot, Walt Whitman and Ralph Waldo Emerson, were inspired by its concepts. Sir William Jones translated a single short Upanishad, the *Isha Upanishad*, into English. Next to do so was Colebrooke, followed by Rammohan Roy, Max Muller and others.

We have already seen Rammohan Roy's pioneering efforts in the nineteenth century in making the Upanishads better known among ordinary people by translating some of them into Bengali and English and organizing readings from the Upanishads through the Brahmo Samaj. The Arya Samaj founder Swami Dayananda Saraswati did quote from the Upanishads, but his focus was the reinterpretation of the Vedic Samhitas. Sri Aurobindo wrote on the Upanishads and incorporated some of the ideas in his own philosophy. Even other philosophers such as Osho commented on these texts. The world-renowned Jiddu Krishnamurti and U.G. Krishnamurti did not acknowledge the Upanishads, but the essence of their ideas can be found in their own thoughts. Swami Vivekananda (1863–1902), founder of the Ramakrishna Mission and a disciple of Sri Ramakrishna, also promoted the Upanishads. He followed the concept of the universal atman and believed that 'In hurting anyone you hurt yourself, in loving anyone you love yourself'.[1] Mahatama Gandhi, known to read the Bhagavad Gita every day, was also inspired by the *Isha Upanishad*.[2] Even Jawaharlal Nehru commented on them in *Discovery of India*,[3] while B.R. Ambedkar quoted the mahavakyas, 'Tat tvam Asi' and 'Aham Brahmasmi', to show how they promoted equality, even though, as he commented, these ideas had not been incorporated into Hinduism.[4]

Today, the Ramakrishna Mission, Chinmaya Mission and other organizations continue to promote the Upanishads, providing new translations and holding classes on them. The Bhagavad Gita, which has passages similar to the Upanishads (particularly the *Katha Upanishad*), is well known. Yet, Upanishadic ideas and philosophy somehow have not formed a part of mainstream thought in India.

In the Bhagavad Gita it is said: 'Among thousands of men perhaps one strives for perfection, and among thousands of those who strive perhaps one knows me in truth.'[5] The Upanishads are for those who want to understand the mysteries of the universe, and of Brahman, that is said to pervade everything, the ultimate cause and ultimate goal.

Acknowledgements

MANY PEOPLE HAVE contributed to this book. To start with, I would like to thank Udayan Mitra for encouraging me to write this, Ranjana Sengupta, Aditya Mani Jha and Shreya Chakravertty for improving the text through their suggestions and expert editing, and all others at Penguin Random House India involved in the book's production and design.

I would also like to thank the several friends with whom I have discussed these texts over the years, and who contributed to my understanding of them.

Finally, I would like to express my deep appreciation of those rishis, yogis and sannyasis who composed and commented on the Upanishads, and to those who continue to share their insights into these profound texts.

Notes

PART I

Chapter 1: An Introduction

1. See S. Radhakrishnan, 'Introduction', *The Principal Upanisads* (Noida: HarperCollins India, 2004).
2. Sri Aurobindo, *The Upanishads: Texts, Translations and Commentaries* (Detroit: Lotus Press, 1998), pp. 6–8.
3. 'Third Anniversary Discourse to the Asiatic Society of Bengal', delivered 2 February 1786, pp. 24–26.
4. See Gregory Possehl, *The Indus Civilization: A Contemporary Perspective* (New Delhi: Vistaar Publications, 2003).
5. Friedrich Max Muller, *The Gifford Lectures on Physical Religion* (Charleston: Nabu Press, 2010), p. 91.
6. M. Winternitz, *The History of Indian Literature, Volume 1* (Delhi: Motilal Banarsidass, 2015), p. 293.
7. Roshen Dalal, *The Vedas* (New Delhi: Penguin, 2014), pp. 292–300.
8. J.J. Clarke, *Oriental Enlightenment* (London: Routledge, 1997), p. 68.
9. Paul Deussen, *Sixty Upanishads of the Veda* (Delhi: Motilal Banarsidass, 2010), pp. 599–600.
10. Ibid, pp. 563–66.
11. Ibid, p. 566.
12. Sri Aurobindo, *The Upanishads: Texts, Translations and Commentaries*, second edition (Pondicherry: Sri Aurobindo Ashram, 1981), p. 1.
13. Signe Cohen, *Text and Authority in the Older Upanisads* (Leiden: Brill, 2008).

14. Patrick Olivelle, *The Early Upanishads* (Oxford: Oxford University Press, 1998), p. 7.
15. Ibid, p. 8.
16. Swami Madhavananda, *The Brihadaranyaka Upanishad* (Kolkata: Advaita Ashram, 1997), p. 500.
17. Michael Witzel, 'Female Rishis and Philosophers in the Veda?' *Journal of South Asia Women Studies* 11.1 (2009).
18. S. Dasgupta, *History of Indian Philosophy, Volume 1* (Delhi: Motilal Banarsidass, 1975), p. 423.
19. S. Dasgupta, *History of Indian Philosophy, Volume 2* (Delhi: Motilal Banarsidass, 1975), p. 251.

Chapter 2: The Philosophical Context

1. C. Sharma, *The Advaita Tradition in Indian Philosophy* (Delhi: Motilal Banarsidass, 2007), p. 124.
2. S. Dasgupta, *History of Indian Philosophy, Volume 2*, p. 667.
3. Ibid, p. 247.
4. N.V. Isayeva, *Shankara and Indian Philosophy* (New York: State University of New York Press, 1997), p. 14.
5. S. Dasgupta, *History of Indian Philosophy, Volume 1*.
6. For more on Shaiva Siddhanta, see S. Dasgupta, *A History of Indian Philosophy, Volume 5*.

Chapter 3: The Main Topics

1. S. Dasgupta, *A History of Indian Philosophy, Volume 1*, p. 36.
2. Sri Aurobindo, *The Life Divine* (Pondicherry: Sri Aurobindo Ashram, 1993).
3. John Woodroffe, *The Serpent Power: Secrets of Tantric and Shaktic Yoga* (New York: Dover Publications, 1941), pp. 346–47.

Chapter 4: The Teachers

1. Patrick Olivelle, *The Early Upanishads* (Oxford: Oxford University Press, 2008), p. 1.

2. S. Dasgupta, *History of Indian Philosophy, Volume 1*, pp. 33–34.
3. F.E. Pargiter, *Ancient Indian Historical Tradition* (New Delhi: Motilal Banarsidass, 2016), p. 141.

PART II

The Texts

1. Sri Aurobindo, *The Upanishads: Texts, Translations and Commentaries* (Detroit, Lotus Press, 1998), pp. 6–8.
2. Swami Veda Bharati, *Subtler than the Subtle: The Upanishad of the White Horse* (Minnesota: Yes International Publishers, 2002).
3. Sri Aurobindo, *The Upanishads: Texts, Translations and Commentaries*, p. 29.

Chapter 5: The Earliest Upanishads

1. Paul Deussen, *Sixty Upanishads of the Veda* (Delhi: Motilal Banarsidass, 2010), p. 392.
2. S. Radhakrishnan, *The Principal Upanishads*, p. 765.
3. A. Weber, *History of Indian Literature* (Montana: Kessinger Publishing, 1988), p. 87.

Chapter 6: Early Upanishads: 2

1. Richard King, *Early Advaita and Buddhism: The Mahayana Context of the Gaudapadiya Karika* (New York: State University of New York Press, 1995), p. 52.
2. Sri Aurobindo, *The Upanishads: Texts, Translations and Commentaries*, pp. 28–97.
3. Paul Deussen, *Sixty Upanishads of the Veda* (Delhi: Motilal Banarsidass, 2010), p. 303.
4. S. Radhakrishnan, *The Principal Upanishads*, p. 793.
5. Signe Cohen, ed., 'Chapter 34' in *The Upanishads: A Complete Guide* (London and New York: Routledge, 2018).

Chapter 7: The Samanya Vedanta Upanishads

1. William K. Mahony, *The Artful Universe: An Introduction to the Vedic Religious Imagination* (New York: State University of New York Press, 1998), p. 271.
2. Paul Deussen, *Sixty Upanishads of the Veda*, p. 577.

Chapter 8: The Deity Upanishads

1. See Paul B. Courtright, 'Appendix' in *Ganesha, Lord of Obstacles, Lord of Beginnings* (New York: Oxford University Press, 1985).
2. Translation based on Sanskrit text and that of celextel.org.
3. Stella Kramrisch, *The Presence of Siva* (Princeton: Princeton University Press, 1981), pp. 187–88.
4. Ibid, pp. 185–88.
5. Arthur Avalon, ed., *Tantrik Texts, Volume XI: Kaula and other Upanishads, with Commentary by Bhaskaraya*, ed., Sitarama Shastri (Calcutta: Agamanusandhana Samiti, 1922), p. 13.
6. Douglas Renfrew Brooks, *Secret of the Three Cities* (Chicago: University of Chicago Press, 1990), p. 16.
7. Ibid, p. 35.
8. Ibid, p. 36.
9. Ibid, p. 39.
10. Paul Deussen, *Sixty Upanishads of the Veda*, p. 815.
11. Ibid, p. 810.

Chapter 11: The *Brahma Sutra*

1. S. Radhakrishnan, *Brahma Sutra, The Philosophy of Spiritual Life* (Montana: Literary Licensing Publishing, 2011), p.22.
2. Andrew Nicholson, *Unifying Hinduism* (New Delhi: Orient BlackSwan, 2016), p. 26.
3. George C. Adams, *The Structure and Meaning of Badarayana's Sutras* (Delhi: Motilal Banarsidass, 1993), pp. 8–9.

Conclusion

1. Swami Vivekananda, *Collected Works, Volume 1* (Chicago: 1893), pp. 389–90.
2. M.K. Gandhi, *Collected Works, Volume 64*, pp. 258–9, www.gandhiashramsevagram.org/gandhi.
3. Jawaharlal Nehru, *Discovery of India* (Calcutta: Signet Press, 1946). He also refers to them in his speeches.
4. See Ashwani Peetush in 'Human Rights and Political Toleration in India: Multiplicity, Self and Interconnectedness', in Ashwani Peetush and Jay Drydayk, eds., *Human Rights, India and the West* (New Delhi: Oxford University Press, 2015), p. 368.
5. Juan Mascaro, trans., *The Bhagavad Gita* (New Delhi: Penguin Books India, 1962).

Glossary

MANY SANSKRIT WORDS have no exact English equivalent, and therefore this book uses a number of Sanskrit terms, most of which are explained within the text. This glossary contains a select list of such words. Sanskrit words have multiple meanings and here those meanings are given which have relevance to this book.

adharma:	unrighteous, against dharma
adhvaryu:	a *Yajur Veda* priest
adhyaya:	chapter, lesson or section; also a term for reading or study, particularly of sacred books
Aditi:	a Vedic goddess, the mother of the gods
Aditya:	a name of the sun god
agneyi:	an agni (fire) sacrifice
agneyadheya:	first installation of the sacrifice
Agni:	a Vedic deity, god of fire; a term for fire
agnihotra:	a Vedic ritual of offerings to fire
agnishtoma:	a Soma sacrifice
ahavaniya:	a sacred fire
ahi:	a serpent
ahitagni:	a dvija (twice-born, a term for the higher castes), who always maintains the sacred fire
ahura:	a term for a deity in Avestan

aitihasika:	legendary; historical; traditional; a traditional historian
ajnana:	ignorance
akasha:	space; ether; sky
amroli:	a yoga technique related to sexual control
anandamaya:	consisting of bliss
annamaya:	consisting of food
anukramani:	list, catalogue or index
anuvaka:	saying after; reciting; repeating; passages for recitation
amrita:	divine nectar, the drink of immortality
antaryamin:	the inner controller
apana:	a type of prana (breath)
apsara:	a divine nymph
Aranyakas:	a class of texts attached to the Vedic Samhitas
aranya:	forest
arthavada:	explanations
arya:	a term meaning noble; used for a group of people in the *Rig Veda*
asat:	untruth, unreality
ashrama:	a stage in the life of a brahmana; a hermitage
ashtaka:	an eighth
ashva:	a horse
ashvamedha:	a horse sacrifice
astika:	a term for philosophical systems that accept the authority of the Vedas
asura:	a divine being, in later texts sometimes demonic
atiratra:	a soma sacrifice
Atri:	an ancient rishi
avidya:	ignorance
avyakta:	the unmanifested
ayas:	metal
bandha:	a lock or hold; a Yogic technique
Brahma:	a deity (pronounced Brahmaa)
brahmachari:	a male student studying with his guru
brahman:	a special priest of the *Atharva Veda*

brahmana:	a member of the brahmana caste, the highest of the four castes
Brahman:	a term for the Absolute; the ultimate creator and underlying substance of the world.
Brahmana:	a class of texts attached to the Vedic Samhitas
Brihaspati:	A Vedic deity
buddhi:	intelligence
chakra:	mystical centre of energy within the body; also a wheel
charana:	a group of people who study one particular shakha of any Samhita
chhanda/chhandas:	metre
chitta:	mindstuff
dakshina:	one of the sacred fires
dana:	donations or gifts
danastutis:	hymns or parts of hymns, relating to gifts.
dasa:	a term for a group of people in the *Rig Veda*; later meant 'slave' or servant
dasyu:	a term for a group of people in the *Rig Veda*
deva:	a god
devayana:	after death, the path leading to the world of the devas
dharana:	concentration
dharma:	righteousness; duty; truth
dharmashastrika:	pertaining to law
dhyana:	contemplation
dvija:	twice-born, refers to the three upper castes
gana (gaana):	song; singing; a part of the *Sama Veda*
gana:	group, flock, troop
gandharva:	a divine being, associated with apsaras; they are said to be divine musicians
garhaptya:	the household fire
griha:	assistant; servant; house; household; householder
grihya:	belonging to a house; domestic; household sacrifices
guna:	a quality; the three main gunas are sattva (purity); rajas (passion and action) and tamas (dullness)

havirdana:	gift of oblation
hotr, hota:	the main priest for the *Rig Veda*
hita:	in Yoga, a term for unseen passages in the body
Indra:	an important Vedic deity, the god of war, also associated with rain and thunder
jalandhara bandha:	the chin lock, a yoga bandha or technique involving the chin
jana:	clan or tribe
jiva:	the individual soul
Jyotisha:	astronomy and astrology, essential to fix the right time for ceremonies and sacrifices
kalpa:	proper; fit; sacred precept, law or rule
Kalpa Sutras:	a category of Sanskrit texts, relating to ritual
kanda (kaanda):	a section, part, portion, chapter or division of a work or book
kandika (kaandikaa):	a part or division of a book
karana:	an astrological division of the day. There are eleven karanas divided into seven movable and four fixed. Two karanas are equal to a lunar day
Karika (kaarikaa):	a concise statement in verse, or a book or work containing such statements
Khanda:	a section of a work, part or chapter
khandaka:	fragment; part or piece; section of a work
khandika:	section or part
khila:	a supplement of a book, or an additional hymn
kundalini:	a hidden power in the body which can be aroused through special practices
mandala:	a circle; wheel; disk; province; in the *Rig Veda*, a division of the text
manomaya:	consisting of the mind
mantra:	instrument of thought; a sacred text, prayer or song of praise; a Vedic hymn; a sacrificial formula
maya:	illusion
muhurta:	a division of time, the thirtieth part of a day; a moment; an instant
nada:	the inner sound

nadi:	a subtle unseen passage in the body, carrying divine energy
Naimisha:	the name of a sacred forest
nakshatras:	constellations through which the moon passes, lunar mansions
nastika:	systems of philosophy that do not accept the authority of the Vedas
neshtri:	a priest at a soma sacrifice
nirukta:	uttered; explained; etymological interpretation of a word
nivid:	proclaim; short formula in a liturgy
pada:	a line or quarter of a verse; a word or stem of a noun; a foot
Padapatha:	a category of texts in which words are arranged in their original form, without following rules of sandhi
Paddhati:	a category of texts
parishishta:	a supplementary section of a text
parivrajaka:	a religious mendicant, a wandering ascetic
parvan:	a section, break, pause or division, particularly of a book; a period or day when the moon changes; a time when the sun enters a new sign; a division of time; a moment
prana:	a term for breath, and also for the life force; there are ten subsidiary types of prana
pranayama:	a method of breath control
prapathaka:	a lecture, chapter or subdivision of a book
prayoga:	a recitation; a sacred text; a connection
pitris:	ancestors
pitriyana:	after death, the path of the ancestors or pitris, leading to rebirth
Pratishakhya:	a class of texts on shiksha
purushamedha:	a human sacrifice, the descriptions of this are probably symbolic
rajanya:	a term for a kshatriya
rakshasa:	a demonic being

ratha:	chariot
rathantara:	the name of a tune mentioned in the *Rig*, *Sama* and other Vedas
rik:	a verse
rishi:	a sage or ascetic
rishika:	a female rishi
sahjoli:	a yoga technique related to sexual control
sandhi:	a conjunction of words, causing a modification of the final and initial letters of the separate words; methods of joining words
saman:	a chant
samhita:	a collection; compilation; usually of knowledge or hymns in a text
shakha:	literally a branch; in the Vedic context, a recension or school
shastra:	hymn of praise; weapon
Shastra (Shaastra):	a class of texts
shiksha:	phonetics or the science of pronunciation
shrauta:	derived from the word shruti, that which is heard; refers to sacred tradition and the three sacred fires
shruti:	literally means 'that which is heard', hence these texts were 'heard' by the composers, conveyed to them from some divine source
smriti:	that which is remembered; a term for texts that are not as sacred as those considered shruti
Soma:	an intoxicating drink that forms part of Vedic rituals; later a name for the moon and the goddess of the moon
Soma sacrifices:	a complex series of rituals described in Vedic texts
stotra:	basic unit of verses to be sung
sura:	a type of wine
sutra:	a short aphorism; a thread or string
svadhyaya:	self-study, particularly of the Vedas

svadha:	a goddess and a sacred exclamation used with offerings to the pitris
svaha:	a goddess and a sacred exclamation, used with oblations to the gods
svara:	accent; sound; note (as in music)
tapas:	religious fervour; intense religious practices
tejas:	splendour
tithi:	a lunar day, the thirtieth part of the lunar cycle which constitutes a little over twenty-seven days
uddiyana bandha:	a bandha or lock, a part of Yoga practice, involving pulling the abdomen inwards and upwards
udgatr:	the main priest of the *Sama Veda*
uktha:	types of verse
ukthya:	a soma sacrifice
upanayana:	ritual of initiation into the Hindu religion, involving the wearing of the sacred thread
uttarayana period:	the period of the sun's progress to the north
Vaikhanasa:	a Vaishnava philosophy
valakhilya:	a term for some supplementary hymns in Vedas; also a class of tiny rishis, of the size of a thumb
vamsha:	lineage, race, family, a dynasty of kings; a list of teachers; an offspring; a son
vanaprastha:	the traditional third stage of life, when the householder's life had been renounced and the person retired to the forest to live the life of an anchorite
vajra:	a thunderbolt, particularly Indra's weapon
vajroli:	a Yogic technique, related to sexual control
varna:	individual sounds; musical sound or note; order or arrangement of a song or poem; caste; colour; species; tribe
vyakarana:	grammar
Vedangas:	subsidiary Vedic texts
vidhi:	rule; ordinance; statute; precept; law
vritra:	a foe or enemy; the name of a demon who may personify drought; he is killed by Indra

yajamana:	sacrificing; worshipping; the sacrificer or person for whom the sacrifice is being conducted
yajnika:	ritualist; performer of many sacrifices; one well-versed in ritual
yajus:	a prose or verse mantra recited with a ritual; a sacrificial prayer or formula; religious reverence or veneration
yoga:	the main star in a lunar asterism; junction; union; joining; yoking; a philosophical system of uniting with the divine
yoni:	in the context of music, of *Sama Veda*, the basic verse; otherwise, the female emblem
yuga:	a time period

The definitions here are selected from M. Monier-Williams's *A Sanskrit–English Dictionary*. In addition, some definitions of advanced Yoga practices mentioned in the book are given here. For further information on esoteric Yoga techniques, those interested may consult Swami Gitananda's book, *Yoga Samyama* (see Bibliography), or any other similar text. Those wishing to practice them must find a guru or teacher.

Select Bibliography

Part I: Secondary Sources

Adams, George C. *The Structure and Meaning of Badarayana's Brahma Sutras: A Translation and Analysis of Adhyaya 1*. Delhi: Motilal Banarsidass, 1993.

Alinei, Mario. 'Towards an Invasionless Model of Indo-European Origins: The Continuity Theory', in *Papers from the EEA Third Annual Meeting at Ravenna 1997, Vol. I Pre-and Protohistory*, edited by M. Pearce and M. Tosi, pp. 31–33. BAR International Series717, 1998.

Anthony, David. *The Horse, the Wheel and Language: How Bronze-Age Riders from the Eurasian Steppes Shaped the Modern World*. Princeton: Princeton University Press, 2007.

Appleton, N. *Shared Characters in Jain, Buddhist and Hindu Narrative: Gods, Kings and Other Heroes*. London: Routledge, 2017.

Arvidsson, Stefan. *Aryan Idols: Indo-European Mythology as Ideology and Science*. Translated by Sonia Wichmann. Chicago: University of Chicago Press, 2006.

Atmashraddhananda, Swami, ed. *The Upanishads in Daily Life*. Chennai: Sri Ramakrishna Math. n.d.

Aurobindo, Sri. *The Life Divine.* 5th imp., Pondicherry: Sri Aurobindo Ashram, 1993.

Aurobindo, Sri. *The Synthesis of Yoga.* 1914-21; reprint, Pondicherry: Sri Aurobindo Ashram, 1998.

Avalon, Arthur , ed. *Tantrik Texts, Vol. XI: Kaula and other Upanishads,* with commentary of Bhaskaraya, edited by Sitarama Shastri. Calcutta: Agamanusandhana Samiti, 1922.

Basham, A.L. *The Wonder That Was India.* Calcutta: Fontana with Rupa & Co., 1971.

Beck, Guy L, ed. *Alternative Krishnas: Regional and Vernacular Variations on a Hindu Deity.* State University of New York Press, 2005.

Bhandarkar, R.G. *Vaisnavism, Saivism and Minor Religious Systems.* Strassburg, 1913; reprint, New Delhi: Munshiram Manoharlal, 2001.

Bharati, Agehananda. *The Tantric Tradition* reprint, New Delhi: BI Publications, 1983.

Bhargava, M.L. *The Geography of Rig Vedic India.* Lucknow: Upper India Publishing House, 1964.

Bhattacharji, Sukumari. *The Indian Theogony: A Comparative Study of Indian Mythology from the Vedas to the Puranas.* Calcutta: Firma KLM, 1978.

Bhattacharya, N.N. *History of the Tantric Religion* 2nd revised edition, New Delhi: Manohar, 1999.

Bhattacharya, N.N. *Tantrabhidhana: A Tantric Lexicon.* New Delhi: Manohar, 2002.

Bhattacharya, N.N. *The Indian Mother Goddess,* 3rd enlarged edition. New Delhi: Manohar, 1999.

Black, B. *The Character of the Self in Ancient India: Priests, Kings, and Women in the Early Upanisads.* Albany, NY: State University of New York Press. 2007.

Bloomfield, Maurice. *A Vedic Concordance* reprint, Delhi: Motilal Banarsidass, 1996.

Boethlingk, O., and Roth, R. *Sanskrit Worterbuch*, 7 vols. St. Petersberg, 1875, reprint, Delhi: Motilal Banarsidass, 1991.

Brooks, Charles R. *The Hare Krishnas in India*. Princeton University Press, 1989.

Brooks, Douglas Renfrew. *Auspicious Wisdom: The Text and Traditions of Srividya Sakta Tantrism in South India*. New Delhi: Manohar, 1996.

Brooks, Douglas Renfrew. *The Secret of the Three Cities: An Introduction to Sakta Tantrism*. Chicago: University of Chicago Press, 1990.

Brown, C. Mackenzie. *God as Mother: A Feminine Theology of India*. Vermont: Claude Stark & Co., 1974.

Bryant, Edwin. *The Quest for the Origins of Vedic Culture: The Indo-Aryan Migration Debate*. New Delhi: Oxford University Press, 2001.

Burghart, Richard and Audrey Cantile. *Indian Religion*. Curzon Press, 1985.

Clarke, J.J. *Oriental Enlightenment: The Encounter Between Asian and Western Thought*. London and New York: Routledge, 2002.

Clarke, J.J. *Jung and Eastern Thought: A Dialogue with the Orient*. London and New York: Routledge, 1994.

Cohen, Signe, ed. *The Upanishads: A Complete Guide*. London and New York: Routledge, 2018.

Cohen, Signe. *Text and Authority in the Older Upanisads*. Leiden: Brill, 2008.

Colebrooke, H.T. *Essays on the Religion and Philosophy of the Hindus*. Delhi: Indological Book House, 1972.

Coomaraswamy, A.K. *Hinduism and Buddhism*. New York: The Wisdom Library, n.d.

Courtright, Paul B. *Ganesha, Lord of Obstacles, Lord of Beginnings*. New York: Oxford University Press, 1985.

Coward, Harold G., and K. Kunjunni Raja. *Encyclopedia of Indian Philosophies, Vol. V, The Philosophy of the Grammarians.* Princeton University Press, 1990.

Dalal, R. *Hinduism: An Alphabetical Guide.* New Delhi: Penguin Books India, 2010.

Dalal, R. *The Religions of India: A Concise Guide to Nine Major Faiths.* New Delhi: Penguin Books India, 2010.

Dalal, R. *The Vedas: An Introduction to Hinduism's Sacred Texts.* New Delhi: Penguin Books India, 2014.

Dalmia, Vasudha and Heinrich von Stietencron. *The Oxford India Hinduism Reader.* New Delhi: Oxford University Press, 2007.

Dandekar, R.N. *Vedic Mythological Tracts.* Delhi: Ajanta, 1979.

Danielou, Alain. *The Myths and Gods of India.* Rochester, Vermont: Inner Traditions International, 1991.

Dasgupta, S. *A History of Indian Philosophy,* 5 vols, 1922–55, reprint. Delhi: Motilal Banarsidass, 1975.

Datta, Amaresh, chief ed. *Encyclopaedia of Indian Literature,* 6 vols. New Delhi: Sahitya Akademi, 1987–1994.

Dayananda Saraswati, Maharishi, *The Light of Truth (Satyartha Prakasha),* translated by Chiranjeeva Bharadwaj, 1988, www.aryasamaj.org.

Deussen, Paul, *The Philosophy of the Upanishads,* 2 vols, authorized English translation, by Rev. A.S. Geden. Edinburgh: T & T Clark, 1906.

Deussen, Paul, *Sixty Upanishads of the Veda,* 2 vols, translated by V.M. Bedekar and G.B. Palsule. Delhi: Motilal Banarsidass, reprint 2010.

Deutsch, Eliot and Rohit Dalvi, ed., *Vedanta: A New Source Book of Advaita Vedanta.* World Wisdom, 2004.

Doniger, Wendy. *Hinduism, An Alternative History.* Penguin, 2009.

Dowson, John. *A Classical Dictionary of Hindu Mythology and Religion,* reprint. New Delhi: DK Printworld, 1998.

Easwaran, Eknath. *Essence of the Upanishads: A Key to Indian Spirituality*. Canada: Blue Mountain Center of Meditation, Nilgiri Press, 2009.

Eliade, M., ed. *The Encyclopedia of Religions*, 16 vols. New York: Macmillan, 1987.

Embree, Ainslee T., ed. *Sources of Indian Tradition, Vol 1*. 2nd edition. New Delhi: Penguin Books, 1992.

Encyclopaedia Britannica, Vol. 28, 1911, Young, Thomas.

Erdosy, George, ed. *The Indo-Aryans of Ancient South Asia: Language, Material Culture and Ethnicity*, Indian edition. New Delhi: Munshiram Manoharlal, 1997.

Farquhar, J.N. *An Outline of the Religious Literature of India*. Delhi: Motilal Banarsidass, 1984; reprint, 1920.

Feldhaus, Anne. *The Deeds of God in Riddhipur*. New York: Oxford University Press, 1984.

Findly, E.B. 'Gargi at the King's Court: Women and Philosophic Innovation in Ancient India', in *Women, Religion, and Social Change*, edited by Y.Y. Haddad and E.B. Findly, pp. 37–58. New York: State University of New York, 1985.

Flood, Gavin, ed. *The Blackwell Companion to Hinduism*. Blackwell Publishing, 2003.

Frawley, David. *Tantric Yoga and the Wisdom Goddesses*. Delhi: Motilal Banarsidass, 1996.

Gandhi, Mahatma. *Collected Works, Vol. 64*. www.gandhiashramsevagram.org/gandhi.

Gitananda, Swami. *Yoga Samyama*. Pondicherry: Ananda Ashram, n.d.

Gonda, Jan, *Vedic Literature: Samhitas and Brahmanas*. Wiesbaden: Harrassowitz, 1975.

Gonda, Jan. *Change and Continuity in Indian Religion*, reprint; New Delhi: Munshiram Manoharlal, 1997.

Gonda, Jan. *Medieval Religious Literature in Sanskrit*. Wiesbaden: Harrassowitz, 1977.

Gopal, Ram. *The History and Principles of Vedic Interpretation.* New Delhi: Concept Publishing Company, 1983.

Goudriaan, Teun, and Sanjukta Gupta. *Hindu Tantric and Sakta Literature.* Wiesbaden: Harrassowitz, 1981.

Griffiths, Arlo and Jan E.M. Houben. *The Vedas: Texts, Language and Ritual.* Leiden: Proceedings of the Third International Vedic Workshop, 2002.

Griswold, Charles. *Self-Knowledge in Plato's Phaedrus.* New Haven, CT: Yale University Press, 1986.

Hastings, J., ed. *Encyclopaedia of Religion and Ethics,* 13 vols. Edinburgh: T&T Clark, 1908–26; reprint 12 vols. New York: Scribner, 1961.

Heehs, Peter, ed. *Indian Religions: The Spiritual Traditions of South Asia—An Anthology.* Delhi: Permanent Black, 2002.

Hemphill, B.E., J.R. Lukacs and K.A.R. Kennedy. 'Biological Adaptations and Affinities of the Bronze Age Harappans', in R. H. Meadow, ed., *Harappa Excavations 1986–1990: A Multidisciplinary Approach to Third Millennium Urbanism.* Madison: Prehistory Press, 1991.

Hersey, Baird. *The Practice of Nada Yoga: Meditation on the Inner Sacred Sound.* Rochester, Vermont: Inner Traditions, 2014.

Hirst, Jacqueline Suthren. *Samkara's Advaita Vedanta.* London and New York: Routledge, Curzon, 2005.

Hopkins, Thomas J. *The Hindu Religious Tradition.* Belmont, CA: Wadsworth Publishing Company, 1971.

Horsch, P. *Die Vedische Gatha-und Sloka Literatur.* Bern: Francke Verlag, 1966.

Isayeva, N.V. *Shankara and Indian Philosophy.* New York: State University of New York Press, 1997.

Jaiswal, Suvira, *The Origin and Development of Vaisnavism.* 2nd edition. New Delhi: Munshiram Manoharlal, 1981.

Jamison, S. *Sacrificed Wife, Sacrificer's Wife: Women, Ritual and Hospitality in Ancient India.* New York/Oxford: Oxford University Press. 1996.

Jones, William. 'Third Anniversary Discourse to the Asiatic Society of Bengal', delivered 2 February 1786, pp. 24–26. in Lord Teignmouth, ed. *The Works of Sir William Jones*. Cambridge: Cambridge University Press, 2013.

Kak, Subhash. *The Astronomical Code of the Rig Veda*, revised and expanded. New Delhi: Munshiram Manoharlal, 2000.

Keith, A.B. *Rigveda Brahmanas: The Aitareya and Kausitaki Brahmanas of the Rigveda*, 1st edition, 1920, reprint. Delhi: Motilal Banarsidass, 1998.

Keith, A.B. *The Religion and Philosophy of the Vedas and Upanishads*. 1st edition, 1925, reprint. Delhi: Motilal Banarsidass, 1998.

King, Richard. *Early Advaita and Buddhism: The Mahayana context of the Gaudapadiya Karika*. New York: State University of New York Press, 1995.

Kinsley, David R. *Hinduism: A Cultural Perspective*. London: Prentice Hall, 1982.

Klostermaier, Klaus K. *A Survey of Hinduism*, 3rd edition, New York: State University of New York Press, 2007.

Knipe, D. *Hinduism: Experiments in the Sacred*. Prospect Heights: Waveland Press, 1991.

Kochhar, Rajesh. *The Vedic People*. New Delhi: Orient Longman, 2000.

Kosambi, D.D. *Myth and Reality: Studies in the Formation of Indian Culture*. Bombay: Popular Prakashan, 1962.

Kramrisch, Stella. *The Presence of Siva*. Princeton: Princeton University Press, 1981.

Lindquist, S.E. 'Gender at Janaka's Court: Women in the Brihadaranyaka Upanishad Reconsidered'. *Journal of Indian Philosophy* 36.3 (2008): 405–26.

Macdonell, A.A. *The Vedic Mythology*. Varanasi/Delhi: Indological Book House, 1971.

Macdonell, A.A. and A.B. Keith. *Vedic Index of Names and Subjects*, 2 vols, reprint. Delhi: Motilal Banarsidass, 1995.

Macdonell, A.A. *A History of Sanskrit Literature*. 1899, reprint. New Delhi: Munshiram Manoharlal, 1972.

Madan, T.N., ed. *Religion in India*. New Delhi: Oxford University Press, 1991.

Mahony, William K. *The Artful Universe: An Introduction to the Vedic Religious Imagination*. New York: State University of New York Press, 1998.

Majumdar, R.C., ed. *The History and Culture of the Indian People*, 11 vols. Bombay: Bharatiya Vidya Bhavan, 1951–69.

Mallory, J.P. *In Search of the Indo-Europeans: Language, Archaeology and Myth*. London: Thames and Hudson, 1991.

Mayeda, Sengaku. *A Thousand Teachings: The Upadesasahasri of Sankara*, 2 vols. Delhi: Motilal Banarsidass, 2006.

Mc Daniel, June. *Offering Flowers, Feeding Skulls: Popular Goddess Worship in West Bengal*. Oxford University Press, 2004.

McGee, Mary. 'Bahinabai: The Ordinary Life of an Exceptional Woman or the Exceptional Life of an Ordinary Woman', in Rosen, Steven J., ed. *Vaisnavi: Women and the Worship of Krishna*. Delhi: Motilal Banarsidass, 1996, pp. 133–69.

Monier-Williams, M. *A Sanskrit–English Dictionary*, reprint. Delhi: Motilal Banarsidass, 1973.

Muller, Max. Gifford Lectures on 'Physical Religion' 1889. London, 1901.

Muller-Ortega, Paul E. *The Triadic Heart of Siva: Kaula Tantricism of Abhinavagupta in the Non-Dual Shaivism of Kashmir*. New York: State University of New York Press, 1987.

Nehru, Jawaharlal. *Discovery of India*. Calcutta: Signet Press, 1946.

Olivelle, Patrick. *The Early Upanishads*. Oxford University Press, 2008 (see Bibliography Pt 2 for details).

Pande, G.C. *Life and Thought of Sankaracharya*. Delhi: Motilal Banarsidass, 1994.

Pandit, M.P. *Upanishads: Gateways of Knowledge*. Wilmot, USA: Lotus Light Publications, 1988.

Parameshwarananda, Swami. *Encyclopaedic Dictionary of the Upanishads*, 3 vols. Delhi: Sarup and Sons 2000.

Patton, Laurie. *Authority, Anxiety, and Canon*. New York: State University of New York Press, 1994.

Peetush, Ashwani and Jay Drydayk, eds. *Human Rights, India and the West*. New Delhi: Oxford University Press, 2015.

Phillips, Stephen. *Yoga, Karma, and Rebirth: A Brief History and Philosophy*. Columbia, 2009.

Phillips, Stephen. *Epistemology in Classical India: The Knowledge Sources of the Nyaya School*. Routledge, 2015.

Radhakrishnan, S. *Indian Philosophy*, 2 vols. New Delhi: Oxford University Press, 1999.

Ranade, R.D. *A Constructive Survey of Upanishadic Philosophy, being an Introduction to the Thought of the Upanishads*. Reprint, Bombay: Bharatiya Vidya Bhavan, 1968.

Ruben, Walter. *Die Philosophen der Upanishaden*. Bern: A. Francke, 1947.

Scott, David. 'The Perennial Message of the Goddess: Enduring Themes down the Ages in Bactria' in *East and West* 48.1–2, 27–39 (1998).

Sedlar, J. *India in the Mind of Germany: Schelling, Schopenhauer, and Their Times*. Washington DC: University Press of America, 1982.

Sen, S.C. *The Mystical Philosophy of the Upanishads*. Delhi: Cosmo Publications, 1937.

Sharma, B.N.K., *History of the Dvaita School of Vedanta and Its Literature*, revised edition. Delhi: Motilal Banarsidass, 2000.

Sharma, C. *The Advaita Tradition in Indian Philosophy*. Delhi: Motilal Banarsidass, 2007.

Sharma, K.S., *Essence of Hinduism*. Mumbai: Bharatiya Vidya Bhavan, 1999.

Singh, M.R. *A Critical Study of the Geographical Data in the Early Puranas*. Calcutta: Punthi Pustak, 1972.

Singh, R. *Schopenhauer: A Guide for the Perplexed*. London: Continuum, 2010.

Sorensen, S. *Index to the Names in the Mahabharata*. Delhi: Motilal Banarsidass, 1963.

Staal, Frits. *Discovering the Vedas*. Penguin Books India, 2008.

Thakur, Upendra. *History of Mithila Circa 3000 BC–1556 AD*. Mithila Institute, 1956.

Vivekananda, Swami. *Collected Works, Vol. 1*. Chicago, 1893.

Walker, Benjamin. *Hindu World*. New Delhi: Rupa & Co, 2005.

Weber, Albrecht. *History of Indian Literature*, translated by J. Mann and T. Zachariae. 2nd edition. London: Tribner, 1882.

Whicher, Ian. *The Integrity of the Yoga Darshana: A Reconsideration of Classical Yoga*. New York: SUNY Series in Religious Studies, 1998.

Winternitz, Maurice. *History of Indian Literature*, vols 1–2, 3rd edition. New Delhi: Munshiram Manoharlal, 1991.

Witzel, Michael. 'Female Rishis and philosophers in the Veda?' *Journal of South Asia Women Studies* 11(1) 2009. http://asiatica.org/jsaws/11-1/female-rishis-and-philosophers-veda.

Woodroffe, John, *The Serpent Power*, 3rd edition, reprint. Madras: Ganesh & Co, 1992.

Zaehner, R.C. ed. *The Hutchinson Encyclopedia of Living Faiths*, 4th edition. Oxford: Helicon, 1994.

Zaehner, R.C. *Hindu and Muslim Mysticism*. London: University of London, TheAthlone Press, 1960.

Zaehner, R.C. *Hinduism*, 2nd edition. Oxford: Oxford University Press, 1966.

Part II: Texts, translations and commentaries: An annotated list (Many of these translations have no date. Unless otherwise stated all translations are into English.)

In the summaries provided in Part II of the book, the Sanskrit texts consulted are mainly those of Upanishad Brahmayogin, along with one or more translations.

Atmapriyananda, Swami, text and trans. *Sannyasa Upanishads.* Kolkata: Advaita Ashram, 2013.

Aurobindo, Sri. *The Upanishads: Texts, Translations and Commentaries,* 2nd edition. Pondicherry: Sri Aurobindo Ashram, 1981 (includes partial and complete translations and commentaries of: *Isha; Kena; Mundaka; Katha; Taittiriya; Aitareya; Prashna; Mandukya; Brihadaranyaka; Chhandogya; Shvetashvatara; Kaivalya; Nilarudra;* the Karikas of Gaudapada; and Sadananda's essence of Vedanta).

Chinmayananda, Swami. *Discourses on Kaivalyopanishad.* Bombay: Central Chinmaya Mission Trust, n.d.

Chinmayananda, Swami. *Discourses on Kathopanishad.* Bombay: Central Chinmaya Mission Trust, n.d.

Deussen, Paul. *Sixty Upanishads of the Veda,* 2 vols, translated from the German by V.M. Bedekar and G.B. Palsule. Delhi: Motilal Banarsidass, reprint, 2010 (includes translations and commentaries on: Part 1: *Aitareya; Kaushitaki; Chhandogya; Kena; Taittiriya; Maha-Narayana; Katha; Shvetashvatara; Maitrayana; Brihadaranyaka;* Part 2: *Isha; Mundaka; Prashna; Mandukya* with Karika of Gaudapada; *Garbha; Pranagnihotra; Pinda; Atma; Sarva; Garuda; Brahmavidya; Kshurika; Chulika; Nadabindu; Brahma-bindu; Amritabindu; Dhyanabindu; Tejobindu; Yoga-shikha; Yoga-tattva; Hamsa; Brahma; Samnyasa; Aruneya; Kantha-shruti; Paramahamsa; Jabala; Ashrama; Atharvashira; Atharvashikha; Nilarudra; Kalagnirudra; Kaivalya; Maha; Narayana; Atmabodha; Nrisimhapurvatapaniya; Nrisimhaottara-tapaniya; Ramapurvatapaniya; Ramaottaratapaniya* (Supplement: the remaining sections and Upanishads of the Oupnekhat).

418   Select Bibliography

Select Bibliography

Duperron, Anquetil. *Oupnekhat: Id est, Secretum Tegendum.* Parisiis 1801–02, 4, 2 vols. Partly translated into the German, Nurnberg, 1808, smaller fragments translated into the German by Othmar Frank, Chrestomathia Sanscrita 1820–21, and Vyasa uber Philosophie, Mythologie, Literatur und Sprache der Hindu. 1826-30.

Gambhirananada, Swami, text and trans. *Taittiriya Upanishad.* Calcutta: Advaita Ashram.

Gambhirananda, Swami, text, trans., commentary. *Mandukya Upanishad, with the Karika of Gaudapada and Commentary of Sankaracarya.* Calcutta: Advaita Ashram, 1979.

Ganguli, K.M., trans. *Mahabharata,* 4 vols, 1904–25; reprint. New Delhi: Munshiram Manoharlal, 2004.

Hume, Robert Ernest. *The Thirteen Principal Upanishads,* translated from the Sanskrit with an outline of the philosophy of the Upanishads and an annotated bibliography . Oxford University Press, 1921 (Translations of *Brihadaranyaka, Chhandogya, Taittiriya, Aitareya, Kaushitaki, Kena, Katha, Isha, Mundaka, Prashna, Mandukya, Shvetashvatara, Maitri*).

Kunhan Raja, C., editorial supervisor, with The Pandits of the Adyar Library, *Dasopanishads with the commentary of Sri Upanishad-Brahma-Yogin, Vol. 1* Madras: Adyar Library, Theosophical Society, 1935 (Sanskrit text of: *Isha, Kena, Katha, Prashna, Mundaka, Mandukya, Taittiriya, Aitareya.* Vol. 2, 1936, Sanskrit text of: *Chhandogya; Brihadaranyaka*).

Madhavananda, Swami, trans. *Uddhava Gita.* Calcutta: Advaita Ashram, 1978.

Madhavananda, Swami, trans. *Aruni Upanishad.* Kolkata: Advaita Ashram.

-----------*Brahma Upanishad.* Kolkata: Advaita Ashram.

-----------*Paramahamsa Upanishad.* Kolkata: Advaita Ashram.

-----------*Sarvasara Upanishad.* Kolkata: Advaita Ashram.

Madhavananda, Swami. *Brhadaranyaka Upanisad, The,* text, trans. and commentary. Madras: Sri Ramakrishna Math, 1951.

Madhavananda, Swami, text and trans. *Sri Sankaracharya's Vivekachudamani.* Kolkata: Advaita Ashram, 2nd edition, 2010.

Mahadeva Sastri, Pandit A., ed. *The Saiva Upanisads, with the commentary of Sri Upanisad-Brahma-Yogin.* Madras: The Adyar Library, 1950 (Sanskrit text of: *Akshamalika; Atharvashikha; Atharvashira; Kalagnirudra; Kaivalya; Ganapatya; Jabala; Dakshinamurti; Panchabrahma; Brihad-jabala; Bhasmajabala; Rudrahridaya; Rudrakshajabala; Sharabha; Shvetashvatara*

Mahadeva Sastri, Pandit A., ed. *The Vaisnava Upanishads, with the commentary of Sri Upanisad-Brahma-Yogin.* Madras: The Adyar Library, Theosophical Society, 1923 (Sanskrit text of fourteen Upanishads: *Avyakta, Kalisantarana, Krishna, Garuda, Gopalatapaniya, Purva* and *Uttara; Tarasara; Tripadibhuti-Maha-Narayana; Dattatreya, Narayana; Nrisimhatapini, Purva* and *Uttara; Ramatapaniya, Purva* and *Uttara; Ramarahasya; Vasudeva; Hayagriva).*

Mahadeva Sastri, Pandit A., ed. *The Yoga Upanisads, with the commentary of Sri Upanisad-Brahma-Yogin.* Madras: The Adyar Library, Theosophical Society, 1920 (Sanskrit text of: *Advaya-taraka; Amrita-bindu, Amrita Nada; Kshurika; Tejabindu; Trishikhi-brahmana; Darshana; Dhyana-bindu; Nada-bindu; Pashupata-brahma; Brahma-vidya; Mandala-brahma; Mahavakya; Yoga-Kundali; Yoga-chudamani; Yoga-tattva; Yoga-shikha; Varaha; Shandilya; Hamsa).*

Mahadeva Sastri, Pandit A., ed. *The Sakta Upanisads, with the commentary of Sri Upanisad-Brahma-Yogin.* Madras: The Adyar Library, Theosophical Society, 1950 (Sanskrit text of: *Tripura; Tripuratapini; Devi; Bahvricha; Bhavana; Sarasvati rahasya; Sita; Saubhagyalakshmi).*

Mahadevan, T.M.P. *Upanishads: Selections from 108 Upanishads.* Delhi: Motilal Banarsidass, reprint 2010 (Includes a brief account of each Upanishad, along with a selection of one or more verses translated into English.)

Mascaro, Juan, trans. *The Upanishads,* reprint. Harmondsworth: Penguin Books, 1971 (Translations of *Isha, Kena, Katha, Prashna, Mundaka, Mandukya, Shvetashvatara;* translations of selected passages from *Maitri, Kaushitaki; Taittiriya, Chhandogya; Brihadaranyaka*).

Mascaro, Juan, trans. *The Bhagavad Gita.* Penguin Books, 1962.

Muller, Max, ed. *Sacred Books of the East* (50 vols); Vol. 1, 15, Max Muller, trans., *The Upanishads;* 2,14, George Buhler, trans., *The Sacred Laws of the Aryas;* 12, 26, 41, 43, 44, Julius Eggeling, trans., *The Satapatha Brahmana;* 25, George Buhler, trans., *Manu Smriti;* 32, 46, Max Muller and H. Oldenberg, trans., *Vedic Hymns* (1887; reprinted New Delhi, Low Price Publications, D.K. Publishers, 1995). Upanishad translations first published 1879, 1884, included in Vol. 1: *Chhandogya, Talavakra, Kena, Aitareya Aranyaka* in three parts, *Kaushitaki, Vajasaneyi Samhita Upanishad (Isha).* 2: *Katha, Mundaka, Taittiriya, Brihadaranyaka, Shvetashvatara, Prashna, Maitri.*

Narasimhananda, Swami, text and trans. *Tripura Upanishad,* in *Traditional Wisdom,* Prabuddha Bharata, January 2016, Vol. 121, No. 1.

Narayanasvami Aiyar. *Thirty Minor Upanishads, Text and Translation.* Madras 1914 (The Upanishads are in three groups: Vedanta Upanishads: *Muktika, Sarvasara; Niralamba; Maitreya; Kaivalya; Amritabindu; Atmabodha; Skanda; Paingala; Subala; Tejobindu; Brahma; Vajrasuchi; Shariraka; Garbha;* Mantra Upanishads: *Tarasara; Narayana; Kalisantarana;* Sanyasa Upanishads: *Bhikshuka; Naradaparivrajaka; Shandilya; Yogatattva; Dhyanabindu; Hamsa; Amritananda; Varaha; Mandalabrahmana; Nadabindu; Yoga Kundali*).

Nikhilananda, Swami. *The Principal Upanishads*, translated and edited in four volumes. Calcutta: Advaita Ashram, 1956 (Translations of *Katha, Isha, Kena, Mundaka, Shvetashvatara, Prashna, Mandukya, Aitareya, Brihadaranyaka, Taittiriya, Chhandogya*).

Nirmalananda Giri. *108 Upanishads*, translated by various scholars with Nirmalananda's commentary on the first ten of the Muktika list (available online, n.d.).

Olivelle, Patrick. *The Early Upanisads, Annotated Text and Commentary.* Oxford University Press, 1998 (Includes translations of the *Brihadaranyaka Upanishad; Chhandogya, Taittiriya, Aitareya, Kaushitaki, Kena, Katha, Isha, Shvetashvatara, Mundaka, Prashna, Mandukya*).

Pandit, M.P. *Upanishads: Gateways of Knowledge.* Wilmot, USA: Lotus Light Publications, 1988 (This provides a general introduction, along with commentaries on the *Isha, Kena, Taittiriya* and *Brihadaranyaka*).

Purohit Swami, Shree and W.B. Yeats. *The Ten Principal Upanishads Put into English*, reprint. London: Faber and Faber Ltd. Mcmlii (free translations of *Isha, Kena, Katha, Prashna, Mundaka, Mandukya, Taittiriya, Aitareya, Chhandogya, Brihadaranyaka*).

Radhakrishnan, S. *The Principal Upanisads.* New Delhi: HarperCollins India, 2004 (Introduction, text in Roman script, translation and commentary of *Brihadaranyaka Upanishad; Chhandogya; Aitareya; Taittiriya; Isha; Kena; Katha; Prashna; Mundaka; Mandukya; Shvetashvatara; Kaushitaki Brahmana; Maitri; Subala; Jabala; Paingala; Kaivalya; Vajrasuchika*).

Roebuck, Valerie. *13 Principal Upanishads.* London: Penguin, 2000.

Sharma, R.N., ed. *Manusmriti*, text, translation and notes. Delhi: Chaukhamba Sanskrit Pratishthan, 2003.

Sivananda, Swami. *Brahma Sutras*, text, translation and commentary. Shivanandanagar: The Divine Life Society, 2008.

Srimad Valmiki Ramayana with Sanskrit text and English translation, three volumes, 4th edition. Gorakhpur: Gita Press, 1995.

Srinivasa Ayyangar, T.R., trans., ed. G. Srinivasa Murti. *Saiva Upanisads, on the basis of the commentary of Sri Upanisadbrahmayogin.* Madras: The Adyar Library, 1953 (Translations of: *Akshamalika; Atharvashikha; Atharvashira; Kalagnirudra; Kaivalya; Ganapatya; Jabala; Dakshinamurti; Panchabrahma; Brihad-jabala; Bhasmajabala; Rudrahridaya; Rudrakshajabala; Sharabha; Shvetashvatara*).

Srinivasa Ayyangar, T.R. trans., *The Yoga Upanishads*, ed., Pandit S. Subrahmanya Shastri. Madras: The Adyar Library, 1938 (has translations of: Advaya-taraka; *Amrita Nada; Kshurika; Tejabindu; Trishikhi-brahmana; Darshana; Dhyana-bindu; Nada-bindu; Pashupata-brahma; Brahma-vidya; Mandala-brahma; Mahavakya; Yoga-Kundali; Yoga-chudamani; Yoga-tattva; Yoga-shikha; Varaha; Shandilya; Hamsa*).

Tejomayananda, Swami. *Ganapati Atharvashirsha Upanishad.* Mumbai: Central Chinmaya Mission Trust, Chinmaya Prakashan.

Tejobindu Upanishad, text: www.sanskritdocuments.org.

Veda Bharati, Swami. *Subtler than the Subtle, The Upanishad of the White Horse: A Paraphrased Translation Based on the Commentary of Shankaracharya.* Saint Paul, MN: Yes International Publishers, 2002. Vedananda, Swami, *The Svestasvatara Upanishad.* Hyderabad: Publisher, Swami Vedananda, 2002.

Vedananda, Swami. *The Kena Upanishad.* Hyderabad: Publisher, Swami Vedananda, 2003.

Venkatesananda, Swami. *The Yoga Sutras of Patanjali*, text, translation and commentary. Shivananadanagar: The Divine Life Society, 2001.

Venkatesananda, Swami. *The Supreme Yoga: A New Translation of the Yoga Vasishtha*, 2 vols. 2nd reprint. Delhi: Motilal Banarsidass, 2013.

Vimalananda, Swami. *Mahanarayana Upanishad*, text, translation and analysis. Madras: Sri Ramakrishna Math, 1968.

Vireswarananda, Swami and Swami Adidevananda. *Brahma Sutras: According to Sri Ramanuja*, text, English rendering, comments, according to the Sri Bhasya of Sri Ramanuja. Kolkata: Advaita Ashram, 2012.

Wilson, H.H. *Visnu Purana: Sanskrit text and English translation*, edited by K.L. Joshi. Delhi: Parimal Publications, 2002.

Translations of the following Upanishads are also available online at www.celextel.org and www.hinduwebsite.org. Many of these were originally published in Chennai by the Theosophical Publishing House.

Avyakta Upanishad, trans., celextel.org.

Bhasma Jabala Upanishad, trans., celextel.org.

Ganapati Upanishad, trans., celextel.org.

Garuda Upanishad, trans., celextel.org.

Gopal Tapaniya Upanishad, trans., celextel.org.

Hattangadi, Sundar, and P.R. Ramachander, trans. *Rama Rahasya Upanishad*. celextel.org.

Kalagni Rudra Upanishad, trans. celextel.org.

Krishna Warrier , A G, trans. *Adhyatma Upanishad*. Chennai: The Theosophical Publishing House.

Krishna Warrier, A G., trans. *Akshi Upanishad*. Chennai: TPH.

-----------*Atma Upanishad*. Chennai: TPH.

-----------*Atma Bodha Upanishad*. Chennai: TPH.

-----------*Annapurna Upanishad*. Chennai: TPH.

-----------*Bahvricha Upanishad*. Chennai:TPH.

-----------*Bhavana Upanishad*. Chennai: TPH.

-----------*Devi Upanishad*. Chennai: TPH.

-----------*Ekakshara Upanishad*. Chennai:TPH.

-----------*Garbha Upanishad*. Chennai: TPH.

-----------*Maha Upanishad*. Chennai: TPH.

-----------*Mantrika Upanishad*. Chennai: TPH.

-----------*Mudgala Upanishad*. Chennai: TPH.

-----------*Muktika Upanishad*. Chennai: TPH.

-----------*Niralamba upanishad*. Chennai: TPH

-----------*Paingala Upanishad*. Chennai: TPH.

-----------*Pranagnihotra Upanishad*. Chennai: TPH.

-----------*Sarasvati Rahasya Upanishad*. Chennai: TPH.

-----------*Saririka Upanishad*. Chennai: TPH.

-----------*Saubhagyalakshmi Upanishad*. Chennai: TPH.

-----------*Sita Upanishad. Chennai:* TPH.

-----------*Skanda Upanishad*. Chennai: Adyar Library, TPH.

-----------*Surya Rahasya Upanishad*. Chennai: TPH.

-----------*Tripura Tapini Upanishad*. Chennai: TPH.

-----------*Tripura Upanishad*. Chennai: TPH.

Narayanasvami Aiyar, K., trans. *Hamsa Upanishad*. celextel.org

-----------*Kali Santarana Upanishad*. celextel.org

-----------*Mandala Brahmana Upanishad*. celextel.org

-----------*Nadabindu Upanishad*.celextel.org

-----------*Sandilya Upanishad*. celextel.org

-----------*Tarasara Upanishad*.celextel.org

-----------*Varaha Upanishad*. celextel.org

-----------*Yoga Kundalini Upanishad*. celextel.org

-----------*Yoga Tattva Upanishad*. celextel.org

Ramachander, P.R., trans. *Advaya Taraka Upanishad*. celextel.org

-----------*Atharvasikha Upanishad*. celextel.org

-----------*Atharvasiras Upanishad*. celextel.org

-----------*Brihad Jabala Upanishad*. celextel.org

-----------*Jabali Upanishad*. celextel.org

-----------*Krishna Upanishad*. celextel.org

-----------*Mahavakya Upanishad*.celextel.org

-----------*Narayana Upanishad*. celextel.org

-----------*Nrisimha Poorva Upanishad*. celextel.org

-----------*Pancha Brahma Upanishad*.celextel.org

-----------*Pashupata Brahmana Upanishad*. celextel.org

-----------*Rama Tapaniya Upanishad*.celextel.org.

-----------*Sarabha Upanishad*. celextel.org

-----------*Vasudeva Upanishad*. celextel.org

-----------*Yogachudamani Upanishad*. celextel.org

Ramanathan, A. A. trans. *Avadhuta Upanishad*. Chennai: The Theosophical Publishing House.

-----------*Bhikshuka Upanishad*. Chennai, TPH.

-----------*Katha Rudra Upanishad*. Chennai, TPH.

-----------*Maitreya Upanishad*. Chennai, TPH.

-----------*Narada Parivrajaka*. Chennai, TPH.

-----------*Nirvana Upanishad*. Chennai, TPH.

-----------*Para-Brahma Upanishad*. Chennai, TPH.

-----------*Paramahamsa Parivrajaka Upanishad*. Chennai, TPH.

-----------*Sannyasa Upanishad*. Chennai, TPH.

-----------*Satyayaniya Upanishad*. Chennai, TPH.

-----------*Turiyatita Avadhuta*. Chennai, TPH.

-----------*Yajnavalkya Upanishad*. Chennai, TPH.

-----------*Yoga Sikha Upanishad*. Chennai, TPH.

Rudra Hridaya Upanishad, trans. celextel.org.

Rudraksha Jabala Upanishad, trans. celextel.org.

Srinivasan, K., trans. *Aksha Malika Upanishad*. celextel.org.

Tripadvibhuti Mahanarayana, trans. celextel.org.

Some useful websites

There are innumerable websites related to Hinduism. A few useful sites are listed below.

www.advaita-vedanta.org texts of Shankara
www.celextel.org Hindu texts.
www.chinmayamission.org
www.indiadivine.org